BY THE AUTHOR

MILITARY HISTORY

Wolfe at Quebec
The Destruction of Lord Raglan
Corunna
The Battle of Arnhem
Agincourt
The Wheatley Diary (Ed.)
Waterloo: Napoleon's Last Campaign (Ed.)

BIOGRAPHIES

The Road to Tyburn
Benito Mussolini
Garibaldi and his Enemies
The Making of Charles Dickens
Charles I
The Personal History of Samuel Johnson
George IV Prince of Wales, 1762–1811

HISTORY

King Mob
The Roots of Evil
The Court at Windsor
An American in Regency England:
the Journal of a Tour in 1810–1811 (Ed.)
The Grand Tour
London: the Biography of a City
The Dragon Wakes: China and the West, 1793–1911

CHRISTOPHER HIBBERT

GEORGE IV

REGENT AND KING

1811–1830

ALLEN LANE

First published in 1973

Allen Lane
A Division of Penguin Books Ltd
21 John Street, London WC1

ISBN 0 7139 0487 9

Printed in Great Britain by
Ebenezer Baylis & Son Ltd
The Trinity Press, Worcester, and London

FOR DAVID AND BARBARA

Contents

Contents

PART TWO, 1821–1830

List of Illustrations

List of Illustrations

Illustration Acknowledgements

The author and publishers are grateful to the following for permission to reproduce photographs: Brighton Art Gallery and Museum for Nos 1, 2, 3, 23; The Trustees of the British Museum for Nos 9, 10; National Portrait Gallery for Nos 7, 8, 12, 13, 16, 17; Guildhall Art Gallery for No 11; Victoria and Albert Museum for No 14; National Galleries of Scotland for No 18; London Museum, Kensington Palace for No 28; Tate Gallery, London for No 31; The Trustees of the Wallace Collection for No 32. A private collection and Courtauld Institute of Art for No 29; No 30 is from an engraving in the Library of the Royal College of Physicians. Nos 4, 5, 6, 15, 24, 25, 26 are reproduced by gracious permission of Her Majesty The Queen. All the caricatures are from the author's collection.

Author's Note

This biography of George IV is based largely upon his papers in the Royal Archives at Windsor, and I have to thank Her Majesty the Queen for graciously allowing me to make use of them. Most of the King's correspondence is now generally available in the eleven volumes comprehensively and meticulously edited by Professor Aspinall to whom all students of the period will be indebted. In addition to this correspondence, I have been granted access to those papers which could not be released at the time Professor Aspinall was compiling his edition, or which concern topics (such as accounts and Queen Caroline's affairs) outside its scope. I would also like to thank Mr Robert Mackworth-Young, Her Majesty's Librarian, and Miss Jane Langton, Registrar of the Archives, and her staff, for their generous help and advice when I was working in the Castle.

Although the Royal Archives provide by far the most vital and abundant sources for the King's life, there are numerous important manuscript sources elsewhere, and I am most grateful to the Duke of Devonshire for access to the Devonshire Collections; to the Marquess of Hertford for access to the Ragley Manuscripts; to the Earl of Halifax for use of the Hickleton Papers; to the Earl of Harewood for use of the Canning Papers; to the Earl of Crawford and Balcarres for use of the Crawford Muniments; to the Earl of Harrowby for use of the Harrowby Manuscripts; to Earl Fitzwilliam and the Trustees of the Wentworth Woodhouse Estate for allowing me to quote from the Wentworth Woodhouse Muniments; to the Earl of Denbigh for permission to quote from the Denbigh Manuscripts; to the Duke of Wellington for use of the Wellington Papers; to the Broadlands Trustees for the use of the Palmerston Papers; to the Trustees of Chequers for permission to consult manuscripts in the library at Chequers; to the Bishop and Dean of Worcester for allowing me to see the Hurd Manuscripts at Hartlebury Castle; to the Director of the Royal Pavilion, for permission to study and quote from various letters in his care; to Mrs Hervé Coatalen for letting me see the correspondence of Sir Walter Farquhar and the Hook Manuscripts; to Lieutenant-Colonel

H. E. Scott for use of some material from the King's papers which are in his possession and for permission to quote from a manuscript in the Eldon Papers; to the Chairman and Secretary of Brooks's for allowing me to consult the records of the club; and to the Directors of Messrs Coutts and Company for permission to use the archives of the bank.

For helping me find the relevant papers I want to thank Mr T. S. Wragg, the Duke of Devonshire's librarian; Mr M. W. Farr, the Warwickshire County Archivist and his staff who have charge of the Ragley Papers; Major T. L. Ingram, Lord Halifax's archivist; Miss Rosamund Campbell, the Earl of Harrowby's archivist; Mr A. R. C. Grant, the Duke of Wellington's librarian; Miss Margaret Cash, Hampshire County Archivist, in whose care are the Palmerston Papers; Mr C. F. Penruddock, Secretary to the Chequers Trust; Mr L. W. Greenwood, librarian at Hartlebury Castle; Mr Derek Rogers of the Royal Pavilion; Mr J. M. Collinson of the Archives Department of Leeds City Libraries where the Canning Papers are now deposited; Mr John Bebbington who, as Sheffield City Librarian, has charge of the Wentworth Woodhouse Muniments; Miss M. V. Stokes, archivist of Coutts' Bank; and Mr N. A. Ussher, the Earl of Harewood's agent.

I have also made use of the Fremantle Collection and the Goderich Papers at Aylesbury; the Finch Manuscripts at the Bodleian, Oxford; the Pretyman Papers at Ipswich; the Waller of Woodcote Manuscripts at Warwick; the Earl Grey Papers at Durham; the Fitzwilliam Manuscripts, the Brooke Records and Lord Dover's papers and diaries at Delapre Abbey; the Markham Papers at York; the Capell Manuscripts at Hertford; the Goulding Papers at Lincoln; and the Brougham Manuscripts in the Library of University College, London. I would, accordingly, like to express my thanks for their help to Mr E. J. Davis, the County of Buckingham Archivist; Mrs Mary Clapinson of the Department of Western Manuscripts, Bodleian Library, Oxford; Mr W. R. Serjeant and Miss Patricia James of the Ipswich and East Suffolk Record Office; Mr J. E. Fagg and Dr J. M. Fewster of the Department of Palaeography and Diplomatic in the University of Durham; Mr P. I. King, Chief Archivist to the Northampton and Huntingdonshire Archives Committee; Mrs N. K. M. Gurney, Archivist at the Borthwick Institute of Historical Research in the University of York; Mr Peter Walne, the Hertfordshire County Archivist; Miss J. A. Cripps of the Lincolnshire Archives Committee; and Mr Joseph W. Scott, librarian, University College, London.

I have also to acknowledge the generous help of Dr F. Taylor, librarian of the John Rylands Library, Manchester; Mr J. N. Allen and his staff at Brighton Reference Library; Miss G. M. A. Beck of the Borough of Guildford Muniment Room; Miss A. Green, the Royal County of Berkshire Archivist; the staffs of the Oxfordshire County Record Office, and of the Public Record Office of Northern Ireland; Mrs Patricia Gill, the West Sussex County Archivist, who kindly answered various questions concerning the Petworth House Archives which are in her care at Chichester; and Mrs L. M. Patterson, the secretary of the Royal Society of Literature, who showed me the Society's papers.

Mr Michael Brock, Vice-President of Wolfson College, Oxford, has been kind enough to read the book in proof and has made several valuable suggestions for its improvement. I am most grateful also to Mrs Joan St George Saunders for working for me in the British Museum and the Public Record Office, to Mrs Stewart Ryan for reading newspapers for me in the Newspaper Library at Colindale, to Miss Barbara Mason for transcribing some of the Wentworth Woodhouse Muniments at Sheffield, to Mrs Frances Hawes, Lord Brougham's biographer, for taking extracts from the diaries and letters of Lady Anne Barnard at Balcarres, and to my son, Tom, and my daughter, Kate, for transcribing various other manuscripts. Mrs Barbro Steele has kindly helped me to translate some of the more obscure letters which Princess Caroline wrote to her husband in her idiosyncratic French. Dr Kenneth Bourne has generously helped me to identify people referred to only by disguised names in Emily Cowper's letters now among the Palmerston Papers. And Mr Edward Miller has provided me with information about the British Museum's acquisition of the King's Library.

For their generous and expert help in a variety of other ways I want also to thank Sir Owen Morshead, Sir Oliver Millar, Mr Geoffrey de Bellaigue, Lord Adam Gordon, Mr David Higham, Mr Cuthbert Fitzherbert, Mr D. A. Hartley Russell, Mr Shevawn Lynam, Mrs Eve Weiss, Dr Clifford Musgrave, Mr Roger Mortimer, Mrs Alan Glendining, Mrs John Rae, Miss Clare Pollen, Mrs Elisabeth Webb, Dr R. J. Hetherington, Mr Anthony Berry and Mr J. R. Rudd of Messrs Berry Brothers & Rudd of St James's Street, Mr Brian Hill, Mr Roger Fulford, Mrs Maurice Hill, Dr A. J. Salmon, Mrs George Onslow and Miss Jane Hoos of the Lord Chamberlain's Office.

Finally I want to say how grateful I am to Mr George Walker and Mr

Hamish Francis for having read the proofs and to my wife for having compiled the index.

C.H.

Quotations from manuscript sources have been given with the original spelling preserved. For the sake of easy reading the punctuation has occasionally been altered, capitalization modified and abbreviations written out in full.

PART ONE
1811–1820

I

Whigs or Tories?
1811–1812

*

'The Prince is excessively nervous'

For months the Prince of Wales had been eagerly looking forward to celebrating the inauguration of his Regency by holding a grand fête at Carlton House. He would have liked to do so immediately after the swearing-in ceremony; yet as long as his father's physicians at Windsor continued to hint that his Majesty's mind might yet be 'roused from its disordered actions', a celebration of his own accession to power would clearly be premature. When the spring of 1811 gave way to summer however, and his father's condition deteriorated, he decided to wait no longer. Twice he fixed a date for the party, but on both occasions was obliged to postpone it because of disturbing reports from Windsor. Then came more reassuring news, and he announced that on 19 June the fête would definitely be given, ostensibly in honour of the exiled royal family of France. Two thousand invitations were hastily despatched, some to people no longer living.

By eight o'clock on the appointed day, Pall Mall, St James's Street and the Haymarket were blocked with carriages, though the guests were not due to arrive until nine. Above the shouts of the coachmen, the crack of whips and the screech of iron-rimmed wheels could be heard the band of the Guards playing in the courtyard of Carlton House beneath Henry Holland's fine Corinthian portico. Beyond the wall that divided the gardens of the house from the Mall, matting had been laid over the smooth grass of the lawns; and covered walks, decorated with painted trellises, flowers and looking-glasses, had been specially built as promenades and supper galleries. The Prince's servants in their dark blue liveries, trimmed with gold lace, hurried about attending to their final duties.

The guests were received in the hall by various members of the Regent's Household and then wandered through the magnificent rooms on the ground floor which few of them had ever seen before.* The Regent himself appeared at a quarter past nine and stood waiting in a room, hung with blue silk and decorated with gold fleur-de-lis, to welcome the Comtes de Lisle and d'Artois, the Ducs de Berri, de Bourbon and d'Angoulême, the Prince de Condé, and Louis XVI's only surviving child, the Duchesse d'Angoulême. He was wearing the richly embroidered and idiosyncratically designed uniform of a field-marshal, a rank to which he had long aspired and from which his father had steadfastly debarred him. He was also wearing the glittering star of the Order of the Garter and a splendid aigrette.

He was forty-eight years old, but looked as though he might well have been several years older. His features, though still quite handsome, were overblown and heavy, and the expensive oils, ointments, creams, pastes and unguents which he bought in such immense quantities from his perfumers and which were applied so assiduously to his almost copper-coloured skin made it look waxlike rather than youthful. He had lost some weight since he had turned the scales at over seventeen and a half stone in 1797, but his well corseted pantaloons could not disguise the fact that he was still extremely fat. His grey eyes were rather watery; the flesh beneath his chin tended to sag into the folds of his immensely high neckcloth; and artificial pieces were required to maintain the luxuriant appearance of the

* Even those who had seen the rooms before had not seen all the furniture, pictures and ornaments in them. For the Regent was continually improving his collections, selling items, acquiring others, exchanging pictures that he no longer much liked for ones he preferred, bringing out of store or down from the attics works which had not yet been displayed or which deserved a reappraisal. 'He changes the furniture so very often,' Lady Sarah Spencer commented, 'that one can scarcely find time to catch a glimpse at each transient arrangement before it is all turned out for some other' (*Lyttelton Correspondence*, 103–4).

thick brown whiskers that adorned his cheeks. But he was as graceful as ever; his manner was still wonderfully easy and courteous, his charm irresistible. As he walked amongst his guests, affable, amusing and urbane, it was difficult not to agree with William Beckford that he was indeed 'graciousness personified'.

The entire entertainment, so Thomas Moore told his mother, was truly 'worthy of a Prince'. 'The extraordinary part of it was, that so large a number should have been served in such a style,' another guest thought; 'tureens, dishes, plates, even soup plates, were everywhere of silver with as many changes as were wanted. There were hot soups and roasts, all besides cold, but of excellent and fresh cookery. Peaches, grapes, pine apples, and every other minor fruit in and out of season were in profusion. Iced champagne at every three or four persons, all the other wines also excellent. There was no crowding, hurry or bustle in waiting; everything was done as in a private house.'

'Nothing was ever half so magnificent,' Moore continued rapturously. 'It was in *reality* all that they try to imitate in the gorgeous scenery of the theatre ... assemblage of beauty, splendour, and profuse magnificence ... women out-blazing each other in the richness of their dress. ... I really sat for three quarters of an hour in the Prince's room after supper, silently looking at the spectacle ... the Prince spoke to me, as he always does, with the cordial familiarity of an old acquaintance.'[1]

At half past two the Regent himself sat down to dinner; the long table was set for two hundred of his most honoured guests beneath ornate lanterns fixed to the fan-vaulted ceiling of the Gothic conservatory. Above him was an illuminated crown with the letters GR; behind him were crimson-draped stands – piled high with silver-gilt plate – and sixty attendants, one of whom stood '*in a complete suit of ancient armour*'. On the table in front of him was a miniature fountain whose waters flowed in a silver-bedded stream to right and left of him. The stream was bounded by mossy banks, water plants and flowers; tiny gold and silver fish swam through the arches of miniature bridges or, sadly, lay dead, floating on top of the water. A model lake was surrounded by miniature urns from which rose breaths of fragrant smoke.[2]

The Duchesse d'Angoulême sat on the Regent's right; the wife of his eldest brother, the Duchess of York, on his left. His mother was not there as she thought it unseemly to hold such a party while the King remained so ill, and had strongly advised her son not to do so during this 'great calamity'.[3] His sisters were also absent, in accordance with their mother's strict orders. Princess Caroline, the Regent's detested wife, had not been invited and had not expected to be invited. Ever since she and her husband had separated she had been 'like an archbishop's wife', she said with characteristic exaggeration and equally characteristic good humour: she did not 'partake of her husband's honours'. But she had not the least objection to the ladies of her Household accepting the invitations they had received, and she even bought them new dresses and ostrich feathers for the occasion.

To her extreme annoyance and disappointment, the Regent's daughter, Princess Charlotte, had not been invited either. She had been longing to go, as she confessed to her former governess, Miss Hayman; it was her 'duty to go'; it was 'proper' that she should go; she thought it 'very hard' that her father had not asked her. She was no longer a child; she was fifteen, tall and well developed for her age. Others, too, thought it hard on the girl. She was admittedly still rather rowdy and gauche; her laugh was sometimes still far too loud and, as John Sanders, the architect, noticed disapprovingly, she had an 'extreme, awkward, neglected manner, lolling and lounging about without any self control'.[4] She was also 'very talkative', Miss Berry thought, and very ill-bred; she did not 'walk any better', and had 'not dignified manners'. Yet she was 'very quick and very lively', and certainly no longer the tiresomely exuberant and ill-mannered, pert little girl who had so exasperated her tutors.[5] And she was, after all, heir to the throne. But the Prince had his reasons, as events were to show, for keeping the girl on a tight rein and as much as possible out of the public eye. As the time for the fête approached, he had sent her down to Windsor to stay with her grandmother.

So neither his wife nor his daughter nor his mother nor any of his sisters were at Carlton House that evening. Nor was Mrs Fitzherbert. She had received an invitation, but when she learned that Lady Hertford – the woman who had usurped her place in the Regent's affections – was to sit at the royal supper-table, she decided to ask him personally whether or not she too would be given a place there. For months past at Brighton she had been humiliated by the Prince's devoted attentions to Lady Hertford at the Pavilion where her own presence had been virtually ignored. Would she be given a place at the Regent's table at Carlton House? she had asked him bluntly. In the past 'to avoid etiquette in circumstances of such delicacy as regarded her own position with reference to the Prince, it had been customary to sit at table regardless of rank'. Would the same rule now apply? Repeatedly since their secret and illegal marriage in her drawing-room in 1785, the Prince had promised formally to establish her position in society as soon as it was in his power to do so. But that was before the advent of Lady Hertford. 'You know, Madam, you have no place', he had replied.

'None, Sir, but such as you choose to give me.'[6]

Though pressed by the Duke of York to admit her to the table, he firmly declined to do so, maintaining that the special privileges accorded to her when he was merely Prince of Wales could no longer apply now that he was Regent; so she had refused to go to the fête at all. They never spoke to each other again.[7]

The Prince was not sorry to see Mrs Fitzherbert go out of his life. She had become increasingly cantankerous of late; at fifty-five she no longer had the resilience to bear his selfishness patiently. In the past she had overlooked or forgiven his waywardness, his faithlessness, his repeated slights, for she had loved him.

Indeed, although she was sorely tried by the silence with which her subsequent letters to him were greeted, she was never entirely to outgrow her love for him.[8] But she knew now that they could never be happy in each other's company again. She demanded a formal separation, and the Regent readily granted it, agreeing without demur to the continuation of her annuity of £6,000. This, having been rather ungraciously accepted, was soon afterwards deemed utterly insufficient. All her pecuniary difficulties, she crossly reminded the Regent, 'originated from . . . the old debts of former times . . . and the very scanty allowance' which he made her. £6,000 was 'not now worth as much as £3,000 was about nine or ten years ago'. The Regent obligingly agreed to increase the pension to £8,000 and then to £10,000, and hoped that with that she would be satisfied and bother him no more.[9] All his thoughts were now centred on Lady Hertford; when parted from her, he confessed, he could only think of presenting her with his 'uggly phizz' once again.[10]

*

Although the Carlton House fête was universally admitted to have been a triumphant success by those who had attended it, it naturally came in for much criticism from those who had not. 'What think you of the bubbling *brooks* and *mossy banks* at Carlton House?' Shelley asked, expressing a widespread indignation. 'It is said that this entertainment will cost £120,000. Nor will it be the last bauble which the nation must buy to amuse this overgrown bantling of Regency.'[11] Many others were equally critical, both of the cost of the fête and of the opulent palace in which it had been held – a palace occupied by a man whose debts, though they were gradually being paid off, still amounted to over half a million pounds. His Household there was reputed to be enormous, as indeed it was. Apart from his Treasurer (Sir Samuel Hulse), his Private Secretary (Colonel John McMahon), his Assistant Private Secretary (General Sir Tomkyns Turner), a Vice-Treasurer and a Vice-Chamberlain, a Keeper of the Wardrobe and a Gentleman Porter, there were, in 1811, two Clerks, five Pages of the Presence, five Pages of the Backstairs, a House-keeper, an Inspector of the Household, a Maître d'Hôtel, a *Tapissier*, a Butler, a Table Decker, and two Surgeons to the Household. The forty-three indoor servants included a silver-scullery-woman, a laundress, two cellarmen, three confectioners, four watchmen, six cooks and ten housemaids.[12]*

The sumptuous interior of the palace in which these people worked came in for even more adverse criticism than the cost of maintaining it. There was 'not a spot without some finery upon it, gold upon gold'.[13] For some it was 'really all too much', 'overdone', 'superfluous', 'vulgar in its opulence'.[14] Yet everyone wanted to see it, of course; and as many as could took the opportunity to do so afforded by the Regent's opening it to the public for three days after the fête. On the third day no less than 30,000 people tried to get in; and, despite the efforts of the Duke of Clarence who stood on top of the garden wall endeavouring to control the crowds in his best quarterdeck manner, there was a stampede in which several distraught women visitors were stripped nearly naked. 'They were to be seen all round the gardens, most of them without shoes or gowns; and many almost completely undressed, and their hair hanging about their shoulders.'[15]

The Regent was reported to be 'exceedingly upset' by the mismanage-

---

* As was shown in the first volume of this biography, the Prince was, and always remained, a kind and considerate master. The Bishop of Lincoln's wife, with whom the Prince was to stay in 1814, was assured by his servants, 'There never was a man more easily pleased than the Prince Regent. Everything is right and he is kind and good to all.' 'How different,' the Bishop's wife commented, 'is all this authentic history to public rumours!' (Pretyman Papers, Ipswich, HA 11a).

ment, and to have relapsed into that mood of strange, unaccustomed withdrawal which observers had noticed during the earlier months of the year. At that time, as though worrying about the political problems with which he would soon inevitably be faced, he had seemed unwontedly distant at private parties and public functions, speaking 'much less, both to men and women than he did'.[16] In March 1811, at a reception at Lady Hertford's, Miss Berry had seen him arrive about midnight from a dinner party at Lord Cholmondeley's. He looked wretched, she had thought, 'with a muddied complexion, and was besides extremely tipsy'. But he was 'gravely and cautiously so', gave her a 'formal grave bow', and spoke little to anyone.[17] It had even been reported, so one of his physicians told Plumer Ward, that he was 'engaged with religion' and was reading a chapter of the Bible every day in the earnestly Protestant company of Lady Hertford.[18] Under her influence, it was supposed, he was now 'affected by Methodistical notions, and Rowland Hill, the Methodist preacher, [had] been with him a second time'.[19]

In the company of those whom he took to be his supporters he had been able momentarily to relax. At the Royal Academy dinner on 27 April, for example, he had appeared at his most attractive; and in one of the best royal speeches that Wilberforce had ever heard, he had, with obvious sincerity, declared that although 'others might be more able to judge the excellence of works of art, [they] could not exceed him in his love of the arts, or in wishes for their prosperity'.[20]

Yet for most of that year he had seemed worried and preoccupied, daunted by the amount of papers to which he was now expected to attend. One day Lord Dundas saw him sitting at a table at Carlton House between his Secretary, Colonel McMahon, and McMahon's assistant, General Turner, 'the one placing a paper before him for his signature, the other drawing it away'. Having dealt with what Dundas believed to be as many as 14,000 papers, the Regent said wearily, 'playing at King is no sinecure'.[21]

'The Prince is very nervous, as well he may be at the prospect before him,' reported George Tierney on 20 July, 'and frequent in the course of the day in the applications to the liquor chest. I much doubt, however, whether all the alcohol, as they call it, in the world under whatever name administered, will be able to brace his nerves up to the mark of facing the difficulties he will soon have to encounter.'[22] The more he drank, indeed, the less decisive he became; and he certainly drank a great deal that

7

summer. According to Lord Hampden he was quite capable of getting through three bottles of wine at dinner, 'besides maraschino, punch and eau de Garuche' which he liked 'excessively strong and hot'.[23]

One of his worst trials was his arch-conservative brother, the Duke of Cumberland, who appeared to follow him wherever he went, warning him against Whigs, against reform, against Catholic emancipation. Princess Charlotte said that her uncle, 'Prince Wiskerandos', whom she heartily disliked, was her father's 'right hand'. In fact, the Regent, who could not bear being pestered, was by now quite exasperated by the Duke – who had been convalescing at Carlton House ever since his valet had tried to murder him at St James's Palace the year before – and he went so far as to move to Stable Yard solely to shake him off. The Duke's society 'is becoming excessively irksome to him,' Lady Holland accurately informed Lord Landsdowne, 'but it denotes a lamentable lack of energy that he can only get rid of a troublesome inmate by flying his own home. The other day when he went to Windsor he took Tommy Tyrwhitt [his former Private Secretary] in his chaise and bid him keep close to the door when they were to come back in order to escape the Duke of Cumberland's importunities, but he had a more dextrous foe than he calculated upon, for the Duke, after the Prince was seated, got up upon the steps upon the pretence of whispering, and instead of getting down, hollowed out to Mr Tyrwhitt that he had better follow in his chaise. The Prince was either too timid or too much confounded to remonstrate.'[24]

In the autumn the Regent escaped to Brighton and there he appeared far happier than he had been in London, charming his guests with his easy, friendly manner, his 'animated and varied conversation', and the delightful way in which, when he went to bed, he would bid them all good night with a graceful wave of his hand and a favourite farewell, 'God bless you all!'

Sir Philip Francis, the reputed author of the *Letters of Junius*, reported him as being 'very gay' at a dinner party at the Pavilion on 30 October, and Thomas Creevey who was there the following day, enjoyed a 'very pleasant evening. About half past nine, which might be a quarter of an hour after we arrived, the Prince came out of the dining-room,' Creevey recorded in his journal. 'He was in the best humour, bowed and spoke to all of us, and looked uncommonly well, though very fat. He was in his full field marshal's uniform. He remained quite as cheerful and full of fun to the last – half past twelve – asked after Mrs Creevey's health, and nodded and spoke when he passed us. . . . He looked much happier and more unembarrassed by care than I have seen him since this time six years. This time five years ago, when he was first in love with Lady Hertford, I have seen the tears run down his cheeks at dinner, and he has been dumb for hours, but now that he has the weight of the Empire upon him, he is quite alive.'[25]

The next evening he was in the same 'high good humour' as he sat in the Music Room, between Giovanni Battista Viotti, the violinist, and Lady Jane Houston, beating his thighs in accompaniment to the band, 'singing out loud, and looking about for accompaniment from Viotti and Lady Jane'.[26] Creevey, a dedicated Whig, listened for some political pronouncement, some indication as to how much longer the Regent intended to keep in power the Tory government which he had inherited from his father. Creevey had hoped that upon assuming the Regency, the Prince would have immediately cast out the Tory Prime Minister, Spencer Perceval, whom, as a former supporter of the Princess of Wales, he did not much like, and call into office those Whigs with whom he had once been on such friendly terms. This was certainly what most Tory Ministers, including Lord Liverpool, had expected.[27] 'We are all, I think,' wrote Palmerston, Secretary at War, to his sister, 'on the *kick and the go*.'[28]

Yet the Prince had not dismissed them, and the Whigs had begun to doubt that he ever would do so. Several Whigs had dined with him at Carlton House on 1 July; but on the 11th he dined with Lord Camden, Lord President of the Council, and on the 24th with the Secretary for War, Lord Liverpool. Also that month, upon passing the windows of Perceval's kitchen, Creevey had been appalled to see 'four man cooks and twice as many maids preparing dinner for the Regent'. He had supposed that the ground was being prepared for maintaining the existing government in office. The Whig leaders, Lords Grey and Grenville, it was by then generally expected, would be 'passed over and the present Ministers continued with the addition of some of the Prince's private friends, such as Lords Moira and Hutchinson and [Lady Hertford's son] Lord Yarmouth, and old Sheridan'.[29] It was certainly Perceval's own view that his government was to be kept in office, though Lord Bathurst, President of the Board of Trade, rather doubted it.[30] Lord Moira agreed with Perceval: the Regent was becoming used to his Ministers; he did not like change anyway and was too lazy to provoke it.[31] Besides, he was finding it

9

extremely difficult to persuade his close friends to serve with the present Ministers. It was the Prince's view that 'his friends ought to come forward whenever he [chose] to call upon them, *without regard to who [was] his [Prime] Minister*'. It was a 'strange fancy', to be sure, but it existed and *'very strongly too'*.[32]

This was one fundamental problem. Another was that the Whigs in general knew that the Prince was far from reliable, and were not at all sure that they could trust him even if they were to negotiate with him. 'I know there are difficulties all round,' said Grenville, 'but I know of none greater than a confidential intercourse where you cannot place confidence.'[33] Even the Prince's personal friends shared this view. As Hutchinson said, there was with him 'a close connection between promise and retraction'.[34]

*

So the summer passed and no changes were made, while the Regent displayed a rash determination to make the most of the still considerable powers of the monarch and to exercise his patronage by granting preferment to his friends, sometimes without consulting Perceval, at others in direct opposition to his wishes. He insisted, for instance, that his faithful servant, Colonel McMahon, should be appointed Paymaster of the Royal Bounty to Officers' Widows, a sinecure worth about £2,700 a year, which was about to be abolished and which the Commons refused to sustain.[35] He was equally insistent that his brother, the Duke of York, who had been forced to retire as Commander-in-Chief in 1809, should be reappointed though the Cabinet warned him against it.[36] He assured his friend the Duke of Northumberland that 'one of the first acts' of his 'emancipation' would be to call up his son, Lord Percy, to the House of Lords, and he promised an appointment in his Household to the Duke's son-in-law, Lord James Murray.[37] He overruled Charles Yorke, First Lord of the Admiralty, in nominating his own candidate to be a Marshal of the Admiralty in place of the Minister's.[38] And he later told Perceval that he was absolutely determined that the brother of his old tutor, Dr Cyril Jackson, should be granted the vacant bishopric of Oxford. 'Perceval then put on one of his little cynical smiles,' so the Regent related, 'and observed, "Your Royal Highness perhaps does not know Dr William Jackson's *character*. He is a notorious *bon vivant*."'

'Oh, as to that,' the Regent replied, 'I know him very well. I have known him all my life. He has drunk a bottle of port in this house before now and I hope that, when he has got his mitre on, that he will drink another.'[39]

At Brighton, however, neither politics nor patronage was discussed, and no members of the government were invited to the Pavilion. Nor were Hutchinson or Moira. Lord Yarmouth was often there with his mother, and so was the persistent and tiresome Duke of Cumberland, looking 'really hideous', in the regimentals of his own German hussar regiment, with 'everybody trying to be rude to him and not standing when he came near them'. Yet although these two, Cumberland and Yarmouth, were suspected to be his 'real advisers', in public at least they were mute. There was 'no intercourse between the Regent and them'.[40]

Reluctant as he was to commit himself, the Regent's political decision could not be delayed much longer. The restrictions on his powers, which had been imposed for a year, were due to expire in February 1812; after that there could be no further delay. The Whigs had reluctantly accepted the fact that it was difficult for the Regent to bring them into office so long as his father's recovery seemed possible; but the reports from Windsor suggested that an early recovery was now highly unlikely. In the middle of July the Duke of Cumberland had written, 'the King has taken 4 jellies, some coco and tea, is totally lost as to mind, conversing with imaginary persons, as he is constantly addressing himself to *Eliza*. . . . 'Tis a most melancholy prospect.'[41] Since then, the prospect had not brightened in the least.

On 17 September the doctors reported that 'His Majesty showed clearly his incapability of maintaining any steadiness in his ideas and conversation for more than an instant. . . . He never failed to decline into some wild unnatural frame of thought after a sentence or two.' They had 'the mortification of hearing him speak of new arrangements which the *late King* was *now* making – and detail accounts of strange and horrible events which he himself was convinced had occurred in the course of the last night'. He was convinced that his sons were also dead, 'or sent away to a distant part of the globe. He was engrossed by the wildest and most extravagant fancies', sometimes imagining that he could call from the dead anyone he chose, at other times that he was an animal in Noah's Ark. In short, he appeared to be 'living in another world', and had lost 'almost all interest in the concerns of this'.[42]

Even so, the Regent hesitated. He did not altogether trust the Whigs any more. Their ideals and aspirations, as exemplified by the stout, uncouth figure of the delightful and sadly missed hero of his youth, Charles James Fox, had held a strong appeal for him in earlier years as an unruly son of a disapproving father. But the case was altogether different now. The loyalty of the Whigs to the Crown he thought questionable, their would-be policies of emancipation and reform too radical. Moreover, as a party they were in disarray, at odds with the radicals, suspicious of one another, without true leaders. Grey, whom the King disliked as much as ever, was unwell and sulky; Holland was also ill; Grenville seemed indifferent to the prospect of office; Lansdowne was considered too inexperienced, Brougham too insincere, Tierney too devious, Whitbread too emotional, Sheridan too profligate. No one thought of George Ponsonby, the official leader of the opposition in the House of Commons as more than a temporary compromise until some more effective spokesman could be found. Above all, in the Prince's mind, was the knowledge that the Whigs were certainly incapable of continuing the war in any state of unity. Many of them were in favour of ending it altogether and of coming to terms with Napoleon. Creevey, for one, was delighted when he thought he detected signs of the Regent's enthusiasm for Portugal and Wellington 'going down', and when Sir Philip Francis assured him, upon the evidence of 'equerries and understrappers', that the Peninsular campaign was now 'out of fashion'. Both Creevey and Francis hoped that the concern that the Regent expressed upon reading the returns of the Army's casualties in the Peninsula would make him 'think of peace'.[43] The Regent was not thinking of peace, though. On the contrary, the idea of a negotiated settlement appeared to him absurd when, after years of sacrifice and struggle, the fortunes of the war appeared to be turning, when Wellington was making headway, and Napoleon was withdrawing troops from the Peninsula to send across the Dnieper into the wastes of Russia.

Difficult as the decision facing him was, the Regent affected not to be unduly concerned about it so long as he remained at Brighton. On 9 November he was still 'very merry and seemed very well'.[44] Three weeks later, however, he was far from merry and very ill indeed.

*

He had gone to Oatlands, the Duke and Duchess of York's country house, to attend a ball held in honour of Princess Charlotte. He had given his daughter a lively demonstration of the Highland fling, had slipped, strained his ankle against the leg of a sofa, and retired to bed. Soon it was clear that he was not merely suffering from a twisted ankle; he 'complained of violent pain' from which he could only obtain relief by lying on his stomach and by taking 'a hundred drops of laudanum every three hours'.[45] Some people talked of gout, but others, better informed, knew that the complaint was far more serious than that. 'The Prince is, I believe, extremely ill,' Lady Bessborough told her lover, Lord Granville Leveson Gower. '[One of his several doctors, Sir Walter] Farquhar says he suffers such agony of pain all over him it produces a degree of irritation on his nerves nearly approaching to delirium. What will become of us, if as well as our King our Regent goes mad? It will be a new case in the annals of history.'[46] Ready as always to make trouble, the Duke of Cumberland, so William Fremantle reported, went about saying that his brother was mad already, that the complaint about his ankle was 'all sham', that he could get up perfectly well if he had a mind to, that the malady 'was higher than the foot, and that a blister on the head might be more efficacious than a poultice on the ankle'.[47] The illness was '*no other* than that he *was mad*'.[48]

Cumberland with great vehemence denied having made these remarks, reports of which led to his brother refusing to see him alone any more.[49] Sir Benjamin Bloomfield, who had been the Regent's Gentleman Attendant since 1808, described to Princess Charlotte a dreadful journey with Cumberland at the beginning of December. He '*never had* passed so *unpleasant* a journey in all his life', Bloomfield avowed, 'as [the Duke] was *vociferating oaths* against the *person* (whoever it was) that *could* set afoot such a lie . . . declared that if he could discover the person he would *destroy him* with his own hands, used the most solemn oaths to declare *his innocence*, in short worked himself up into a sort of frenzy that [I] hardly knew what [I] would do next, as there were firearms in the carriage – and this conduct the whole way up to town.'[50]

Whether or not the Duke had said his brother was mad, Fremantle was himself inclined to suppose that the Regent's brain was indeed sadly affected, and he told the Marquess of Buckingham that he thought that this was because he was so desperately 'worried and perplexed' by the problems of the now imminent unrestricted Regency. These had harassed 'his mind and rendered him totally incapable, for want of nerves, of doing anything'.[51]

For several weeks he continued 'very ill' with agonizing 'pains in his arms and fingers' and 'the loss of all power in them'. On 23 November he complained to Lady Hertford that he had passed a night so bad that 'it surpassed in every respect everything' that she could form herself 'the smallest idea of'; the day before he had been 'incapable of moving a a single joint' in his 'whole frame'.[52] One of his doctors, Sir Everard Howe, told Thomas Lawrence that he was now taking as many as 250 drops of laudanum a day, and even so could get only three hours' sleep.[53]

. By 1 December Princess Charlotte found him looking much better, but obviously 'suffering a great deal of pain still'. For two hours he 'talked entirely of the King and gave a *most distressing* and lamentable *account*'; nevertheless he was '*more easy in his manner*' which the Princess thought was '*a step*' at least.[54] A fortnight later he was suddenly and unexpectedly back in London, still 'nervous to the greatest degree', so George Tierney thought, as he was bound to be if the stories about the quantities of laudanum he took were true.[55] According to Princess Charlotte he was also taking 'a great quantity' of hemlock which was now his only means of getting any sleep.[56] However, Sir Walter Farquhar assured her on 18 December that the danger was over, though he could not declare when his patient would be '*quite recovered* as he had retarded his recovery himself so much owing to his playing with his constitution', disobeying the doctors' instructions, dosing and treating himself as he thought fit.[57] He was still excessively nervous, and when he heard accounts of the murders in Ratcliffe Highway, he was 'so much alarmed' that he gave orders that no strangers should be admitted to Carlton House after eight o'clock at night, to the great disappointment of his servants, 'who had made preparations for entertaining their friends at Christmas'.[58]

It was 'much believed' that the attack in the arm was 'paralytic';[59] and, according to Princess Charlotte, he himself attributed the weakness and twitching in his hands to paralysis. This was a likely enough diagnosis, Princess Charlotte thought, since huge quantities of opium were 'liable to cause that'.[60] He could hardly write on account of three 'of his fingers being compleatly numbed and useless', which made his friend and physician, Sir Henry Halford, think that the Regent might be suffering from palsy.[61] A year later he was still complaining that his 'poor right paw' could still hardly hold a pen,[62] and that he had the *'greatest pain and difficulty in writing, having the gout all over him but particularly in both his hands'*.[63]*

* It has been suggested that the Prince Regent was suffering from porphyria, that rare hereditary metabolic disorder which, in a far more severe form, afflicted his father and which, endemic in the Stuarts, was transmitted to the Hanoverians by the Electress Sophia, granddaughter of James I and mother of George I. The Prince's symptoms seem consistent with such a diagnosis, though he was never subject to the extreme mental derangement which characterized his father's case (Macalpine and Hunter, 229–46). He always took great trouble to conceal his illnesses when he feared that they might be reported as hereditary afflictions of the brain; and an article in the *Sunday Times* which guardedly made this suggestion drove him to demand that the Attorney-General should lose no time in attending to the 'infamous attack' made upon him. He also wrote to the Home Secretary, 'Why not treble the duty upon all Sunday newspapers?' He read everything of this kind, feeling it 'a duty to do so', hence he could well 'judge of the mischief resulting from this abused liberty of the press'. His observations equally applied 'to obscene prints in the form of caricatures'. There was scarcely a shop in London dealing in such trash in which he was 'not exposed in some indecent ridiculous manner'; and it was 'high time' that a stop was put to it (Parker, i, 336–7). During this illness in 1811–12, and all subsequent illnesses, he was extremely reluctant to allow any bulletins to be issued since, he insisted, they only led to gossip. During a severe illness in 1824, when for three days he never spoke and his life was despaired of, Sir Henry Halford was desired to travel to Windsor by night and to go back to his London patients in the morning, so that all might be 'kept in the most profound secrecy' (Buckingham, *Memoirs of the Court of George IV*, ii, 77).

2

An Adonis of Loveliness
1812-1814

*

'This (or else my eyesight fails),
This should be the Prince of Whales'

The Regent's general recovery was slow, and was rendered all the more prolonged by the political problems he was now urgently called upon to settle. He had postponed his decision as long as he possibly could, seeking advice from every quarter, then discussing the advice with yet other advisers, keeping all contenders for office in the dark as to what he intended to do, hoping that after wearisome, exhausting negotiations a strong government acceptable to himself would eventually emerge. Ideally this government would 'unite as many persons of talent ... as possible'.[1] It would include moderate men of both parties, as well as his personal friends; it would carry on the war in the Peninsula with renewed energy; and it would postpone the problem of Catholic emancipation.[2]

In the past, during Fox's lifetime, the Regent had always looked upon Catholic relief with sympathy, as his friends Lord Moira, Lord Hutchinson and Lord Hutchinson's brother, Lord Donoughmore, still did. But now – due largely to the influence of the Hertford family, it was supposed – the Prince was more inclined to agree with the Duke of Cumberland that it would be a most dangerous innovation. Not wanting to be accused of having broken faith, he maintained that he still favoured relief, yet he could not see his way to granting it so long as the King was alive. After all, his argument ran, he was only acting as Regent in the King's name; the King had had strong feelings that to give way to the Catholic claims would be to violate his coronation oath; the King's feelings must be respected.

As Prime Minister in his ideal government the Prince favoured the claims of the Duke of Wellington's brother, Lord Wellesley, the Foreign Secretary, that 'Spanish grandee grafted on an Irish potato', in the Regent's characteristically acute description. Lord Wellesley himself had no doubts as to his own suitability for the post; and on 16 January he tendered his resignation on the grounds that Perceval was incompetent and that neither he nor the rest of the Cabinet were pursuing the war with sufficient vigour. The Regent persuaded him to remain for the time being, holding out the hope that he might soon find himself at the head of a coalition government; and the next month the Regent sat down to write a letter to the Duke of York – an intermediary known to be strongly against Catholic emancipation – who was to take it to Lord Grey who was, in turn, to make its contents known to Lord Grenville.[3]

Neither Grey nor Grenville was in the least disposed to consider the coalition which the letter, in a calculatedly wounding way, proposed. The Regent was merely offering the Whigs a few ministries in return for their acknowledgement that the Tories deserved to remain in office in recognition of their 'honourably distinguished' conduct of the war in the Peninsula.[4] In their rather haughty reply, Grey and Grenville pointed out that they differed from the present administration on 'almost all the leading features of the present policy of the empire', particularly Ireland, and they refused to consider joining it unless there were to be a clear understanding that Catholic relief would be granted.[5] In any case, neither Grey nor Grenville was convinced that it would be wise to accept office even if it were to be definitely and unreservedly offered them, irrespective of the differences over Catholic emancipation. As Grenville said, there was a 'total want of confidence in the Prince's steadiness and good faith'.[6]

Having thus skilfully broken with the Whigs without actually refusing to offer them office, the Regent turned back to Perceval whose government was confirmed in power, to the profound satisfaction of the Duke of Cumberland to whom his brother was now reconciled. The Regent's difficulties, however, were far from over. Lord Wellesley, disappointed in his hopes of succeeding Perceval, reiterated his determination not to serve under him any longer, and advised the Regent to strengthen the government by bringing in both Lord Castlereagh and George Canning.

When this advice was passed on to the Cabinet, they unanimously decided to resign unless Wellesley did so. His ambitions frustrated, Wellesley did resign, proceeding to Carlton House 'in the highest style, state liveries and full dress', to deliver up the seals to the Regent who 'was or, appeared to be, *deeply* affected and almost unable to speak'.⁷ Then, to the Regent's further chagrin, he was asked to accept the admission to the government of Lord Sidmouth as Lord President of the Council. 'Is it possible Mr Perceval, that you are ignorant of my feelings and sentiments towards that person?' he exclaimed angrily when the Prime Minister explained the necessity of bringing Lord Sidmouth in. 'I now tell you, I will never have confidence in him, or in any person who forces him upon me.' The Regent thoroughly disliked Sidmouth, his father's conscientious and prudish former Prime Minister, whom he blamed for his past failure to obtain the military promotion upon which he had set his heart. 'If you choose to employ him, be it so,' he went on. 'But I warn you that you must take all the responsibility of the measure upon yourself.'⁸ In the end, however, the Regent was forced to give way.

While the Cabinet, thus strengthened, were far from satisfied that they had the Regent's confidence, the Whigs were outraged by his treatment of them. Even Lord Moira, who for years had been one of his most intimate friends – and had, in consequence, become almost bankrupt – was for a time estranged from him, unable to reconcile his personal friendship with loyalty to Whig principles.⁹ Lords Hutchinson and Donoughmore were also estranged; so was the Duke of Norfolk.¹⁰ 'It grieves me to the soul to tell you, Sir,' Moira wrote to him on 28 February, 'that the general astonishment at the step which you have taken is only equalled by a dreadful augury for your future security. It is not the dissatisfaction of disappointed expectants to which I allude. A disinterested public views with wonder your unqualified and unexplained departure from all those principles which you have so long professed. It observes with a still more uneasy sensation your abandonment of all those persons for whom you had hitherto proclaimed esteem, whose adherence you had spontaneously solicited, and of whose services (rendered at the expense of foregoing their private advantages) you had for years availed yourself.'¹¹

At the St Patrick's Day dinner at the Freemasons' Tavern on 17 March, when the Prince was normally the 'reigning and rapturous toast', his name was loudly hissed. Sheridan loyally stood up to defend it; but, as was so often the case now, Sheridan was drunk, and his speech was received with shouts of protest and hisses louder than ever.¹²

Very few other Whigs remained faithful to the Regent. Lord Forbes, his aide-de-camp, thinking that his political opinions did not 'in the least degree accord with those of the Ministers, in whom his Royal Highness the Prince Regent thought it expedient to repose his confidence', felt it his duty to submit his resignation from the Household.[13] The Regent declined to accept it;[14] but Creevey, who attended a dinner party at Michael Angelo Taylor's house in Whitehall, a favourite rendezvous of the Whigs, recorded that Lord Forbes came to the table 'with the yellow lining and the Prince's buttons taken away from his coat. He said never again would he carry about with him so degrading a badge of servitude to such a master.'[15]*

Forbes's indignation was common throughout the Whig party. Deprived of all the pleasures, power and perquisites of office, its members rounded with fury on the Regent and on the Hertfords, the Duke of Cumberland and the Queen, whom they believed chiefly responsible for turning his mind against them. Creevey was vehement in his condemnation of 'this madman', 'this most singular man . . . doomed, from his personal character alone, to shake the throne'.[16] Brougham attacked him in even stronger terms; so, too, did Whitbread. As Lord Holland later observed, they all 'charged his Royal Highness with ingratitude and perfidy', encouraging 'every species of satire against him and his mistress'.[17] Indeed, Lady Hertford, 'the old lady of Manchester Square', was quite as savagely attacked as he was himself. Lord Grey, who declared that he would never take office until 'this destructive influence' had been abolished, referred in the House of Lords to an 'unseen and separate influence which lurked behind the throne . . . an influence of [an] odious character, leading to consequences the most pestilent and disgusting'.[18] Another Member of the House described a similarly pestilential figure 'issuing forth from the inmost recesses of the gaming house or brothel and presuming to place itself near the royal ear'.[19]

Enraged, the Regent retaliated. At a banquet at Carlton House he launched 'a furious and unmeasured attack' upon his erstwhile political friends by whom he persuaded himself, as he so often did persuade himself, that he had been monstrously ill-used. So angry with the Whigs did he become, in fact, that Princess Charlotte burst into tears and had to be led out of the room by Sheridan.[20] It had once been her father's proud

---

* Lord Forbes's host, Michael Angelo Taylor, had formerly been a close friend of the Regent. They had recently fallen out because – so it was said – the Regent had tried to seduce Mrs Taylor. Her husband had discovered him in the process and knocked him down (*The Rising Sun*, ii, 157–9; BM *Sat*, viii, 481).

boast that he had 'bred up his daughter in the principles of Mr Fox'.[21] Now it had come to this.

Worse was yet to come. On 11 May Perceval was shot through the heart in the lobby of the House of Commons by John Bellingham, a deranged commercial agent ruined by the war; and the Regent had another ministerial crisis on his hands. Lord Liverpool, formerly Secretary for War, succeeded Perceval as Prime Minister; and Lord Castlereagh became Leader of the House of Commons as well as Foreign Secretary. The Regent tried to give the government further strength by asking Wellesley and Canning to rejoin it. Canning, however, refused to work with Castlereagh, and declared that he would not join a government which was not committed to Catholic emancipation. Wellesley, his eye still on the leadership, also refused; and, in any case, Liverpool and his colleagues made it clear that they would refuse to have either him or Canning back.[22]

An exasperated backbencher now proposed a motion of 'no confidence' in the present administration; the motion was carried, and Lord Liverpool's government resigned on 22 May.[23] Once again the Regent turned to Wellesley and through him halfheartedly approached the Whigs with renewed proposals for a coalition; but this time, too, as he surely hoped they would, the negotiations came to nothing. Then, professing to be desperately in need of the reassurance and advice of his old, estranged friend, Lord Moira, he sent for him and 'flung himself upon his mercy'. When Moira dutifully called at Carlton House, the Regent 'hung round his neck in tears' and 'seems to have been very nearly in convulsions'.[24] Moira said that perhaps it would be better if he called another day to discuss the situation when the Regent was 'more composed'.[25] The next day, however, he was just as agitated as ever; but, after a long discussion, Moira agreed to attempt yet another approach to Grey and Grenville. He was no more successful with them, though, than Wellesley had been. They demanded the resignation of the Regent's Household, including, of course, Lord Hertford, and his son, Lord Yarmouth; and this the Regent loyally refused to consider. Lord Moira then set about composing a government with the help of the Tories; yet although a brave soldier he was 'the greatest political coward in the world', and in the end his nerve failed him.[26] The Regent, having used him as he had used Wellesley to get rid of the Whigs, now decided that the time had come to 'fall back upon his old government' and to reappoint Lord Liverpool as Prime Minister. At last, by a combination of wearying procrastination and cunning manoeuvre, he had got the government he had all along been endeavouring to establish: Perceval's government without Perceval, a government that would pursue the war with vigour, and leave the Catholic question alone.[27]

*

Throughout the protracted negotiations which had taken place since Perceval's murder, the Regent had appeared to be in 'a state of agitation beyond description'. Sheridan 'described the Prince's state of perturbation of mind as beyond anything he had ever seen'.[28] He sought relief in drink as well as in laudanum. As Princess Charlotte commented disapprovingly, 'too much oil was put into the lamp'.[29] It was not only the harassing negotiations with government and opposition that had bothered him. There had also been a series of anonymous letters, signed 'Vox Populi' and 'An enemy of the damned Royal Family', which threatened him with 'the same fate as Mr Perceval' if he did not see to it that bread was cheaper and that Bellingham was reprieved. In the north, where anger over what was felt to be his betrayal of the Whigs was particularly strong, walls and doors had been placarded with notices offering a hundred guineas as a reward for the Regent's head. In addition, there had been angry scenes in Parliament over his continuing to employ Colonel McMahon as his Private Secretary at a salary of £2,000 a year, an office which the opposition condemned as unconstitutional, since no British sovereign, except King George III when he was nearly blind, had ever had a Private Secretary before.[30] There had above all been the constant importunity of numerous claimants who looked to him, now that his powers were unfettered, to fulfil old promises, not to mention the worry of his debts.

At the end of 1811 his debts amounted to £552,000; and he had wanted the Cabinet to appeal to Parliament to settle them. He had also asked for £150,000 for what he termed 'Regency services'. The Cabinet had insisted that he must be content with £100,000 for 'Regency services';[31] and as for his debts, it had been suggested to him that Parliament would never agree to pay off so immense a sum; he must endeavour to do so himself by means of his own economies. This had been the 'decided and unanimous opinion' of the Cabinet, 'most reluctantly and unwillingly adopted'.[32]

There had also been strong opposition to the Regent's requests for

£196,000 a year for the establishments of the King, the Queen and the Princesses.[33] And the Regent had not only had serious differences with the government about this, he had also had to contend with the objections of his increasingly ill-tempered mother. If the Princesses were to have their own establishments – which she was very much opposed to their having – the Queen wanted to know why she herself could not have a 'separate and distinct establishment'.[34] It was all very well to argue that, in the event of the King's recovery, he would want to find 'his government, his family and his everything exactly *eo ipso* as he left them';[35] in the meantime she had to confess that she was 'very uneasy'. She wanted 'a certain sum' stipulated for herself alone so that she could never 'be either suspected or accused of incroaching upon the King'.[36]

She was 'voracious', the Regent's former Secretary, Tyrwhitt, complained, 'and had tormented the Prince in his worst illness, at Oatlands, with a visit to prevent his giving the Princesses an independent establishment'.[37] However, she was not able to prevent it. He remained firm in support of his sisters' cause; and although the Queen was eventually promised her own establishment, so, too, were the Princesses. They were to receive £9,000 a year each, in addition to £4,000 a year from the Civil List, and were thus to become independent of their parents at last. They had had to wait an inordinately long time. Since the eldest, Princess Charlotte had married the Hereditary Prince (now King) of Württemberg in 1797, not one of the other sisters had found a husband. Augusta was now forty-four, Elizabeth forty-two, Mary thirty-six and Sophia thirty-five. They all looked to their eldest brother for his future help, and all wrote affectionate letters to thank him for the great kindness he had always shown them in the past. He was still, and was ever to remain, their '*dearest, dearest* brother' whose 'angelic behaviour' towards them would always be remembered.[38]

It was rarely that anyone else referred to him in such terms. He was as unpopular with the people as a whole as he had ever been. The Marquess of Buckingham was informed by William Fremantle, that when he went to the Queen's Drawing-Room at the end of April 1812, there were 'upwards of ten thousand people in Pall Mall through which he passed, but there was not one single token of applause. It was a dead silence throughout.' 'At the play the other night,' Fremantle continued, 'when *Henry V* was acted, all the allusions to his breach of promise when Prince of Wales were thundered with applause and in the new play which is now acting at the Lyceum there are some allusions to female influence in government which are constantly met by clapping and applause.'[39]

After the St Patrick's Day dinner at the Freemason's Tavern, where the drunken Sheridan's amphibological remarks in defence of the Regent's name were drowned in the general hissing, the *Morning Post*, which had been purchased on behalf of Carlton House some years before,[40] wishing to make amends for this 'ungenerous conduct', referred to the Prince in ludicrous hyperbole as 'the Glory of the People', 'the Maecenas of the Age', an 'Adonis of Loveliness'.[41]

These 'astounding eulogies' were altogether too much for the *Examiner* which briskly responded with the assertion that this so-called 'Glory of the People' was, in fact, 'the subject of millions of shrugs and reproaches', that 'this Adonis of Loveliness was *a corpulent gentleman* of fifty! In short, that this delightful, blissful, wise, pleasurable, honourable, virtuous, true *and* immortal PRINCE [was] *a violator of his word, a libertine over head and ears in debt and disgrace, a despiser of domestic ties, the companion of gamblers and demireps, a man who has just closed half a century without one single claim on the gratitude of his country or the respect of posterity'*.[42]

The author of this attack, Leigh Hunt, and his brother John, editor of the *Examiner*, were arrested and charged 'with intention to traduce and vilify his Royal Highness, the Prince of Wales, Regent of the United Kingdom'; and, despite a spirited defence by Henry Brougham who, enthusiastically welcoming the case as an excellent opportunity for damaging the Regent, 'fired for two hours very close and hard into [him] on all points, public and private', they were found guilty, fined £500 each and sentenced to two years' imprisonment.[43]

The sentence caused widespread indignation and made the Prince more unpopular than ever. Shelley, who visited Leigh Hunt at Horsemonger Lane Gaol, and proposed a subscription for the 'brave and enlightened man', furiously condemned the Regent as a 'crowned coward and villain', an 'infernal wretch', constantly demanding more money – and for what? 'For supplying the Augean stable . . . with filth which no second Hercules could cleanse.'[44] Keats lamented that 'kind Hunt was shut in prison'; and Charles Lamb's anonymous verses on 'The Prince of Whales' were repeated with renewed conviction:

> Not a fatter fish than he
> Flounders round the polar sea.

See his blubbers – at his gills
What a world of drink he swills . . .
Every fish of generous kind
Scuds aside or shrinks behind;
But about his presence keep
All the monsters of the deep . . .
Name or title what has he? . . .
Is he Regent of the sea?
By his bulk and by his size,
By his oily qualities,
This (or else my eyesight fails),
This should be the Prince of Whales.[45]

Benjamin Haydon expressed the general view when he commented that although Hunt's libel was impudent enough, the 'debauched Prince . . . amply deserved it'.[46] And although writers were inclined to be more circumspect thereafter, the number of attacks upon the Regent were by no means diminished. A few weeks after the Hunts were sentenced, Thomas Moore, lending his pen to the Whigs' attack, published anonymously *Intercepted Letters or the Twopenny Post-Bag* in which the 'R–G–T' was held up to a ridicule even more wounding than Hunt's savagery.

It was at this time that the Prince had the mortification of quarrelling finally with Beau Brummell whose elegance and caustic wit he had for so long, if rather jealously, admired. There had been numerous petty quarrels in the past, since Brummell had always declined to mark his friendship with the Regent with that deference expected of the intimate Carlton House circle. The rule was that the Regent might treat his friends familiarly, but that they must not presume upon this to be familiar in return, either with him or with distinguished guests in his presence. It was a rule that Brummell had often broken. Captain Gronow recorded one particular occasion when Brummell, dining at the Marine Pavilion at Brighton, 'incurred his master's heavy displeasure in the following manner. The then Bishop of Winchester, perceiving Brummell's snuff-box within his reach, very naturally took it up and supplied himself with a pinch; upon which Brummell told his servant, who was standing behind his chair, to throw the rest of the snuff into the fire or on the floor. The Prince [who had a great reverence for bishops] all the while looked daggers: he gave Master Brummell a good wigging the following day, and never forgot the insult offered to the Bishop.'[47]

Soon afterwards there came that fatal day when the Regent, arriving at a ball at the Argyle Rooms, spoke to their mutual friend, Lord Alvanley, but ignored Brummell. 'Alvanley,' Brummell called out, 'who is your fat friend?' That question – there are conflicting reports as to the circumstances in which it was asked – marked the end of their friendship.

Brummell was later asked to a dinner at Carlton House but merely, so General Sir Arthur Upton, one of the other guests, thought, in order that the Regent – who could never forgive ridicule of his personal appearance – might take his revenge. Brummell, elated at not having been cut off the Prince's invitation list after all, drank too much wine at dinner. His host, turning to the Duke of York, said that perhaps it would be as well to ring the bell and ask for Mr Brummell's carriage before he became quite drunk. Brummell stood up, left the room, and never spoke to the Regent again. [48]

Twice more at least they saw each other, once when the Regent's carriage stopped outside the picture gallery in Pall Mall. Brummell was standing in the doorway. He raised his hat to the sentries, pretending that their salute had been intended for him, then turned his back as the Regent stepped out of his coach. Some time later they were forced together by a crush outside the opera as they were waiting for their carriages. They looked straight into each other's eyes, but neither spoke. Brummell backed away when he could do so, coolly staring into the Prince's angry face. [49]

*

Although he found it only too easy to make enemies, the Regent had not lost the art of making friends, both with men of his own age, such as the rich art patron, Sir John Fleming Leicester, and with men much older, like the Russian-born merchant and philanthropist, John Julius Angerstein, whose collection of pictures was to form the nucleus of the National Gallery. He could be as charming as ever when he chose. Maria Edgeworth once saw him at Mrs Hope's, talking with most attractive animation, 'one third of the night', in the centre of the room to Lady Elizabeth Monk. [50] On another occasion he had a conversation almost as long and quite as intense with Mme de Staël who thought that no one could have been more '*aimable*', and who thereafter lost no opportunity of 'saying flattering things' about him. [51] John Constable who met him at a dinner before the opening of the Reynolds exhibition at the British Institution found his easy friendly manner most agreeable.[52] Lord Byron, whose *Childe Harold's Pilgrimage* was published in March 1812, the same month as Leigh Hunt's libel in the *Examiner*, was introduced to him at a ball and was delighted to find 'a finished gentleman from top to toe . . . with fascination in his very bow'.[53] They spoke together for more than half an hour about 'poetry and poets'. Byron reported the conversation to his publisher, John Murray, who in turn wrote to another of his authors, Walter Scott, to tell him that the Regent had displayed 'an intimacy and critical taste which at once surprised and delighted Lord Byron. But the Prince's great delight was Walter Scott, whose name and writings he dwelled upon and recurred to incessantly. He preferred him far beyond any other poet of the time, repeated several passages with fervour, and criticized them faithfully. He spoke chiefly of *The Lay of the Last Minstrel* which he expressed himself as admiring most of the three poems. He quoted Homer, and even some of the obscurer French poets, and appeared, as Lord Byron supposes, to have read more poetry than any Prince in Europe. He paid, of course, many compliments to Lord Byron, but the greatest was "that he ought to be offended with Lord Byron, for that he had thought it impossible for any poet to equal Walter Scott, and that he had made him find himself mistaken" '.[54]

Impressed as he was by the Regent's charm of manner, and flattered as he was by his gratifying taste in literature, Byron did not hesitate to join in the general vilification. He was the author of 'To a Lady Weeping' which appeared anonymously in the *Morning Chronicle* in the month that *Childe Harold's Pilgrimage* was published. Sympathizing with Princess Charlotte's distress at her father's outburst against the Whigs during the dinner party at Carlton House, it bids her

> Weep, daughter of a royal line,
>   A sire's disgrace, a realm's decay:
> Ah, happy! if each tear of thine
>   Could wash a father's fault away!
>
> Weep – for thy tears are virtue's tears –
>   Auspicious to these suffering isles;
> And be each drop in future years
>   Repaid thee by thy people's smiles.[55]

Two years later, when opposition to the Regent was even more vehement than it was in 1812, Byron had these lines republished over his name. Both then and on their first appearance they reflected the public mood towards the Regent far more accurately than the portrait of the gracious, cultivated 'Prince of Princes' in *Don Juan*.

For a time at the beginning of 1814 the Regent had enjoyed a brief spell of popularity when it transpired that Andrew James Cochrane Johnstone, an unscrupulous Member of Parliament who had been insisting in the House of Commons that the evidence given against the Princess of Wales in the 'Delicate Investigation' of 1806 was perjured, was himself a perjurer.[56] But the tide had soon turned against the Regent once again. Indeed, throughout 1814 discreditable stories about him circulated widely in London society, and many were true enough, for he was drinking more heavily than ever. In January much was made of his visit to Belvoir Castle where he had stood as godfather to the Duke of Rutland's heir and where he had helped himself far too generously from the fifty-gallon cistern of punch which the Duke had provided for his guests.[57]

Yet the picture so often drawn of a constant sot was grossly distorted. On his way back from Belvoir Castle to London the Regent stayed for the night in Huntingdon at Buckden Palace, the episcopal residence of the Bishop of Lincoln, where both the Bishop and his wife were entranced by his friendly and gracious behaviour. Mrs Tomline had taken the greatest pains to ensure that her distinguished guest should be properly welcomed and correctly treated. She had written to a knowledgeable friend, Princess Charlotte's Lady Companion, for advice; and she had been told exactly how to receive him, how to light him to his room, what to wear, and whom to invite to dinner. 'You need not attend him to his room more than once,' she had been informed. 'The best thing would be for him to choose his place at table. . . . You might write to Lord Lowther [who was to be in attendance] say what company there is in the neighbourhood and ask whom the Prince would like to meet. I think he likes to meet company. . . . The Prince has no water (or finger) glasses at his table, neither has any royal personage here, except the Princess of Wales. . . . The more you are dressed the better, certainly with diamonds. . . . A handsome morning dress for breakfast is quite sufficient. . . . *No* livery servants must wait, except his own . . . His valet, Dupaquier, must have a bed in a room as near him as possible. . . . He will make all easy to you; he is so well bred.'[58]

So that there should be no mistakes or misunderstandings, Mrs Tomline wrote down the most precise instructions for her own servants and for those she was to borrow for the occasion from her neighbours. They were told exactly where to stand during dinner and given instructions, as detailed as those in a military drill book, as to how to serve the dishes and the wine. 'The Prince's own two pages stand behind his chair and do not move,' they were informed. 'But whatever the Prince asks for is handed to them to give to him, and his plates are taken from their hands. . . . The Prince to be served before the ladies on all occasions.' They were told when to remove the upper of the two table-cloths – 'after the cheese has been handed around and the epergne taken away' – when to leave the room – 'after the ices are taken off and the dessert plates changed and the wine set upon the table' – and when to bring the coffee, tea and liqueurs into the drawing-room – 'after the Prince is served, coffee is to be brought as usual for the company, tea ½ an hour afterwards, liqueurs ½ an hour after that'.

In an immensely long letter to her sister, Mrs Tomline described how she stood at the bottom of the staircase waiting for the Prince to arrive, 'dressed in diamonds, according to the custom'. It was dark outside, and servants were posted with flambeaux on either side of the entrance gates, on top of the main gateway, beside the entrance porch and on the porch roof. Ten more servants were stationed at strategic points within the house, where forty-four people, including the Prince's two pages, his valet and four footmen, were to sleep that night.

At the sound of carriages in the drive, the Bishop, who had once been Pitt's tutor, and his eldest son, who had come down from Cambridge for the night, walked down the porch steps. The Prince alighted, shook the Bishop and his son by the hand, apologised for being late, and approached Mrs Tomline who made 'a very *profound* courtsey which HRH returned with a very "beautiful and respectful bow", as it was said to be by bystanders'.

'I then took one candle from a servant in waiting,' Mrs Tomline continued, 'and the Bishop took another to light HRH upstairs (according to *ceremony*, not *necessary*, for I had procured *plenty* of lamps for all the passages and appartments). . . . The Prince said something *very graciously* and took my hand, begged I would not trouble myself and said a something about the weather. At the Drawing Room door I stopped for him to enter first which he did with a sort of *apologising* bow, and walked to the fire as people usually do. By this time his attendants [Lord Lowther, General Turner and Sir Carnaby Haggerston] were come into the room, and the usual sort of introductions took place, in the most familiar, easy way possible on his part. He made me sit down almost immediately, but he and everyone else continued standing . . . I was exceedingly delighted by the Prince's inimitable manner – such mingled condescension and dignity I had no idea of before. . . .

'When the Prince went from the Drawing Room to dress, the Bishop and I conducted him to his room. He begged I would not give myself this trouble, but in a way that showed it was proper I should go, and then said, "If it must be so, allow me your hand." On the landing at the dressing room door he turned to stop my proceeding any more, and in the most obliging manner possible thanked me for my most flattering attentions. . . . He expressed himself instantly delighted with the room, and the Bishop left him to dress. It is singular that he *never* uses a dressing room *anywhere*, but always dresses in his bedroom which he likes to be *very* warm. . . . He brings his own sheets everywhere . . . Instead of the *ten* blankets you heard of he sleeps even *this* weather with *only* two and no counterpane or quilt. What can possess people to frame such fibs for no purpose?' [59]

Having dressed for dinner, the Prince returned to the drawing-room where the other fifteen guests were now assembled. He offered Mrs Tomline his arm on dinner being announced, asked her where she usually sat and took the chair on her right. He talked to her about her family, about the recent festivities at Belvoir, 'a good deal about the present state of Europe', and told her an anecdote concerning Napoleon, repeating in French 'with a sort of shudder', an exceptionally vainglorious remark the Emperor was alleged to have made. Mrs Tomline confessed that she was utterly captivated by him and felt completely at ease in his company.

'I was not at all nervous, somehow or other,' she told her sister, 'though I hardly know how to account for not being so on such a great occasion. I do not think I ever felt more *self-possessed* than I was during the whole visit. . . . The Prince's manner was so very gracious and encouraging as to set me at ease. . . . Strange as it may appear, the Bishop was more nervous than I was.'

When the dinner – a 'most capital' one, the hostess was proud to say – was over and the ladies had retired, the Prince asked the Bishop to come to sit next to him, talked to him of 'parliamentary subjects' and of the problems of Catholic emancipation to which the Bishop was rigidly opposed. 'Nothing could equal the grace and kindness of his manner to the Bishop,' reported Mrs Tomline, who was proud 'yes, *properly proud* of the honour done' to her 'beloved husband'.

29

The Prince retired to bed at half past twelve – he usually went about one o'clock – and the Bishop lighted him to his room once more. 'I offered to go also,' Mrs Tomline said, 'but he took hold of both my hands with a grace which is quite indescribable, saying this could not be permitted and that he must be allowed to wish me good-night *here* with many thanks for my most obliging attentions to him in every way. . . . When he got to the door of the Drawing Room he turned round and made a *grand* bow of leave to the company that seemed to excel in grace and dignity and condescension. . . . Really the Prince Regent's manners are most *fascinating*! And his correctness here was perfect. . . . You can scarcely conceive the impression made by him.' [60]

On his return to London, however, he began to drink heavily again and the impression he gave was far less favourable. Within three weeks of his return, one of his doctors, Sir Henry Halford, had never seen him so ill 'in all his life before', and confided in Princess Charlotte that another 'such attack' would be '*fatal*'. Sir Henry attributed the attack to excessive drinking, of which the Regent had been doing a 'vast deal'. [61] A few weeks later, Charles Greville recorded a characteristic story in his diary: 'The Regent was very near dying in consequence of a disgraceful debauch, about ten days ago. He sent for Mr Colman [George Colman, the dramatist and theatrical manager] of the Little Theatre, from the King's Bench [debtors' prison] and sat up the whole night with him, and others of his friends, drinking, until he was literally dead drunk. He was saved with some difficulty by Sir W[alter] Farquhar.'[62]

Neither the British victories in Spain, nor even the end of the war and Napoleon's abdication in April affected the Regent's unpopularity to any noticeable degree. When, on the day that Napoleon left for Elba, he escorted the cumbersome figure of Louis XVIII into London after his long exile in Buckinghamshire, he aroused no marked enthusiasm; and though the white flags of the Bourbon dynasty and fleurs-de-lis fluttered from hundreds of windows, beside the national flag of Britain, though there were scattered cheers as the impressively escorted procession made its way down Piccadilly to Grillon's Hotel in Albemarle Street where the French King was to stay, no one could pretend that either of the two stout gouty gentlemen in the state carriage drawn by eight white horses was being acclaimed as a hero. Despite his Army's victories the Regent was still no more than a 'graceful *en-bon-point* Adonis, Prince of modern Macaronis'. Whenever his yellow carriage with its maroon blinds swung through the park, pulled by superb bay horses and escorted by galloping Life Guards, it was watched by the people in pointed silence, and sometimes even actually booed.[63] One day as it drove into the City, which it was never to do again, it was surrounded by a hissing mob who called out threateningly, 'Where's your wife?'

'Prinny is exactly in the state one would wish,' Creevey commented vindictively. 'Nothing can equal the execrations of the people who recognise him. *She*, the Princess, on the contrary, carries everything before her. . . . All agree that [he] will die or go mad. He is worn out with fuss, fatigue and *rage*. He came to Lady Salisbury on Sunday from his own dinner beastly drunk, while her guests were all perfectly sober.'[64]

But still, whether the people wanted him to or not, the Regent could not avoid taking a leading part in the victory celebrations, as it was not only his taste but his duty to do so, and a duty, it was grudgingly allowed, that he did perform well. 'Our Prince Regent is never so happy as in show and state,' commented Lady Vernon, 'and there he shines incomparably.'[65]

Having invested the new French King with the Order of the Garter and buckled the Garter round Louis's elephantine knee – it felt just like 'fastening a sash round a young man's waist' – the Regent wished him well on his journey from Dover. Standing at the end of the pier, he bowed as the *Royal Sovereign* headed for the French coast and Louis XVIII rested his vast unsteady legs in his cabin.

Returning to London, the Regent prepared himself to receive the Tsar Alexander I and Frederick William III, King of Prussia, who, with Prince Metternich, representing the Emperor of Austria, were due to arrive on 7 June. The Regent was not looking forward to their coming. He had already met the Tsar's recently widowed sister, Catherine, the Grand Duchess of Oldenburg, whom he heartily disliked. The Grand Duchess, an ugly, vivacious, clever, mischievous and self-important little woman, had arrived at the end of March and had been installed in the Pulteney Hotel in Piccadilly, which had been taken over for her by the Russian ambassador at a cost of 210 guineas a week. The Regent had arrived to welcome her to England before she had had time to change out of her travelling clothes; they had met on the staircase and had taken an instant dislike to one another.

During the next month the Prince's dislike had grown more intense from day to day. The Grand Duchess had done all she could to annoy the

Prince by receiving the leaders of the opposition, and by announcing that she would go to see the Princess of Wales, which she no doubt would have done had not the Russian ambassador prevented her by threatening to resign. She had also welcomed Princess Charlotte and had spent hours alone with her in her room.

A dinner given for her at Carlton House had been a lamentable disaster. She had begun by demanding that the band be sent away as music made her feel sick; and when her host, in an attempt to smooth over this embarrassment, had ventured to hope that a woman of her charm would not continue to wear mourning for long, she had 'answered by an astonished silence and looks full of haughtiness'. She had then made some criticisms of the Regent's treatment of his daughter to which he had unwisely responded, 'When she is married, Madam, she will do as her husband pleases. For the present she does as I wish.' This reply had given the Grand Duchess the opportunity of observing with a smile, 'Your Highness is right. Between wife and husband there can only be one will.' The Regent had turned to Countess Lieven, the Russian ambassador's wife, and whispered in her ear, 'This is intolerable.'[66]

'Handsome as he is,' the Grand Duchess had subsequently reported to her brother, 'he is a man visibly used up by dissipation and rather disgusting. His much boasted affability is the most licentious, I may even say obscene, strain I have ever listened to. You know I am far from being puritanical or prudish; but I avow that with him . . . I do not know what to do with my eyes and ears – a brazen way of looking where eyes should not go.'[67]

The situation became even more strained and embarrassing when the Tsar himself arrived. He was far from being predisposed in the Regent's favour. He had read with extreme annoyance of the reception that had been accorded in London to Louis XVIII who, ignoring Alexander's own contribution to the downfall of Napoleon, had had the effrontery to reply to the Regent's congratulations by declaring, 'It is to the counsels of Your Royal Highness, to this glorious country, and to the steadfastness of its inhabitants, that I attribute, after the will of Providence, the re-establishment of my House upon the throne of my ancestors.'[68]

Declining to stay in the Duke of Cumberland's apartments at St James's Palace, which had been prepared for him, the Tsar accepted the advice of his sister, who had great influence over him, and put up instead with her at the Pulteney Hotel. Immediately on his arrival there he stepped out onto the balcony to acknowledge the rapturous cheers of the crowds who had gathered in Piccadilly to acclaim him. This was particularly galling to the Regent who, having ridden out to Shooter's Hill to welcome his guest, would now be obliged to drive all the way through the crowds to the Pulteney Hotel to see him, instead of being able, as he had planned, to slip quietly down the Mall to St James's. Eventually he decided not to risk exposing himself to the insults of the crowd, and sent a message to the Tsar that he could not come to his hotel. The Grand Duchess, who had been waiting for hours with her brother to receive him, angrily exclaimed, 'This is what the man is like.'[69]

Over the next few days the relationship between the Regent and the Tsar rapidly deteriorated. They kept each other waiting; they scarcely looked at each other when they did meet. Fancying himself as a despot upon whom the rays of enlightenment had descended, the Tsar went out of his way to talk to the Whig leaders as well as the Tory Ministers, and actually went to see Jeremy Bentham. He caused yet further offence when he showed himself to be rather attracted by Lady Jersey, with whom he waltzed energetically around Lady Cholmondeley's ball-room, and when he refused to enter the Regent's coach unless the Grand Duchess accompanied them, though the Regent carefully explained to him 'that no woman ever went into the same carriage as the Sovereign when he appeared in public as such'.[70]

The blunt, reserved, down-to-earth King of Prussia did not antagonize the Regent in the same way as the mystically ruminating, liberal-minded Tsar; but he, too, was a difficult guest, insisting on sleeping on a rough camp bed instead of the state bed that had been provided for him at Clarence House, and behaving generally like 'a sulky bear'.[71]

Overlooking these slights, the Regent commissioned portraits of both his guests from Thomas Lawrence – whose great gifts demanded an indulgent attitude towards his former escapades with Princess Caroline at her house at Blackheath – and accompanied them on various visits to the sights of London and to Oxford where they were to receive the honorary degree of Doctor of Civil Law and where the honorary degree of Doctor of Laws was to be bestowed upon Metternich.

The Regent, who had himself been honoured with the degree of D.C.L. in 1810, following his gift to the University of the fruits of the Herculaneum Mission, arrived at Magdalen Bridge wearing his scarlet robes and was met there by the Mayor and the Chancellor. He and his fellow sovereigns were escorted to the Sheldonian Theatre, the Divinity School, the Clarendon Press, the Bodleian Library, and then to dinner in the Radcliffe Camera where spectators were admitted to the gallery to watch the feast, at which the King of Prussia's celebrated General, the bluff Prince von Blücher, got extremely drunk on strong beer and cognac. On the last day of the visit, at dinner at Christ Church where the Regent was staying, Blücher was guilty of similar misbehaviour, and when his health was drunk he mumbled a response in his guttural German. 'The Prince, perceiving the indecorum of this, at once rose,' an undergraduate recalled, 'and announced that so excellent a speech should not be lost upon the greater part of the company, who could not be expected to understand German, and that, therefore, in the absence of a better interpreter, he would volunteer for that office himself. . . . He then delivered an extremely neat and tactful address of thanks to the University.' The undergraduate considered this behaviour characteristic of the Prince's 'peculiar grace and elegance' which had 'shown in its best lustre during the whole visit'.[72] Maria Edgeworth confirmed that the Prince's visit to Oxford had been a great success and that he had entered the Sheldonian Theatre to 'loud applause'.[73]

In London, though, the rude behaviour of the people towards him sometimes made it impossible for him to remain pleasant and composed. Carlton House was illuminated during the celebrations with green and yellow flares placed between palm trees in painted tubs; yet it was outside the windows of the Tsar and the Prussian King that the crowds gathered. The cheers that greeted the visitors when the Regent accompanied them in public were not too hard to bear for he could flatter himself that he had a share in them, though the Tsar's hail-fellow-well-met response to the acclamations was mighty irritating. But he could not hide from the fact that he was more likely to be hissed than cheered when he went out alone.

Towards the end of the visit there was a splendid banquet, costing £20,000, at the Guildhall. On proceeding to his place on the dais through an aisle between the seven hundred standing guests, the Regent had to wait while the Tsar stopped to chat with Lord Holland and Lord Grey. He then had to suffer the further embarrassment of hearing the Grand Duchess insist that the singers from the Italian Opera stop their performance since they, like the Carlton House band, made her feel sick. It was only with the most sulky reluctance that she agreed to 'God Save the King' being played softly after the loyal toast.

By this time Ministers and opposition alike had grown decidedly tired of both her and her brother. 'When folks don't know how to behave,' Lord Liverpool murmured to Countess Lieven, 'they would do better to stay at home.' Lord Grey decided that the Tsar was a 'vain, silly fellow', after all.[74]

What had been most intolerable of all to the Regent during these weeks, when London had been celebrating the end of the war with such enthusiasm, had been the rapturous applause invariably accorded to his wife. He had debarred her from attending all official functions but he could not prevent her going to Covent Garden, where she was greeted with loud clapping, with shouts of 'Three hearty cheers for an *injured woman*', and with demands that the orchestra should strike up God Save the King, the 'good King, the protector of outraged innocence'.[75] The Regent turned pale when he saw the artfully timed entrance of the Princess, who contrived to arrive in a black wig and many diamonds just as the applause for the Regent's royal guests was subsiding. A friend of Thomas Moore had never seen 'anything so pointed as the manner in which the entire audience turned to her and cheered her'.[76]

After the performance her carriage was cheered more wildly than ever as it made its way through crowds who shouted to ask her if she would like them to burn down Carlton House.[77]

3

Princess Caroline
1812-1814

*

'The poor Princess is going on headlong to her ruin'

For all the public's support of her, the Princess of Wales was now a lonely and dispirited woman. She was 'very large and coarse', in Joseph Farington's opinion, 'exhibiting nothing of feminine grace or dignity, nor was there any taste shown in her manner or in her dress'.[1] For a time after her formal separation from the Prince she had lived happily enough at Kensington Palace, which the Regent was rumoured to be anxious to close down as a hotbed of Jacobinism. She had given dinner parties and dances which had been attended by guests whom any ambitious hostess would have been proud to have at her table. Writers came and politicians, musicians and scholars; and if she really preferred the racy gossip of such guests as Lady Oxford, whose children by a variety of fathers were known as the Harleian Miscellany, she could nevertheless enjoy the conversation of Charles Burney, Lord Byron, William Lamb, Samuel Rogers and George Canning. Nor was she entirely neglected by the royal family. To the Regent's profound annoyance the Dukes of Kent, Sussex and Gloucester accepted her invitations; the Duchess of York called upon her regularly; even the Queen, disapproving and distant as she was, asked her to the Queen's House when her mother, the Duchess of Brunswick, was also to be of the company. But as time went on she grew increasingly bored by the life she was forced to lead and the limitations imposed upon her conduct. She was 'always seeking amusement,' Lady Charlotte Campbell commented, 'and unfortunately often at the expense of prudence and propriety'.[2] After unwillingly suffering the company of some tiresome guest she would exclaim – though in less fractured English than that in

36

which Lady Charlotte chose to record her remarks – 'Mine Gott, dat is de dullest person Gott Almighty ever did born!' Sometimes she would suddenly get up in the middle of a particularly boring party, and leave for the theatre where a box had been provisionally booked for her. On other occasions, fancying a drive might relieve the tedium, she would step into her carriage and, without telling the coachman where she wanted to go, would point in the appropriate direction. At other times she would give a ball and would bounce up and down crying out '*Vite! Vite!*' if her partner, though exerting himself to the utmost, did not dance quickly enough for her satisfaction; or she would lead her guests all over her apartments in a dance of her own invention.[3] She did these extraordinary things, Lady Charlotte Campbell thought, for no other purpose than to make people stare.[4]

Occasionally she would make a tour of Bayswater, knocking on doors and asking if there were rooms inside to let. She did in fact take a cottage in Bayswater where she spent whole days pretending to be an ordinary private person, as Marie Antoinette had done at her Hameau at Versailles. In the evenings she made up extravagant fantasies about her past life with which she regaled her astounded ladies, or she sang – and sang very badly – to the accompaniment of a weird and grasping family of Italian musicians, named Sapio. 'The poor princess is going on headlong to her ruin,' wrote Lady Charlotte Campbell. 'Every day she becomes more imprudent in her conduct, more heedless of society. . . . The society she is now surrounded by is disgraceful.' Lady Charlotte, much alarmed by a 'change in the shape' of the Princess's figure, thought that she might be pregnant until reassured that the change was due to her Royal Highness 'having left off stays – a custom which she [was] very fond of'.[5]

The dreadful Sapio, whom Lady Charlotte called the 'Ourang-Outang', was one of the worst of the Princess's new friends. He came to dinner one evening when the 'music mania' was at its 'highest pitch' and was 'more free and easy and detestable than ever. . . . Then her Royal Highness sang – Squall – Squall . . .' During a subsequent musical evening the 'horrible din of their music hardly ever stopped the whole evening, except when it was interrupted by the disgusting nonsense of praise that passed between the parties'.[6]

Lady Elizabeth Foster, who had married her lover, the Duke of Devonshire, after Georgiana's death, thought that no one now had any 'doubt of the Princess having had attachments and even intrigues'. For the past 'seven or ten years' everybody was in agreement as to her 'imprudence of conduct, indelicacy of manner and conversation, and criminal attachments'.[7]

'I daresay they think me mad!' Princess Caroline commented carelessly; and her mother certainly thought her so. 'She has this excuse,' the old Duchess confided to Lord Redesdale, touching her head and bursting into tears. 'She is not quite right *here*.'[8]

Unbalanced she may have been, but she was still astute. And when the clever and ambitious lawyer, Henry Brougham, and Samuel Whitbread, the enthusiastic, impetuous and eloquent champion of reform, took up her cause, she realized that they had other motives than her own defence.[9] Whitbread, the hero of the Whig left in the House of Commons, was undoubtedly more sincere in his championship than was Brougham, who did not even like her any more; but both of them, as she well knew, saw in her an invaluable weapon with which to beat the Regent and the Tories. Brougham had seen and seized his opportunity in June 1812 when the Regent had used his now unshackled powers to restrict even further the number of visits his daughter was allowed to make to her mother. Ever since the 1806 'Delicate Investigation' into the Princess's strange conduct at Blackheath, Princess Charlotte, with the King's approval, had been forbidden to see her mother more than once a week. In 1812 the Regent decided that she was not in future to be allowed to see her more than once a fortnight.

The Regent had sound reasons for imposing this restriction on his daughter, far better reasons than all but a few people knew. Even those who disregarded the evidence against the Princess submitted to the King's Commissioners in 1806, or who believed she had since reformed her life, could not convincingly argue that the Princess of Wales was an ideal parent for a high-spirited, impressionable sixteen-year-old girl. The conversations at her dinner-table were notorious – at least amongst those who had first-hand knowledge of them; and the Regent knew that no attempts had been made to curb them when Charlotte was a member of the party. It was not only society scandals and illicit amours, such as Mrs Clarke's affair with the Duke of York, that were openly discussed in her presence; she was also introduced to the company of men like Sir William Drummond, the diplomat, who assured her that the Christian view of the Bible was all nonsense, that priests had always been the 'most corrupt and contemptible of mankind'.[10] Moreover, the Princess knew all about her mother's supposed lovers, past and present, and was encouraged to be friendly with those loose young men who were often to be found strutting about her rooms at Kensington and Blackheath.

The King himself had attempted to put a stop to his granddaughter ever paying a visit to the Princess of Wales unless suitably chaperoned; but as Princess Charlotte herself confessed, 'notwithstanding that order, she generally saw her mother alone and had witnessed many things in her mother's room which she could not repeat'.[11] Later the King had ordered that she 'should never meet any society whatever there'; but this injunction had also been flouted.[12]

It was not that Princess Charlotte was particularly devoted to her mother. Indeed, Lady Charlotte Campbell said that Princess Caroline was 'too quick-sighted' not to be perfectly aware 'that her daughter did not care three straws for her'.[13] In letters to her best friend, Margaret Mercer Elphinstone, Princess Charlotte wrote of her '*duty*' calling her to Kensington, of her having to go to 'a very disagreeable dinner' where she would be 'most horribly tired'. 'I shall be ... just in time', she told Miss Elphinstone in a characteristic note on 6 January, 'to set off for dinner [with my mother] which shall be *humdrum* enough.'[14] Although she did not see him very often, and was never entirely at ease with him when she did, Princess Charlotte appears, indeed, to have preferred the company of her father, more and more so as she grew older. He was '*very kind*' when he went to see her one day while she was staying at Bognor, and she drove him out 'by his *own desire* in the phaeton'.[15] She would have enjoyed his visits to her much more, she confessed, if her fearful uncle, Cumberland, had not always accompanied him and spoiled it all with his rude banter and indecent jokes, his way of bullying her. When her father had been due to dine with her at Warwick House on 24 September 1811, for example, 'the *charming* D. of Cum' who had been to see her the day before and had been 'as disagreeable as usual' had told her that he would come too, and this she was sure would 'spoil it'.[16]

If Princess Charlotte was never very anxious to visit her mother, the mother did not display any marked affection for the daughter. Princess Caroline made a great fuss when the Regent forbade their meeting more than once a fortnight. She protested to her 'ever beloved Charlotte' that she was being deprived of 'the only happiness' which was left to her 'to enjoy upon this earthly world'; she told her that she would never relinquish the right to see her; she said that her pen was too feeble to express her 'deep felt regret'.[17] But her protests were made largely because Brougham advised her to make them and because, as she confessed to her intelligent and amusing Lady-in-Waiting, Lady Charlotte Lindsay, a confidante of Brougham's, she derived great 'fun' from her 'warfare with the royal family', keeping them 'in hot water', 'teazing and worrying them'.[18]

This 'warfare' entailed several visits to Windsor, where she followed Princess Charlotte, insisting that she must see her there if she were not allowed to see her once a week at Kensington. Charlotte herself dreaded these visits to Windsor where she felt 'banished and in prison'.[19] Her ill-tempered grandmother, constantly sniffing snuff, was so fearfully disapproving; and though the 'old girls', her aunts, were always 'very happy' to see her and *'in their different ways'* to *'do them justice'* were always as 'attentive or endeavouring to be *civil'* as they could possibly be, their life was so 'dreadfully dull' that they had become dull too.[20] The noisy visits of her flamboyant mother – who was never dull whatever else she was – might, therefore, have been welcome in the staid and tedious atmosphere of the Windsor Lodges. But her mother was never admitted.

Princess Caroline protested to her mother-in-law about her husband's cruel rules, and asked if they could not be modified on her instructions; but Queen Charlotte, entirely unsympathetic, refused to interfere and told her son what his wife had done. He expressed himself most gratified by the 'very kind and considerate and well judged and most prudent method' that she had adopted to 'baffle this not only extraordinary . . . but most impudent fresh attempt on the part of this most mischievous and intriguing infernale' to affect a fondness for her daughter 'which she never did feel and [was] totally incapable of feeling to create a discord or confusion in the family under the pretence of seeing her'.[21]

Undeterred by rebuffs, the Princess and Brougham decided to make a formal protest in writing to the Regent. Brougham drafted the letter; she signed it and sent it off. It was returned to her unopened, since the Regent, having 'some years ago declared that he never would receive any letter or paper from the Princess, intended to adhere to that determination'. She then despatched it to Lord Liverpool who also sent it back: no direct communication from her to the Prince could be received under any circumstances. Eventually she prevailed on Lord Liverpool to read it to the Prince who was 'not pleased to signify any commands upon it'.[22]

Ultimately, though, he did relent; and gave permission for the Princess to see her daughter on 11 February, less than a fortnight after her previous visit. This did not suit Brougham's book at all. The more intractable the Regent was made to appear the better. So, before Princess Charlotte's next visit to her mother took place he arranged for the letter of protest to be published in the leading Whig newspaper, the *Morning Chronicle*, with the Princess of Wales's entire approval.[23]*

The Prince's immediate reaction was to submit to the Privy Council, the Archbishops, the Speaker, the Master of the Rolls and other lawyers, the evidence collected during the 'Delicate Investigation' of 1806, together with the question 'whether it is fit and proper that the intercourse between her Royal Highness, the Princess Charlotte and the Princess of Wales should continue under restriction and regulation'. The Regent went to Warwick House to tell Princess Charlotte what he had decided to do. It was 'a very serious investigation', he warned her, but that 'whatever way it ended', his treatment of her 'would be equally kind and considerate, as he should not consider her accountable for the faults of her mother'.

---

* For several years past, both the Regent and the Princess had been conducting their feud with each other through the Press and had been doing all they could to win over journalists and newspapers to their respective sides. The Princess, who was supported by the *Morning Chronicle*, the *Pilot* and the *Star*, gave occasional sums of money to the *Sunday Review*; while her friend, Lady Perceval, supplied the *News* with forged letters (Aspinall, *Politics and the Press*, 306–11). McMahon and Charles Arbuthnot were both active on the Regent's behalf. In 1812 McMahon supplied the *Morning Chronicle* with copies of documents damaging to the Princess's reputation; and in 1813, so Lady Charlotte Lindsay told Brougham, a proprietor of the *Evening Star* was offered £300 a year if he would turn against the Princess; but championing the Princess was far more profitable than supporting the Regent, and the offer was declined (Brougham MSS, March 1813: Aspinall, 93). Peter Stuart, a former proprietor of the *Morning Post*, claimed 'some permanent situation under government' on the grounds that he had been promised that his small annuity 'would be doubled or tripled as a permanency whenever His Royal Highness by the accession of power was enabled to do so'. The egregious Rev. Henry Bate Dudley also demanded a reward for services in the past when he had defended the Regent in the pages of the *Morning Herald*. He was granted a baronetcy and a stall in Ely Cathedral, and, although his claims to further church preferment were refused, he obtained by blackmail an annuity of £300 (Aspinall, *Politics and the Press*, 168). Another journalist, Thomas Ashe, claimed to have been 'seduced, at a time of dire distress, to abandon the services of the Princess of Wales' and to have thereafter received 'upwards of 1,000 guineas' for elevating 'the husband at the expense of the wife' (RA Geo IV, Box 12: Asp/K. ii, 36). This Thomas Ashe was imprisoned as a debtor in 1814 in the King's Bench from which he was evidently released by an official from the Home Department who paid off his debts for him (RA Geo IV, Box 12, 1 November 1820).

As she listened to her father's words, Charlotte, standing by the fireplace, appeared to be 'dreadfully overcome'; she 'looked penetrated with grief and spoke not a word'.[24]

Towards the end of February the Privy Council reported that 'after a full examination of all the documents' before them, they were of the opinion 'that under all the circumstances of the case' it was 'highly fit and proper . . . that the intercourse between her Royal Highness, the Princess of Wales, and her Royal Highness the Princess Charlotte should continue to be subject to regulation and restraint'.[25]

As soon as he could, Whitbread leapt to the Princess of Wales's defence in the House of Commons, pointing out that in 1807 the Cabinet had virtually cleared her of the charges made the year before. The Regent thereupon riposted by publishing the evidence that her servants had brought against the Princess, to which Brougham then responded by republishing *The Book*, Spencer Perceval's defence of the Princess which had been printed in 1806. By this time, so Lady Melbourne said, it had become the 'fashion amongst ladies to burn their newspapers that the servants may not read such improprieties'.[26]

Newspaper proprietors themselves were delighted to have such material to publish. Although the Whig *Morning Chronicle* had printed the Princess of Wales's letter of complaint to the Regent, it did not support Brougham and the Princess unquestioningly since to do so was not in keeping with the general party line. Other papers, however, found it highly profitable to support them. *The Times* had not done so at first; but a bad fall in circulation suggested a change of policy. After the change the circulation was rapidly made up again. The *News*, a strong supporter of the Princess, had increased its circulation by over a quarter by the end of the first four weeks of Brougham's campaign.[27]

But if newspaper readers, while taking delight in all the scandal, were generally not prepared to have the Princess presented in a bad light, Princess Charlotte was deeply disturbed by all the stories which were spread abroad about her mother and which she knew were far from groundless. She liked Brougham, who was fond of her in turn; and she shared his hatred of the Tories; but she could not feel as he did about his war with them over the restrictions imposed upon her mother's visits to her. One day, after the restrictions had been imposed, she met her mother in the Park. And as soon as she got home she wrote to her father to explain to him that the Princess, who was on her way to visit the dying

Duchess of Brunswick, had stopped her carriage and spoken to her for five minutes. 'I trust this circumstance will not happen again,' she told him, 'but as it was entirely unexpected by me I wished to give you the earliest intelligence, as I make it a point *never* to have *any concealments* from *you*. I hope you will soon come to me.'[28]

Relations between mother and daughter had grown progressively worse throughout 1813 and by the spring of 1814, so Lady Charlotte Lindsay told Brougham, Princess Charlotte 'seemed to be in despair about any possibility of reconciliation'.[29] She knew that her mother 'found very great fault with her to everybody, and said that "she could not think she was her daughter, as she showed such want of character", and that "she had no spirit or steadiness"'.[30] Princess Charlotte also knew that her mother, tired of the campaign that was still being waged on her behalf, was thinking of leaving the country, but *she* had not been consulted; and it was a matter, as Brougham apprehensively advised her, that concerned her intimately. If her mother went to live on the Continent, the Regent might well find grounds upon which to divorce her. He would then be free to marry again, perhaps have a son, and Princess Charlotte would no longer be heir to the throne. Yet Princess Caroline's desire to live abroad, despite all the appeals that were made to her, was growing stronger month by month; and by the time the visit of the Tsar and the King of Prussia to England was over she felt that she should delay no longer.

*

The Princess of Wales had been outraged to receive from the Queen notification of the Regent's command that she must not attend the drawing-rooms to be held in honour of the foreign sovereigns as he himself would be present. She had been told that it must be 'distinctly understood, for reasons of which he alone [could] be the judge', that it was the 'fixed and unalterable determination' of the Regent 'never to meet the Princess of Wales upon any occasion, either public or private'.[31] The Princess had protested; she had reminded the Queen of how she had been treated 'up to the period of his Majesty's indisposition'; she had declined to surrender her 'right to appear at any publick drawing-room' to be held by her Majesty. She had also written to the Regent declaring that she would 'not submit to be treated as guilty' having 'been declared innocent'. 'Can your Royal Highness have contemplated the full extent of your declaration?' she asked him. 'Has your Royal Highness forgotten the approaching . . . possibility of our coronation?'[32] But in the end, for all her indignation, she felt obliged to give way and to 'yield in the present circumstances to the will of his Royal Highness'.[33]

Forbidden to attend official functions, care had also been taken to ensure that she did not see the foreign sovereigns in private. Every possible obstacle had been placed in her way; even the Duchess of York, the King of Prussia's sister, had been prevailed upon to suspend her visits to her during King Frederick's visit.[34] So, while everyone else was enjoying themselves, she was left at home frustrated, making wax models of her detested husband, sticking horns in their heads and pins in their bodies, and gloomily watching them melt in front of the fire.

At the opera, which Brougham had urged her to attend, the supremely tactless Tsar, who had repeatedly asked if he could have a look at the King, had peered at her through his binoculars, and had said that he would call upon her whether the Prince liked it or not. She had waited in for him all afternoon, wearing her best dress, anxious to talk to him about her father who had died fighting in the Tsar's cause; but he had never come.

It was the final disappointment. Foreign kings and emperors ignored her; her husband hounded her; most of his family avoided her; her former friend and protector, the King, her uncle, though even he had been less indulgent of late, was now unable to help her; her mother had died; and, as for her supporters, the Whigs, why all they did was 'for the gratification of the *party*' not for *her* gratification! They ordered her about, told her where to go and what time to arrive, tormenting her with their selfish advice. 'No child was ever more thwarted and controlled than she.' As for all this cheering by the people in the streets and the audience at the opera, it was 'of no consequence' to her 'but to Mr Whitbread. And that's the way things always go and always will go until I can leave this vile country,' she concluded sadly. She did not know who plagued her more, her friends or her enemies.[35]

Anxious that every inducement should be given to his wife to fulfil her intention of going abroad, the Prince agreed that Lord Castlereagh should assure her that an annuity of £50,000 would be made available to her immediately, in place of her present income of £22,000 a year. Whitbread and Brougham were strongly against her accepting the 'insidious offer' of so large a sum lest it should appear that, by doing so, she was abandoning her claims and grievances for money. They drafted a letter which was to be sent by the Princess to the Speaker of the House of Commons refusing it; but before Whitbread had had time to take the draft to her, she had already, to his 'infinite surprise', written to Castlereagh accepting the offer – as Canning, almost alone among her advisers, had hoped she would[36] – adding that she did so 'in order to prove to Parliament' that she was 'never averse to any proposal coming from the Crown to replace her in the proper splendour adequate to her situation, and to throw no unnecessary obstacles in the way to obstruct the tranquility or impair the peace of mind of the Prince Regent'.[37]

Whitbread, 'much chagrined and disappointed' by these comments, told the Princess that he 'exceedingly' disapproved of them, that she had 'surrendered everything' by them, that they would be used against her 'whenever she wished to assert the rights of her station'.[38]

She replied that 'she meant to relinquish nothing, and particularly that she meant to go to St Paul's' to the thanksgiving service at which, it had been made clear to her, she would not be welcome.[39] She demanded a seat in the Cathedral 'upon the same level with the seats of the rest of the royal family';[40] but she was curtly informed by the Lord Chamberlain that her request could not be granted without the authority of the Regent, and his Royal Highness had not 'been pleased to give his authority for this purpose'.[41]

Lady Charlotte Lindsay, who had burst into tears when told that the Princess had accepted the offer of £50,000 a year,[42] told Brougham that she seemed quite unaware of her folly and of her having forfeited all claim to his 'advice and assistance'.[43] Brougham, indeed, felt 'fully justified in giving her up'. 'I suppose you have heard of Mother P. bitching the thing so completely in snapping eagerly at the cash, and concluding with a civil observation about unwillingness to "impair the Regent's tranquility"!! etc.' he wrote to Creevey, 'This was all done on the spot and in a moment, and communicated to Sam and me next day . . . However, tho she deserves death, yet we must not abandon her, in case P. gets a victory after all.'[44]

The next week Brougham saw and seized his opportunity to deprive the Regent of his victory. 'Mrs Prinny's' request for a seat in St Paul's for the thanksgiving service had been refused and all was 'alive' once more: now a letter could be written complaining of her continued ill-treatment, pointing out that her acceptance of the offer of £50,000 a year was 'wholly misconstrued', and that she now spurned it.[45]

But although Whitbread easily persuaded her to inform the government that she did not need £50,000 – £35,000 would be sufficient – Brougham found it a much more difficult task to persuade her to change her mind about leaving England where she was proving so valuable a weapon in his war with the Regent and his Tory ministers. 'Depend upon it, Madam,' he warned her, 'that there are many persons who now begin to see a chance of divorcing your Royal Highness from the Prince. . . . As long as you remain in this country I will answer for it that no plot can succeed against you. But if you are living abroad and surrounded by base spies and tools who will be always planted about you, ready to invent and swear as they may be directed, who can pretend to say what may happen?'[46]

Margaret Mercer Elphinstone added her pleas to those of Brougham. 'Let me entreat you to use every exertion of your influence for Princess Charlotte's sake,' she urged Lady Charlotte Lindsay, 'to induce the Princess not to make a long absence, which would be ruinous, both to the interest of mother and daughter.'[47]

4

Princess Charlotte
1812-1814

*

'If she were mine, I would lock her up'

For many months now Henry Brougham had been assiduously fostering the idea that the Regent thoroughly disliked his daughter, that he was jealous of her, that he would be glad to have her out of his way. 'He is jealous of her to a degree of insanity, and has been for some time,' Brougham had assured Lord Grey at the beginning of 1813. 'I believe the Dukes of Cumberland and Yarmouth have actually been feeding him with hopes of getting rid of her by divorcing his wife, and this he is fool enough to believe. It seems too absurd, but you may rely on it some such thing has been broached.'[1]

It was true, of course, that the Regent could not fail to be exasperated by those enthusiastic shouts which almost invariably greeted her carriage – 'God bless you! Never forsake your mother!' – that, detesting Princess Caroline as he did, he could not but find distasteful in their daughter all that reminded him of his wife. Charlotte was better looking than her mother, but she was already rather showily full-blown. She was talkative and on occasions rather coarse. Her governess had had to remonstrate with her about the immodest way she wore her clothes and showed her drawers and her legs as she got in and out of carriages. 'I don't care if I do,' she had responded, proud of her legs which were certainly very pretty. Her conversation had been 'forward and dogmatical on all subjects, buckish about horses, and full of expressions very like swearing'.[2] In short, as Miss Berry had observed, she had been 'very ill brought up'.[3] Her manners were 'so odd', the Grand Duchess of Oldenburg told the Tsar, that they took your breath away. She looked like a plump boy,

47

'or rather like a young rascal, dressed as a girl', the Grand Duchess thought. But she had 'much wit and doggedness in her nature', 'a will of bronze in the least things, a searching reasoning power'; she had 'great intelligent eyes of pale blue' which, unfortunately, sometimes had 'the fixed look of the House of Brunswick'.[4]

She was also warm-hearted and emotional, and obviously attracted to men. The Regent conceived it his 'duty as a father' to ensure that she was kept firmly in hand, that she was closely watched from morning to night by those who had been appointed to supervise her upbringing. He repeatedly reminded her governess, Lady de Clifford, of her duties in this respect and on one occasion at least felt obliged to give 'her ladyship a severe lecture'.[5] Eventually Lady de Clifford resigned. It was given out that she had done so on the grounds of ill health, but the real reason was a quarrel over her charge's association with Captain Charles Hesse of the 18th Hussars, a handsome womanizer who was said to be an illegitimate son of the Duke of York.[6] The Prince, who was always extremely well-informed about Princess Charlotte's friends and behaviour, had heard disturbing rumours about Hesse which Lady de Clifford herself partially confirmed.[7] It was not until after Lady de Clifford's resignation, however, that Princess Charlotte confessed the full story to her father. Her aunt, Princess Mary, was present when the confession was made and she afterwards made a record of what her niece had said.

Princess Charlotte had made the acquaintance of Captain Hesse one day when she was out riding at Windsor where his regiment was quartered, Princess Mary wrote. 'Lady de Clifford had allowed him to ride by the side of the open carriage morning and evening for six weeks before she reprimanded her for it. . . . And after the regiment moved from Windsor and was quartered at Portsmouth and Lewes, the Princess Charlotte confessed to her father she always met him at her mother's at Kensington, and had private interviews with him . . . with the Princess of Wales's knowledge and connivance. . . . The Princess of Wales used to let him into her own appartment by a door that opens into Kensington Gardens, and then left them together in her own bedroom, and turned the key upon them saying, "*À present je vous laisse, amusez vous.*"'[8]

'I can tell you what is more,' the Princess continued as her father stood 'horror struck' by this revelation that his wife had virtually invited their daughter, then aged sixteen, to make love with Captain Hesse. 'My mother carried on a correspondence for us, and all the letters backwards and forwards went through her hands.' Presents had also been exchanged, and Princess Caroline, without her daughter's knowledge, had given him a portrait of her. 'God knows what would have become of me if he had not behaved with so much respect to me,' Princess Charlotte concluded. She had never really been able to make out whether Captain Hesse was her mother's lover all the time, but she supposed Princess Caroline's 'object was to draw her into this scrape to bring the boy [her adopted son, William Austin] forward as heir to the throne'. She added that her uncle, the Duke of Brunswick, who had often put her on her 'guard on the subject of [her] mother's conduct', told her that he was 'sure that the boy was her child'.[9]

The Prince, who was relieved to learn that no promise of marriage had ever been given to Hesse but dismayed that he had not so far returned her indiscreet letters or presents as he had promised to do, told her how appalled he was by the 'dreadful situation in which she had been placed'. But if she concealed nothing from him he would not reproach her; on the contrary 'his object must be to save her' and to 'prevent the possibility of such a thing happening again'.

He was kind to her and she was grateful. That evening after dinner she went to Princess Mary's room 'and said that her mind was greatly relieved since she had *told all* she had in her *mind* to her father, that she had been miserable and never had courage before this to do so'.[10]

This was Christmas Day, 1814; but at the time of Lady de Clifford's resignation in 1812, when her father suspected, though did not know for sure, what was happening between Hesse, herself and her mother, Princess Charlotte had been far less amenable and not in the least contrite.

She had, in fact, been excessively cross when she learned that Lady de Clifford was to be replaced by another governess, the Dowager Duchess of Leeds. The last thing she wanted was another governess. Now that she was nearly seventeen she felt entitled to her own Household with Ladies-in-Waiting, and on 10 January 1813 she wrote to her father accordingly.[11] He replied that she could not possibly have a Household of her own until she got married. Undeterred by this refusal, she repeated her request to Lord Liverpool.[12]

The Prince was furious by this '*deceit* and duplicity', by her having gone behind his back to his Prime Minister. He drove down to Windsor with Lord Eldon, the Lord Chancellor, a particularly unfortunate choice in his daughter's opinion, since Eldon was not only a pompous man of extremely humble parentage – risen from the coal wharfs of Newcastle upon Tyne and known in the royal family as 'Old Bags' – but, of all the members of the Cabinet, the most unlikely to have any sympathy with her case.

How could she be so impertinent as to demand her own Household at her age? her father wanted to know when she had been called down into the Queen's room to confront him. He told her that he knew 'all that passed in Windsor Park' and it was, therefore, utterly out of the question for so 'stiff-necked, stubborn and silly' a girl to have her own establishment. Lord Eldon then reminded her what the English law had to say about the Sovereign's power over members of his family and, upon being asked what *he* would do if he had such a daughter, he maintained, 'If she were mine, I would lock her up.'[13] The Princess listened to all this in silence; but later on in the room of one of her aunts, she burst into tears and sobbed, 'What would the King say if he could know that his granddaughter had been compared to the granddaughter of a collier?'[14]

'Things were in a most uncomfortable state after this scene,' commented Cornelia Knight, the Queen's tall, touchy, and humourless companion who had been asked to chaperone Princess Charlotte, and never to let her 'go out of her sight for one moment', pending the arrival of the Duchess of Leeds. The Princess fell ill with a heavy cold and a 'little nervous fever, occasioned by all she had gone through'. But at least she could comfort herself with the reflection that, although she would have to accept the Duchess of Leeds as her Governess, the Duchess's principal assistants were not to be known as Sub-Governesses but as Lady Companions. The appointment of Lady Companion was offered to Miss Knight who badly wanted to accept it since she found life at Windsor 'every year more and more confined', and had grown unutterably bored with having to listen to all 'the complaints and private quarrels' of the royal family. Life at Warwick House – 'miserably out of repair and almost falling into ruins', as she was to discover it to be – would have its disadvantages, yet it would certainly be less tedious than life with the Queen.[15]

Her Majesty, however, did not want to lose Miss Knight's company, though she would not actually commit herself to saying so, wishing her companion 'to take the refusal' on herself so that the Queen might thus avoid offending the Prince. Eventually Miss Knight had 'an hysterical fit', and then barred herself in her room having aroused the Queen's fury

The Banqueting Room of the Brighton Pavilion: lithograph from Nash's *Views of the Royal Pavilion*.

The Great Kitchen of the Brighton Pavilion: lithograph from Nash's *Views of the Royal Pavilion*.

3 The east front of the Brighton Pavilion: lithograph from Nash's *Views of the Royal Pavilion.*

4 The Prince Regent, Tsar and King of Prussia in Hyde Park: engraving by Alexander Sauerwied.

by attempting to buy herself out of her employment. She had tried to do this with the offer of a loan of £1,000, which she 'knew the Queen was very desirous to procure', and which, added to the salary Miss Knight was to give up, would have 'set her Majesty completely at ease in respect' of the expense of various improvements she wanted to make at her retreat at Frogmore. It was not until the Regent had written to his mother and she, in turn, had commanded Miss Knight to leave her employment for Princess Charlotte's, that the matter was resolved.[16]

If Miss Knight was anxious to move to Warwick House, the Duchess of Leeds was certainly not, and was very unhappy when she arrived there.[17] She found her charge quite as difficult as Lady de Clifford had done, and she was so upset by the prospect of having to scold her that she cried in her sleep. Charlotte's petticoats were too short; she nodded at people instead of bowing to them; she whispered to the maids of honour at Chapel between the prayers and the sermon; she bought her friends expensive jewellery which she could not afford. The Duchess knew that she ought to reprimand the girl for these offences; but she 'did not like to venture on anything herself unless driven to the last extremity'. Above all, the Duchess was harassed by the Prince's strict instructions about her supervision of the Princess's correspondence, since she found it impossible to ensure that her charge was not in touch with proscribed friends and relations. Indeed, the Princess, an inveterate letter-writer, sent and received numerous communications without her Governess's knowledge, a selection of them being passed to her on one occasion in the Duchess's presence by her mother who had concealed them in a parting present of a pair of shoes.

Once the Regent had won his point that visits between mother and daughter must continue to be subject to restrictions, his rules governing Princess Charlotte's conduct were somewhat relaxed. 'What is passed is passed and gone by,' he assured her, 'and therefore let us think no more of it; and pray do not let it give you any further uneasiness. . . . God bless you, my dearest child.'[18] To show her that all disagreements between them were now truly in the past, he invited her to a dinner at which he was as kind as she could have wished.

The dinner was given on the day that an unidentified coffin had been opened in St George's Chapel at Windsor and had been found to contain the remains of King Charles I. Having elaborately demonstrated upon Miss Knight's tense neck the way in which King Charles had been beheaded, the Regent presented to his daughter the centre sapphire from the Stuart crown, which he had received from Paris together with some Stuart papers. Soon afterwards he asked his daughter for a portrait of her for which she gave several sittings to George Sanders. Then came another invitation to dinner and the Prince was once again in excellent humour, though before Miss Knight left he said to her, tapping her on the shoulder, 'Remember, however, my dear Chevalier, that Charlotte must lay aside the idle nonsense of thinking that she has a will of her own; while I live she must be subject to me as she is at present.'[19]

So, indeed, she was; and at the least sign of insubordination there was trouble. It was clear to Miss Knight that the Regent was determined to keep her 'as long as possible *a child*'. Whenever he suspected that there was the possibility of a scandal such as the Hesse incident had threatened to become, he renewed all his orders, made complaints to her attendants, and declined to see her for weeks on end. First of all there was a fuss over her supposed interest in the Duke of Gloucester, a particular *bête noire* of the Regent, who knew that he had been in the habit of attending Princess Caroline's parties with his cousins the Dukes of Kent and Sussex. One evening at the Duke of York's, when the Regent saw his daughter and Gloucester sitting next to each other on a sofa, he told Lady Liverpool to go over to her and ask her to change places with Lady Bathurst. Charlotte declined to do any such thing. She got up, left the room and returned home 'indignant and hurt at having been watched and worried'.

After this there was a fuss about the Princess going to Sanders's house for her sittings instead of giving them at Warwick House. Warwick House was too dark, it was explained; but that was a most unsatisfactory excuse: the Prince knew that she was likely to meet the most unsuitable people in the artist's studio. Then there was trouble over the Princess's supposed attraction to the Duke of Devonshire.[20] The Duchess of Leeds assured the Regent that the Princess had never 'written a line to the Duke of Devonshire or stopped at Chiswick in her life or sent any message there'.[21] But the Regent thought that the Duchess was not taking her duties conscientiously enough, and he sent Sir Henry Halford over to Warwick House to reprimand her and Miss Knight for having driven twice in one day down the Chiswick Road when the Duke was giving a 'great breakfast' at Chiswick House, an outing suggested by Miss Knight who had been concerned to find some sort of amusement for the Princess whose 'life was so monstrous, that any other young person must have felt it excessively dull'.

'Young P. and her father have had frequent rows of late, but one pretty serious one,' Brougham contentedly informed Creevey. 'He was angry with her for flirting with the D. of Devonshire, and suspected she was talking politics. . . . P. will put on his dignified air on which he piques himself, and then say, "Your Grace will be pleased to recollect the differences between you and my daughter."'[22]

Frustrated and unhappy, Princess Charlotte was reported to be 'in a bad state of health', with a fixed pain in her side for which she wore 'a perpetual blister';[23] she was also putting on weight. At a big party at the new Military College at Sandhurst her father did not even talk to her, and she in turn turned her back on her grandmother to show her general distaste for the entire proceedings which ended with her father, the Duke of York and the Sovereign Prince of Orange collapsing drunkenly under the dining-room table.[24]

The Prince of Orange's son was soon to be the cause of the worst row that she and her father had yet endured.

*

Prince William of Orange was not a prepossessing young man. Endeavouring to compensate for an unhealthy, sallow appearance and a frail physique he adopted an excessively hearty manner, drank too much and shook people by the hand with intemperate vigour. Brougham referred to him as 'Young Frog'. He had spent two years at Oxford, had served on the Duke of Wellington's staff in Spain, and was shortly, at the age of twenty-two, to be given a command at Waterloo which he was to execute with notable incompetence. But despite his many faults he was not an entirely unattractive young man. Princess Charlotte was for a time to feel for him a kind of affection, and to decide that her father's obvious wish that she should marry him was not as unacceptable as she had at first declared it to be.

'I think him so ugly,' she commented soon after first meeting him, 'that I am sometimes obliged to turn my head away in disgust when he is speaking to me. Marry I will, and that directly, in order to enjoy my liberty; but not the Prince of Orange.'[25]

Since there was no question of her being allowed to marry the Duke of Devonshire, she would have preferred the Duke of Gloucester although he was so tiresomely self-satisfied and getting on for forty. It was 'perfectly true', she admitted, that she did not particularly care for him; but she could never expect 'to marry from inclination', anyway; and at least the Duke was good-natured: she 'might reasonably look forward to being treated with kindness'. She discussed the matter with her father's chosen messenger, Sir Henry Halford. Sir Henry reported her preferences to the Regent who did not care for the idea at all, replying that he would have to go down to Windsor to talk to the Princess himself. When he arrived he was in a better mood than had been expected, and Charlotte, whose stammer usually grew much worse during her painful interviews with her father, had reason to feel thankful after this one that he had not been cross with her. He began by saying that he would be 'very calm and very affectionate' and that although he could never consent to her marrying the Duke of Gloucester he would not bring any pressure to bear on her with regard to anyone else. He could not forbear making a few favourable remarks about the Prince of Orange, but he made it clear that he would not force her hand in that direction. All the same, his wishes were unmistakable.

In her predicament Princess Charlotte turned for advice to Lord Grey. After complaining that she was '*secluded* from all society almost entirely' and felt 'threatened with more restrictions if possible from the few friends' that she did see, she went on to tell him of Sir Henry Halford's frequent visits to her. These visits were not welcome, but as Sir Henry came 'from the Prince and by his orders' she could not always refuse seeing him, though sometimes she had done so when she thought that she could without causing offence.[26] Miss Knight had tried to put a stop to his coming and his endeavouring to influence the Princess in lengthy private interviews; but the Regent had declared that Sir Henry was 'the friend of the family'; he had no objection to his daughter being left alone with him.[27] Since, therefore, Halford could not be prevented from coming to Warwick House with his messages and orders from the Regent, how should she answer him? She was 'decidedly against the Prince of Orange'; but how long could she go on maintaining her resolution not to marry him?[28]

Lord Grey replied that while no law, human or divine, gave her father the right to coerce her into marriage, she ought to 'avoid, by all proper means, the appearance of a public opposition to his pleasure, and that she should dispose herself as much as possible to a compliance with it'.[29]

This was not the advice for which she had been looking, and she wrote to Lord Grey again, evidently hoping for stronger support. Grey contented himself with the observation that he had always felt sure she would not be pressed to a marriage against her inclinations, and the Regent's assurances to her had made it clear that he would never require of her 'so painful a sacrifice'.[30]

There the matter was left for a time; but as 1813 drew to a close, further hints were dropped at Warwick House about the advantages of a marriage to Prince William. One day the persistent and persuasive Sir Henry Halford called and had 'a long interview' with the Princess on the subject; and gradually she came to view Prince William in a different light. Looking at a print of him, she decided that perhaps he was not so ugly after all; he was 'certainly adored in the army'. Invitations to Carlton House followed; and, as Brougham told Lord Grey, the Princess was once more 'on perfectly good terms' with her father. 'She has completely altered her language as to the Prince of Orange, and I am quite clear she will take him if they offer him to her. . . . I always thought that the best . . . part of her character was the spice of the mother's spirit and temper; but I fear she has a considerable mixture of the father's weakness and fickleness. Indeed what can you expect? Her behaviour to Lady de Clifford [was] such as I almost defy her father to surpass, accomplished as he is in such walks.'[31]

At one dinner party the Regent, in the brightest of good humours, presented his daughter with a diamond-studded belt which he had been sent from Turkey and to which he had added a diamond clasp. At a subsequent Carlton House party the Prince of Orange was present and after dinner the Regent took him and Princess Charlotte into the conservatory where they walked up and down together, the Regent doing most of the talking, Princess Charlotte looking pale in an unbecoming violet satin dress trimmed with black lace. She confessed to a friend afterwards that she was 'more agitated' than she could express. Having marched them up and down for some time, the Regent took Charlotte to one side and said to her enquiringly, 'Well, it will not do, I suppose.'

'I do not say that,' she replied. 'I like his manner very well, as much as I have ever seen of it.'

Taking this as a declaration of consent, the Regent, 'overcome with joy', took her back to the Prince of Orange and 'joined their hands immediately'. Prince William was 'so much affected, but so happy',

Charlotte thought; and as for herself it all appeared 'like a dream'. Back at Carlton House after midnight, she told Miss Knight what had happened, that she was engaged. Prince William had turned out to be 'by no means as disagreeable' as she had expected.[32]

Two days later, accompanied by her father, Prince William arrived at Warwick House and they were left alone together for the first time. He was 'naturally dying of shyness and fear', and was even more perturbed when his talking of their having a home together in Holland as well as in England reduced the Princess to tears.

She had not before considered this aspect of her marriage, and after the Regent had tactfully hurried the Prince of Orange away to another engagement the thought of living abroad with him preyed on her mind. Shortly before Christmas she went to Windsor where she was to be confirmed on Christmas Eve, and there the congratulations, the 'little jokes and witty sayings', the expressions of pleasure that could not conceal the '*sorrow*' of her maiden aunts, all increased her disquiet. When she returned to London she was 'quite ill for some days afterwards'.[33]

The day after her eighteenth birthday, on 8 January 1814, Lady Charlotte Campbell came to visit her at Warwick House and found the Princess 'very gracious', yet she had talked in a most desultory way, and it would be difficult to say of what. 'Her hands and arms are beautiful,' Lady Charlotte decided, 'but I think her figure is already gone, and will soon be precisely like her mother's: in short it is the very picture of her, and *not in miniature*.'[34]

Lady Charlotte was a rare visitor. 'We scarcely saw anyone,' Miss Knight said, 'the days passed quietly . . . ' The Duchess of Leeds's daughter lived in the House, but she was younger than the Princess who, in any case, did not like her. Charlotte grew more and more depressed. Her father had not been able to come to see her on her birthday as he had gone up to Belvoir Castle to stay with the Duke of Rutland for the christening of his godson. And she was conscious that he was once again displeased with her. Miss Knight certainly found him so when, at his request, she called at Carlton House one morning after his return from Belvoir Castle. He was ill in bed, having celebrated the Rutland baby's christening with such excessive enthusiasm that his doctors had felt obliged to exhaust him by bleeding him and keeping him 'low for several days'. He complained first of all that Princess Charlotte was having an exceptionally fine carriage built for herself by a man called Birch instead of by his own coachbuilder, that she had consulted the Duke of Kent about this instead of himself, that she was having it painted green and not, as it should have been, yellow, like his own. He went on to complain that his daughter spent too much on jewellery, and that it was shameful of 'young ladies of immense fortunes', like Mrs Thrale's granddaughter, Margaret Mercer Elphinstone, to accept valuable presents from her.

Miss Knight, anxious to exculpate herself from any possible blame in this, assured him that she herself had made an agreement with the Princess to accept no presents from her, as she had also done with Princess Amelia. The mention of his beloved dead sister was too much for the Prince to bear in his weakened condition, and he burst into tears. Recovering himself, he enjoined Miss Knight to ensure that Princess Charlotte did 'not now think of frivolity'. 'She was to be married, and must think of the duties of a wife.'[35]

The more Princess Charlotte thought about becoming a wife, however, the less the idea appealed to her since it seemed to entail her living abroad. It was far from her wish to retract her consent to the marriage, she told Lord Grey; but she was 'too much an Englishwoman' not to feel most reluctant at leaving this country, 'both from affection and a sense of duty'.[36]

Lord Grey agreed that it was 'unquestionably of the utmost moment' that she should not be pressed to leave against her inclinations; it was 'no less important to the public' that her 'habits should be formed amongst the people she was to govern'. However, everything that he had heard of the Prince of Orange, particularly from officers who by living with him had the best means of forming an opinion about him, justified the choice which her Royal Highness had 'so happily made'.[37]

In her next letter, Princess Charlotte enclosed one she had received from the Prince at The Hague which had made her even more apprehensive. The Prince told her that he was 'daily more tired' of Holland and wished himself 'a thousand times back to England' since the formalities and etiquette that had to be observed at the Dutch court were quite against his nature. Yet it was clear from his letter that he would be expected to spend six months every year in Holland, where they were to have a nice summer house outside The Hague as well as a town house in the capital. He had 'nothing more at heart' than to make her happy, so he hoped that she would bring English ladies of honour with her. After all, every place was 'almost alike if one lived with friends'.[38]

57

Princess Charlotte did not mention her reluctance to live abroad to her father when he summoned her to Carlton House on 2 March. With a gouty leg resting on the seat of a nearby chair, he handed her a letter from Holland in which a formal proposal of marriage had been made. But to her friend, Priscilla Burghersh, she strongly objected: 'As to going abroad, I believe and hope it to be quite out of the question, as I find by high and low that, naturally, it is a very unpopular measure in England, and as such of course (as my inclinations do not lead me either) I could not go against it, and besides which, I have now no manner of doubt that it is decidedly *an object and wish of more than one* to get rid of me if possible in that way. . . . You are far too sensible not to know that this [marriage] is only *de convenance*, and it is as much brought about by *force* as anything, and by deceit and hurry; though I grant you that, were such a thing absolutely necessary, no one could be found so *unexceptionable* as he is. I am much more *triste* at it than I have ever chosen to write; can you be surprised?'[39]

She was strongly urged to stand firm against living abroad not only by her sympathetic girl friends, but also by Henry Brougham and by the Duke of Sussex, who approved of the marriage but thought the question of her going to Holland ought to be discussed by Parliament. Lord Liverpool believed that the representatives of the Russian Court were also intriguing against the threatened close alliance between the House of Orange and the English royal family which did not suit Russian policy. 'She has been induced to insist upon conditions being inserted in the contract of marriage of which she never thought until recently, and which (to the extent to which she is desirous of pushing them) cannot be admitted,' Liverpool told Castlereagh. 'The object is to break off the marriage with the Prince of Orange and to form a connection between the Princess and one of the Grand Dukes of Russia.' Liverpool had 'the strongest reason to believe' that Mme de Tatischeff, wife of a Russian diplomat and a woman often in Princess Charlotte's company, was engaged in this intrigue.[40] It was furthermore supposed that the Emperor of Russia's sister, the Grand Duchess of Oldenburg, had also been involved in the intrigue, an additional cause of the Regent's dislike of her family.[41]

Princess Charlotte's visit to the Grand Duchess at the Pulteney Hotel had so disturbed the Regent that he had sent Sir Henry Halford to Warwick House with instructions to Miss Knight not to let the Princess and the Grand Duchess meet so often. The Regent's concern was understandable, for the Grand Duchess was 'a great favourite of Princess Charlotte'. Their conversations had been quite uninhibited, the Grand Duchess always having spoken with the utmost candour, telling Charlotte how vulgar she found the Duke of Clarence and that, having now seen the Prince Regent, she could 'never think of marrying *him*'.[42]

At the suggestion of Lord Grey, Princess Charlotte wrote to her father on 15 April politely requesting to see the marriage contract, which she heard from the Prince of Orange had been shewn to him and the terms of which he found 'most liberal'. She begged that she, too, might see the contract, at the same time asking for an article to be inserted in it preventing her being taken or kept out of England against her inclinations.[43] She felt, she said, a 'decided repugnance to a removal from this country'.[44]

On receipt of the Princess's letter, the Regent immediately sent for Miss Knight who was to present herself at Carlton House at twenty minutes past eleven on 17 April. According to Miss Knight's long account of this interview, it was an extremely painful one. 'The Prince was very angry,' Miss Knight wrote. 'He asked me whether I knew of the letter he had received from Princess Charlotte on Friday, which I answered in the affirmative: he said it was an impertinent letter from a daughter to a father, that she had no right to ask to see the contract; that a sketch of it had been sent over to the father of the Hereditary Prince of Orange, not to himself – that I must tell Princess Charlotte that the marriage was her own choice, and her own proposal and that when he had told her of the probability of her going to Holland she had made no objections.'

The Regent went on to say that he would forgive his daughter if she would withdraw the letter; but if she would not do so it would have to be laid before the Cabinet and Privy Council as the House of Orange would naturally insist on the marriage treaty being broken if she persisted in her determination not to leave England. As to her demand for a house for herself and the Prince in England, 'he said, with much displeasure that he could not find one to purchase in a moment, and that perhaps he must build one; and that I might quiet her mind by assuring her that she would not be an exile from England, that she would not have to stay more than 7 or 8 months at a time in Holland, though perhaps if she were in a family way it might be imprudent for her to remove from The Hague, but that provision would be made in the contract that her eldest son (as intended for the throne of England) should be brought up here from the age of three or four, and the second in Holland. . . . That they had fitted up a splendid residence for her at The Hague and in the country, that he would visit her there, and she and her husband might be his guests in England. He said she had already more liberty than was prudent and should have less if she broke off the marriage by persisting in not going to Holland. He said she might be popular for a short time by obtruding that reason on the publick, but that her popularity would not last.'[45]

The next day Princess Charlotte replied that it gave her the 'very deepest concern' to have incurred her father's displeasure. 'But I cannot with all that respect and affection retract one word of my determination,' she continued. 'I was astonished to hear from Miss Knight you thought the marriage was first proposed by me, and that it was to gratify my wishes you gave your consent.'[46]

Although Lord Grey supported the Princess in her determination that there should be an article in the marriage treaty preventing her being taken out of the country against her will, he was alarmed by reports that, even if it were to be conceded, she would break the engagement anyway. 'I would earnestly dissuade the Princess from [taking this step], except in the last and most unavoidable necessity,' Grey wrote to Margaret Mercer Elphinstone. 'The connection is much approved of by the country . . . its failure would create general disappointment, and if it could be presented as arising from levity or capriciousness in the Princess would injure her in the public estimation.'[47]

This was the Regent's view entirely; and, knowing that Charlotte was being encouraged to make difficulties and that she had 'legal advisers', he was very cross to receive his daughter's demands for what he considered to be wholly unnecessary and unreasonable stipulations in the marriage contract. Feeling that he could do no more himself, he asked the Duke of York to go to Warwick House to reason with her. The Duke wrote to tell his niece that he was coming, but she desired him not to come 'as she did not wish to have any unpleasant discussion with him'. Undeterred, the Duke called at the house, where he told Miss Knight that he wanted to see the Princess. She declined to come down, and the Duke was forced to go away without seeing her, expressing the regret 'that she had ill advisers from amongst those who were not well disposed towards government'.

When he had gone the Princess wrote him a letter explaining her objections to the marriage, objections which she once more repeated on

22 April, saying that she was 'perfectly ready to communicate' them to the Prince's Ministers if he deemed it requisite to send them to her. She would not see the Lord Chancellor, however, as they were 'not on speaking terms'.[48]

'If these have ever been your sentiments, dearest Charlotte,' the Duke of York replied sternly, 'it is much to be lamented that you did not make them known sooner, and that you allowed the most formal publick acts to take place, and every preparation to be made, when in your own mind, or at least after a moment's consideration, you must have been aware that the whole was nugatory on this determination.'[49] The Princess denied that she had allowed any public acts to take place, whereupon the Duke reminded her of her having granted an audience to a representative of the Dutch government to whom she confirmed her acceptance of a formal offer of marriage, and of her having ordered diamonds with money transmitted to her by the Prince of Orange.[50] This elicited another long letter from Princess Charlotte in which she reiterated her denial that the marriage had been first proposed by her and her determination that, if it were to take place, she would not leave England.[51]

Three days after this letter was written, early on the morning of 30 April, there arrived at Warwick House a young man who gave his name as Colonel St George. Miss Knight came down the rickety black staircase to be confronted by the Prince of Orange who asked to see the Princess. He was told she was still in bed; he said he would wait; he was then informed that she could not see him before three o'clock; he begged to be allowed to see her earlier than that; very well, she would see him at two.

He then wrote her a note which was sent up to her bedroom: 'Dearest Charlotte, I am extremely disturbed at your not wishing to see me; but I ask it once more as a particular favour that you will allow me to wait till you are up. If you insist upon a refusal I must follow your wish and return at two o'clock. I am most desirous and anxious to be able to speak to you freely.'[52]

Having read this note, Princess Charlotte got up at last and came down to see the Prince. He asked her if he had offended her in any way and was assured that he had not. But there was still the problem of where they were to live. So the Prince said he would go to see the Regent.

He left immediately, then hurried back within an hour or two to announce excitedly that the Regent wanted them both to go over to

Carlton House to see him: there had never been any intention that she should live 'chiefly abroad'; all past differences would be forgotten. But Charlotte declined to go. Her spirits were so much overcome, she said, and her nerves so shaken. And when the Prince had left she wrote to tell him that she trusted they would not meet again until she had 'every possible assurance and satisfaction' that her conditions to the marriage were 'fully agreed to'.[53] She must be 'complete mistress' of her own actions, she wrote in a subsequent letter after the Prince had asked her categorically what her conditions were, whether she was 'determined never to leave England' or whether she meant 'occasionally to visit Holland and other parts of the Continent' with him.[54]

So the inconclusive discussions went on, Princess Charlotte insisting that she must never be required to leave England without her consent, Lord Liverpool, now a frequent caller at Warwick House, endeavouring to persuade her – since The Hague was 'not as far from London as Edinburgh or Dublin' – to give some indication that she would be prepared to gratify the Prince of Orange's family by visiting Holland.[55]

But it was all to no avail. Princess Charlotte was intractable; and her Whig advisers were evidently anxious that she should remain so, thus causing as much embarrassment to the government as she could.

The Duke of Sussex was one of these advisers who encouraged her not to give way. During a long conversation with Lord Grey about the marriage, Sussex said that the Princess was 'much irritated against the Duke of York' who, so she had been warned, 'aimed at the Regency in the event of the Prince's death'. Princess Charlotte had also got it into her head that the Duke of York was trying to prove 'the Prince's marriage with Mrs Fitzherbert which had been solemnized twice, i.e. by clergymen of both churches'. The Duke of Sussex professed that he could not conceive how Charlotte had come to believe such things; but in a memorandum of his conversation Lord Grey noted that he had 'reason to believe' that Sussex himself was responsible.[56]

As well as receiving advice from Lord Grey and mischievous warnings from the Duke of Sussex, Princess Charlotte was also constantly in touch with Brougham and with her mother, though her mother seemed more concerned that she should display her disapproval over her own exclusion from the Queen's court at the time of the visit of the foreign princes to London than that she should put an end to the marriage proposals by declining to leave the country. 'It is not for me to give you my advice upon such a delicate subject,' her mother wrote to her; 'but all those friends as Lord Grey, Lansdowne, Mr Whitbread, Brougham and Co. are particularly anxious that you should manifest your feelings very publicly at the great insult your mother has received from the Queen and that you ought to refuse your attendance at Court which would raise you very much in the estimation of the world to take publicly the part of your oppressed and persecuted mother. However you are perfectly at liberty to act after your own judgment.'[57]

Princess Charlotte, much annoyed that she herself had been invited to so few of the great functions that summer, was quite prepared to take her mother's side over this; and when her father, hoping that his daughter would soon be persuaded to come round to his view, sent to Warwick House a list of wedding guests among which Princess Caroline's name was not included, she immediately returned it to him.

At the same time Princess Charlotte informed the Prince of Orange that her mind was unalterably made up on the point: she would not go to Holland after marriage, and she would never leave England at all unless she wanted to. If Prince William could not convince the British government that these were essential conditions she would call the marriage off altogether.

Ultimately, towards the end of May, the Prince of Orange told Princess Charlotte confidentially that his father would consent to everything 'for the sake of his happiness'; and on 5 June 1814 she was informed that *her* father and the government were also prepared to give way. It was agreed that she should never leave the country without her own consent and that whenever she did consent to go abroad she could always come home 'at her own pleasure'.[58] On 10 June she wrote to Lord Liverpool to accept these terms.[59]

The matter did not rest there, however. Soon after this stipulation in the marriage contract had been approved, the Regent, 'greatly out of humour', arrived at Warwick House with the Bishop of Salisbury. He hoped and trusted that his daughter would give up the stipulation 'as a mark of civility to the House of Orange'. Politely but firmly Princess Charlotte declined to give way. Brougham had successfully impressed on her the vital necessity of her remaining in England immediately after the marriage, for if she went abroad her mother would no doubt go too; and this might well result in that dreaded sequence of events: a divorce, the Regent's remarriage, a new heir and her loss of the throne. Moreover, the nearer the marriage approached the less disposed she felt to go through with it at all. She and the Prince of Orange had not been 'on comfortable terms for some time'. It continued to rankle with her that during the visit of the foreign sovereigns to England he had gone everywhere, regardless of the fact that she had been invited scarcely anywhere.[60] She had gone to a boring reception given by her grandmother and to a dinner at Carlton House, and that was all. All the foreign sovereigns and most of the princes had called on her at Warwick House but none of them had stayed even to take tea with her. She had been left to drive about in her carriage to look at the crowds and the decorations, the arrivals and departures, the guards of honour and the escorts, staring at everything and everyone 'with perfect sang-froid'.[61]

To make matters worse, when the Prince of Orange found time to call on her their differences seemed deeper at each succeeding visit. One day, for instance, she said that at their future house both her mother and father must be equally welcome; but, knowing well what the Regent would have to say to this arrangement, Prince William replied that he thought it ought to be open only to her father. Then there was the unpleasant business of Prince William's heavy drinking at the parties to which he went and she was not invited. Brougham reported him as having been made 'remarkably drunk' by her cousin, the wild young Prince Paul of Württemberg for whose behaviour his stepmother, the Regent's oldest sister, was obliged to apologize.[62] The Prince of Orange was again very drunk on 10 June at Ascot Races and had returned to London clinging to the outside of a stage-coach.[63] Princess Charlotte, already 'quite enraged' at not being allowed to go to the Races herself, was disgusted at the reports of his condition.[64]

She felt the time had come for a 'thorough explanation' with him. Although no arrangement had been made for a house for them in England, preparations for the wedding were going on apace: the Queen was already making fussy arrangements about the trousseau; the Regent, so she learned from her aunt, Princess Mary, was intending to ask the Orange family over to England as soon as the other royal guests had gone home. Princess Charlotte told the Prince that she would like to see him immediately he returned from the celebrations in Oxford. He accordingly presented himself at Warwick House on 16 June.

Lady Charlotte Lindsay was there at the time and immediately afterwards submitted one of her lengthy reports to Henry Brougham: 'While we were talking the Prince of Orange was announced: she went to him, and desired that I should remain where I was to hear the result of their conference, which has ended in her *positive declaration* that she *will not leave England now*, but will avail herself of the discretionary power promised her in the contract; and gave as her reason the situation of the Princess of Wales, whom she thought herself bound in duty not to leave under her present circumstances. He appeared to be very unhappy, but seemed to admit that if Princess Charlotte adhered to this resolution the marriage must be off. He begged her to reconsider it, and left the house in much agitation.'[65]

That same evening Princess Charlotte wrote to him to tell him that she now considered their engagement '*to be totally and for ever at an end*'.[66] Until he received this final letter he had continued to believe that she might repent; but he had to recognize now that his hopes of marrying her and of becoming Prince Consort of England were not to be fulfilled. He replied that he had informed his family of her decision but that he was not prepared to tell her father, an unpleasant duty which she must perform herself.[67]

The night before he left England he attended a ball at Devonshire House; he went up to Lord Castlereagh's niece, Lady Emma Edgcumbe, wrung her hand with his customary force, and said, 'Goodbye, God bless you, Lady Emma. I am off tomorrow.' There were tears in his eyes, she said. 'He appeared miserable.'[68]

At Warwick House, Princess Charlotte awaited her father's reactions to the information she had had to impart to him. So far, all he had done was to write to tell her that he had received her letter with 'astonishment, grief and concern';[69] but she could not be in any doubt that there was bound to be a far more violent reaction than this.

5

The Warwick House Affair
1814

*

'Like a bird let loose from its cage'

Creevey, for one, looked forward to the next instalment of the drama with anticipatory delight. 'Well, my pretty,' he told his wife. 'We have now a new game for Master Prinny. . . . Whitbread has shown me Princess Charlotte's letter to the Prince of Orange. By God! It is capital. . . . The marriage is broken off and . . . the reasons are – first, her attachment to this country which she cannot and will not leave; and, above all, her attachment to her mother, whom in her present distressed situation she likewise cannot leave. . . . What think you of the effect of this upon the British publick? . . . And what do you suppose has produced this sudden attachment to her mother? It arises from the profound resources of old Brougham.'[1]

There was a further reason which Creevey did not know but which the Regent suspected, and that was that Princess Charlotte's eye had lighted upon other Princes who were in London at that time and were more attractive than Prince William of Orange. There was Prince Augustus of Prussia, there was Prince Frederick of Prussia, and there was Prince Paul of Württemberg, all of whom, the Regent sourly noted, had called at Warwick House and none of whom was notably virtuous. After Prince Paul's call, the Regent demanded a full report from the Duchess of Leeds who replied that both herself and Miss Knight had been present during the interview and added, 'I am extremely concerned and surprised at your Royal Highness not condescending to take the slightest notice of me last night at Lady Hampden's for I can with truth assure you, Sir, I have served your Royal Highness most honestly and faithfully in the most difficult situation in which human being ever was placed. My resignation is always ready to be laid at your feet.'[2]

Another caller at Warwick House was the bland and good-looking Prince Leopold, third son of the Duke of Saxe-Coburg-Saalfeld, who had come over to England in the suite of the Tsar and who had served with the Russian army against Napoleon. Princess Charlotte invited him to breakfast; and it was thereafter rumoured in London, so Mrs Tomline, the Bishop of Lincoln's wife, was assured, that it was this 'new fancy' which was the 'real cause for the breaking off of the marriage' to the Prince of Orange.[3] The Regent, who was not informed of the invitation to breakfast, did not believe that Prince Leopold would be guilty of any impropriety: he was 'a most honourable young man' and had written him a letter perfectly justifying himself.[4] But the Regent did not trust Prince Paul or either of the Prussian princes, particularly the handsome, disreputable Prince Augustus who, as the Duke of Kent said, was the 'black sheep in his family'.[5] The Regent had good reason not to trust the assured and experienced Prince Augustus, for between 11 June and the end of the month there had been at least two clandestine meetings between him and Princess Charlotte at Warwick House. On one of these occasions when the Princess's astute and managing friend, Margaret Mercer Elphinstone, called she was told by a thoroughly alarmed Miss Knight that the two of them were alone together in the Princess's room. Miss Elphinstone said that they must be interrupted, and when Miss Knight refused to interfere she went upstairs to disturb them herself.[6]*

Hearing rumours of what was going on, the Bishop of Salisbury, the Princess's former preceptor, whom she had never liked, went to Warwick House to suggest that she should write a submissive letter to her father holding out a hope that she might, even now, be prepared to marry the Prince of Orange within a few months. If she did not do so 'arrangements would be made by no means agreeable to her inclinations'. She wrote a submissive letter couched in affectionate terms; but it contained no suggestion that she was prepared to reconsider marriage to the Prince.[7]

---

* Throughout this period, so Mrs Tomline was reliably told by one of her London correspondents who was well informed about the activities at Warwick House, Miss Knight behaved 'very indiscreetly'. There was 'no intrigue' on her part to break off the marriage to the Prince of Orange; but she had little control over her charge and was certainly guilty of an 'improper yielding' to the Princess's strong will (Pretyman Papers, Ipswich, HA 119).

Two days later she and Miss Knight received a summons to Carlton House. The Princess asked to be excused, on the grounds that she had not been well for some days and was still suffering from intermittent excruciating pain in her knee. So Miss Knight went to see the Regent by herself. Miss Knight, whom he knew to have connived at Charlotte's meetings with Prince Augustus, found him 'very cold, very bitter and very silent'.[8] On her return to Warwick House she told the Princess how angry her father was about the Prussian Princes. Believing that the hateful old Bishop had spread the suspicions at Carlton House, Charlotte seems to have supposed that the best response would be a display of outraged innocence. She wrote a furious letter to the Bishop in which she boldly declared the '*whole allegation to be false* and *a base lie*' and assured him that 'no such violent accusation or measures' would have any effect on her.[9] Fearing that this defiant letter would doubtless provoke a furious reaction at Carlton House, the Princess warned her page after she had sent it that 'it was possible all the servants might be sent away, but that she would never forget them whenever it was in her power'.

Her fears were fully justified. At six o'clock the next evening, 12 July, the Regent was seen emerging from Carlton House. He marched across the courtyard with the Bishop of Salisbury and four ladies and entered Warwick House. Leaving the Bishop and the ladies downstairs, he walked up the staircase and into Charlotte's room where he found her lying on a sofa. It was clear that this latest rebellion of his daughter's, following so soon on the numerous frustrations and humiliations he had undergone that summer, was more than he could bear with any pretence to composure. To be hissed in the streets while his foreign guests were cheered was bad enough, to know that his wife, despite all her gross misbehaviour, was the heroine of street mobs and theatre audiences while he was their villain – this was worse; but now to have an insubordinate daughter, manipulated by his political enemies, flirting with a most undesirable young man and rejecting a highly desirable marriage which she had formerly welcomed and which would remove her from the evil influence of her mother – this was intolerable.

He told her that her servants were all to be dismissed, that the ladies he had brought with him were to take over Warwick House, that she herself was to be confined at Carlton House for five days and then taken to Cranbourne Lodge in Windsor Forest where she was to see no one but her grandmother once a week, and that she was to leave immediately.

He was with her alone for three-quarters of an hour, then called in the Bishop of Salisbury who remained with them for a further quarter of an hour. Already, before her father's arrival, so Miss Knight told Mrs Tomline, Princess Charlotte was 'so agitated and wretched, and her eyes so swelled with crying' that she was quite unfit to leave the house. By the time the interview was over she was more distraught than ever. She ran from the room 'in great distress', fell on her knees before Miss Knight and cried out, 'God Almighty! Give me patience!'[10]

But she did not remain kneeling long. Suddenly she made up her mind: she would run away. She dashed into her bedroom, asked her maid for her bonnet and shawl, and rushed down the backstairs, across the courtyard, past the sentries at the gate and out towards Charing Cross. At Charing Cross she jumped into a hackney coach and told the driver that she would give him a guinea to drive her as fast as he could to her mother's house at Connaught Place.

Her mother was not there. She had gone to Blackheath for the day and had not yet arrived home. Fully in command of the situation and of herself, indeed evidently relishing the drama which she had called into being, she sent a groom to fetch her mother back, despatched another messenger to bring Brougham to Connaught Place immediately, and scribbled a scarcely legible note to her uncle, the Duke of Sussex. This note she handed to a third servant, then asked a fourth to serve her dinner.

While Charlotte was waiting for the meal to be brought up to the drawing-room, Brougham arrived in answer to her summons. He had been at a dinner party at Michael Angelo Taylor's and, having spent most of the previous night working on a brief, was tired out; he had fallen asleep in the carriage and was 'still half-asleep' as he stumbled upstairs to the drawing-room. Princess Charlotte ran up to him, and said, 'I have just run off.' Before he had had time to find out why, Princess Caroline and Lady Charlotte Lindsay came into the room, followed by the servants with a meal. Princess Charlotte asked Brougham to sit down with them, but he declined the invitation, explaining that her message had arrived just as he was finishing dinner at a friend's house.

'You may eat a little bit with us,' Charlotte said. 'And at any rate you can carve.'

She was in excellent spirits, Brougham noticed, 'like a bird let loose from its cage'. She talked away cheerfully, laughed a great deal and was obviously enjoying herself enormously.

69

During the meal Miss Elphinstone arrived in a hackney coach with the Bishop of Salisbury. Charlotte sent the Bishop back to Carlton House with a message stating her terms for submission: the reinstatement of Miss Knight and her maids and no restrictions to be placed upon visits to her by Miss Elphinstone who, for the moment, remained at Connaught Place to join the merry party in the drawing-room.

From time to time various of the Regent's representatives were announced as being at the door. Their names were greeted with shouts of amusement and they were not invited in. The Lord Chancellor, Lord Eldon, arrived, and it was decided that he should be left to wait in his carriage outside in the street. Then Lord Ellenborough came, bringing with him a writ of habeas corpus. Brougham put in a word for him as his chief; but the ladies decreed that he must remain outside 'as well as Old Bags'. Ellenborough was followed by John Leach, a pernickety and affected King's Counsel whose name evinced cries of 'Little Bags!' 'Reticule!' 'Ridicule!' Even the Duke of York was kept waiting downstairs, though Princess Caroline did go down after dinner to have a word with him.

The Duke of Sussex, as a known sympathizer, was asked upstairs immediately, fell into conversation, in German, with Princess Caroline and was then introduced to Brougham whom he had not previously met.

'Pray, Sir,' the Duke asked him directly. 'Supposing the Prince Regent, acting in the name and on behalf of His Majesty, were to send a sufficient force to break the doors of the house and carry away the Princess, would any resistance in such case be lawful?'

'It would not.'

'Then, my dear,' he said turning to Charlotte, 'you hear what the law is. I can only advise you to return with as much speed and as little noise as possible.'

This was not at all the kind of advice that Charlotte was hoping to receive; and her father's reply to her message, which the Bishop of Salisbury now brought her and which required her to 'submit unconditionally', made her more than ever determined not to do so. She believed that if she were to submit, she would be forced to go through with the marriage to the Prince of Orange, though Brougham repeated the assurance he had often given her, that it could never take place 'without her consent truly given'.

'They may wear me out by ill-treatment,' she protested, 'and may represent that I have changed my mind and consented.' She could only be sure of remaining safe, if she held to her determination to remain with her mother. But her mother – though she did not say so – was apparently not so taken with that idea as her daughter was: she had made up her mind to leave England and did not want her daughter to interfere with her plans.

What should she do? Princess Charlotte asked Brougham. She was now growing rather nervous, not so sure of herself. Brougham replied that she really ought to go back to Warwick House or Carlton House. At this she began to cry. Did he too, she asked him pitifully, refuse to stand by her? Quite the contrary, Brougham assured her. As to the marriage she 'must follow her own inclination entirely', but 'her returning home was absolutely necessary'. Yet she would not give way: she would never go back, she said; nothing and nobody would induce her to do so. The discussion went fitfully on; and it grew late; the night passed, and dawn came. Brougham wearily took the Princess to the window and asked her to look out into the Park. 'Look there, Madam,' he said. 'In a few hours all the streets and the Park, now empty, will be crowded with tens of thousands. I have only to take you to that window, and show you to the multitude, and tell them your grievances, and they will all rise on your behalf.'

Brougham could not remember exactly what she said in reply to this, but it was something like, 'And why should they not?'

'The commotion will be excessive,' he told her. 'Carlton House will be attacked – perhaps pulled down; the soldiers will be ordered out, blood will be shed; and if your Royal Highness were to live a hundred years, it never would be forgotten that your running away from your father's house was the cause of the mischief; and you may depend upon it, such is the English people's horror of bloodshed, you never would get over it.'

This was an argument to which she could not fail to respond. She looked at Brougham with an expression he could only describe as one of 'stupefaction'. But before she submitted she insisted that he should prepare a document which declared that she was 'firmly resolved' that the proposed marriage between herself and the Prince of Orange should 'never take place', 'that *this* was her voluntary avowal, and to be considered as such, whatever she might afterwards be represented to have said, she being now at liberty and about to be taken back to Carlton House'. If ever there should be an announcement of the marriage 'it must be understood to be without her consent and against her will'. Brougham did as she wished; he then made six copies of the document which her mother, Lady Charlotte Lindsay, the Duke of Sussex, and himself all signed. Then, towards five o'clock in the morning, she drove back with the Duke of York to Carlton House.[11]

She was delivered into the charge of her four new ladies, Lady Ilchester, Lady Rosslyn and two of Lady Rosslyn's nieces, who in due course accompanied her to Cranbourne Lodge where they were joined by her former governess, Mrs Alicia Campbell. At Cranbourne Lodge she felt 'quite hopeless and spiritless'. It was as though she had been cast into prison. She was closely watched all day; and at night one or other of her ladies slept in her room or in an adjoining room with the connecting door left open. She was forbidden to receive or to send letters; her only permitted visitor was Margaret Mercer Elphinstone, who her father believed would prevent her from doing anything stupid. Miss Elphinstone was a convinced Whig but, as Lady Charlotte Lindsay knew, did not encourage her to support her mother.[12] And, as far as the Regent was concerned, that was all important.

The only parties Princess Charlotte was allowed to attend were her grandmother's tiresome musical evenings at Frogmore; the only change to which she could look forward was a visit to Weymouth for the recruitment of her health.

It was during this miserable time in Windsor Forest that she received a letter from her mother which caused her so much 'distress and agitation' that Miss Elphinstone had never seen her so 'deeply affected and apparently mortified' in her life. Miss Elphinstone felt she would never forget the 'dreadful effect' this letter had had upon the Princess. 'Even when I left her two days after,' she said, 'her pulse continued at 98.'[13] For her mother had written to say that she was definitely going abroad. She had indicated that she might return one day, but she did not say when that day might be.[14] 'She decidedly deserts me,' Princess Charlotte complained to Miss Elphinstone. 'After all if a *mother* has not *feeling* for her child or children are they to *teach it to her* or can they *expect to be listened to* with any *hopes of success?*'[15]

All that Brougham had foretold now seemed likely to transpire: there would be a divorce, a second marriage, a new heir, and her title to the throne would be gone.

*

For days past, Brougham had been doing his utmost to make Princess Caroline change her mind;[16] but at length he had had to accept the fact that she would be deterred no longer. Nothing could stop her now, he was informed by Lady Charlotte Lindsay, who had never seen 'so fixed a determination'.[17] Declaring that since she was deprived of the honour of being Princess of Wales, she would be plain Caroline, 'a happy, merry soul', she made the final preparations for her departure.

At the end of the first week in August she rode down to the Sussex coast where she presented herself at Worthing in a satin pelisse with huge golden clasps, and one of those tall military-style hats which she so unfortunately favoured, a great construction of violet and green satin surmounted by a plume of green feathers. She drove along the front with Lady Charlotte Lindsay and William Austin, a brash, though rather vacant-looking boy, now fourteen years old. Also in attendance were Lady Elizabeth Forbes, as Lady-in-Waiting, and, as her three Chamberlains, Colonel John St Leger's younger brother, Anthony Butler St Leger, Keppel Craven, and the odd, good-natured, gregarious archaeologist and traveller, Sir William Gell, known as 'Topographical Gell', 'a coxcombe', in Thomas Moore's opinion, 'but rather amusing'. Her equerry was Captain Charles Hesse; and her doctor was Henry Holland, a young man of twenty-five whose taste was for travel rather than medicine, whose favourite prescription was 'the frequent half-hour of genial conversation', and whose reputation in later life, having married the witty daughter of the Rev. Sydney Smith, was that he was 'unfit to attend a sick cat'.

With these ill-assorted attendants and a train of servants, stewards and couriers, the Princess, who had assumed the name of the Countess of Wolfenbüttel for the duration of her journey, stepped aboard the frigate *Jason*, characteristically creating an air of mystery about her by displaying peculiar concern for the contents of a certain metal case, on which was painted in large white letters, '*Her Royal Highness the Princess of Wales, to be always with her*'. As the *Jason* sailed out to sea it was noticed that she was crying.[18]

*

With his detested wife out of the country at last, and his unruly daughter safely restrained at Cranbourne Lodge, the Regent, during the late summer of 1814, might reasonably have looked forward to an easier and happier life. But his enemies declined to leave him in peace. When his daughter's flight from Warwick House to Connaught Place became public knowledge, Francis Horner, the Whig Member of Parliament for St Mawes, declared that he thought the Regent's conduct was that of a Prussian corporal;[19] and Henry Brougham wanted to know whether 'anything so barbarous' as the Regent's treatment of his daughter could be found outside Turkey.[20] To be sure the *Morning Post* blamed the daughter rather than the father for her 'unnatural rebellion', and castigated Miss Knight as one of Princess Charlotte's 'obnoxious associates';[21] but Brougham was quite right when he wrote contentedly that the affair was 'buzzed over town, of course', and that all were 'against the Prince'.[22]

Brougham wrote out five questions for the Duke of Sussex to ask in the House of Lords. Was the Princess enjoying the same freedom of communication with her friends which she had had at Warwick House? Was she allowed to send and receive letters as before? Was she 'in that state of liberty which persons considered not in confinement ought to be in'? Was she to be allowed to undergo that course of sea-bathing which her physicians had prescribed for her? And was she to have an establishment suitable to her rank?[23]

The Whig party as a whole, however, would not give Brougham and Sussex the support they needed, and Lord Grey came to the conclusion that it would be better if the matter were dropped. Lord Liverpool assured the House of Lords that Princess Charlotte was being given all the freedom that was reasonable and compatible with an education pleasing to 'God, nature and the laws of the country'; and although many Members doubted that this was so, no further steps were taken to free her from the Regent's strict control.[24]

6

Impresario, Collector and Patron
1814-1815

*

'The country will have cause to be grateful'

Having temporarily settled the problem of Princess Charlotte without undue embarrassment, the Regent now turned his attention to the more congenial task of arranging a fête at Carlton House as a personal tribute to the Duke of Wellington, the signing of the warrant for whose pension he had been pleased to make 'the first act of his unrestricted regency'.[1] For this fête he had a special polygonal building put up in the garden. It was a solid structure, one hundred and twenty feet in diameter, built of brick with a leaded roof; but the interior was to give the impression of summer light, airiness and festivity. This effect was achieved by painting the umbrella-shaped ceiling to resemble muslin and by decorating it with gilt cords, by fixing looking-glass to the walls and hanging them with muslin draperies, and by the sparkling illumination of twelve chandeliers. On the day of the fête huge banks of artificial flowers were arranged on the floor in the shape of a temple behind whose walls of petals and foliage were concealed two bands.

A covered promenade, its interior decorated with draperies and rose-coloured cords, led to a Corinthian temple where the guests could admire a marble bust by Turnerelli of the great Duke placed on a column in front of a large mirror engraved with a star and the letter W. The walls of a second covered walk, decorated in green calico, were covered with transparencies representing such appropriate subjects as 'Overthrow of Tyranny by the Allied Powers' and 'Military Glory'. Elsewhere in the garden were supper tents and refreshment rooms hung with white and rose curtains, and with regimental colours printed on silk.

75

The first of the two thousand guests began to arrive at nine o'clock in the evening and were received at the grand entrance by equerries who conducted them to the fanciful rooms and tents and corridors on the garden front. The Regent himself appeared in his field marshal's full-dress uniform, wearing his English, Russian, Prussian and French orders, looking extremely content and welcoming.

The fête was all that he could have hoped for. Even the Queen, who did not sit down to supper until two o'clock, stayed on until half-past four; and there were many guests still there at dawn.[2]

While the Regent had been planning this fête at Carlton House, he had also been supervising the preparations for a most elaborate gala in the London parks to celebrate the anniversary of the Battle of the Nile and the centenary of the accession to the English throne of the House of Hanover. For weeks past the newspapers had been reporting on the strange and exotic buildings which were appearing in the parks – in St James's Park, a Chinese pagoda and a picturesque yellow bridge ornamented with black lines and a bright blue roof; in Green Park, an embattled Gothic castle over a hundred feet square; in Hyde Park, ornamental booths and stalls, arcades and kiosks, swings and roundabouts. The trees were hung with coloured lamps; lanterns lined Birdcage Walk and the Mall; railings and dwarf walls were torn down to widen the entrances. The *Sun* reported that five hundred men had been at work for a month to produce the 'most brilliant fireworks ever seen in this country'. The *Morning Post* promised spectacles of unparalleled splendour. Only *The Times* struck a gloomy note, remarking that the public would 'first gape at the mummery, then laugh at the authors of it and lastly grumble at the expense'. *The Times*, having piously complained of the preparations continuing on a Sunday, also condemned the gingerbread stalls, the facilities for selling ale and gin, and the scanty precautions against the intrusion of a violent mob. 'Was there not something in the shape of a promise given that no fair should take place?' an editorial demanded. 'And was not the just outcry against its debauchery, drunkenness, and mingled and various abominations silenced only by the distinct pledge that nothing of their cause should be permitted?'

It seemed on the morning of the appointed day, 1 August, that *The Times*'s peevish prophecies of disaster were about to be fulfilled when a heavy rain began to fall. Between ten and eleven, however, the sun came out and the celebrations began.

First there was a spectacular ascent from Green Park when Windham Sadler's colourful balloon 'sprang into the air with its usual velocity and Mr Sadler, who had taken up with him 'a vast number of programmes of the jubilee . . . flung them down again from the sky with much industry and profusion'. Then there was a regatta on the Serpentine, followed by a splendid naumachia representing the Battle of the Nile which ended with the French fleet being destroyed by fireships. This was followed by a display of fireworks even more magnificent than the *Sun* had predicted. From the battlements of the Gothic castle in Green Park there blazed an amazing array of maroons and serpents, Roman candles and Catherine wheels, fire-pots and girandoles. Rocket after rocket shot into the sky, each one containing 'a world of smaller rockets'. And when the dense clouds of smoke, which hid the sombre canvas castle from view for a minute or two, had blown away there was seen standing in its place, as though 'placed there by magic', a brightly illuminated Temple of Concord, its walls displaying allegorical pictures prominent amongst which was *The Triumph of England under the Regency.*

The crowds cheered; the Japanese lanterns shone gaily against the yellow and black walls of the Pagoda; the gas jets spluttered on its blue roof; and when at ten o'clock the whole building burst into flames and fell into the waters of the lake, killing a lamplighter and injuring five other workmen, this was supposed by most of the crowd to be yet another brilliantly contrived spectacle. The royal family looked on approvingly from the windows and lawns of Buckingham House where the Queen had invited three hundred guests to a banquet.

The proceedings were universally agreed to have been an enormous success. There had been no riots; the crowds were in excellent humour; the few troops on duty were not required; and even *The Times* agreed that the celebrations had gone off very well, that 'it was an indisputable fact that so immense a number of the people had never before been brought together by any description of public rejoicings or any of the great events which have so often gilded the pages of British history'.[3]

The Regent could congratulate himself upon being personally responsible for this particular 'description of public rejoicings' which had proved so successful and so enjoyable. For a time, indeed, now that Princess Caroline was safely out of the country and Princess Charlotte was secluded from the public eye, now that he had proved himself so inspired an impresario, he began to lose some of his unpopularity. Two days after the great gala in the parks, the *Courier*, always a strong supporter of the royal family and the government, fulsomely reported: 'Among the many instances which have come to our knowledge, so honourable to the character of the Prince Regent as a man of feeling, one occurred at the levee on Thursday last' when a man, who had lost a leg, stooped to kneel before him. 'No, no,' the Regent protested, knowing of the man's disability from having met him previously at Brighton, 'No, no, you will hurt yourself.' 'It is in these little traits of character,' the *Courier* commented, "that one discerns the goodness of his heart and it is our greatest pride, whenever we meet with them, to be the humble instrument of recording them.'[4]

This sort of unctuous compliment was scarcely to the taste of the readers of *The Times*, but it did reflect a gradual, if shortlived, change in the public attitude towards the Regent which became noticeable at this time. To the Regent's own taste no compliment seemed too outrageous; and if the public were reluctant to give him the full credit to which he felt entitled, he was never sparing of praise himself. Indeed, it later became one of his rather engaging idiosyncrasies to suggest that he was personally responsible for the military and naval triumphs which were being celebrated that summer, and were to be celebrated the next.[5] The Duke of Wellington usually listened to such tales in silence, though once, after hearing the Regent relate how he had made a body of troops charge down a particular sharp declivity, the Duke was heard to observe, 'Very steep, sir'.[6]

An extremely vain man, the Regent had always endeavoured to evade the painful realization of his own unpopularity by pretending that it did not exist; and sometimes he seems actually to have succeeded in persuading himself that it did not exist, for he had extraordinary powers of self-deception. He once, for instance, solemnly assured Lady Cowper that he had visited her mother, Lady Melbourne, every day as she lay dying and that she had expired in his arms, when Lady Cowper knew perfectly well that he had never been near the house.[7] To his doctors, when suffering from an exceptionally severe hangover, he would explain, 'By God, it is very extraordinary . . . for I live very abstemiously and went to bed in good time,' though they knew as well as he did that he had been drinking maraschino until two o'clock that morning.[8]

He had once, at the height of the public outcry against his supposed ill-treatment of Princess Caroline, astounded Lord Moira by remarking with evident self-satisfaction that 'no prince was ever idolized by the people of this country as himself'.[9] Sir Philip Francis gave an example of this remarkable self-deceiving vanity when recounting an after-dinner conversation at the Pavilion one evening during the early days of the restricted Regency, when the Prince had not been free to make peers as he wished. The guests, following the Prince's complaint about this restriction, had amused themselves by inventing titles and testimonials for each other. Sir Philip suggested as an appropriate citation for Sheridan, at that time in more than usually straitened circumstances, 'The Man Who Extends England's Credit'.

Everyone laughed, but the Prince, noticing how upset Sheridan was, said to him, 'Don't mind him, old fellow! His penalty shall be to find a name for *me*, and woe betide him if I'm not content with it.'

'Name, name,' everybody shouted.

'*The* Man,' proposed Sir Philip with heavy emphasis on the first word.

'Go on,' said Sheridan.

'I've done,' said Sir Philip.

The Regent said, 'I'm content' and bowed 'gracefully round'.[10]

The compliment, he clearly thought, was not overdone. When the news of Napoleon's abdication arrived in London he wrote to his mother to tell her that he was 'really quite bereft of the means of expressing' himself, or of giving vent to feelings which surpassed 'all discription'. And he added, 'I trust my dearest mother that you will think that I have fulfilled and done my duty at least, and perhaps I may be vain enough to hope that you may feel a little proud of *your son*.'[11] For, after all, as he put it in another letter, the victory could not have been won without his own 'original and indefatigable endeavours'.[12] The boast, of course, was not altogether unjustified. His decision to keep the Tories in office in 1812 and his support of them since certainly did give him good reason to feel entitled to share the credit of victory. But to arrogate to himself the lion's share seemed to his critics absurd.

His 'indefatigable endeavours', he liked it to be supposed, were largely responsible for the final overthrow of Napoleon who, having landed in France from Elba in February 1815, was defeated by the armies of Wellington and Blücher in June at Waterloo; and he used to say with pride of his achievements, 'I set them all to work'. Of course, he did not always expect to be taken seriously. When he heard that after Waterloo the country's revenue exceeded by 'many, many, many millions, that of any former year, ever yet known', he 'could not help telling the Chancellor of the Exchequer that the balance should be transferred to his "private coffer" in consideration of his exertions' and all that he had done for the country 'as well as the whole world'.[13]

The Regent was at a party at Mrs Boehm's in St James's Square when Major the Hon. Henry Percy, bloodstained and dusty, arrived to announce the victory and to lay the eagles of the French army at his feet. His hostess was 'much annoyed with the battle of Waterloo as it spoilt her party'; but the Prince delighted in the scene. He asked the ladies to leave the room while Lord Liverpool read out the despatch which Major Percy had brought with him. When Lord Liverpool had finished reading, the Regent turned to Major Percy and in his most good-natured, gracious manner said to him, 'I congratulate you, *Colonel* Percy.'

Soon afterwards, however, reflecting upon the great number of men who had been killed, tears began to run down his cheeks. 'It is a glorious victory,' he said, 'and we must rejoice at it, but the loss of life has been fearful, and *I* have lost many friends.'[14]*

*

Waterloo *was* a glorious victory, the people agreed; but they declined to acknowledge that the Regent had had any part in it. In any case, military triumphs on the Continent were of less concern to them than the price of bread at home during the post-war slump. The Corn Law of 1815, which aimed to restore agricultural prosperity at the expense of the consumer, enraged the London poor. Members of Parliament known to be in favour of it were attacked on their way to the House; and, in the mistaken belief that the Regent himself was an active supporter of the Bill, a crowd of demonstrators deposited a blood-stained loaf on the parapet of Carlton

---

* The Allies declared that Napoleon was their prisoner and England was made responsible for selecting his place of confinement. Napoleon himself asked if he could live in England, a request which Lord Holland and the Duke of Sussex publicly urged should be granted. But the Regent agreed with the government that there could be no question of his living in England where as Lord Liverpool said, 'he would become an object of curiosity immediately, and possibly of compassion in the course of a few months'. So the request made in a personal letter to the Regent was refused with the agreement of the other Allied powers. The Regent, however, noting that Napoleon had referred to him as 'the most powerful, the most constant and the most generous of [his] enemies', declared approvingly, 'Upon my word, a very proper letter: much more so, I must say, than any I ever received from Louis XVIII' (Holland, *Further Memoirs*, 220).

House which had to be protected by troops from a threatened assault by the mob.

Nor was it, of course, only the poor who were bitterly offended by the contrast between the squalor in which tens of thousands of people in the slums of London had to live and the ever increasing splendours to be seen behind the Corinthian portico and garden wall of the Regent's palace. George Tierney, one of the more extreme Whigs, complained in 1815 that the furniture for Carlton House had cost the nation £260,000; charges for upholstery were £49,000 in a single year; plate and jewels cost about £23,000 each year. Yet Carlton House was constantly being improved, refurnished and redecorated; and it was the tax-paying middle classes who had to bear most of the cost. A new Gothic dining-room, divided into five apartments with walls of varnished wood decorated with the arms of the Kings of England, was added at the east end to complement the conservatory; a second Gothic library was installed as well as several new Corinthian rooms including a golden drawing-room; and if some of the buildings that appeared from time to time in the gardens were found to have other uses – like the polygonal structure erected for the Wellington fête, which was moved to Woolwich to serve as a weapons museum and armoury – there were many others that were merely demolished and carted away. Five days after the Wellington fête it was announced in *The Times* that the Regent would shortly take possession of the Duke of Cumberland's apartments at St James's Palace, which had been prepared for the Emperor of Russia, 'previous to the commencement of grand alterations at Carlton House'.[15]

The Regent's reckless expenditure would have been considered rather less censurable had he been content with his London palace; but he continued to lavish money on other equally extravagant enterprises elsewhere, though his debts, while gradually being reduced, still amounted in May 1814 to £339,000. At the beginning of 1815 work had begun on rebuilding the Marine Pavilion at Brighton, the existing structure by Henry Holland being now considered rather humdrum; and the Regent's Treasurer dreaded to think what the ultimate cost of this new work would be.

Some years before, James Wyatt had submitted an estimate which suggested a likely figure of £200,000.[16] Wyatt was the architect of the Pantheon in Oxford Street, described by Horace Walpole as 'the most beautiful edifice in England', and of Fonthill Abbey, William Beckford's fantastic mansion in Wiltshire. He had done a good deal of work for George III and, for the Regent, had designed the second library at Carlton House. But before any work on the new Pavilion could be begun, he was killed in a carriage accident; and the Regent, 'very much affected ... even to shedding tears', had to find another architect to fulfil his plans.[17] He soon found one in John Nash.

He already knew Nash well. It was he who had been responsible for the new Corinthian rooms at Carlton House, as well as the buildings in the gardens for the Wellington fête in 1814 and the pagoda and bridge in St James's Park that same year. The Regent had also been closely involved with Nash's plans for a massive redevelopment scheme which was eventually to transform the face of central London. In fact, it was widely believed that the relationship between Nash and the Regent was something more than that of architect and patron. For Nash, the son of an impoverished Lambeth millwright, had risen with remarkable speed in the architectural profession. Trained in the office of Sir Robert Taylor, he had launched out and bankrupted himself as a speculative builder before going into partnership with Humphry Repton. But in 1798 he had married a woman much younger than himself, a woman who was supposed to have been one of the Prince's mistresses. And thereafter he became much more successful and much richer, arousing a good deal of dislike by his self-satisfaction and display, his snobberies and affectations. 'A great coxcomb', Robert Finch recorded in his diary. 'He is very fond of women ... attempted even Mrs Parker, his wife's sister. He lives in Dover Street, has a charming place on the Isle of Wight and drives four horses.'[18]

Coxcomb or not, Nash was an architect of exceptional talent whose emergence as the Regent's favourite architect was fully justified by his performance. The Regent eagerly discussed with him the plans for an extensive development in Marylebone Park – an expanse of open land north of Portland Place which had just reverted to the Crown from the noble families to whom it had formerly been let – and for a new road that was to sweep up to this new development from Pall Mall. The development in Marylebone Park was to be known as Regent's Park; the road that led to it as Regent's Street. These were both impressive schemes for the improvement of the capital that remained, throughout their gradual realization, close to the Regent's heart. Indeed, without the Regent's support and his influence over the apathetic and hidebound

5 (*above left*) Edward, Duke of Kent, by George Dawe.

6 (*above right*) Augustus Frederick, Duke of Sussex, by G. H. Harlow.

7 (*below left*) Frederick, Duke of York, by David Wilkie, 1823.

8 (*below right*) Ernest Augustus, Duke of Cumberland, by George Dawe.

9 The revolving Temple of Concord erected in Green Park for the display of a 'Grand Firework' to celebr the Peace on 1 August 1814: engraving by R. W. Smart after James Pain.

10 The Chinese pagoda and bridge built across the canal in St James's Park for the illumination of 1 Augu 1814: engraving by J. Gleadah after T. W. Edy.

Commissioners for Crown Lands they could never have been realized at all.[19]

At the time many people wished that it had not been possible to realize them. The stucco and cast-iron terraces were widely condemned as meretricious. Prince Pückler-Muskau described Nash's architecture as 'monstrous';[20] Maria Edgeworth was 'properly surprised by the new town . . . built in Regent's Park – and indignant at plaister statues and horrid useless *domes* and pediments crowded with mock sculpture figures which damp and smoke must destroy in a season or two'.[21]

The charges were understandable. There was much in Nash's work that was grandiose, extravagant and showily exuberant; but for all their audacious – sometimes even outrageous – panache, his buildings were eventually seen to be as delightful as the Regent had found them from the beginning. Their influence spread all over England, from seaside resorts on the south coast, to inland spas such as Cheltenham, from the outer suburbs of London to the market towns of the country.[22]

Admiring Nash's gifts and sharing his panache, the Regent had no hesitation in asking him to work with him on the designs for yet another architectural adventure, a romantic country house in Windsor Great Park. This new residence was known at first as The Cottage; and then, since this seemed scarcely appropriate for the large building it eventually became, as the Royal Lodge, or, as his enemies preferred, 'The Thatched Palace'.

The Royal Lodge, originally a modest house occupied by the Deputy-Ranger, was converted by Nash into an enchanting and imposing Gothic *cottage orné*. Its roof was thatched and its windows mullioned; its brick walls were rendered in coloured plaster; a thatched verandah, supported by rustic columns entwined with ivy and honeysuckle, extended along the south front at the western end of which there was a large glass conservatory. Tall, elegantly shaped chimneys rose above the reeds of the roof; the larch trees and pines that encircled the lawns secluded the house without keeping the sunlight from its windows. By the end of 1814 over £52,000 had been spent upon it, including £17,000 for furniture. It was to be constantly altered, renovated and enlarged; and a new dining-room – the only part of the rambling house to survive *in situ* today – was still not completed at the time of its owner's death.[23]

*

Robert Smirke, a practical, methodical, rather staid architect, examples of whose work were soon to be seen all over London, was highly critical of the Regent's fanciful taste and extravagant expenditure. He condemned the apartments at Carlton House, for example, as being 'so overdone with finery, and superfluous as, supposing the owner not to be known, would give an unfavourable idea of the kind of mind he must have'.[24] Yet even Smirke conceded that the Regent's patronage of the arts and artists, of scientists and scholars, was to be commended as compensation for his many faults and follies, and that he was a truly discerning connoisseur as well as a generous patron. Richard Westmacott, the sculptor, gave evidence of this when he unpacked, for the Regent's inspection at Carlton House, some fine casts of the group of Niobe which had been sent to London by the Grand Duke of Tuscany. The Regent commented that one of the statues did not belong to the group. 'I was pleased at the Prince making this remark without any observation from me,' Westmacott reported to Lawrence. 'The Prince's remarks . . . were not only judicious but expressed with a feeling and in a language of art that I was not aware he was master of.'[25] When Thomas Lawrence was knighted in April 1815, having fulfilled the Regent's commission to paint the various allied sovereigns, ministers and generals who had contributed to Napoleon's downfall, Smirke wrote that 'no act of our Regent Sovereign was ever more just', and that if he kept up to that, the country would have 'cause to be grateful'.[26] The Regent himself assured Sir Thomas that he was proud in conferring a mark of his favour on one who had raised the character of British art in the estimation of all Europe.[27]

Lawrence had been in France when the Regent recalled him to London to begin painting those portraits of the allied leaders which now hang in the Waterloo Chamber at Windsor. He had gone over to Paris to see the works of art which Napoleon had brought together in the Louvre from all over the Empire. These works of art included the Apollo Belvedere and various other statues which had been taken from Rome and which the Pope now offered to the Regent on the grounds that the expense of bringing them back would be too heavy for the Papacy to bear. Much as he would have liked to possess 'these inestimable productions', the Regent replied that he could not take advantage of their owner's necessity, and he offered to pay for their return to Rome himself.[28]

The generosity did not go unrewarded. The Regent was sent in return a number of casts from marbles in the Vatican museum which were immediately offered to the Royal Academy, whose President was informed that 'if casts from any other of the fine antiques in Rome should be considered desirable for the School of the Royal Academy, His Royal Highness would, on their being specified, use his influence to obtain them'.[29] This offer was followed by the loan to the Royal Academy school of the Raphael cartoons, 'one at a time for a few months each', and of *Rembrandt and Saskia about to go out*. The Rembrandt was a picture he had recently acquired as a companion piece to Rembrandt's *Shipbuilder and his Wife* which Lord Yarmouth had bought for him some years before.[30]

While Lawrence was working for the Regent in London, Antonio Canova was at work on his behalf in Rome. Canova had been sent to Paris by the Pope to superintend the return of various Italian treasures, and after his work there was completed he had gratified a long-felt wish to visit London. The Regent had greeted him warmly, presented him with a valuable snuffbox and commissioned from him various works, including a group of Mars and Venus, a statue of a nymph, and later, to the horror of the Whigs, an expensive statue in Rome to the memory of the exiled Stuarts whom the Regent profoundly revered.*

The Regent's 'fine taste, sound judgment, and extensive information' made a deep impression on Canova who used to say that of all the sovereigns he had met in the course of his career – and he had talked to almost all the crowned heads of Europe – there was not one 'in whose address were more happily combined, the suavity of the amiable man, and the dignity of the great monarch'.[31] He particularly respected the Regent for the support which he had given to the nation's purchase of the marble friezes from the neglected Parthenon brought back from Greece by the seventh Earl of Elgin. These friezes, the Elgin marbles, had been subjected to much ignorant criticism from the kind of self-professed

---

* When part of James II's remains were discovered during the rebuilding of the parish church at St Germain-en-Laye in 1824, they were removed in great state on the express instruction of George IV and placed beneath the altar before being solemnly reinterred in the newly completed church (Campana de Cavelli, *Les derniers Stuarts à St Germain-en-Laye*, Paris, 1871, i, 99). The marble group of Mars and Venus was completed in 1817 and placed, rather inappropriately, in the Gothic conservatory at Carlton House in 1824. Together with another group by Canova of a girl and cherub which reached Carlton House in 1819, the Mars and Venus group is now at Buckingham Palace (*Buckingham Palace*, 183).

connoisseur satirized by James Gillray; but Canova confirmed their supreme merit and welcomed the Regent's interest in their purchase.*

As in art, so in the sciences, the Regent's patronage was eagerly sought and gratefully welcomed. He was President of the Royal Institution, which consequently became 'more the *ton* than anything' and attracted 'ladies of all ages' to its lectures. He bestowed an unsolicited knighthood on the chemist, Humphry Davy, subsequent inventor of the safety lamp; he also knighted William Herschel, the astronomer; he endowed readerships in mineralogy and geology at Oxford; he championed William Congreve, inventor of the Congreve rocket, at a time when he was being much ridiculed, made him one of his equerries, and would no doubt have knighted him too had he not succeeded to his father's baronetcy.

He also professed himself anxious to promote the cause of literature. He was a patron of the Literary Fund, regularly subscribed to it, and obtained for it a Charter of Incorporation. He was particularly anxious to give his personal encouragement to the work of Jane Austen. He frequently read her novels, so she was told by her brother's doctor who was also one of the Regent's physicians, and he kept a set 'in every one of his residences'. One day in 1815 she was invited to Carlton House where she was conducted round the library by Stanier Clarke, the Regent's librarian, who told her that his master had 'read and admired' all her publications, and that she was free to dedicate a novel to him if she wished

* Canova's colossal marble statue of Napoleon, in the pose of a naked Roman emperor, 11 feet 4 inches in height, also came to England at this time. Canova had been commissioned by Napoleon to execute the work in 1802 and had completed it in 1810. Napoleon did not like it, however, since the winged figure of Victory in the statue's right hand does not return his stern gaze but seems about to fly away from him. The statue was consequently packed away out of sight. It was bought in 1816 for less than £3,000, a figure which nevertheless enabled the Louvre to complete the installation of the Salle des Antiques. The Regent presented it to the Duke of Wellington, and it now stands in the staircase vestibule at Apsley House (Archives Nationales o³ 1430: *The Wellington Museum* (HMSO, 1964, 37). After Canova's death in 1822, George IV bought his two last works for 5,000 guineas. The King's agent, W. R. Hamilton, Minister at the Court of Naples, could not say that Canova's brother was '*perfectly* satisfied' that the sum paid represented 'the full amount' which the sculptures were worth, nor what the artist would have expected for them; but Hamilton was fully persuaded that the 'Abbato Canova was highly flattered that these his brother's latest finished works should be deposited in the palace of the King of Great Britain' (RA 27064 12 August 1825).

to do so. She did wish to do so, and told her publishers that her next novel, *Emma*, which was already advertised for publication, was to be 'dedicated by permission to HRH the Prince Regent', and that it was her 'particular wish that one set should be completed and sent to HRH two or three days before the work [was] generally public'.[32]

7

Cranbourne Lodge and Claremont Park
1814-1817

*

'Is there any danger?'

While Jane Austen had been at work on *Emma*, Princess Charlotte had been languishing in her close confinement at Warwick House, Cranbourne Lodge and Weymouth. The people she was allowed to see were limited to the names on a list drawn up by her father who insisted that though she was permitted to go to the theatre once or twice a week she must not sit at the front of the box or stay till the very end of the performance. 'Nothing can be so wretchedly uncertain and uncomfortable as my situation,' she complained miserably to Priscilla Burghersh. 'I am grown thin, sleep ill and eat but little. Bailly [Dr Matthew Baillie] says my complaints are all nervous, and that bathing and sailing will brace me; but I say *Oh no*! no good can be done whilst the mind and the soul are on the rack constantly, and the spirits forced and screwed up to a certain pitch.'[1] It was not that she missed her mother. Indeed, she told her aunt Mary that she thought the best thing that Princess Caroline could do would be to stay abroad, and that she did not mind if she never saw her again.[2] What she complained of most, so Margaret Mercer Elphinstone informed Brougham, was that one of the ladies was 'obliged either to sleep in the room with her, or in the next with the door open, and that many of her letters have been kept back'.[3]

In a long letter to Lord Grey, Miss Elphinstone had given a worrying account of the Princess's health at Weymouth during the late summer of 1814. She had become 'worse daily', and the pains in her knee had been so severe that she had been unable to sleep for nights on end. 'To make her sejour at the seaside as disagreeable as possible,' Miss Elphinstone had continued, 'the Prince has positively refused to allow her to drive her ponies there, as he says it would collect a mob at the door every time she went out. He has also prevented her Sub Tutors from going with her, though she asked to have them as a favor, so that she will be literally deprived of every amusement and occupation that could for a moment divert her thoughts from her present melancholy situation. . . . Her allowance, which used to be paid regularly (every month I believe) has been withheld from her, ever since she left Warwick House. A tradesman sent in his bill to her a few days ago, begging to be paid as he was in great distress for money – to accomplish this, and to pay some little pensions that were due to poor people, she protests she was obliged to part with some of her diamonds – surely this tyranny cannot last long.'[4]

So far as the Princess's allowance was concerned, Miss Elphinstone did not know the full facts. On the day after she had written to Lord Grey, the Regent had written to his mother from Ragley asking her to let Charlotte have £200 which he would pay the Queen back as soon as he returned to London.[5] He had added that, 'strange as it may appear', he had never in his life known what the amount of her allowance was. He had presumed the King had made adequate provision for her, and had told Lady de Clifford that he 'wished that Charlotte should at all times be liberally supplied with money, and not stinted in the least, and that the allowance should be proportioned to her years, increasing of course as she grew more advanced in her years; and that if hereafter the sum thus allowed by the King was not sufficient for affording what was proper for Charlotte for her pocket', Lady Clifford had but to apply to him and he would do 'all that was necessary' so far as his means would admit.[6]

In fact, the amount of the pocket money was £10 a month.[7] In addition she was allowed £1,000 a year for her other expenses, excluding the house and stable accounts.[8] But this had proved far from enough for her. By the end of 1814 she had become involved in debt to Colnaghi for nearly £600 for prints, and to various dressmakers and jewellers to the astonishing amount of over £20,000. This had been largely due to her excessive generosity to her friends all of whom had received expensive presents of jewellery from her at the time of her engagement to the Prince of Orange; she had hoped that the bills would be paid out of the sum which she expected to receive from Parliament on the occasion of her marriage.[9]

His knowledge of the great amount of her debts had not prevented a happy reconciliation of the Regent and his daughter five months after her flight from Warwick House when she had confessed to him for the first time the full story of her association with Captain Hesse and her mother's active encouragement of the affair. Her father's kindness and understanding about all this had impressed her deeply; she had told the Duke of York 'with great glee' of the happiness she felt 'at being upon so cordial and affectionate a footing' with her father once again.[10]

But the narrow escape she had had with Captain Hesse and the other unsuitable young men who had been allowed to be alone with her made her father all the more certain that she ought to get married as soon as possible. Her recent capricious behaviour had, he felt sure, done much harm to her reputation abroad; and if she were left unattached much longer it might be difficult to arrange a suitable match for her at all.

Princess Charlotte agreed with him about the desirability of an early marriage. 'My character, my dear father, you must believe is no matter of indifference to me. . . . Having entered upon this subject I cannot conclude it without begging you to take into consideration how much a matrimonial connexion would be likely to remove me and my reputation from all this present distress.'[11] Yet Princess Charlotte could not agree that a renewal of the engagement to the Prince of Orange, as her father proposed, was at all acceptable.

The Regent still considered that Prince William would prove a highly suitable husband. He believed that she had been prejudiced against him by Lady Jersey and Brougham, by the Duchess of Oldenburg and Whitbread, and that he was far from being the wastrel that they said he was. To be sure he drank rather a lot; but that was understandable in his present distress. It was not an incurable fault. The British Minister at The Hague had always entertained a good opinion of him.[12]

The Regent invited Margaret Mercer Elphinstone to the Pavilion where, as she admitted, he was 'more than gracious' to her; but she 'soon discovered the motive of all this mummery'. 'I was catechised and sermonised for two hours,' Miss Elphinstone reported to Lord Grey. 'His grand plan is still to bring about the Orange marriage to which he wished to make me instrumental. . . . I at once declined, stating that it was a subject so disagreeable to the Princess that I dare not venture to touch upon it. . . . [Only a few days ago she said that] so far from repenting of the step she had taken in refusing the Prince of Orange she would rather continue to suffer all the privations and restraints she had [recently undergone]. "Well," said the Prince, "it is just as I thought. When she once takes a thing into her head she is as obstinate as the devil. However, as this is the case I desire you will not repeat any part of this conversation to her. At all events it is a subject *I* can never again mention to my daughter after what has passed – it can only come from her own good sense or the counsel or influence of her friends."' [13]

Soon afterwards Princess Charlotte raised the matter herself. She wrote to her father from Cranbourne Lodge to tell him that she understood it was still his wish to secure her marriage with the Prince of Orange: 'Pardon me if I say *that* information greatly pained me. . . . There is no act of obedience, no sacrifice you could wish me to make that I am not ready for, if it is necessary to prove my sense of duty. But where the future (and I may add) the whole happiness of my life is concerned . . . I think I cannot be too plain in humbly stating my strong and fixed aversion to a match with a man for whom I can never feel those sentiments of regard which surely are so necessary in a matrimonial connexion. . . . I hope you will not love me less for thus laying open the sentiments of my heart, as you told me you would never urge any union that would make me miserable'. [14]

Undeterred by this letter, the Regent replied that he did, indeed, want her to reconsider the House of Orange match which, he reminded her with some exaggeration, she had formerly 'so earnestly and so ardently' asked him to approve. As she herself had admitted, she was not free to choose a husband as the rest of the world did. Was it not then extremely fortunate to find 'youth, character, power, rank, consequence, national interests and actual national alliance, all united in one', as they happily were in the Prince of Orange? [15]

Princess Charlotte did not think this fortunate in the least. She had no such high opinion of the character of the Prince of Orange whom she 'could not esteem, regard, or look up to as a wife should her husband'. [16] So, the Regent at last accepted that there was nothing more that could be done. He told her that her precipitate reply to his letter, written before 'there was time for reason to operate on the representations' which he had made, had given him 'no inconsiderable degree of pain', yet she could rest assured that he would not press 'the matter further'. [17]

Relieved and thankful, Princess Charlotte grew more and more cheerful as the weeks went by. Her health improved; her knee 'benefitted much from fomentations of hot salt water'.[18] At Weymouth, aboard the Queen's yacht, she could be heard laughing again and calling out with familiar gusto for a luncheon of 'cold beef, with plenty of mustard'.[19] At Cranbourne Lodge, Lady Ilchester noticed 'an air of happiness' about her which she had not seen before.[20] As her friends knew, this happiness was due to the fact that she had found a man she wanted to marry and who wanted to marry her.

*

Prince Leopold of Saxe-Coburg-Saalfeld was good-looking and charming in a rather solemn kind of way. Talented and respected, he was as smart as the Prince of Orange was slovenly, though some people found him a little unctuous and shifty, noticing, as Lady Charlotte Campbell did, that he never looked at the person to whom he was talking.[21] His virtues had been extolled to the Princess by the Duchess of Oldenburg, whose Russian relatives would be delighted to see her married to the son of a petty German princeling rather than to the future King of the Netherlands on whom they had designs themselves and to whom they eventually succeeded in marrying the Tsar's sister, the Grand Duchess Anna Paulowna.

Princess Charlotte had not at first been unduly excited at the prospect of marrying Prince Leopold, except as a means of escape from her present seclusion. If she did so it would be 'with the most calm and perfect indifference', though she admitted to Margaret Mercer Elphinstone that he had 'the highest and best character possible in every way', and was 'extremely prepossessing in his figure and appearance'. Of the men available to her, he would be her first choice if the choice were left to her. Certainly he was most attentive and made it flatteringly clear to her how much he liked her. 'At all events,' she said, 'I know that *worse off*... I *cannot* be than I am *now*, and after all if I end by marrying Prince L., I marry the best of all those *I have seen*, and that is some satisfaction.'[22]

Her father was not at all taken with the idea of having him as a son-in-law. It was not only that he was of no importance whatsoever in European politics, that he was so poor he had had to rent lodgings over a grocer's shop in Marylebone High Street, but there was something in the ingratiating suavity of his manner which was decidedly distasteful. He was gifted admittedly; his service in the Russian army as a very young cavalry general had been quite distinguished; he would no doubt treat

Charlotte well, but it was difficult to regard him as other than a calculating careerist. The Regent, who was extremely adept in choosing nicknames, called him *le Marquis peu à peu.* The less inventive Lord Frederick Fitzclarence dismissed him as a 'damned humbug'.[23]

In the end, however, the Regent allowed himself to be persuaded. It was no recommendation to him that the Duke of Kent – through whose hands the correspondence between Prince Leopold and Princess Charlotte had passed – advocated the match. But the Duke of York was also in favour of it; so was Lord Castlereagh, on whom Prince Leopold had made a good impression at the Congress of Vienna; and Princess Charlotte assured him that no one would be 'more steady and consistent in this . . . engagement' than herself.[24] So it was settled; and in January 1816 both Charlotte and Leopold were invited to Brighton.

It was a very happy time. Her grandmother, much better tempered than usual, was there; so were her aunts; and they all 'seemed delighted to have her under her father's roof. It certainly was a gratification to the [Regent] to find it really gave so much pleasure to the Princess,' Lady Ilchester reported, 'for he had been led to suspect that she did not like to come, which was a complete mistake, and of which he [was] now convinced.'[25]

He could not have been kinder, Charlotte herself thought, although he was suffering so badly from gout that he had to wheel himself about in a Merlin chair in which he sat the whole evening talking to Lady Hertford, his sisters and selected friends, or listening to the band. The Queen played cards and others of the guests played backgammon or strolled up and down between the cast-iron and bamboo staircases at either end of the Chinese gallery, their brilliant suits and dresses illuminated by the coloured lanterns and reflected in the panels of looking-glass on the doors.

'The Chinese scene is gay beyond description, and I am sure you would admire it, as well as the manner of living at the Pavilion,' Lady Ilchester told a friend, 'though the extreme warmth of it might, perhaps, be too much for you. Everyone was free in the morning of all Court restraint, and only met at six o'clock punctually for dinner to the number of between thirty and forty, and in the evening as many more were generally invited; a delightful band of music played till half-past eleven, when the Royal Family took their leave, and the rest of the company also, after partaking of sandwiches. The evenings were not in the least formal.'[26]

Throughout her visit the Regent was in 'high spirits and good humour', Charlotte wrote contentedly; and she told her aunt Mary that his kindness towards her made her 'as happy as possible'.[27] 'He is grown thinner and his legs considerably reduced. . . . There is not a soul that is not in extacies at my fate and choice.'[28]

She was obviously so herself. For in the comforting atmosphere of her family's friendliness and her father's evident affection, she had fallen in love. Her previous indifference was quite forgotten. She had 'not one anxious wish left'; she was now 'thoroughly persuaded' that Prince Leopold would 'do all and everything' he could to please her and make her happy. A Council was held at the Pavilion and the Regent gave his formal consent to the marriage.

Soon afterwards Princess Charlotte went to visit the Queen at Windsor 'with the happiest face imaginable'. She 'talked of the event in a very quiet and reasonable way', looking forward to 'more real happiness in this expected union than in the former choice she had made'. 'In my humble opinion I believe she truly means what she says,' the Queen reported to the Regent, 'and if it is possible to make her feel before marriage that though the Prince becomes an object of consequence by marrying her, he must be the head of the family and she submit to him as his wife, all will do well. And on his side, he must be carefull not to give her too great an idea of her own consequence, nor be drawn in to make promises before marriage which he might (being ignorant of the customs and manners of the country) find difficulty to fulfill afterwards.'[29]

Having delivered herself of this advice, the Queen entered eagerly into the arrangements for the marriage, offering advice about the trousseau, about a country house for the bride and bridegroom, suggesting that Cranbourne Lodge should be given to Princess Augusta, and proposing that Princess Charlotte's Ladies should have £400 a year, not £500 as the Regent had suggested, since 'the Queen's Ladys [had] only five' and they might claim more.[30] Above all, the Queen busied herself about the Princess's jewels, having a passion for jewels herself. She ordered Bridge, the jeweller, to come to Windsor with those the Princess had ordered – which far exceeded in price the sum that Parliament had voted for them – so that the girl could be given proper guidance in choosing the best.[31]

It had been agreed that Charlotte and Leopold should be allowed £60,000 a year 'to maintain an establishment which without being either extravagant or profuse' would be 'suitable to their rank and station',[32] and that they should, in addition, be granted a capital sum of the same amount, '£40,000 for furniture, plate, etc., £10,000 for personal equipment and £10,000 for jewells'.[33] It was also agreed that, in addition to a London home, Marlborough House, they should be provided with a house in the country. So Claremont Park at Esher in Surrey, which had been built by Lord Clive, was bought for them from Charles Ellis, the rich Member of Parliament for Seaford, for £69,000. The Regent would have liked to bestow a further favour by creating Prince Leopold Duke of Kendal; but he was dissuaded from doing so on the grounds that 'nothing could be more inconvenient, *personally*, to the Consort of the future Queen, and also to the public, than his having a seat in the House of Lords'.[34]

On the day of the wedding, 2 May 1816, Princess Charlotte dined at the Queen's House with her grandmother and aunts. After dinner she put on her shimmering silver wedding dress and the wreath of diamond roses which the Queen had helped her to select from the ample stock of Messrs Rundell, Bridge & Co. She was ready just before eight o'clock when she came down the staircase with Princess Augusta and stepped into the carriage that was to take her to Carlton House.

Looking out of the window as she drove through the Park she saw the hundreds of people who had spent the afternoon cheering and clapping outside Clarence House, calling for the bridegroom to show himself on the balcony. 'Bless me!' Charlotte exclaimed. 'What a crowd!'[35]

The wedding was conducted at Carlton House with the splendour associated with all the functions that were held there. The bride and bridegroom knelt on crimson velvet cushions, beneath candlesticks six feet high; and when the ceremony was over, the Princess knelt to her father for his blessing which he gave her with such a 'good hearty, paternal hug' that Lady Liverpool was delighted.[36] During the ceremony there was one unfortunate incident, so Lady Charlotte Campbell was told: when Prince Leopold repeated the words, 'With all my worldly goods I thee endow', 'the royal bride was observed to laugh'.[37] After the ceremony there was another embarrassing moment: the Queen, insisting that it would be 'so improper' for the bride and bridegroom to drive away together, asked Mrs Campbell, Princess Charlotte's former governess, to sit between them in the carriage. Mrs Campbell was brave enough to refuse.

*

From the beginning, Princess Charlotte was ideally contented with her husband, though naturally there were occasional differences, as when, for instance, he wanted to go to bed but she did not choose to do so, and he had to wait until she was ready.[38] 'We lead a very quiet and retired life here,' she wrote from Claremont, 'but a very, *very* happy one.' They spent nearly all their time together, walking arm in arm through the gardens, driving out side by side, close to each other, their heads almost touching, singing duets in the drawing-room after dinner, reading to each other.[39] Only when he went out shooting were they apart, and when he returned she would brush his hair. For the first time in her life she took criticism without resentment. '*Doucement, ma chère, doucement,*' he would say to her, endeavouring to cure her of her natural impetuosity and rough ungainliness, and she would smile and try to please him. When he corrected her in his meticulous, pedantic way, she would listen patiently; when he scolded her for lightheartedly making fun of someone, she tearfully promised not to offend him in such a way again.

One of his suite, a young German doctor of Swedish descent, Christian Stockmar, thought that his master was quite right to correct her, for she had 'most peculiar manners, her hands generally folded behind her, her body always pushed forward, never standing quiet, from time to time stamping her foot, laughing a great deal, and talking still more'. She was 'astonishingly impressionable and nervously sensitive', and she could be very rude: on Stockmar's being presented to her for the first time she examined him intently 'from head to foot'. His own first impressions of her were 'not favourable'. Yet he soon grew deeply fond of her and she of him. She took to calling him 'Stocky' and to confiding in him the unhappiness of her past. 'My mother was bad,' she once told him, 'but she would not have become as bad as she was if my father had not been infinitely worse.'[40]

But all that unhappiness, all those quarrels with her father were now truly in the past. 'Harmony, peace and love' reigned at Claremont, Stockmar said, and on her visits to Carlton House and the Pavilion she and her father were perfectly at ease. 'Happily for me,' she had assured her father not long before her marriage, 'we are now upon the most comfortable and confidential terms possible'; and so they still remained. She contentedly told Dr Baillie how 'affectionate and tender' her father had been to her of late.[41] He visited her at Claremont on 16 October, and it was a happy day. 'You must be well soon for my sake,' she wrote to him that autumn, hearing he was unwell again. 'Pray don't forget me and believe me a devoted child, my dearest Father, your very affectionate Charlotte.'[42]

Princess Charlotte's one concern seemed to be her difficulty in having a baby. She conceived twice, but on both occasions she miscarried; and when she became pregnant for a third time it was considered that Dr Baillie should have the benefit of the advice of a specialist, in the tall, thin, elegant shape of Sir Richard Croft.

Croft, as the leading and most fashionable *accoucheur* of his day, was a highly self-confident, though far from skilful physician. He took upon himself the sole responsibility for his patient's care, bleeding her regularly and imposing on her a thin, weak and most unappetising diet, mainly composed of liquids. He believed this treatment necessary because of her 'morbid excess of animal spirits'.[43]

The pregnancy, however, continued satisfactorily; and on 9 October it was announced that a baby would be born in nine or ten days' time. No complications were expected, though to the Queen's experienced eye her granddaughter's figure appeared so unnaturally immense that she could not help being 'uneasy to a considerable degree'.[44] By 21 October she was still 'well'; and in spite of her suffering the next day a 'little from headache', as a cure for which 'blood was ... several times ... drawn from a vein at the back of the hand', the doctors thought there remained no cause for alarm.

Princess Charlotte did not share their confidence. Moods of excessive excitement alternated with periods of deep despondency. On 10 October she wrote a gloomy letter to her 'dearest mother', though before her marriage she had promised her father never to do so again and had, in fact, told Princess Mary that she hoped all intercourse would *'entirely cease'*.[45] 'Why is not my mother allowed to pour cheerfulness into the sinking heart of her inexperienced and trembling child?' she asked miserably. 'I have but one mother and no variation of place or circumstance can remove her from my mind. ... Should it be the pleasure of Providence that I survive the hour of approaching danger, I may at some future period be endued with power to restore you to that situation you were formed to embellish. But if an all wise decree should summon me from this sphere of anxious apprehension, not for myself but for my mother a pang of terror shoots across my bewildered brain. ... Believe me, my adored mother, I fear less to die than to live, the prospect of protracted existence is so blended with dangers and difficulties, so shadowed with clouds and uncertainties, so replete with anxieties and apprehensions that I must shrink from the contemplation of it, and fly for refuge even to the probability of my removal from so joyless an inheritance.'[46]

On 3 November her labour began. It continued for fifty hours. She was in great pain; but she said to one of the nurses, 'I will neither bawl nor shriek,' and she did not do so. She bore 'all without a murmur'.[47] Sir Richard Croft remained with her, allowing into the room neither Dr Baillie nor an assistant *accoucheur*, Dr John Sims. He advised his patient not to eat anything.

'Nothing can be going on better,' he announced at three o'clock on the afternoon of 4 November to General Sir Robert Gardiner, Prince Leopold's principal equerry. And at a quarter to eight the next morning he reported to the Cabinet Ministers, who had been summoned to Claremont so as to be present when the child was born, that his patient had made 'a considerable, though very gradual progress throughout the night'. The labour was 'so very slow' that he could not determine when it would be accomplished. Nevertheless, her 'pulse and general appearance' were good.

She continued in labour throughout the day, the pains 'in some degree relaxed'; and it was not until nine o'clock that night that she was at last delivered. The baby, 'a beautiful fine boy . . . very large', was dead.[48]

The mother, however, continued to do 'extremely well', though there seemed something strange about her 'unnatural composure, not to say cheerfulness', and the way in which she had accepted her suffering almost as if she had been too elated to feel it.[49] Yet 'no unfavourable symptoms' had occurred; there was 'no apparent danger'. The Ministers left the house and returned to London. Prince Leopold and the doctors went to bed.

At midnight Princess Charlotte complained to her nurse of a singing in her head and of feeling suddenly cold. She tried to drink some gruel, but she could not swallow it and was sick. Then she felt a sudden, agonizing pain. 'Oh what pain,' she cried, clasping her hands to her stomach, 'it is all here.'[50]

Croft and Sims, who were hurriedly summoned from their beds, found her pulse alarmingly rapid and irregular. They put bottles of hot water and warm flannels in her bed, poured brandy, hot water and wine down her throat until she scarcely knew what was happening any more. 'They have made me tipsy,' she complained pathetically to Dr Stockmar. She had a pain in her chest now as well as in her stomach and could scarcely breathe. 'Is there any danger?' she asked and was told to compose herself. She then went into convulsions. Afterwards 'she could not articulate, but sunk into a calm composure, until . . . with a gentle sigh, she expired'.[51]*

*

The Prince Regent himself had been seriously ill again in September. 'We have been near losing him,' Lady Holland reported, 'and as the physicians mistook his disorder, they have probably curtailed his length of life, for the disease was treated as inflammatory and they took 60 ounces of blood. When Baillie saw him he declared it to be spasm, and gave laudanum and cordials. The consequences are likely to produce dropsy.'[52]

He was convalescing at a shooting party at Sudbourne in Suffolk with the Hertfords when he heard from Sir Robert Gardiner that his daughter had been in labour for twenty-seven hours, that the exertions of the womb were 'less vigorous than they ought to be', and that some 'artificial assistance' might become necessary.[53] He left for London immediately, refusing to wait for fresh horses to be put into the post-chaise, and asking every time the carriage stopped whether there was any further news. Once he was told that the Princess continued in

* The mysterious causes of Princess Charlotte's death have been long debated. It has been recently suggested that she may have inherited porphyria. 'Cases have been observed where a fulminating attack of porphyria set in a few hours after confinement with signs of cerebral irritation, spreading paralysis, convulsions and finally respiratory failure' (Macalpine and Hunter, 246). At the time the doctors were blamed, and in particular, of course, Sir Richard Croft, who had taken upon himself so much of the responsibility for the case. In subsequent generations Princess Charlotte's case was cited as a classic example of the danger of not using instruments soon enough, though Croft's reluctance to use 'artificial assistance' was strictly in accordance with contemporary obstetric practice. Croft never recovered from the disgrace and from the cruel attacks that were subsequently made on him. The Regent kindly tried to make amends for these attacks by thanking him publicly for the 'zealous care and indefatigable attention manifested by Sir Richard towards his beloved daughter', and by assuring him that he was entirely satisfied with the 'medical skill and ability which he displayed, during the arduous and protracted labour, whereof the issue, under the will of Divine Providence, had overwhelmed His Royal Highness with such deep affliction' (Asp/K ii, 212–13). Few of Croft's former patients shared this professed confidence. And on 13 February 1818, while attending a woman whose difficulties in labour resembled those he had witnessed at Claremont, he took a pistol from the wall and shot himself in her house (*Gentleman's Magazine*, lxxxviii, i, 277).

labour. A messenger with a letter informing him that his grandson was stillborn passed him on the road.[54]

He arrived at Carlton House between three and four o'clock in the morning, and having ascertained that although the baby was dead, his daughter was 'doing extremely well', he went exhausted to bed. Soon afterwards he was roused by the Duke of York and Lord Bathurst who told him that Princess Charlotte also was dead. He 'struck his forehead violently with both hands, and fell forward into the arms of the Duke of York'.[55] His doctors were called and thought it necessary to bleed him with their customary immoderation.

He recovered sufficiently to drive over to Claremont where Prince Leopold, overwhelmed with grief, did not feel up to seeing him. He drove over again five days later, all the blinds of his carriage drawn, and saw Leopold and the bodies of his daughter and grandson, both of which, to Prince Leopold's 'surprise and sorrow', had been embalmed.[56] Leopold was still very distressed. But, so the Queen said, much was to be 'expected from the mildness of his character to contribute towards the recovery of his spirits'.[57] And as Princess Mary observed, though evidently 'much affected', he remained 'completely calm and composed'.[58] The Regent asked him if he would like to come to stay at Carlton House where he might feel less unhappy; but he preferred to stay where he was, protesting that he would live for the rest of his life at Claremont, forbidding anybody to remove the Princess's watch from her mantlepiece or her cloak and bonnet from the screen in the sitting-parlour on which she had placed it after their last walk together.[59]

In contrast to the unhappy yet composed Prince Leopold, the Regent was so overcome with emotion that it was 'impossible to attempt to describe' the condition into which he worked himself; it could 'scarcely be imagined'.[60] His shock was 'so intense as to excite great apprehension and alarm'.[61]

On leaving Claremont he drove over to see his mother, who had returned to Windsor from Bath where, since Princess Charlotte had not wanted her fussing about at Claremont,[62] she had gone, on Sir Henry Halford's advice, to take the waters. Seriously ill and very tired, she had broken out into a fit of compulsive sobbing when told of her grand-daughter's death, for she had grown fond of her in recent months; and as soon as she felt able to do so she had taken up her pen to tell her son how deeply she felt for him in his present loss and misery, how fully she shared his grief. She had tried to comfort him by telling him that he had done all he possibly could to make his 'child completely happy by granting her to marry the man she liked and wished to be united to', and by giving her a house where she had enjoyed 'to the very last almost complete felicity'.[63]

Yet the Regent seemed beyond the reach of sympathy. When his sister Mary went to visit him at Carlton House she was so upset by his condition that she was obliged to go into an anteroom to regain her composure before leaving the house. She later acceded to his urgent entreaties to go down and keep him company at Brighton where he hoped to recover his spirits.[64]

His recovery was very slow. 'All his thoughts and conversation turn upon the late sad event,' Croker told Lord Whitworth on 14 November. 'He never stirs out of his room, and goes to bed sometimes at eight or nine o'clock, wearied out, and yet not composed enough for sleep.'[65] He was 'still very much and very truly indisposed', he confessed to his 'dearest mother' on 16 December when explaining to her why he had not written to her for some time past. 'I do not know under what denomination to class the attack,' he told her, 'or by what name regularly to define it and call it, for it seems to me to have been a sort of mishmash, Solomongrundy, Olla podrida kind of business in itself that is quite anomalous; a good deal of rheumatism, as much of cold, with a little touch of bile to boot, not a very pleasant mixture on the whole, and composed of as unpleasant ingredients, as can well be thought of or imagined. In short all this potpourri has rendered me both bodily as well as mentally very unfit.'[66]

A fortnight later he was feeling somewhat better, at least his 'poor stomach' did, which he attributed to his taking Brandish's medicine twice a day, a medicine strongly recommended to him by Sir Henry Halford. It agreed with him perfectly and alleviated 'in great measure all those dreadful sufferings' he had 'experienced for some time past'.[67] He was still, however, far from well in the summer; and on 27 July his speech to Parliament had to be read by commission as it contained references to his daughter's death and he could not bear to read these out himself.[68] *

---

* Prince Leopold, who rarely missed an opportunity of blackening the Regent's character in the eyes of their niece, Queen Victoria, assured her in 1839 that 'it was observed that for years he had not been in such good spirits than by the loss of his daughter. She was more popular than himself. That, since her marriage, was her only crime' (RA Y65/60917, 18 January 1839).

8

Royal Marriages
1815-1818

*

'The damnedest millstone about the neck of any government that can be imagined'

Princess Charlotte's sudden death had stunned the country 'as if by an earthquake at dead of night', Henry Brougham recorded. 'This most melancholy event produced throughout the Kingdom feelings of the deepest sorrow and most bitter disappointment. It is scarcely possible to exaggerate, and it is difficult for persons not living at the time to believe how universal and how genuine those feelings were. It really was as if every household throughout Great Britain had lost a favourite child.'[1] This was not quite true. In the opinion, for example, of the Duke of Wellington, whom Princess Charlotte annoyed by calling 'Arthur', *tout court*, 'her death was a blessing to the country'. She 'would have turned out quite as her mother. . . . In addition to her mother's inclinations she had an exceeding bad manner.'[2] Nor had Lord Holland entertained a very favourable opinion of her. 'Little had appeared in this young lady,' he thought, 'to justify the inordinate grief at her death . . . she had shown even in the nursery, and still more in the months preceeding her marriage, that she inherited, together with the Prince Regent's quickness of apprehension and feeling, some of his greatest defects, *viz.*, a love of exaggeration, if not a disregard of truth . . . a passion for talebearers and favourites, and all those petty failings and practices which lead to what the French call *tracasseries.*'[3]

But certainly in the country at large the death of Princess Charlotte was looked upon as a tragedy.

For a long time before her death the public had been in an irritable, restless humour. 'The general spirit of the country,' wrote Robert Peel,

Chief Secretary for Ireland, 'is worse, I apprehend, than we understand it to be.'[4] At the beginning of the year the Regent was reported to have been so much hissed by the mob as to be 'quite disgusted'.[5] He had driven to Parliament through a crowd which was 'animated by a very bad spirit', and which was 'amazingly increased both in numbers and violence' upon his return to Carlton House. As he passed down Pall Mall, his carriage window was shattered and he felt a missile of some sort fly past his face. The Duke of Sussex reported the incident with a kind of malicious pleasure to Lord Holland, adding in a significant whisper, 'He himself *pretends* he was shot at.'[6] According to Lord James Murray it was not pretence at all. Lord James, who had accompanied the Regent in the carriage as Lord in Waiting, 'spoke distinctly [of] two small holes . . . within one inch of each other through an uncommonly thick plate glass window; and the space between the two holes was not broken'.[7] He believed that 'the holes spoken of were made by bullets from an air-gun'.[8]

There were many people who would have been glad enough if the missile, whatever it was, had killed the Regent who was widely held responsible for the repressive measures which the government adopted in their efforts to quell the national disturbances. 'At present we have a starving population,' Mrs Leadbeater was told by a friend in March, 'an overwhelming debt, impoverished landholders, bankrupt or needy traders; but we have fine balls at the Regent's.'[9] In June he opened Waterloo Bridge, on the second anniversary of Napoleon's defeat. It was a lovely sunny day, and a 'glorious, beautiful, gratifying spectacle';[10] but the cheers were for Wellington, not for him, not for that 'uncommonly huge mass' which, so Cobbett estimated, weighed 'perhaps a quarter of a ton'.[11] He had let loose his stomach now, so Lord Folkestone observed, and it reached his knees.[12]

For a time the attitude of the public towards the Regent was shocked into change by Princess Charlotte's death, though it was widely reported that he did not share the general grief, that his neglect of her was in some way responsible for her death, even that he and the Queen had poisoned her. But by the end of November, as Croker told Peel, the grief was wearing off and the public was returning to its 'sulky humour, waiting for any fair or unfair excuse to fly into a passion. . . . If there should arise any division in the Royal Family, it will be the match to fire the gunpowder. *Apropos* of royal matches, I hear that Ministers have been a little puzzled how to deal with the avowed readiness of the Duke of Kent to sacrifice himself and jump into the matrimonial gulf for the good of his country, but they have hit upon a scheme which seems politic. They propose to marry the Duke of Clarence, as the eldest unmarried Prince, and he who has a right to the first chance; and also to marry the Duke of Cambridge, the youngest unmarried Prince, from whom the country has the best chance; and having thus resolved to burn the candle at both ends, Vansittart [the Chancellor of the Exchequer] discovers that he cannot afford to burn it in the middle too, and therefore Kent and Sussex cannot have the wedding establishments etc., suited to their rank.'[13]

It was certainly true that Vansittart – having been compelled to abolish the property tax, which was considered in Parliament appropriate only to a time of war, and to discontinue the war malt tax, which was no longer acceptable to the country Members – was loath to provide expensive households for those various members of the Royal Family who were now taking it into their heads to get married. 'My God!' exclaimed Wellington when Creevey mentioned to him 'the proposals to augment the establishments' of the royal dukes, 'they are the damnedest millstone about the necks of any government that can be imagined. They have insulted – *personally* insulted – two thirds of the gentlemen of England, and how can it be wondered at that they take their revenge upon them when they get them in the House of Commons? It is their only opportunity, and I think, by God, they are quite right to use it.'[14]

*

Within the Royal Family there were far deeper divisions than Croker supposed. The Prince and his sisters were on those happy, close, affectionate terms that they had always enjoyed. They took it in turns to write to him to send him what little news there was ever worth conveying from Windsor, to give him bulletins on their father's condition, on their mother's and their own varying states of health, to thank him for presents and for being so kind to them during their holidays at Brighton to which they looked forward with such eagerness. In her tiny writing Princess Sophia would report on the 'dear King's occasional bursts of passion', or his favourite sister, Princess Mary, a more regular correspondent, would reassure him that his Majesty's days were generally 'very quiet' and 'composed', though he was sometimes 'rather high at dinner time'. Mary would also send frequent reports about her sisters, particularly Sophia, whose frequent illnesses distressed them all, for it was 'a sad house to be ill in'. Princess Elizabeth would tell him about a cricket match which had been arranged 'for the Eatonians', or of a rare, enjoyable evening party: 'I wish you had been here with us to-night for we have laughed in a manner we rarely do now unless occasioned by you. Dundas's manner of speaking French is beyond everything ridiculous and in telling my mother a story in which he was to mention Soissons he pronounced it with such an English accent that it was enough to kill me. He said, "in the town of *So is son*"; and my mother's quiet way of answering "Soissons" was so ridiculous that when she was gone we all of us were in fits.'[15]

It was very rarely that their mother reduced them to laughter; more often she drove them to tears. She had grown very fat, so enormous, indeed, that one cruel observer said that she looked as though she were bearing all her fifteen children at once; she suffered from occasional attacks of erysipelas which not only reddened her face but made it swell to a distressing size. And, correspondingly, she grew ever more cantankerous and difficult until, as Lord Glenbervie said, her irritability became so 'intolerable' that her daughters were driven 'quite miserable' by it. She refused to see the King alone, finding him frightening as well as embarrassing, and Princess Mary said that when she did go to see him, taking one or other of her children with her, her manner towards him as he rambled on was to say the least 'unfortunate'. This manner, Princess Mary thought, was attributable partly to 'extream timidity', partly to an innate deficiency in 'warmth, tenderness, affec'.[16]

In protest against their mother's treatment of them, the Princesses constantly appealed to the Regent, who did all he could to help them. The first of his sisters' appeals had been addressed to him almost as soon as the restrictions imposed upon his Regency had expired. Princess Augusta, then aged forty-three, had written to him to ask him to grant her her heart's desire by consenting to her marriage to the man whom she had now loved for nine years, Lieutenant-General Sir Brent Spencer, one of her father's equerries, a brave Irish soldier eight years older than herself. She had confided in the Prince her love for him several years before and he had been kind and understanding; but there was nothing at that time that he had been able to do to help her, for their father would never have consented to the match. Now that the King no longer had the power to prevent it, she had approached her brother again: 'I now beseech you my dearest to consider *our situation*. If it is in your power to *make us happy I know you will.* Of course it will be necessary to keep it a secret and it must be quite a *private marriage.* . . . No consideration in the world . . . shall make me take such a step unknown to *her.* I owe it to her as my mother, though I am too honest to affect asking for *her consent as it is not necessary.* . . . I am certain the Queen *cannot approve* if she *merely* thinks of my birth and station, but that is *the only reason* she can object to it. . . . But when she considers the character of the man, the faithfulness and length of our attachment, and the struggles I have been compelled to make, never retracting from any of my duties, though suffering martyrdom from *anxiety of mind* and *deprivation* of happiness. . . .'[17]

The Queen, as all who knew of Princess Augusta's secret might have expected, had been appalled when she had heard of it. She had refused to talk about it; she would not hear of her daughter's marriage to such a man. Over the next few months the atmosphere at Windsor had become so strained and insupportable that the Princesses had threatened to quit 'the paternal roof' unless their mother gave them more freedom.[18]

The crisis had been reached in December 1812 when the Queen had sulkily grumbled that her daughters' wish to go to London more often than they did at present displayed a want of 'delicacy and affection towards the King'. There had been a 'dreadfull scene', Princess Augusta reported. 'Upon my honor my sisters [Elizabeth, then aged forty-two, and Sophia, thirty-five, and Mary, thirty-six] were perfectly respectful both in manner and words, though she was too violent to allow it and even when she told them that she would never forgive them, Eliza said, "*May God* forgive you for saying so." She won't allow that *any of us* feel for the King's unhappy state of mind. . . . She has declared that after to-night the subject is *never* to be *mentioned again* and that she COMMANDS us to be silent upon it. I am ashamed to have written so much on so *painfull* a subject because I love the Queen with all my heart; but I *feel* the *injustice most deeply* with which she treats *us all four*. It is undeserved – and our lives have not been *too* happy. . . . Never was a daughter more faithfully attached than Eliza to the Queen – and she really has sacrificed every comfort in life to prove it, and sad and cruel is the abuse she has met with. I am miserable that you my dearest brother that you should have so much vexation on our account. We are all gratitude to you.'[19]

Princess Elizabeth wrote by the same post to tell her brother how deeply she had been hurt by the Queen's words, how it quite broke her heart to be told that she was wanting in delicacy and affection towards the

King after all the sacrifices she had made and all the sacrifices she was still prepared to make to ease her mother's mind and try to give her some happiness. The blow of being thought unfeeling haunted her. It was quite impossible for her to go to London now with a heart so ill at ease.[20]

The Queen also wrote that same night to excuse herself, to say that she quite understood that her daughters might want to go to London 'sometimes', but not every week, as if they were to do so she would be 'almost left quite alone'. She went on to complain that she had been 'amazingly offended' by the 'easy manner' in which Lord Liverpool had disposed 'of the royal family appearing in public'. 'As to the representation your sisters have made of what did pass on Sunday night before they left Windsor I am ignorant of,' the Queen continued in rising anger. 'But . . . when Elizabeth, by defending her own conduct, struck in a most violent manner upon a Holy Book, saying she would have an oath that she had done all in her power to please, it so provoked me that I did say after that violence I should not be surprised at her giving me a box at the ear, which gave her an hysterick fit, and they left me determined to report it the moment they came to town. . . . Whether this conduct is what a mother ought to expect from her children I leave to the judgements of those who have any. In short this last journey of theirs has given me a blow which can not be easily effaced, for the coming to ask my advice and hearing my objections and not following is treating me like a fool. The telling me that the living with me here in my distress is disagreeable, and to repeat to anybody what concerns the interior of a family is more than imprudent. . . . The Dukes of York and Cambridge's impertinent behaviour to me on a former occasion I can never forget, and as to Ministers they can have nothing to do with it. At least if they do, I shall stop them short.'[21]

The Regent immediately went to see the indignant Queen and, having soothed her ruffled feelings, persuaded her to accompany her daughters to Carlton House. Before Christmas he had managed to bring peace once more to the squabbling family, and Princess Augusta thanked him warmly for the 'very kind part' he had taken on their behalf. 'I am very certain that it is to *your good offices* that we are indebted for her assurances that she had misunderstood us', Augusta wrote, 'and I only hope that we shall not have any occasion to plague you with our applications for redress.'[22] It was a hope that was not to be realized.

*

Scarcely had the Regent temporarily patched over the differences between his mother and his sisters, than he was called upon to settle a quarrel between the Queen and the Duke of Cumberland who, in 1815, selected as his bride her niece, Princess Frederica of Mecklenburg-Strelitz. The Regent might well have felt some reluctance in helping his brother for he had heard from Princess Elizabeth who had had 'volumes from Royal' – their eldest sister, Princess Charlotte, Queen of Württemberg – about Ernest's characteristic mischief-making while he was in Germany where he had spoken 'so improperly' of the Regent that it was 'quite abominable'. Charlotte, who detested their brother Ernest, had said, 'If it was one person that told me I would not believe it, but all say the same.'[23] The Regent, however, chose to disregard the reports of his brother's indiscreet gossiping. He had thought it advisable to supersede him by appointing their more tractable younger brother, the Duke of Cambridge, Governor of Hanover, a disappointment which had reduced Cumberland to tears.[24] And he was now anxious to make amends by helping him, even though he did not consider Princess Frederica a very suitable choice. She had been married twice before, first to Prince Frederick of Prussia and then, when she was engaged to the Duke of Cambridge, hurriedly to Prince Frederick of Solms-Braunfels by whom she had discovered herself pregnant.

The Queen at first approved the match, but after learning more from her daughter, Charlotte, in Württemberg, she decided that Princess Frederica was, after all, a most unfortunate choice. So did the House of Commons, which rejected the government's Bill to increase the Duke of Cumberland's allowance from £18,000 to £24,000 a year. Despite his mother's opposition and Parliament's disapproval, the Duke married Princess Frederica at Strelitz, but when he proposed to bring her over to England the Queen warned the Regent that she would on no account receive her.[25]

The Regent drove over to Windsor in the hope of inducing her to change her mind; but she was obdurate.[26] This had made the Duke's blood boil in his veins, so he said, and his mother would soon find out that he was 'pretty *decided*' when he resolved 'on any thing'.[27] He brought his bride over to England on 27 August 1815 and their marriage was solemnized according to the rites of the Anglican Church two days later at Carlton House in the Regent's presence, and in the conspicuous absence of the Queen and her daughters. The bride was enchanted by the Regent's kindness. He embraced her warmly, gave her, 'in a way that was simply lovable', a present of his portrait in enamel, mounted in 'beautiful large stones', and held her left hand 'throughout the entire ceremony'.[28] His consent to the marriage earned the Duke and Duchess's 'heartfelt gratitude';[29] but it led to serious trouble with the Queen and with the government.

The Queen's anger was much increased when she received from the bride's brother, her eldest nephew, Prince George of Mecklenburg-Strelitz, a letter *'couched in terms so offensive and so insulting'* that she could not *'with any regard to decency shew it to any individual'*. 'I have too frequently experienced proofs of your kindness and affection,' she wrote to the Regent, 'to allow myself to believe upon this occasion that you could ever have invited or encouraged any proposal for bringing my nephew to this country if you could have foreseen that he was to be brought here for the purpose of *bullying* and *insulting* your mother. . . . But I cannot deny that I have felt most acutely the want of support which I might have expected.'[30]

The Regent wrote a long, pained reply in which he denied the unreasonable accusations, saying that he had hoped that his conduct through life would have protected him from the suspicion that he was 'capable of tamely submitting to an offer of insult or disrespect' to his mother.[31]

But the Queen was not to be placated. She was more determined than ever now not to receive her niece; and, in a subsequent letter, reiterated the impossibility of ever doing so.[32] So overwrought did she become, indeed, that she fell seriously ill; and Lord Bathurst, on behalf of the government, thought it advisable to suggest that Cumberland should take his wife back to Germany, for if the Queen's malady were to 'end fatally' the people would attribute it to the Duke's continuing in England. 'Mischievous persons' would then 'be able so to work on the public feelings as to expose her Royal Highness most unmeritedly to personal insult and reproach.'[33]

The Regent agreed that it would be advisable for his brother to leave the country before more harm was done; and when the Duke protested that he could not afford to do so, money was offered him for the purpose.[34] The Regent asked the Duke to call on him at Carlton House where, 'in the most emphatic manner', he told him that 'his decided opinion was that he should, with his Duchess, immediately leave England – that the Prince Regent could not separate himself from the Queen, that time might yet heal their distresses, and circumstances might arise which might enable him to receive them in the manner all must wish'.[35]

Yet the Duke remained as obstinate as his mother. Alternately protesting that the Duchess's health was 'very precarious', that he could not leave by himself for 'such an act would be a desertion of the Dutchess whom he was resolved at all hazards to protect', and that 'a departure would be immediately held forth as a *proof of conscious guilt and fear of shewing*' themselves, he refused to leave.[36] And the Queen, despite a letter of protest from the King of Prussia to the Regent, still refused to receive his wife.[37]

The Regent told the King of Prussia that he wished to God he could shake his mother's 'unfortunate determination', but 'by the laws and customs' of the country she was 'wholly independant' of him and he could not oblige her to 'receive any person, whether of the Royal Family or otherwise, against her own inclination'.[38] The Regent patiently continued in his efforts to change his mother's mind, while at the same time endeavouring to persuade his brother to go back to Germany should he not be successful. He even considered giving him the Governorship of Hanover in place of the Duke of Cambridge; but Count Münster, the Hanoverian Minister, was rigidly opposed to the idea.[39]

Once again the Regent and his brother fell out. The Duke called at Carlton House and for five minutes the two men sat in studied silence without looking at each other.[40] The Duchess, forgetting all her brother-in-law's past kindness, refused to believe that he could not insist on her being received by the Queen. 'Oh, really, sire,' she exclaimed in irritation when he tried to explain the situation to her. 'The coal-heaver is master *in his* own house.'[41] He endeavoured to make amends by inviting her to dinner at Carlton House with all the most fashionable ladies in London; but when Lady Stafford told her that the Regent hoped that after this grand dinner she would find it easier to leave the country with honour, she was more indignant than ever.[42]

As late as April 1818 the Regent was still strongly urging his mother to receive the Duchess. But the Queen remained adamant: she would not in any circumstances receive her, and expressed 'an anxious wish that she would not again be urged upon this painful subject'.[43]

The Duke of Cumberland stubbornly stayed on in England until the end of July 1818 when he and the Duchess returned at last to Germany. The Regent came to say goodbye, and the Duchess thought that his guilty conscience would not allow him to look her straight in the eye.[44] But although the Duke was deeply disgruntled with the rest of his family he was in the end prepared to recognize that his eldest brother had done all he could to help him, and he wrote to tell him so, from the York Hotel, Dover, on the morning of his departure: 'I cannot leave my native shore without . . . expressing to you my sincerest and most heartfelt gratitude for all your brotherly kindness to me during my stay in England which believe me will never be effaced from my recollection. In short you ALONE among eleven *brothers* and *sisters* have proved to me that you are really a *brother* and *friend*. God bless you for it.'[45]

*

To everyone's surprise the Queen raised no objection to the next marriage in her family, that of her daughter, Mary, to the Duke of Gloucester, whose mother, the illegitimate daughter of Sir Edward Walpole, had also been denied entrance to the Queen's court. But if his mother approved of this match, the Regent did not. He had never liked his cousin Gloucester, and he had grown to like him even less since he had, with the Duke of Sussex, openly sympathized with Princess Caroline and taken it upon himself to champion Princess Charlotte at the time of her rebellion over the proposed match with the Prince of Orange. He had not taken seriously the stories he had heard about his daughter's considering Gloucester as a husband for herself, stories which were characteristically spread about by the Duke of Cumberland who said it looked as though she were going to choose the Cheese instead of the Orange. For who could really want to marry the Cheese? Princess Mary can have wanted to do so, he supposed, only as a means of escape from 'the Nunnery', where her painfully restricted life was made all the more unbearable in winter by 'dreadful chilblains'.[46] She had never been attracted by men in the way that her sisters were; and the idea of anyone falling in love with the Duke of Gloucester seemed to the Regent absurd.

Prince Leopold's friend Stockmar shared the Prince's distaste, and described Gloucester as being 'large and stout, but with weak, helpless legs . . . prominent meaningless eyes; without being actually ugly, a very unpleasant face with an animal expression'.[47] But if she did not love him, Princess Mary had, unaccountably, always been quite fond of him; and since she was the Regent's favourite sister, 'the most of an angel he ever knew', he gave his consent to the marriage when she asked him for it, and took great trouble to negotiate satisfactory terms.

The wedding, which ultimately took place at the Queen's House on 23 July 1816, was a most disorderly affair. The room was excessively hot and overcrowded; the seating so badly arranged that only a few people in it could see what was happening; the congregation so restless and talkative that the Lord Chief Justice called out jocularly, 'Do not make a noise in that corner of the room. If you do, you shall be married yourselves.'

The bride looked as though she were about to faint; her sisters and her ladies could not stop crying; nor could Lady Eldon. The Regent, who was giving his sister away, 'several times had recourse to his pocket hand-kerchief'. The Queen seems to have been almost alone in remaining dry-eyed throughout the lengthy and disorganised proceedings.[48]

*

While the Duke and Duchess of Gloucester settled down to a quiet country life at Bagshot Park, the Duke of Clarence continued his erratic search for a suitable wife for himself. He had separated from Mrs Jordan, the mother of his ten illegitimate children, in 1811; but he had not yet succeeded in finding anyone to take her place. The Regent had once told him that he doubted that anyone *would* marry him;[49] but debts of £56,000 made a wife an urgent necessity.[50]

He had considered numerous heiresses, both foreign and domestic, only to have his overtures rejected. He had first wanted to marry Catherine Tylney-Long, a 'lovely nice little angel' worth over £40,000 a year; but she had preferred the more obvious charms of Wellington's nephew, William Wellesley-Pole. He had then proposed to the equally rich Margaret Mercer Elphinstone, 'who, in the most decided and peremptory terms, rejected him'. He had then offered himself to Lady Charlotte Lindsay who had turned him down with similar promptitude. Unsuccessful overtures to the Dowager Lady Downshire were followed by a firm decision to marry the Earl of Berkeley's widow. But the Regent had declined to accept a butcher's daughter, whom he considered decidedly vulgar, as a sister-in-law; and she herself had considered the proposal 'impossible'; so the search went on. The next quarry was the Tsar's sister, the Grand Duchess of Oldenburg. He asked the government for his travelling expenses to pay court to her; the government declined to pay them; so, generous as ever, the Regent gave his brother £1,000. He might have saved his money. The Grand Duchess found him quite as vulgar as the Regent thought Lady Berkeley. He was 'awkward, not without wit, but definitely unpleasant', and wholly wanting in 'delicacy'. The Duke had then turned his attention to Princess Sophia, the Duke of Gloucester's sister, who married neither him nor anybody else. After that match was ruled out he announced to the Regent that he was indefatigably 'ready and happy to set out for the Continent' as he had 'not any doubt that the eldest daughter of Landgrave Frederick of Hesse [was] a lady in every respect fit for [his] wife provided pecuniary matters [could] be arranged and the lady's consent obtained'. The lady's consent was not obtained, however; and a few weeks later the Duke had transferred his attention to Caroline, the eldest daughter of the Electoral Prince of Hesse-Cassel, whose youngest daughter, Augusta, was to be married in 1818 to the Duke of Cambridge. Nothing came of this proposal either; and the Regent suggested to his brother that he might care to consider 'the only daughter of the King of Denmark'. In fact there were two daughters; but neither of them became the Duchess of Clarence.[51]

By this time the Duke's protracted and capricious search had long since led Lord Auckland to suppose that the King's 'mad doctors,' the Willises, had another patient in need of their attentions.[52] The search, however, was now nearly over. At the beginning of 1818 the Regent learned from his sister, Princess Mary, that their mother was half 'distracted' by a letter from the Duke in which he announced that he had proposed to and been accepted by Miss Wyckham, a 'fine vulgar miss', heiress to the Oxfordshire estate of Lord Wenman.[53] 'On this being told to the Regent, his Royal Highness *groaned*,' Lady Jerningham reported, 'which is, it seems, his way of disapproving.'[54]

The Duke had informed Princess Mary that whatever his mother or brother might think about the match, he was determined to go through with it. '*Nobody* could *prevent* his having Miss Wyckham if he *chose it*, he had but to apply to Parliament. He was in perfect good humour but most decided on the *subject*. . . . He said . . . the Prince's consent will be *rung from him* at last, so he better give it at once. . . . ' 'I told him it would break the Queen's heart,' Princess Mary informed the Regent. 'He said I love her very much but a man must judge for himself in this world . . . and then wanted to convince me in *your* heart you approved of it *now*, only that Ministers would not let you approve.'[55]

The Ministers, indeed, were unanimous in their condemnation. When the Regent handed the Cabinet his brother's petition, they replied that it was 'their indispensable duty' to declare that it would not be in 'the best interests of the State' to accede to the Duke's request.[56] To their surprised relief, the Duke gave way without further ado, merely asking that a barony should be conferred upon Miss Wyckham, though this, as Lord Liverpool pointed out when declining the request, would lay her open to the accusation that she had purchased a peerage by releasing the Duke from his obligation to her.[57]

At last a bride was found in the small and far from prepossessing person of Princess Adelaide, the eldest daughter of the Duke of Saxe-Coburg-Meiningen. She was 'frightful', Charles Greville thought, 'very ugly with a horrid complexion'. But the Queen knew her to be a good-natured woman, and her own widowed mother was happy enough to find a husband for a daughter who would soon be twenty-six and who might be considered to have made a good match with a man, admittedly a man in late middle age, with some prospects of becoming King of England.

There was some little difficulty over the Duke's increased income on his marriage. He wanted an additional £10,000 a year at least, as well as a town house, extensive repairs to his house at Bushey, his debts paid and handsome provision for his illegitimate children.[58] But Parliament declined to grant so large an addition to his present income of £18,000 a year; whereupon the Duke said that if he could not have the income he would not take the wife. The problem was eventually settled however, and on 11 July 1818 the marriage took place at Kew. On the same day the Duke of Kent was also married at Kew.

*

The Duke of Kent had experienced almost as much difficulty in finding a suitable bride as the Duke of Clarence. He had been looking about for one since 1816 when, still in company with Mme St Laurent, he was living modestly in Brussels, having made an assignment of most of his property in favour of his creditors. He had managed to obtain a loan of a thousand guineas from the Tsar to pay for a journey of inspection to eastern Europe, but the excursion had been fruitless.[59] The Duke did not particularly want to marry. He was perfectly happy with Mme St Laurent, who choked convulsively over her breakfast one morning soon after Princess Charlotte's death, when she read an article in the *Morning Chronicle* on the subject of her lover's duty to marry and to provide an heir which the Duke and Duchess of York had not succeeded in doing and the Duke of Clarence might also fail to do.

'Before anything is proceeded with in this matter,' the Duke confided in Thomas Creevey one day in December 1817 in Brussels, 'I shall hope and expect to see justice done by the nation and the Ministers to Mme St Laurent. She is of very good family and has never been an actress, and I am the first and only person who ever lived with her. . . . As to my own settlement, as I shall marry (if I marry at all) for the succession, I shall expect the Duke of York's marriage to be considered the precedent. That was a marriage for the succession and £25,000 for income was settled, in addition to all his other income, purely on that account. I shall be contented with the same arrangement. . . . You have heard the names of the Princess of Baden and the Princess of Saxe-Cobourg mentioned. The latter connection would perhaps be the better of the two, from the circumstances of Prince Leopold being so popular with the nation.'[60]

So, in this businesslike way Prince Leopold's sister, Victoria, the thirty-one-year old widow of the Prince of Leiningen-Dachsburg-Hardenburg, was chosen. The marriage took place at Coburg in May 1818; and after it had been solemnized by the Anglican church at Kew in July, the Duke and Duchess returned to Germany. They came back to England the following spring for the Duchess's confinement. Her baby girl, her only child, the future Queen Victoria, was born at Kensington Palace on 24 May 1819.*

*

---

* The Duke of Kent, claiming that he did not have enough money for the journey, borrowed £5,000 from Lords Fitzwilliam and Dundas for the purpose of bringing his wife home so that their baby could be born in England. He also received assistance from Lord Darnley and Alderman Matthew Wood, whose baronetcy was the first conferred by Queen Victoria. The Prime Minister did not think there was any reason for the Duchess of Kent or any of the other royal Duchesses who happened to be abroad at the time to come home for their confinements. 'It would be a most severe burden upon the royal family', he considered, and an unnecessary one, though it might be '*advisable*' for 'some British subject' to be in the house at the time of the delivery (Twiss, ii, 319). Prince Leopold, when King of the Belgians, assured his niece, Queen Victoria, more than once that her uncle the Regent had done all he could to prevent her being born in England. 'Arrived in London, we were very unkindly treated by George the 4th *whose great wish was to get you and your mama out of the country*,' he told her emphatically. 'And I must say without my assistance, you could not have remained. You know now sufficient of the value of money to be aware that no royal Duchess with child can live on £6,000 a year, particularly when she had not a spoon or napkin

While the Dukes of Clarence and Kent had been preparing for their marriages, so also, at the age of forty-seven, had their sister, Princess Elizabeth.

The Princess had dreaded telling her mother of her plans, for the Queen was seriously ill now as well as cantankerous.[61] Her treatment at Bath in November 1817 had not done her much good;[62] and on her return to Windsor she was 'dreadfully low' and found such difficulty in getting her breath that Princess Elizabeth was really frightened to be with her. 'I cannot possibly stand it,' Elizabeth told the Regent on 25 January 1818; 'thank God, she cannot bear me with her, though I entreat her to cry as I am sure when her spirits are in that state it is better to give vent to tears than choke herself by swallowing them.'[63]

---

of her own.' King Leopold – who was always assuring Queen Victoria how unpleasant was her uncle's character, how strongly marked it was by 'extreme selfishness, a great spirit of revenge and intrigue, and a complete absence of anything manful' – told her in subsequent letters that he did not know what would have become of her had he not been alive to protect her after her father's death: 'I know not what would have become of you and your mama, if I then had existed no longer. George the IVth hated your father.... He did all to prevent your *being born in England*' (RA Y67/30, 22 January 1841; RA Y71/63, 17 May 1845; RA 74/69, 2 September 1848). This was not strictly true. Certainly the Regent disliked both the Duke and the Duchess of Kent and curtly refused to comply with the Duke's long list of demands, including 'pecuniary assistance', for the satisfactory accomplishment of the Duchess's confinement in England. He agreed with the Prime Minister that there was no necessity for the Kents to come home, despite the Duke's protestations that there was 'a total want of convenience' at his house at Amorbach, and that it would be too expensive to spend the period of the Duchess's confinement at Brussels. But once the Duke had made arrangements to pay his own expenses he withdrew his objections, sending the royal yacht to wait for the Duke and Duchess at Calais and making arrangements for apartments to be prepared for them at Kensington Palace (RA 22293, 6 April 1819; Woodham-Smith) 21–5). The Duke, however, had never forgiven his brother for not insisting that he should be reappointed to his military command in 1811, though he had done everything he could for the Duke of York (RA 46504–5, 31 July 1811; RA 46519–20: Asp/P, viii, 371–3). He now felt he had further grounds for resentment. He declared that his brother had been extremely selfish, and he was most indignant about being told that he must not, in the circumstances, expect to meet 'a *cordial* reception' on returning home. Before his return he wrote a long letter from Cologne setting out his complaints which, so he informed his correspondent, he did not 'wish to be concealed from the world'. 'You have therefore my sanction,' his letter concluded, 'subject to your usual prudence and discretion, to make what use you please of the information I have given you' (RA M3/1, 5 April 1819).

Two days later, however, the Queen was so much better that she felt able to take a long drive; and on the 29th Princess Elizabeth plucked up courage to tell her of the offer that had been made to her by the Hereditary Prince of Hesse-Homburg. At first the Queen had seemed resigned to it. 'You always wished to settle,' she had said to her daughter encouragingly on being told of her intentions, 'and have always said that you thought a woman might be happier and more comfortable in having a home.'[64]

But that very evening, as her mind dwelled on the unpleasant prospect of being deprived of her daughter's company on which she had been able to rely for so many years, she began to be difficult, 'flurried and vexed'. When Count Münster called at the Castle to discuss the arrangements for the proposed marriage she refused to see him: he had come to see her daughter not her. She grumpily refused to go into dinner or to play cards; she said she did not care what Elizabeth did. 'Do as you please,' she told her, 'you are of age.'[65]

'I have done everything that can be done to make her happy,' Princess Elizabeth complained sadly to the Regent, 'but I am hardly used.'[66] 'Believe me I am nearly distracted,' she continued the next day. 'My mother is so angry that it frightens me. . . . [She] says she is so incensed by my conduct that she cannot bear to see me.'[67] Princess Augusta tried to comfort her sister by telling her that their mother was a 'spoilt child'; their father had spoilt her 'from the hour she came' to England; and they themselves had continued doing so from the hour of their birth. She was just vexed that she could not manage this her own way. Elizabeth told her brother all that Augusta had said, and added that she felt sure he would soothe it all out and 'soften' their mother.[68]

The Regent went down to Windsor to try to do so. He spoke to her for a long time, and before leaving assured Elizabeth that everything would now be all right.[69]

'Alas! Good humour and all our prospect of bringing the Queen round vanished as your carriage drove off,' Princess Sophia told him the next morning. 'The irritation in her mind continues very great, and now will be greater as I verily believe that until yesterday she still had hopes that Eliza had not made her final irrevocable decision. . . . I cannot say that I perceive any material difference in the symptoms of the Queen's disorder, but it is impossible not to suppose that this violent agitation must be productive of some ill effects. . . . I find from our friend Sir Henry [Halford] who saw her this morning that her suppressed anger made it difficult for him to judge correctly of her pulse and her breathing.'[70] As for Elizabeth she had by now decided that her mother was not nearly so ill as she liked her daughters to suppose: 'She has been very comfortable with others when I am away, before me she tries to be worse.'[71]

The day after the Regent's visit, the clouds at Windsor were 'as thick if not thicker' than ever; and by 9 February Princess Elizabeth could scarcely write to him for her eyes were 'compleatly blinded for tears'.[72] After a second visit, however, their mother was induced to behave less unreasonably on condition that she was not deprived of her daughter's companionship immediately after the marriage. She sent Elizabeth a diamond necklace by way of truce; and at a subsequent interview, though 'some things of course' hurt the Princess's feelings, 'upon the whole' the conversation went off well. On leaving her mother's room, Elizabeth sat down to write to her brother to thank him for all he had done: she could 'never express how deeply' she felt his affection which had supported her more than she could say.[73]

A week later *The Times* announced that the marriage was 'at length finally determined upon', and that it had been 'definitely fixed, that, instead of leaving this country immediately, as was originally proposed', her Royal Highness would remain in England for some time. This arrangement had 'been brought about for the satisfaction of her Majesty to whom her illustrious daughter [had] in a peculiar degree, endeared herself by a long series of filial attentions, and from whom the Queen, in her declining years, felt it impossible to endure the pang of separation'.[74]

The marriage took place on 7 April at the Queen's House; and some of those who saw the bridegroom there for the first time were surprised by Princess Elizabeth's anxiety to marry him. For the Hereditary Prince of Hesse-Homburg, who had vainly proposed himself as a husband for Princess Augusta in 1804, was now forty-nine and far from attractive. A much-decorated soldier, with those flamboyant whiskers favoured by German generals and the Duke of Cumberland, he was immensely fat, was reputed to wash at the most infrequent intervals and smelled of garlic and tobacco.[75] Yet Princess Elizabeth disregarded his personal appearance, and grew increasingly fond of her 'kind and affectionate better half'.[76] She had every reason to be grateful, she assured her brother, for the prize she had drawn.[77] There was, indeed, something rather endearing about him. He was known to the public as 'Humbug', but his wife referred to him more affectionately as her 'beloved Bluff'.

It was as touching as ridiculous that on bending down to pick up a fan which the Queen had dropped at her levee, his stout bottom rent the seat of his trousers.

The wedding was free of such incident, though on their way to the Royal Lodge at Windsor, which the Regent had lent them for their honeymoon, the bridegroom was sick and was obliged to spend the rest of the journey sitting outside in the dicky. The Princess had ordered a new carriage, but the journeymen employed in its manufacture had gone on strike, and she had had to make use of her old bumpy landaulet.[78]

During the honeymoon the Prince spent a good deal of his time smoking in the conservatory.[79] But his wife was ideally happy. Before leaving for her new home in Germany, she wrote a letter of thanks to the Regent. He had been prevented from attending the wedding by an attack of gout so severe that he could not walk; the *Morning Post* declared that he would not have attended it anyway, 'owing to a similar scene having been fresh in his recollection in the marriage of his beloved daughter, the Princess Charlotte'.[80] His sister thanked him effusively for making it possible for her to marry 'so excellent a being' whose 'one thought' was to make her happy. As always her brother's conduct had been 'so delicate, so angelic, so like himself'. He was, and was to remain, her 'beloved and dearest angel'.[81]

9

Repasts and Riots
1818–1820

*

'The pomp and magnificence of a
Persian satrap'

With the Queen also the Prince was now on the best of terms. Past quarrels had been quite forgiven; and his mother recognized that her eldest son was 'all goodness and ever ready to forward the happiness of his family'. Towards herself in her declining years he could not have been more considerate, more understanding. He knew only too well how much his sisters had had to endure because of her selfishness and increasing ill temper; but in taking their side when necessary he had always behaved with the greatest kindness, gentleness and tact. Guests at Carlton House and at Brighton noticed with what affectionate deference he treated his mother, waiting upon her himself, making sure she was comfortable and had everything she wanted. She was duly grateful, and always thanked him most warmly for his 'really unbounded kindness' towards herself and his sisters during their visits.[1] In her turn she took special pains to make each year's celebration of his birthday at Frogmore the kind of event which he would appreciate. Once she had had a collection of splendid tents, which had been presented to her by the Sultan of Mysore, erected for him in the gardens; she had had Chinese lanterns hung from the trees and, while a band played in a shrubbery, she had walked up and down on the lawn with him, holding his arm. On another occasion she had invited him to a party at the Queen's House. It would not be 'à la manière de Carlton House', she had warned him, 'but about 150 or 200 people, and if you should like to take a quiet dinner with me en famille I will order it at six that we may have a little time to breathe before the company comes.'[2]

On the plain sheets of cheap paper which all the Royal Family at Windsor used, she had written to him regularly to give him advice about Princess Charlotte, to congratulate him upon the 'good news from the Continent', to keep him informed about the health of the King and the rest of the family, to offer her sympathy when he was ill, to warn him against taking insufficient care of himself and of taking too much laudanum, to urge him to consult Sir Henry Halford of whom she had a much higher opinion than she had of his other doctors. She had given him news about the activities of the Court at Windsor; she had sent him occasional presents – 'four of the finest smoked geese' she had ever seen, 'to be eaten raw', or the 'March of a Cossack Division', 'painted in gouache therefore requiring glass to prevent its pealing off'. She had suggested days of national thanksgiving for such events as the restoration of Hanover, and had made her wide knowledge of etiquette available to him when, for instance, the Duchess of Brunswick died: 'As one of the Royal Family you will of course have her buried in one of the royal vaults, either Westminster or Windsor, the latter place, Colonel Taylor [Herbert Taylor, her trusted private secretary since the establishment of the Regency] thinks was the King's desire she should be deposited. Your mourning of course must be that for a mother, and Charlotte's the same with bombazine. The public places must be shut, as she is one of the family, until the interment and of course you will have no levee during that time. . . . I advise this the more as every little trifle in the conduct of the Royal Family is at present so severely censured.'[3]

*

The Queen attended her daughter's marriage to the Hereditary Prince of Hesse-Homburg; but it was her last public appearance. She was seventy-three, frail and doddering, and it was clear that she did not have long to live. After Elizabeth's departure for Germany in July she became subject to fits of uncontrollable weeping in which she found it difficult to get her breath and, therefore, grew 'alarmed about herself'.[4] According to Charles Greville, these spasms of breathlessness could also be induced by fits of anger as, for instance, when she heard that the Duchess of Cambridge had met the Duchess of Cumberland in Kew Gardens and had actually embraced her. 'She was in such a rage that the spasm was brought on and she was very near dying.'[5]

In the autumn of 1818 she was moved to Kew where she was looked after by Princess Augusta and by Princess Mary whose husband, the Duke of Gloucester, had had to agree that she should not forsake her filial duties because she was his wife.

From Kew, Princess Augusta wrote to the Regent to prepare him for her approaching death. Augusta had told their mother that the doctors had given warning that she was '*very ill*'. The Queen had murmured, 'So!' and laying her head on the pillow had 'cried very much indeed'. 'I wish to God I could see *your brothers*,' she had said to Augusta when recovered. 'Tell them I love them, but I am too ill. I can only see you and Mary.' 'She then said, "I pray from night till morning and from morning till night. I think a great deal, I assure you, I wish I was near the dear King where I ought to be at dear, dear Windsor."' She put her head on the pillow and Augusta thought that she had gone to sleep, but her hands kept moving up and down gently as if she were praying.

She told Sir Herbert Taylor, who saw her on 31 October, that she was praying constantly when people thought that she was asleep. Her sufferings were 'very great', she said, and their influence on her mind was 'very distressing'. Sir Francis Milman, who was assisting Sir Henry Halford in the case, considered that she was 'in a state of such nervousness and agitation' that it was absolutely essential 'to hold no unnecessary language' to her concerning her condition or the possibilities of a cure. Yet, when Taylor went to see her a fortnight later to discuss her will, she was calm and collected. Taylor suggested that Frogmore should be left to Princess Augusta and the Lower Lodge to Sophia and she said, 'Yes, Sir. I think that would be very right. You will put it so.'[6]

Taylor went to see her on 16 November with the will ready for signing. When he arrived at the door he was told that Halford had informed her of her 'immediate danger'. Halford was kneeling beside her, holding her left hand and feeling her pulse, 'with a most anxious expression of countenance. . . . The perspiration was running down her face, her eyes were moist, she breathed quick and appeared to be in great suffering.' She recognized Taylor, gave him her right hand 'with a most affectionate look and a painful smile', and pressing his hand, continued to hold it in hers. He asked her if she was ready to sign the will, but being deaf in the right ear, she did not hear him and had to ask Halford what he said. Halford told her and, when she had signed the will, he asked Taylor, speaking in Latin, to send immediately for the Regent.

The Regent drove down to Kew post-haste, and he was there, sitting by her bed and holding her hand, when she died the next day, 17 November 1818.[7]

He was 'extremely affected' by her death, Croker said;[8] and Lady Jerningham heard that he was so distressed that it was feared he would not be able to 'go through with the outward pageantry' of the funeral.[9] For several days he did not move from Carlton House. 'There is no one who will feel [the Queen's death] more than you, who was ever so devotedly and tenderly attached to her,' Princess Elizabeth wrote to him, 'and with reason for no parent was ever more wrapt up in a child than she was in you, and I firmly believe that she would with pleasure have sacrificed her life for you.'[10]

His doctors advised him to go to Brighton to recuperate. But he could not bring himself to move; and it was not until the beginning of December that he left London. Even then, so he told his brother, William, he could not describe what his feelings still were; they existed 'to the utmost extent of the bitterest anguish in the deepest recesses' of his heart. Ever since their mother's death he had not been able to hold up his head in the least; in short he had been 'incapacitated for everything'.[11]

*

The Pavilion to which the Regent returned in December 1818 was no longer the long, low cream-coloured Graeco-Roman house which Henry Holland had designed in the 1780s. The designs for a new Pavilion in the Indian style, which Humphry Repton had presented to the Prince in 1807, had been temporarily set aside; but the idea of a Moghul palace had never been completely abandoned, and in 1815 John Nash had borrowed from the Regent's library at Carlton House various books containing plates of Indian scenes painted by Thomas Daniell and his nephew William.[12]

Inspired by these scenes, Nash had prepared drawings and plans for the Regent which had gradually been put into effect. The transformation had been very slow. By the middle of 1816 little work, other than the enlargement of the Chinese corridor, had been completed; for the Regent's finances were in an even more precarious state than normal. In March he had received a strong warning, signed jointly by Liverpool, the Prime Minister, Castlereagh, the Foreign Secretary, and Vansittart, the Chancellor of the Exchequer. These Ministers had warned him of the 'unprecedented difficulties' which were thrown upon the government 'in all financial discussions in the House of Commons at the present moment in consequence of the temper of the times, and more particularly of the distress' which was 'so severely felt by most classes of His Majesty's subjects'. They had been 'fully persuaded' that no government which did not 'enforce a system of economy and retrenchment' and which did not abstain from every expense not 'indispensably necessary', could hope to continue in existence. No subject was 'viewed with more jealousy and suspicion than the personal expenses of the Sovereign or his representative at a time when most of the landed gentlemen of the country [were] obliged to submit to losses and privations as well as to retrenchment.' 'Your Royal Highness's servants humbly submit', the ominous letter had concluded, 'that the only means by which [there] can be a prospect of weathering the impending storm is by stating on the direct authority of your Royal Highness and by your command, if it should be necessary, that all new expenses for additions or alterations at Brighton or elsewhere will, under the present circumstances, be abandoned. Your Royal Highness's servants are perfectly convinced that Parliament will never vote one shilling for defraying such expenses, if unfortunately they were to be persevered in.'[13]

Of this there could be no doubt. Whig Members had long been complaining in the strongest terms about the expensive alterations begun and contemplated at Brighton. One of them had expressed the hope that Parliament would hear 'no more of that squanderous and lavish profusion which in a certain quarter resembled more the pomp and magnificence of a Persian satrap, seated in the splendour of Oriental state, than the sober dignity of a British Prince, seated in the bosom of his subjects'.[14] Henry Brougham went even further and in what Castlereagh termed 'a most violent speech' condemned the Regent's 'profligacy' and 'extravagance' in terms which would not have been too strong, in Samuel Romilly's opinion, to have used in describing the days of the Emperor Tiberius.[15]

Faced with such criticism, the Regent had been obliged to call a halt to the work at Brighton; and it was not until a year later, after the Queen had 'most graciously and liberally contributed to the promotion of the splendid improvements of the Palace by a grant of £50,000 from her private purse', that the labourers and craftsmen had taken up their tools again.[16] Thereafter the work had continued steadily and the Regent's vision of an Indian palace had gradually taken shape. At first two big wings had appeared at north and south with oriental windows and sharply pointed battlements, topped by tall pagodas and minarets; then, between these wings, a huge new onion-shaped dome built on a cast-iron frame had been lifted into position where once Holland's low classical dome had stood. Other oriental domes had appeared; then screens of Indian columns, graceful colonnades, pierced stone lattice work, delicate cornices, cast-iron pillars wreathed with iron serpents, overhanging eaves and fretted battlements had taken shape until the splendid edifice that so astonished the Regent's contemporaries was complete.[17]

Inside, the Chinese decorations remained, though they were continually being altered and refined, made less exuberant, more stately. Under the direction of Robert Jones and the Craces, father and son, new wallpapers went up, ceilings and domes were freshly painted, chandeliers were hung, rich curtains cascaded from bamboo pelmets, Chinese and Japanese lacquered cabinets and tables were arranged in the rooms, Chinese banners were fixed to the walls. And all the while the Regent came and went, offering advice, making criticisms, demanding alterations: in one single six-month period the decorations of the southern wing were changed four times.[18] The bills mounted year after year. Nearly £9,000 was spent in 1814, over £22,000 in 1815, almost £10,000 in 1816, £15,000 in 1817, £33,000 in 1818, over £40,000 in 1819 – the year in which £30,000 was raised on mortgage through Coutts's Bank – and over £25,000 in 1820, a total of more than £155,000 in seven years.[19]

Nash's two great new apartments were the Music Room and the Banqueting Room, both with huge chandeliers like waterlilies and enormous wall-paintings, Chinese landscapes of scarlet, gold and yellow lacquer in the Music Room, Chinese figures in the Banqueting Room. The domed ceilings of both rooms were elaborately painted, the Music Room with green and gold shells, the Banqueting Room with a spreading and fruiting palm tree, a silver dragon appearing among the leaves.

Croker, who visited the transformed Pavilion in December 1818, was not much impressed by it all. Nash's two new rooms were 'both too handsome for Brighton', though he later admitted that the Banqueting Room, when lighted up at night, was 'really beautiful'. The outside was 'said to be taken from the Kremlin at Moscow'; but it seemed to him to be 'copied from its own stables, which, perhaps were borrowed from the Kremlin'. Anyway, it was 'an absurd waste of money' and would be 'a ruin in half a century or sooner'.[20]

Dorothea de Lieven, wife of the Russian ambassador, was not much impressed either when she went over 'the Kremlin' with the Duke of York. 'We were shown a chandelier which cost eleven thousand pounds sterling,' she told Prince Metternich, who had become her lover during the Congress of Aix. 'I write it out in full because it is really incredible. The chandelier is in the form of a tulip held by a dragon. . . . How can one describe such a piece of architecture [as] the King's palace here? The style is a mixture of Moorish, Tartar, Gothic and Chinese, and all in stone and iron. It is a whim which has already cost £700,000; and it is still not fit to live in.'[21]

However the kitchens and larders, which were under the expert direction of Jean Baptiste Watier, were 'admirable – such contrivances for roasting, boiling, baking, stewing, frying, steaming and heating; hot plates, hot closets, hot air, and hot hearths, with all manner of cocks for hot water and cold water, and warm water and steam, and twenty saucepans all ticketed and labelled, placed up to their necks in a vapour bath'.[22]

The Regent, a dedicated gourmet and gastronome, was a frequent visitor to these kitchens which he had had ornamented with fanciful cast-iron columns in the guise of palm trees, and with elaborate bronze smoke canopies and hexagonal lanterns. Occasionally he would give informal parties here; and once, during the Christmas holidays in 1817, he gave a supper party for the servants. A scarlet cloth was thrown over the stone floor; 'a splendid repast was provided, and the good-humoured Prince sat down with a select party of his friends, and spent a joyous hour. The whole of the servants, particularly the *female portion*, was delighted with this mark of royal condescension.'[23]

For eight months, until homesickness drove him back to France, the great chef, Antonin Carême, worked here; and one evening in January 1817 he provided a menu of thirty-six *entrées*, as well as four soups, four *relevés de poissons*, four *grosses pièces pour les contre-flancs*, ten *assiettes volantes de friture*, eight *grosses pièces de pâtisserie*, thirty-two *entremets* and four *plats de rotis – les coqs de Bruyères, les canards sauvages, les poulets gras bardés, les gelinottes.*[24]

Life at the Pavilion followed much the same pattern as it had done in the past. About twice a week there was a dinner party to which twenty or so guests were invited, many of them complaining, as guests at the Pavilion had always had cause to complain, of the excessive heat of the rooms. They assembled just before 6.30, and the Regent on entering the room walked round to shake hands and exchange a few words with them all. He then led the lady or ladies of highest rank to the dining-table.

After the meal the band struck up as usual; the Regent occasionally played patience, and Croker was 'rather amused' one evening 'to hear him exclaim loudly when one of the kings had turned up vexatiously, "Damn the King".' 'The supper,' Croker added critically, 'is only a tray with sandwiches, and wine and water handed about.'

In fact, Croker did not think the evening entertainments at the Pavilion were as agreeable now as they had been. 'The dinners are dull enough,' he recorded on 15 December 1818. 'They are too large for society and not quite crowded enough for freedom, so that one is on a sort of tiresome good behaviour. How much pleasanter it used to be with a dozen at a circular table in the old dining-room. His Royal Highness not looking well today. The fineness of the weather does not tempt him abroad; his great size and weight make him nervous, and he is afraid to ride – I am not surprised at it. I begin to fear that he will never ride again. He says, "Why should I? I never had better spirits, appetite, and health than when I stay within, and I am not so well when I go abroad." He seems as kind and gracious as usual to everybody.'[25] In the company of the Duke of Wellington, though, he affected an air of excessive bonhomie which the Duke found most distasteful. 'By God, you never saw such a fellow in your life as he is,' Wellington exclaimed to Creevey in response to a question about him. 'Then he speaks and swears so like old Falstaff, that damn me if I was not ashamed to walk into a room with him.'[26] When the earnest-minded William Wilberforce was a guest, however, the Regent took care to be more delicate. Wilberforce had heard rumours that the talk at the Pavilion was commonly such as he would dislike to hear. But he found '*the direct contrary was the fact.* . . . The Prince [was] quite the English gentleman at the head of his own table.'[27]

Although, as he told Croker, the Regent spent most of his time indoors, sleeping late and sitting quietly in the afternoon with Lady Hertford, he had not given up riding altogether. Sometimes in the mornings he could be seen trotting about the Pavilion lawn or more often in the Riding House, having mounted his horse by means of a complicated mechanism described by a *Times* correspondent: 'An inclined plane was constructed, rising about the height of two feet and a half, at the upper end of which was a platform. His Royal Highness was placed in a chair on rollers, and so moved up the ascent, and placed on the platform, which was then raised by screws, high enough to pass the horse under; and finally, his Royal Highness was let gently down into the saddle.'[28] This was, of course, a most tiresome process, so complicated a manoeuvre that the Regent could rarely be troubled to go through it merely to get astride a horse. And when the caricaturists took to ridiculing the method he was obliged to adopt, he instantly abandoned it, declining to ride at all except when he was sufficiently recovered from his gout to mount his horse unaided. Then he could be seen, as Lord William Gordon saw him, in January 1819, riding out 'almost every day'.[29] For the rest of the time he contented himself with driving about in the yellow Berlin which Thomas Moore used to see on its way to Lady Hertford's house in Manchester Square, or in a tilbury, a small two-wheeled gig, which he drove with his groom sitting beside him. This riding in a gig with a groom, however, was considered as vulgar as being cranked into the saddle was ludicrous. 'Grave men,' Charles Greville commented, 'are shocked at this undignified practice.'[30]

*

In June 1819 the Regent left Brighton for London to attend the christening at Kensington Palace of the daughter of the Duke and Duchess of Kent. He had been asked to stand as godfather and, without much relish, he had agreed to do so. He was much displeased to learn that the other godfather was to be the Tsar Alexander. The names her parents had suggested for the child were Victoire Georgina Alexandrina Charlotte Augusta, and these did not please him either. He told his brother that the name of Georgina could certainly not be used, 'as he did not chuse to place the name before the Emperor of Russia's – and he could not allow it to follow'.[31] He added that he would discuss the other names with him at the ceremony which he had decided must be a private family affair so that the Kents could not make a grand occasion of it.

But, according to the Duchess, no satisfactory discussion took place. The Archbishop of Canterbury had the child in his arms before the Regent pronounced the name he had selected from those offered for his consideration – 'Alexandrina'. There was a long pause while the parents and the Archbishop waited for him to give another name. The father reminded him that, after Georgina which he would not allow them to use, they had suggested Charlotte. The Regent firmly shook his head. The Duke then proposed the name Augusta; but his brother did not approve of this either. Nor did he approve of Elizabeth which the father finally put forward. There was now only one name left of the five the parents had proposed. Looking at the Duchess, who had been reduced to tears, he said, 'Give her the mother's name also then, but it cannot precede that of the Emperor.' So she was baptized Alexandrina Victoria.[32]

Thankful to escape from the company of the tiresome Kents – whose self-importance as parents of the heir to the throne was profoundly irritating – the Regent now set out for Cowes where in August he was seen to be in 'excellent health' enjoying his first visit to the Regatta aboard the *Royal George*. A sailor's life suited him 'admirably', and he was 'received everywhere with enthusiasm'.[33]

*

While the Regent was enjoying himself at Cowes, between 50,000 and 60,000 people assembled in St Peter's Field, an open space near the centre of Manchester, to hear the radical orator, Henry Hunt, voice their demands for parliamentary reform. News of this proposed meeting had deeply disturbed the Cabinet in London. All over the country, ever since the Corn Law riots of 1815, there had been intermittent outbreaks of violence, revolutionary gatherings, fierce threats against the established order. At a huge meeting in Spa Fields, London, a tricolor flag and a revolutionary cap had been paraded before the cheering crowds who had later broken into a gunsmith's shop and marched towards the City. The French Revolution was too recent in men's memories for such disturbances not to cause the greatest alarm. Throughout 1816 isolated disturbances had seemed to threaten national revolution. On many occasions troops of Yeomanry were attacked by the mobs which they had been called out to disperse. In Devon and Cornwall they had to be rescued by Dragoons; at Norwich they were stoned and attacked by fireballs; in Essex they were thrown back by rioters who took shelter behind tombstones and pelted them with rocks.[34]

The Cabinet had earlier refused the demands of Lord Sidmouth, the Home Secretary, to prohibit all public meetings; but after these and other riots, they had felt compelled to act decisively and to suspend the Habeas Corpus Act. Protest against the Government's measures led to further disturbances and to a march towards London from Lancashire of hundreds of petitioners, known as 'The Blanketeers' from the coverings they carried with them for their night shelter.

In 1817 a good harvest and a revival of trade had helped to restore the country to a relative quiet. But in 1819 the troubles had started again; and when on 16 August both Yeomanry and Hussars were used against the largely peaceful crowd in St Peter's Field, Manchester, and several people, including two women, were killed, revolution appeared to threaten once more. Lord Sidmouth had little doubt that the 'clouds in the north' would soon burst, and he wrote to Lord Eldon, the Lord Chancellor, to tell him that he wished he could persuade himself of the 'sufficiency of the means either in law or force', to curb the spirit of the revolt and 'crush its impending and too probable effects'.[35]

Lord Grey felt sure that 'the leaders of the popular party' wanted revolution rather than mere reform; and that, 'inflamed' as they were by distress, the people were ready to support them.[36] The Regent shared this view. At Lord Sidmouth's request he wrote a letter approving the action of the Manchester magistrates in St Peter's Field and commending the 'forbearance' of the commander of the regular troops.[37] He approved the measures known as the Six Acts by which the government endeavoured to curb the activities of the revolutionaries, and read with approval letters from the Duke of Cambridge who protested that 'nothing but firmness' could quell the 'abominable revolutionary spirit now prevalent in England'.[38] On his return to London from Cowes, the Regent was made only too well aware of the strength of this revolutionary spirit. He was 'hissed by an immense mob' around his front door; and Lady Hertford was all but tipped out of her chair into the street and had to be rescued by Bow Street Runners.[39]

It was at this time that Arthur Thistlewood, a former estate agent who had been arrested after the trial of the Spa Fields rioters, conceived in his disordered brain the bizarre and monstrous plan of assassinating the entire Cabinet. He and thirty-odd followers planned to execute their murders at Lord Harrowby's house in Grosvenor Square, where the intended victims were due to dine on 23 February 1820. They were to be slaughtered in the dining-room and the heads of Lord Sidmouth and Lord Castlereagh, one of the Home Secretary's strongest supporters, were to be carried off in a bag. Having been told about the plot by an informer, the government were able to have Thistlewood and his associates arrested at their headquarters in a ruined stable in Cato Street on 23 February

1820. Lord Sidmouth, who had personally supervised the operation with his habitual calm and courage, was praised by the Regent as 'the Duke of Wellington on home service'.[40]

'The Ministers have had a narrow escape,' Lord Althorp wrote to Lord Milton two days after Thistlewood's arrest, 'for nothing would have been more easy than to have murdered them in the way it was intended.' Both Althorp and Milton had opposed the more repressive of the government's Six Acts on the grounds that 'if you prevent the people from meeting in the open you will drive them to plots and assassinations'; and they feared that further disorders were inevitable.[41]

Their fears were justified. The Cato Street Conspiracy was followed by a number of alarming incidents, particularly in the north. Accounts of insurrectionary movements were received from Barnsley and Sheffield; over a thousand armed men assembled at four different points around Huddersfield intending to attack the town on the night of 31 March; and artillery was ordered to Wakefield in April. But as in 1817, so now as the spring of 1820 advanced, the disturbances died down with the general improvement of the economic situation, and a revulsion amongst the more moderate reformers against the savage plans of the extremists.

Before the summer was over, however, the government were threatened from a new and unexpected quarter; and the Regent was to face an adversary far more destructive of his peace of mind than either Hunt or Thistlewood.

IO

The Milan Commission
1814–1820

*

'Two young and hot lovers could not have done as much'

Ever since her arrival in Brunswick in August 1814, Princess Caroline had been providing Europe with scandalous stories about her astonishing behaviour. She had exhausted her hosts and her attendants by her restless energy, by going to balls and masquerades, to supper parties and gambling parties night after night, by refusing to go to her bed and by having the musicians dragged from theirs to play on until dawn. She had provided her Gentlemen with a startling new livery of gaudily embroidered coats and plumed hats. At Geneva she had appeared at a ball 'dressed *en Venus*, or rather not dressed, further than the waist'; at Baden, at the Opera, she had pranced into the box of the mourning, widowed Margravine, shouting with laughter and wearing an outlandish peasant headdress ornamented with spangles and fluttering ribbons; later at Baden, so Miss Wynne was told by Lord Redesdale, 'when a *partie de chasse* had been made for her, she appeared with a half pumpkin on her head', explaining to the astonished Grand Duke that it was the 'coolest sort of coiffure'. At Genoa she was drawn through the streets in a gilt and mother-of-pearl phaeton dressed in pink and white, like a little girl, though exhibiting a large expanse of middle-aged bosom and showing two stout legs in pink top boots; at Naples where she went in defiance of the urgent advice of Lord Liverpool, she had been so obviously captivated by the virile, arrogant swagger of Napoleon's hirsute brother-in-law, Joachim Murat, that men said she had induced him to make love to her; and at a ball there she was alleged to have appeared 'in the most indecent manner, her breast and her arms being entirely naked'. At Athens she had 'dressed almost naked and danced with her servants'; on Elba she had made a flamboyant pilgrimage to the house where Napoleon had lived in exile.*

The Hon. J. W. Ward imagined in November 1815 'that "Injured Innocence" which made such a run two years ago would now be hissed off the stage'.[1] On a visit to Milan, Robert Southey heard that the Princess was reported to be insane.[2] And Walter Savage Landor repeated stories of indecent paintings on the walls of her villa, of orgiastic balls that were given there, of the 'Deptford boy' (William Austin) spitting in the face of his tutor. Landor himself had seen Austin at a theatre in Italy, 'and all the time he was there he was employed in scratching his head and examining the success of the operation'.[3]

'I cannot tell you how sorry and ashamed I felt as an Englishwoman,' Lady Bessborough, who saw the Princess at a ball, told Granville Leveson Gower. 'In the room, [dancing], was a short, very fat elderly woman, with an extremely red face (owing I suppose to the heat) in a girl's white frock-looking dress, but with shoulder, back and neck, quite low (disgustingly so) down to the middle of her stomach; very black hair [in fact, a black wig] and eyebrows, which gave her a fierce look, and a wreath of light pink roses on her head. . . . I was staring at her from the oddity of her appearance, when suddenly she nodded and smiled at me, and not recollecting her, I was convinced she was mad, till William Bentinck [the British envoy], pushed me and said, "Do you not see the Princess of Wales nodding to you?" . . . I could not bear the sort of whispering and talking all round about the Principessa d'Inghilterra.'[4]

But the Principessa seemed not to care, nor even to notice it. It was as though she were revelling in her freedom to behave as badly as she felt inclined to behave, and, in so doing, to insult and infuriate her husband.

One by one her English attendants had left her, first Colonel St Leger,

---

* Count Münster, the Hanoverian Minister, whose agents were employed to watch her movements and activities, thought that 'her predilection for everything connected with the Bonaparte family' deserved 'as much and even more notice as her love affair'. The Marchese Circello reported to Prince Castelcicala, in the year of Waterloo, that the Princess had examined the house in which Napoleon had lived on Elba 'with the utmost attention and minuteness, expressing her admiration of every corner of it, especially those rooms which Napoleon had been reported to have preferred'. Before his portrait she had announced, 'Napoleon, I salute you. I always had and have now the greatest esteem for you.' She asked if she might keep his ebony billiard cue as a 'precious memento' (RA Geo IV, Box 8, 9 December 1815).

then Lady Charlotte Lindsay and Lady Elizabeth Forbes, then Sir William Gell and Keppel Craven, finally Captain Hesse and Dr Holland.* Their places were taken by an extraordinary collection of retainers including French chambermaids and French cooks, Arab footboys, Austrian postilions and Italian footmen, whose 'overbearing insolence' was 'beyond description' and whose 'entrance into any territory [was] as much dreaded as the incursion of freebooters'.[5] Over them all presided the swarthy, robust and handsome figure of Bartolommeo Bergami. Bergami – or Pergami as he preferred the name to be spelled – was thirty-two at the time of his appointment, and separated from a sullen, silent wife whose dialect was difficult to understand even in the very few sentences which ever escaped her. He had formerly been a soldier, a quartermaster in a regiment of Hussars, and afterwards a courier on the personal staff of General Pino; he had served in the Russian campaign of 1812, and in the subsequent wars of 1813 and 1814. His family, so he claimed – and so it was afterwards confirmed – was an old and respectable one which had fallen on hard times through the extravagance of his father, the son and grandson of well-to-do physicians.[6] Certainly Bartolommeo Pergami himself, English observers agreed, though a man of no education and little talent, had the manners of a gentleman. It had not, therefore, seemed inappropriate when Princess Caroline had appointed him her *valet de place*. What had seemed wholly objectionable was Pergami's rapid promotion to Chamberlain, the appointment of numerous friends and relations of his to her Royal Highness's staff, his evidently welcome presence at her dinner table – where his former fellow-servants waited on them both. With the Princess's help, her handsome, sturdy Chamberlain acquired a country estate near Milan, assuming the title of Baron della Francina; also with the Princess's help he was created a Knight of Malta. His little daughter, Victorine, often slept in her bedroom and called her 'Mamma'.

It was in the company of this attractively vigorous and attentive companion that the Princess, by now an intrepid and resourceful traveller, set out upon her famous pilgrimage to the Holy Land. Since she had

---

* Captain Samuel George Pechell, R.N., who was later to be a witness against the Queen at the enquiry into her conduct in the House of Lords, said that Lady Charlotte Campbell had 'made no scruple of giving as her reason for leaving [the Princess] that she had daughters and would not allow them to stay where there was such an example' (Journal of J. A. Powell, 5 August 1818–3 July 1820, RA Geo IV, Box 23).

already sailed to Sicily and drunk tea with the Dey in his seraglio at Algiers, had explored the Greek islands and the mosques of Syria, had driven through Constantinople and inspected the defences of Acre, no one in London was unduly surprised when it was learned that, accompanied by a horde of attendants and hangers-on which now numbered over two hundred persons, she had ridden into Jerusalem on an ass. Nor was any great surprise evinced by the report that the increasingly eccentric Princess had there established the Order of St Caroline of Jerusalem whose Grand Master was 'the Colonel Bartholomew Pergami, Baron of Francina, Knight of Malta and of the Holy Sepulchre of Jerusalem', whose most honoured Knight was William Austin, and whose motto was 'Honi soit qui mal y pense'.

On her return to Europe, via Jericho, the Princess moved into a villa on Lake Como which she greatly enlarged and named the Villa d'Este after the distinguished family from which she was descended. From there she moved to the Villa Cassielli on the Adriatic near Pesaro where she was told that her daughter was dead. She realized then that her husband would have no further compunction in initiating proceedings against her in order to secure a divorce. So long as her 'ever beloved daughter was still alive,' she wrote to Henry Brougham, 'such proceedings would never have taken place to make such false and foul accusations upon my character'.[7] But now that Charlotte was dead, she supposed that the Prince would do all he could to rid himself of her.

*

For months past, indeed, the Regent had been closely following his wife's wild progress with intentness and disgust. Foreign rulers had been made aware that any favours granted her would cause grave displeasure in London. British diplomats had been asked to watch and report on her movements; and the letters that were consequently received in London tended to confirm all that the gossipmongers said. From Hanover came reports of her 'very incongruous conduct' which 'created general astonishment and justly merited indignation': those with opportunities of observing her closely 'fully confirmed whatever [had] been generally circulated about the indecorous public and private conduct of the Princess', mentioning particularly her glaring very intimate connection with a certain Bergamo.[8] Similar reports came from Vienna; and from Florence came letters about her continuing 'exceedingly prodigal behaviour', her 'intimacy' with Pergami which was 'the subject of conversation everywhere', her carrying about a baby in her arms, the belief that she was insane.[9]

Faced by such reports as these and encouraged by his friend Sir John Leach, now Vice-Chancellor, the Regent felt that he had no alternative but to ask the government to authorize an official enquiry into the Princess's conduct. The government agreed to pay the costs of such an enquiry on condition that 'whatever might be the nature of the evidence obtained, however decisive as to criminality, the question of the expediency of any proceedings must always be considered as an open question'.[10]

The three men chosen to undertake the investigations were William Cooke, of Lincoln's Inn, 'one of His Majesty's Counsel learned in law', Major Thomas Henry Browne, an Italian-speaking officer who had served in Spain under Wellington, and John Allan Powell, a solicitor, also of Lincoln's Inn. They were sent out to Milan – at that time under the rule of Austria – with instructions 'to engage all such assistance either legal or otherwise' as they considered expedient and to place themselves 'in communication with the governments of the several countries' to which their enquiries might lead them.

They left for Italy in the summer of 1818, and before the end of the year had examined and taken down the 'voluntary answers' of numerous servants, sailors, innkeepers, gamekeepers, fishermen, postilions and gardeners, who all seemed in general agreement about the Princess's unbecoming conduct. The evidence was not always easy to collect. The Austrian authorities in Milan afforded Powell and his colleagues 'every possible protection and countenance'; but when they moved south into the Papal States they had cause to complain that officials there were 'very lukewarm', not to say 'inimical'.[11]

'I fear the police and authorities near you are too much disposed to favour the person in question', Thomas (recently promoted Colonel) Browne wrote to Baron Ompteda, Hanoverian Minister at the Vatican, who had attempted to collect evidence upon the Regent's behalf before the arrival of the 'Milan Commission'. 'The Papal Government would appear to be more inclined to withhold than to assist in discovering the truth, which is rather singular when it is no secret how much devotion to the Prince Regent is always expressed by Cardinal Gonsalvi [the Papal Secretary of State]. Were we to require what is unreasonable, or to seek for evidence or facts which had never existed, the case would be different and we should justly meet with difficulties from the Roman authorities but as this is not the case we are not a little astonished to find that all the authorities civil and military are at her disposal.'[12] It had also required 'much management to induce' the witnesses to give their evidence without the promise of reward, the Italian character being 'keenly alive to interest'. Moreover, their dread of assassination was great. 'The Princess', Browne went on, 'is at this moment so completely surrounded by the family of Pergami, and they are such a determined set of Ruffianos that they would not scruple at any act, however desperate, against those whom they might suspect of acting to their prejudice.'[13]

Nevertheless, before the end of November 1818, Browne had 'no doubt of everything being completely proved';[14] he had 'collected sufficient evidence to warrant a public enquiry', and felt that the case was 'already made out'.[15] By July of the following year, when a total of eighty-five persons had been examined, William Cooke felt able to report: 'From this comparison of evidence and from the cool, clear, and distinct manner in which these persons delivered their testimony, we should give credit to the truth of what they have said. We are under the necessity, therefore, of humbly stating that in our opinion this great body of evidence established the fact of a continued adulterous intercourse' between the Princess and Pergami.[16]*

---

* The charges of wholesale bribery later to be levelled at the Milan Commission were unjustified. Indeed, the papers in the Royal Archives show how careful the members of the Commission were to follow the orders they had received from Sir John Leach, who had ordered Cooke to conduct the enquiry with the utmost caution and impartiality and 'to assimilate the examination of the witnesses as nearly as might be to the principles of a British Court of Justice'. Leach had 'in the strongest terms impressed upon the Commissioners that not only were they not to offer or promise bribe or reward but were to forego the most important testimony rather than hold out any expectation of benefit to the witness'. These instructions appear to have been carried out. Care was taken to enquire into the character of possible witnesses; and the testimony of those who were discovered to be of bad character was not accepted. The evidence of thirty witnesses was rejected on the grounds that their accounts were improbable or their characters were suspicious. Of the £10,000 allowed to the Commission, not more than £120 was paid out 'as a recompence for their loss of time and trouble' to the eighty-five witnesses whose evidence was considered worth recording. Having rejected the evidence of an untrustworthy sailor, Browne reported to London that it had 'been the uniform practice of the Commission to reject everything which did not bear decided marks of unimpaired recollection and sincerity'. It cannot be doubted

One of the earliest witnesses to be examined was Giuseppe Sacchi, a former cavalry captain, for nine months courier to the Princess and for three subsequent months her equerry, who had entered her service at the Villa d'Este in November 1816 and had left it at Pesaro at the end of November 1817. He was later to swear that he had often seen the Princess and Pergami walking about arm in arm and kissing each other, and that the balls which were given at Pergami's villa near Milan – and of which several other witnesses were to speak in similar terms – were 'quite brothels', attended by women of 'very low condition'. Male servants in the Princess's employment would frequently leave the ballroom with these women 'according to their pleasure and will'; and the Princess once jokingly chided Sacchi, 'I know, you rogue, that you have gone to bed with three of them and how many times you have had intercourse with them.' Pergami, 'who was present, began to laugh and to cry aloud, "It is true! It is true! It is true!"'.

Sacchi went on to depose that he had seen Pergami more than once enter the Princess's room late at night and that he had heard her call him, 'mon ange', 'mon amour', 'mon cœur'. They travelled by night in the same carriage where 'two or three times' Sacchi found them in the morning 'both asleep and having their respective hands upon one another. Her Royal Highness had her hand upon a particular part of Mr Bergami and Bergami had his own upon that of Her Royal Highness . . . Once Bergami had his breeches loosened and the Princess's hand was upon that part.'[17]

References to the festivities at Pergami's villa near Milan and at the Villa d'Este were also made by numerous other witnesses including Teodoro Majocchi who had entered the Princess's service in December 1817 after having been first postilion to General Pino. Majocchi described in particular the obscene dances performed for the Princess on these occasions by one of her servants, a mulatto from Jaffa named Mahomet. Like Sacchi, Majocchi had seen Pergami enter the Princess's bedroom, and he described how intimate they were; how he held her round the waist when lifting her onto her ass and held her hand while she was riding it; how, when they travelled together, they shared the same carriage in

that the Milan Commissioners were far more scrupulous than the Queen's agents nor that their witnesses were generally much more reliable (RA Geo IV, Boxes 8, 9, 10, 11, 13, 23).

which Pergami kept a bottle 'to make water in'; how they took great care to have rooms as close as possible to each other in all the inns where they stopped for the night, and alternately wore the same blue silk bed-gown.[18]

Majocchi, who had accompanied the Princess on her pilgrimage to Jerusalem, gave an account of the sleeping and bathing arrangements on board the polacca which were later to become a subject of heated discussion at dining-tables all over Europe, and were to give rise in London to the much quoted verse about Pergami:

> The Grand Master of St Caroline
> has found promotion's path.
> He is made both Night Companion
> and Commander of the Bath.[19]

According to Majocchi, the Princess found it so hot on the polacca that she had a tent fitted up for her on deck, and in this tent she used to sleep with Pergami. She also had him in her cabin when she was having a bath for which Majocchi was in the habit of supplying the water; 'then the door was shut, and Bergami and the Princess remained alone in the cabin.'[20]

Vincenzo Gargiullo, the captain of the polacca, confirmed that the Princess and Pergami had slept together under the tent and that he was present when she had her bath. Indeed, he accompanied her 'for anything she did, for any other thing she did', even when she went below to go to the water-closet. Gargiullo recalled how Pergami had made the Princess laugh by 'putting some pillows or cushions under his Grecian robe' to make himself look pregnant. And both he and his mate, Gaetano Paturzo, had seen Pergami sitting on a gun on deck, kissing the Princess who sat on his knee.[21]

Other members of the crew and the Princess's entourage claimed to have been witnesses of these and worse improprieties; but the most damning evidence of blatant intimacy came from Louisa Demont, the Princess's smartly dressed, sly-looking *femme de chambre* who was also aboard the polacca.

Mlle Demont testified that Pergami was usually present when the Princess was at her toilet, when she was almost entirely undressed with her breasts quite bare, and that he would often go into her room at night scantily clothed, once presenting himself in nothing but his shirt and slippers. Sometimes in the night Mlle Demont would hear the Princess's door open and close; and, in the morning, when she went into her mistress's room to make the bed she would find that it had not been slept in. The Princess had herself painted as a penitent Magdalen with her hair disordered, her eyes heavenward, naked to the waist. She gave the finished portrait to Pergami.[22]

So the evidence accumulated and was elaborated. Outdoor servants and workmen who had had opportunities to see Pergami and the Princess at the Villa d'Este and elsewhere, waiters and maids who had observed them on their travels were found to provide more and more evidence of her Royal Highness's guilt.[23] They had been seen kissing and 'caressing each other with their hands', lying together in a boat on Lake Como; Pergami had been observed with his hands on her naked breasts and on her thigh; he had been surprised coming out of her room 'with only his drawers on'.[24] Month by month, as the piles of depositions mounted, the three commissioners felt increasingly confident not only of the Princess's guilt but of their being able to offer enough unshakable evidence for it to be proved in an English court of law. The Regent could not have felt other than satisfied by the results of their unpleasant work, yet he had cause also to feel concerned by the enquiries at the same time being undertaken by the Princess's advisers.

*

Although she had so dismissively spurned his urgent advice to her not to go abroad in 1814, Henry Brougham had ever since been keeping a careful watch on the Princess's activities, expecting the time would surely come when she would feel obliged to call once more on his services. When reports of her scandalous conduct made it clear that the Regent would be induced to take action against her, Brougham had asked his brother James to go out to Italy to help her to sort out her financial problems and, at the same time, to provide him with a first-hand report about the Princess's behaviour and intentions.

James Brougham arrived at Pesaro in the spring of 1819 and was received by the Princess with the 'greatest attention and kindness'. In two long letters to his brother, written towards the end of March, he first of all described the Princess's establishment. This consisted of eighty people in all, over sixty of whom lived in the villa. She had '48 horses and

God knows how many carriages of different sorts', Brougham reported, ' – some of the horses the finest Arabians I ever saw – and all *good*. A ship with a captain and eight men.' It was all very '*hospitable* and *plentiful*'; indeed, it was very surprising that the Princess was not more deeply in debt than she was, particularly as she had even less idea of the value of money than her husband had. She had added two large wings to the Villa Cassielli, which she had bought and given to Pergami, yet 'she *says* the addition wont cost more than £500!!' She had paid £7,500 for the Villa d'Este 'and laid out upon it in building and furniture upwards of £20,000, and above £2,000 in making a road, you may say altogether £30,000'.

She was very generous, and well enough liked. But she was full of complaints. She said that her English servants had cheated her outrageously, and the general behaviour of English people towards her had been abominable. The Royal Family, under the Regent's influence, had cut all connection with her. 'Leopold never wrote to her *at all*. The courier who went round Europe came here on his way to Naples, with a common circular letter telling her of Princess Charlotte's death. The Queen's death was never announced to her *at all*. The Duke of Gloucester was near, and never took the smallest notice of her. And all her old friends cut her in the same way.' The Regent's Milan Commission annoyed her 'most terribly', especially the evidence of her maid, Louisa Demont, who was 'a great Whore'. She insisted that people had been paid to poison her and the kitchens were watched accordingly; two servants paraded the hall all night; Baron Ompteda, who had been in the district trying to get people to bear witness against her, was not only the Regent's spy, but was also at the bottom of this plot to poison her.

As to the stories about her conduct with Pergami, Brougham was sorry to have to say that there was certainly enough 'to justify reports'. '*Le Baron*' admittedly appeared to be a '*remarkably good sort of man* . . . very active – quite a different man' from what he had expected. But their relationship was undeniably most irregular. Pictures of Pergami were in every room of the villa and all the plate in the dining-room, except for a few things which she had brought over from England with her, bore his arms. 'Nothing can appear more revolting to propriety than the Princess of Wales, with her large fortune using another person's plate,' Brougham thought. 'Certainly the whole thing tells badly. *His* house and grounds, *his* plate, his ordering everything, he even buys her bonnets, this I saw, and all his family quartered upon her!!!' His brother, Louis, was first equerry; his sister, an ill-bred woman known as Countess Oldi, was 'Lady in Waiting', his old mother superintended the linen, his daughter called the Princess 'Mamma'. 'In fact, they are to all appearances man and wife, never was anything so obvious. *His room* is close to hers, and his *bed room* the only one in that part of the house. The whole thing is apparent to everyone, though perhaps there might be difficulty in proving the fact to find her guilty of high treason, yet I should think all the circumstances being stated would completely ruin her in the opinion of the people of England, that once done, the Prince might get divorce, or at any rate prevent her being Queen if she wished it.'

For this reason James Brougham strongly recommended that some sort of settlement should be made with the Princess so that a public enquiry into her conduct could be avoided. 'I should propose that she write a letter to the Prince stating her reasons for wishing a divorce or Parliamentary separation. . . . You must give me the style of this letter, because she will ask me to write it for her, and it must be well done, as there is no saying what may be made of it hereafter. She should begin by asserting innocence . . . high toned in the style of Mary Queen of Scots . . . accusing the Regent of plaguing her by these inquisitions, and concluding by saying as her daughter is dead, and there is no hopes of her having any pleasure in England she thinks it better for both to separate. I am quite convinced that it is the very best thing that can be done on every account, and the sooner the better, before she loses more character, or in fact before England knows more of the matter.'

Brougham felt sure that the Princess would be happy to settle for a divorce. She told him that long before Princess Charlotte's death she had resolved never to go to England again; she had no ambition to be Queen *'and never had'*. The only thing that might have induced her to return would be to pay the Duke and Duchess of York a visit as she liked them both. She would be quite content, she said, to settle for £100,000 and to 'give up her annuity and everything', and although this 'would be madness – *not three years income!*' Brougham was confident that he and his brother between them could arrange a satisfactory figure for her with the Regent's advisers; and the more she got the more she would be obliged to them both.[25]

But the matter could not be settled so simply. Henry Brougham accepted his brother's advice and formally proposed that, provided her present annuity were guaranteed to her for life, she would agree to the ratification by Parliament of the terms of a separation and would renounce her right to become Queen, taking some other title after the Regent's coronation, such as Duchess of Cornwall.[26]

This solution was not considered practical, however. In the first place Brougham was advised by Lord Lauderdale, a shrewd if eccentric Scotsman trained in the law, that Parliament could not pass an Act ratifying the separation unless the Princess were proved guilty of infidelity or confessed to it. And for her to confess was, she insisted, 'impossible'. Nor would she agree to a less formal separation by mutual consent: that was 'doing nothing'.[27] Moreover, the Regent would not agree to separation by mutual consent either. He wanted to be more securely rid of the woman: there must be a divorce. It was Lord Lauderdale's opinion that he was actually contemplating getting married again.[28] Certainly Prince Alexander of Soms wrote to him to suggest that it might be a good idea for him to marry a daughter of Victor Emmanuel, King of Sardinia, who was a great-grandson of Anne of Orleans, the granddaughter of Charles I, and thus the Stuart claimant to the throne of England. Also, a story later got abroad, so W. H. Fremantle told the Marquess of Buckingham, 'that they are trying to cook up a match for the King with a Princess of Tours and Taxis (I believe a sister of the Duchess of Cumberland) and a sister of the Princess Esterhazy. Metternick is at the bottom of it.'[29] But the Regent never spoke of marriage himself; he wanted a divorce merely to be free of that 'vilest wretch this world ever was cursed with'.

The Cabinet were very reluctant to agree to a divorce, which could not be obtained 'except upon proof of adultery, to be substantiated by evidence before some tribunal in this country – and such a proceeding could not . . . be instituted without serious hazard to the interests and peace of the Kingdom'.[30] Moreover, the Cabinet doubted that the evidence collected by the Milan Commission, damning though it was, was strong enough to prove the Princess's adultery. The body of it consisted 'almost exclusively of the evidence of foreigners most of them not above the rank of menial servants and that of masters and attendants in hotels wholly unacquainted with the English language'.[31] The Cabinet also feared that the Regent's marriage to Mrs Fitzherbert would be raised again and that the further damaging gossip about his past mistresses and present companions would be spread about by his enemies to increase his unpopularity. Above all, it was feared that the Princess's legal advisers would produce equally damning recriminatory evidence against the

Prince; they even suggested that to air so much dirty linen in public would have a serious effect upon public morals.[32]

While the Cabinet hesitated and held back, taking 'the whole case', as Castlereagh put it, 'into their mature consideration', the Regent became more anxious for a divorce than ever, dreading what the Princess might do unless action were taken against her while she still *was* a Princess and had no claim to be Queen. And in his anxiety, as so often in times of stress, he once more fell seriously ill.

The Queen on Trial
1820

*

'No other subject is ever talked of'

The Regent's anxiety was much increased by the disturbing bulletins which the Duke of York had for some time past been sending him from Windsor. His father, now in his eighty-second year and 'greatly emaciated', though still finding 'amusement in the inexhaustible resources of his distempered imagination', was slowly dying.[1] Scarcely had the doctors been summoned to the Prince's own bedside than he was given the news, which he received 'with a burst of grief',[2] that 'his Majesty expired at 32 minutes past 8 o'clock PM, 29 January 1820'. At the age of fifty-seven, he was King himself at last. The proclamation of his accession was delayed for a day, however, as 30 January was the anniversary of the execution of King Charles I; and it was not until Monday, the 31st, that accompanied by the royal Dukes and by Prince Leopold, he emerged from Carlton House to stand in the cold air while the aged Garter King of Arms read out the traditional formula in a slow and quavering voice.[3]

The next day the new King was attacked by an inflammation on the lungs, and a bulletin was issued with the grave news that his Majesty was 'severely indisposed'. He could not sleep; he had a racing pulse and pains in the chest; he experienced great difficulty in breathing. It was feared that he might be suffering from pneumonia or pleurisy; but whatever the disorder was, he came close to death. Wellington told Lady Shelley that he thought the King might slip through their fingers.[4] 'Heavens, if he should die!' Princess Lieven wrote to Metternich. 'Shakespeare's tragedies pale before such a catastrophe. Father and son, in the past, have

145

been buried together. But two Kings! I hope this one will recover.'[5] Thomas Creevey for one did not think that he would. 'He is, I apprehend, rapidly approaching death,' Creevey told Elizabeth Ord – 'and then for the Queen and Bruffam!'[6]

Brougham, in fact, was praying heartily for the King's recovery, for he dreaded the idea of his successor, King Frederick I, who would turn out to be a 'shady Tory-professional King' and would never give 'these villains', the present Tory Ministers, 'the least annoyance'. Frederick I would not long survive, nor would 'that Prince of Blackguards, "Brother William",' so, 'in the course of nature', the Whigs would live only 'to be *assassinated* by King Ernest I or Regent Ernest'.[7] Even if Regent Ernest were not to survive, the Whigs could hope for little from other members of the family.

The Duke of Kent had adopted Whig opinions late in life but only in opposition to the King; and Kent had died a few days previously. The Duke of Sussex's political opinions were more sincerely held, but as the Hon. H. G. Bennet said, Sussex was in the habit of talking 'very sad stuff'; and, as Creevey decided, though Sussex never said anything that made you think him foolish, and was 'civil and obliging, there was a *nothingness* in him that [was] to the last degree fatiguing'.[8] In any case, the likelihood of a King Augustus I was very remote indeed.

While the Whigs discussed the possible consequences of the King's death, he began slowly to recover, despite the loss of a total of 150 ounces of blood at the hands of Sir Henry Halford and Sir Matthew Tierney.[9]

He felt himself sufficiently recovered by 14 February to wish to attend his father's funeral the following day; but his physicians, 'scarcely yet relieved from that state of anxiety and alarm' which his 'dangerous illness had given rise to', viewed his expressed intention with 'absolute dismay' and most strongly urged him 'to forego that satisfaction' to his feelings that he naturally attached to 'a performance of the last act of filial piety to the late King'.[10]

The King gave way to their entreaties and remained indoors, 'terribly' worried about the woman he declined to call the Queen.[11] The previous week, despite his debilitated condition, he had spent a whole evening in 'very serious agitation', studying all the prayer-books in the Carlton House library, hoping to find a precedent that would support his determination not to allow Church congregations to pray for the well-being of

11 The Guildhall Banquet of June 1814, by George Clint.

12 The Regent by Sir Thomas Lawrence, *c.* 1814.

13 Princess Charlotte, an unfinished watercolour by Thomas Heaphy.

14 Warwick House, Warwick Street, Princess Charlotte's residence: aquatint from *Ackermann's Repository of Arts*, 1811.

Queen Caroline and to exclude her name and title entirely from the Liturgy.[12]

He could not find a precedent, but he was determined that they should be excluded anyway.[13] Although not all the members of the Cabinet concurred, and the Archbishop of Canterbury was also opposed to their exclusion, the government agreed after lengthy deliberations that she should not be mentioned in the Liturgy and that she ought not to be crowned Queen. They went on to say in a memorandum of extraordinary length that, while they deprecated her conduct, they could not recommend the King to proceed to a divorce. They suggested instead that 'the Princess', as they were careful still to refer to her, should be given an allowance on condition that she remained abroad, which they confidently expected she would do rather than return to face the accumulating evidence of the Milan Commission.[14]

The King read this memorandum with 'some surprise and much regret'. He recognized perfectly well that the Princess's counsel would rake up 'recriminations of every kind', but he was prepared to face this if only he could once and for all rid himself of his unspeakable wife. He believed that the evidence against her was entirely convincing, and was struck by 'the extraordinary coincidence of testimony of different witnesses who [had] been separated from each other for years'. The general tendency of the evidence was confirmed 'by several English persons'. Having made up his mind 'to all the discomfort to which' he could be exposed, he was determined on a divorce, even if he had to go to Hanover to obtain one, and, encouraged by Sir John Leach, who had carefully studied the Commission's evidence, he threatened to dismiss Lord Liverpool's government. 'The King has declared his determination to look for other servants if we do not agree to bring forward a Bill for Divorce,' Canning, President of the Board of Control, noted in his diary on 10 February. 'Be it so!'

In acrimonious discussions with his Ministers he ordered the Prime Minister out of the room; he commanded Wellington 'to hold his tongue'; and in a subsequent quarrel with the Lord Chancellor he said to him insultingly, 'My Lord, I know your conscience always interferes except where your interest is concerned.'[15] When Canning, 'after two sleepless nights trying to make up [his] mind', offered his resignation on the grounds of his former friendship with the Queen – 'no doubt one of

the *many favoured*', Castlereagh rudely commented[16] – the King declined
to accept it, so Canning withdrew to France and resigned later.[17]*

Nor was the divorce the only question which divided the King and his
Ministers; for he was thoroughly dissatisfied with their refusal to sanction
a Bill providing for an enlarged Civil List. 'He has been pretty well
disposed to part with us all because we would not make additions to his
revenue,' Eldon noted in a memorandum on 26 April.[18] And part with
them he certainly would have done had he been able to do so. But to find
an alternative government proved impossible. He asked Sidmouth, now
his most favoured Minister, to replace Lord Liverpool; but Sidmouth
declined even to consider the proposition and advised the King to stick
to his present administration.[19] No responsible potential minister could
be persuaded to form or to join a government brought about in these conditions. So the King was obliged to give way. He sent for Lord Liverpool,
apologized to him for his hastiness, and took what comfort he could from
the Cabinet's promise to institute proceedings for a divorce should 'the
Princess' return to England.[20] As for his disappointment at being refused
an increased Civil List, he wrote to the Prime Minister: 'The King is
fully sensible of the importance of publick economy and is desirous to
make every personal sacrifice on his part for that object, and the King
will never require that the intended arrangement shall be disturbed unless
it shall be found to be inconsistent with the dignity and splendour of the
Crown which the King considers to be inseparable from the public
interest.'[21]

*

James Brougham had believed Princess Caroline to be quite sincere
the year before in her protestations that she had no wish to return to
England, but since then she had begun to change her mind. When she
had learned that her father-in-law was likely to die she had written to
Henry Brougham to say that she *might* return if the country would

---

* If, as the King suspected, Canning had been Princess Caroline's lover before his
marriage, the affair was evidently a brief one. Canning met the Princess for the first
time on 22 June 1799. He found her 'most extraordinary and most delightful'; he was
'charmed with her beyond measure'. Just over a year later, on 8 July 1800, he married
the heiress, Joan Scott. After the marriage he was a frequent guest at Blackheath,
sometimes alone but often with his wife. The Princess was also a frequent guest of
Mr and Mrs Canning at their country house (Canning's MS diaries in the Canning
Papers, 29d, 29di).

protect her. Excited by the possibilities of this, the Duke of Sussex woke Henry Brougham at two o'clock on the morning of 30 January to tell him that the King indeed was dead.[22]

Soon after dawn a courier was despatched to Italy to advise the Queen to come north to Brussels or Paris, or even to Calais, and to demand a yacht to bring her to England.[23] It seems unlikely that Brougham really wanted her to come all the way to England, even though her presence would prove a useful weapon with which to overthrow the Tories and so bring the Whigs and himself to power. In August he had written to the King's friend, Lord Hutchinson, to say, 'Her coming would be pregnant with every sort of mischief (not to mention the infernal personal annoyance of having such a devil to plague me for six months). I think it would expose things to the risk of clamour and violence which no one can hope to estimate, far less to direct, or, in case of necessity, disarm. . . . Therefore I am disposed to prevent her coming by every means in my power.'[24]

Since this letter had been written, George III's death had admittedly transformed the situation. The risk of 'clamour and violence' was just as great, perhaps even greater: memories of Peterloo might be fading, yet the unrest and discontent in the country were as threatening as ever. But Princess Caroline was now Queen, and her uses as a threat to the Tories were incalculably more valuable.

Yet it was probably only as a threat that Brougham envisaged her. 'It would be *frightfully dangerous* for her to come here all at once,' he warned Lady Charlotte Lindsay on 18 February. 'All now depends on her coming to Brussels or some near and handy spot. If she arrives plump on you at Paris, make her either stay there or at Calais till I come out to her.'[25]

For the moment the Queen herself did not appear to be particularly inclined to hurry home. She had been in Leghorn when the news of the King's death reached her; but despite Brougham's summons to 'Brussels or Calais', she was unfortunately 'absolute obliged' to turn her back on 'dear old England', so she told her former physician, Walter Farquhar. She had to 'go first to Rome to Mr Torlonia, my banker, which usual received my letter of credit from Coutts House in London'.[26] She would return to England eventually, though. 'Any merchant ship or frigate' would be 'quite sufficient' for her, she assured Farquhar; and she told Brougham that she would reside at 'the old Queen's palace in the Green Park without any alternations and expence for the nation'.[27]

While the Queen remained in Rome, the King and the government discussed the terms that should be offered to her to induce her to stay on the Continent. It was felt that almost no sum would be too great provided that she could be prevented from returning to England. Eventually it was agreed that she should be offered £50,000 a year if she would relinquish the title of Queen or any other title indicating her relationship with the English Royal Family, and if she would undertake not to come into 'any part of the British dominions'.[28]

Before this offer was made to her, however, she left Rome for France by way of Geneva. Exasperated on the journey by news of her omission from the Liturgy and by her treatment at the hands of the representatives of the foreign courts who, in deference to the known wishes of King George IV, declined to accord her the recognition to which she felt entitled, she entered France quite fixed in her determination to return to England and demand to be accorded her rights. She was accompanied by Alderman Matthew Wood, an extreme radical Member of Parliament for the City of London and twice its Lord Mayor, who had sailed out to meet her and to offer her the doubtful benefit of his far from disinterested advice.

The son of a Devonshire serge-maker, Wood had left Exeter to seek his fortune in London where he was now in a thriving way of business as a chemist and hop merchant. A consistent supporter of the more advanced Whigs, he saw in what he no doubt took to be the sad case of Princess Caroline those political opportunities that had appealed to Henry Brougham. Unlike Brougham, though, he knew little of the evidence that was mounting against the Queen whom he vehemently urged to return to London where she would receive the welcome due to an injured heroine.

Brougham, accompanied by Lord Hutchinson, left for France on 1 June and, on the afternoon of the 3rd, arrived at St Omer, where the Queen had agreed to meet him. It was immediately clear that she was not in the least disposed to listen to the government's proposals, and she informed Brougham of her intention of proceeding straight to England. 'I entreat your Majesty once more earnestly and patiently to reflect upon the step about to be taken,' Brougham implored her the day after his arrival at St Omer. It would be far better, he advised her, to accept the generous annuity that was offered her on the understanding that it would be granted 'without any renunciation of rank or title or right' and with a pledge on the part of the government that she should be 'acknowledged and received abroad by all diplomatic agents' according to her 'rank and station'. If she *did* return to England she ought to do so secretly, and to dispense with 'such marks of popular favour' as were more suitably displayed towards a parliamentary candidate at an election than towards a Queen of England. 'My duty to your Majesty binds me to say very plainly,' he continued, 'that I shall consider every such exhibition as both hurtful to your Majesty's real dignity and full of danger in its probable consequences.'[29] When this plea proved ineffective he sent another at seven o'clock the same evening. 'I earnestly implore you to refrain from rushing into certain trouble and possible danger.'[30]

But it was all to no avail. The Queen sent Brougham a curt note commanding him to inform Lord Hutchinson that it was 'quite impossible' for her to consider the government's proposals.[31] Then, without waiting to consult Brougham further or waiting for Hutchinson's reply, in which he said that he would send a courier to London for further instructions, she got into her carriage and left for Calais. In fact, she had already written to Lord Liverpool from Villeneuve-le-Roi on 29 May, to inform him that she intended arriving in London 'next Saturday the 3thd of Juin'. She had asked for one of the royal yachts to be ordered to take her across the channel, and had ended her letter with the ominous words, 'I desire . . . also to be informed of his Majeste's intentions what residence should be alloted to me, either phermenent or temprory: I trust that his Majeste is recovered from his severe illness. Caroline Queen of England.'[32]

'It is impossible for me to paint the insolence, the violence and the precipitation of this woman's conduct,' Hutchinson reported in exasperation to Bloomfield. 'I never saw anything so outrageous, so undignified as a queen, or so unamiable as a woman. . . . She has really assumed a tone and hauteur which is quite insufferable, and which nothing but the most pure and unimpeached innocence could justify. . . . We have at length come to a final and ultimate issue with this outrageous woman. She has set the King's authority at defiance, and it is now time for her to feel his vengeance and his power. Patience, forebearance and moderation have had no effect upon her. I must now implore His Majesty to exert all his firmness and resolution: retreat is impossible. The Queen has thrown down the gauntlet of defiance. The King must take it up.'[33]

Hutchinson was convinced that Brougham possessed 'no real authority or power over the mind or decisions' of the Queen. 'I do not think that he ever made the slightest impression upon her or that she ever listened to him for a moment with the serious intention of following his advice,' Hutchinson reported. 'Before our arrival she had organized everything for stage effect: her chief informer was that enlightened mountebank, Alderman Wood.'[34]

Her demand for a yacht to convey her across the Channel having been ignored, she arrived at Dover on 5 June in the ordinary packet. 'This brave woman', as *The Times* referred to her, was clamorously welcomed by a royal salute from the Castle and by a crowd even larger than Alderman Wood had promised her.[35] To the triumphant strains of a raucous band, she was escorted to her hotel by tradesmen and fishermen carrying banners and shouting suitable slogans. The next day she left for London by way of Canterbury and Greenwich, collecting ever larger and more enthusiastic crowds of supporters as she approached the capital. She drove over Westminster Bridge in an open carriage, the purple silk pelisse she had worn on landing having now been changed for a more sombre mourning dress with an Elizabethan ruff, donned in respect for her late father-in-law and uncle, George III. Next to her, so delighted by the cheers that he occasionally stood up to return them at the top of his voice, sat Alderman Wood; opposite was her Lady-in-Waiting, Lady Anne Hamilton, and an Italian servant; behind, in a second carriage, rode William Austin, accompanied by Alderman Wood's son; a third carriage contained an assortment of Italian attendants. 'Her progress was slow through the countless populace,' reported Thomas Denman, the handsome, sociable and eloquent lawyer who had been appointed her Solicitor-General, 'her travelling equipage mean and miserable, her attendants appeared ill-calculated to conciliate good-will in this country. Hardly a well-dressed person was to be seen in the crowd. Two or three men on horseback assumed a rather more respectable appearance, but one of these was my bankrupt cousin.'[36]

There was no gainsaying, though, the general enthusiasm with which she was greeted. Charles Greville, who rode out to watch her enter London, found 'the road thronged with an immense multitude the whole way from Westminster Bridge to Greenwich. Carriages, carts and horsemen followed, preceded, and surrounded her coach the whole way. She was everywhere received with the greatest enthusiasm. Women waved pocket handkerchiefs, and men shouted wherever she passed.'[37]

The cavalcade proceeded unsteadily up St James's Street, where she 'bowed and smiled to the men who were in the windows' of White's Club, and then on to Alderman Wood's house in South Audley Street where she showed herself to a wildly excited mob that 'streamed through the streets all night with torches, making passers-by shout, "Long Live the Queen!"', and roaring their support of 'Queen Caroline and her son, King Austin'.[38] For two days the mob surged round the house, occasionally retiring to demand illuminations in her honour or to break the windows of people deemed less than enthusiastic in her support. Lord Sidmouth, going 'home from Cabinet with the Duke of Wellington, could not get into his own house,' Croker reported, 'and the mob broke the windows of the Duke's carriage'.[39] Lady Hertford's house was assaulted and her windows broken; the mob also stoned Sidmouth's house from which Admiral Lord Exmouth rushed out armed with sword and pistol and drove them away.[40] 'The fermentation encreases much,' Sir Thomas Tyrwhitt told Coutts, the banker. 'It has got amongst the soldiery, who skirmish in their barracks.'[41] The Marquess of Buckingham's correspondents shared Tyrwhitt's apprehensions. Thomas Grenville told him that the rumours about the military were increasing 'daily and frightfully';[42] while W. H. Fremantle wrote, 'I have great doubts if the troops are not infected. The Press is paid abundantly [to support the Queen] and there are some ale-houses open where the soldiers may go and drink and eat for nothing provided they will drink, "Prosperity and health for the Queen!" ... The City is completely with her. ... The King grows daily more unpopular.'[43] Lady Jerningham decided that the spirit of the times was most alarming; the country was nearer to disaster than it had ever been since the time of King Charles I.[44] Lord Grey had already informed Holland that they would see, if they lived, 'a Jacobin Revolution more bloody than that of France'.[45]

On 8 June the Queen moved to a quieter house in Portland Place, before establishing herself at Brandenburg House in Hammersmith, a mansion built for one of his mistresses by Charles I's nephew, Prince Rupert. Meanwhile the King, bitterly castigating her disgraceful entry into London sitting next to 'that beast Wood', was forced to conclude that he had never been more disliked. To his surprise and obvious elation he was fitfully cheered when he went to the Chapel Royal on Sunday 18 June, and allowed himself to be persuaded by his companions that the shouts indicated a significant change in public opinion. The Cabinet, therefore, 'thought it highly necessary, in consequence of the feeling betrayed by the Guards, the known bias of the lower orders of the metropolis, particularly of the women, in favour of the Queen, and the cry of "No Queen, no King!" which had been heard in the country as well as in London, that the King should be undeceived on this point, and deputed Lord Sidmouth to wait on his Majesty for this purpose.'[46] Soon afterwards, insulted by mobs shouting 'Nero!' beneath the windows of Carlton House, the King retired to the Royal Lodge in Windsor Park, a move which heightened the feeling against him for, as Lord Liverpool said, he was condemned as 'a coward afraid of showing himself'.[47]

Before his departure he had sent messages to both the House of Commons and the House of Lords recommending to their 'immediate and serious' attention the contents of a certain green bag. This bag, soon to become a favourite subject of almost every caricaturist and lampoonist in London, contained the most important of the Milan Commission's papers. The King trusted that, having examined these papers, Parliament would 'adopt that course of proceedings which the justice of the case, and the honour and dignity of His Majesty's crown' required.

A Secret Committee of the House of Lords was accordingly appointed to study the documents in the green bag; and in due course this Committee, which included the Archbishop of Canterbury, the Lord Chancellor and various other members of the Cabinet, came to the conclusion that the papers, containing as they did allegations 'of the most licentious' conduct on the part of the Queen, regrettably called for 'a solemn enquiry'.

Since Pergami was Italian and not subject to English law, and since the alleged offences had not taken place in England, it was impossible to institute a trial for high treason which would have otherwise been the appropriate procedure. It was therefore considered necessary to introduce a Bill of Pains and Penalties, a parliamentary method of punishing a person without resort to a trial in a court of law. The Bill, which was technically a private Bill, the Law Officers acting for an unnamed person whom everyone knew to be the King, was read for the first time in the House of Lords on 5 July. It accused the Queen of having conducted herself towards Bartolommeo Pergami with 'indecent and offensive familiarity and freedom', and of having carried on 'a licentious, disgraceful, and adulterous intercourse' with him; it sought to 'deprive her Majesty Caroline Amelia Elizabeth of the title, prerogatives, rights, privileges, and pretensions of Queen Consort of this realm, and to dissolve the marriage between his Majesty and the said Queen'.

Rather than proceed to these lengths, and to the scandal of a public enquiry, Members of both Houses endeavoured to arrange a settlement. Brougham and Denman, representing the Queen, and Wellington and

Castlereagh, on behalf of the King, met to discuss this possibility; but from the outset their talks had been unpromising: the Queen – 'the most impudent devil that ever existed', in Wellington's opinion[48] – had been insistent that her name should be restored to the Liturgy, and on this point, as Castlereagh remarked, the King 'was immovable as Carlton House itself'.[49] Eventually a deputation from Parliament, led by William Wilberforce, who sympathized with both the King and the Queen, had begged her Majesty to yield, on the understanding that she did so not because she feared the results of a public enquiry, but because she had the interests of the country at heart. She had agreed to consider this petition, yet on 24 June – influenced by Wood, so Denman thought – she had rejected it, to the evident satisfaction of the mob who abused Wilberforce as 'Dr Cantwill' for ever having put it forward.[50]

As they waited for the public enquiry to begin, people throughout the country lost no opportunity of displaying where their sympathies lay, toasting the Queen in taverns and ale-houses with such vigorous thumping on the tables that half the glasses were smashed.[51] An exhibition – 'through the channel of optical illusions' – of 'the grandest display of LIKENESS OF EMINENT CHARACTERS (forty in number) ever introduced to the public' went on show in various towns and was an immense success. King George the Third – 'God bless him!' – was the first figure displayed, 'accompanied by a figure of Fame'. He was followed by 'a small full length study of his present Majesty', preceded by 'Henry 8th of England, whose Queen he caused to be beheaded', and succeeded by 'Witch of Endor'. Then came 'Her Present Most Gracious Majesty QUEEN CAROLINE; God bless her!!!'; and she in turn was followed by 'an Italian Female Wretch, an Accuser of the Innocent Queen Caroline', 'No friend to the Queen – THE POPE!!', 'A Turkish Bribed Accuser of Royal Female Innocence', and various other villains intent upon her destruction. A fine finale included 'The SPIRIT of the basely persecuted, innocent, injured Queen Caroline, ascending in glory to Heaven for PROTECTION!!', 'The Angel of Innocence', 'A heavenly Messenger', 'Mr Brougham', and, last of all Queen Caroline once more, this time 'magnanimously, gracefully, condescendingly saluting her good subjects'.

Although the Queen had her detractors in all classes and even in Whig families like the Hollands, where Lady Holland was very far from agreeing with her husband's support of her,[52] there were many more people in the country at large who shared Lord Holland's view rather than his wife's.

Even those who agreed with Byron that there was 'not the slightest doubt about the Queen and Bergami', agreed also with Brougham that after 'the treatment she had received ever since she came to England, her husband [had] no right to ... the punishment sought against her'.[53] As Cobbett put it, 'the people, as far as related to the question of guilt or innocence, did not care a straw'.[54] They were prepared to champion her anyway. 'The common people, and I fear the soldiers, are all in her favour and I believe the latter more than is owned,' Emily Cowper told her brother. 'As for her virtue, I don't think they care much about it, for tho they call her innocent, the Mob before her door have repeatedly called out "A cheer for Prince Austin".'[55] Lord Carlisle testified that 'the infatuation for the Queen prevails equally in the most secluded valleys of our moors as at Hampstead and Highgate';[56] and Sir James Mackintosh went so far as to say, 'All the world is with her'.[57] The 'military in London' were now showing more and more 'alarming symptoms of dissatisfaction', Charles Greville recorded, 'so much so' that it was doubtful how far even the Guards could be trusted. A battalion of the 3rd Guards refused to give up their ball cartridges when coming off duty and were hastily marched out of the capital. On their way through Brentford they were heard drunkenly crying out, 'God save the Queen!' Henry Luttrell said to Greville, 'The extinguisher is taking fire.'[58]

Sir Thomas Williams told Grey-Bennett that he, too, had heard the 3rd Guards shouting 'God save the Queen!' and 'The Queen for ever!' as they marched out of London. 'As usual all this was denied by the Government and the officers,' Grey-Bennett recorded in his diary; 'but it is true. ... Even the 10th Hussars, the King's Own Regiment showed ... a strong feeling of compassion for the Queen; and a person of credit told me that he walked into the Toy Tavern, Hampton Court, where the Regiment was quartered, and passing by the tap saw twelve or fourteen soldiers sitting in it, where, one of them taking up a pot of porter said, "Come, lads, the Queen!" when they all rose and drank her health.'[59]

Those who had known the Queen personally in the past had little doubt that she was guilty. Thomas Lawrence wrote of her 'daring profligacy',[60] and Scott of her 'shockingly irregular' conduct.[61] But these were views which most people thought it prudent not to express in public. Even in the King's stronghold of Brighton the manager of a theatre told Lord Darlington that he dared not permit the singing of 'God Save the King' any more for fear of provoking a riot;[62] and Brighton ladies were apt to say to each other, 'Well, if my husband had used me as hers has done, I should have thought myself entitled to act as she has done.'[63] Apart from the crowds at Ascot who always cheered the King when he drove to and from the races, it seemed to Croker that it was only a few 'people of fashion at the west end' of London who did not support the Queen against her husband, and they, like everyone else, talked of nothing else.[64] 'No other subject is ever talked of,' Charles Greville wrote. 'If you meet a man in the street, he immediately asks you, "Have you heard anything new about the Queen?" All people express themselves bored with the subject, yet none talk or think of any other. . . . Since I have been in the world I never remember any question which so exclusively occupied everybody's attention, and so completely absorbed men's thoughts.'[65]

An unprecedented number of caricatures and satirical pamphlets appeared in the shops and were sold in the streets. William Hone, George Cruikshank and a host of other satirists and artists championed the Queen and ridiculed the King; while only one printseller ventured to produce loyalist prints.[66] 'The most remarkable aspect of this fierce encounter', wrote Richard Rush, the American Minister in London, 'was the boundless rage of the Press and liberty of speech. Every day produced its thousand fiery libels against the King and his adherents, and as many caricatures, that were hawked in all the streets. This tempest of abuse . . . was borne for several months without the slightest attempt to check or punish it.'[67]*

* In fact, the King, excessively sensitive as he was to all forms of ridicule, made many attempts to check the abuse. William Hone claimed to have been offered 'up to £500' for the suppression of 'The Queen's Matrimonial Ladder', a pamphlet which depicted the King in the worst possible light (Rickword, *Radical Squibs and Loyal Ripostes*, 27). Certainly, through Bloomfield, the King bought up the plates and copyrights of particularly offensive prints, and obtained undertakings from artists and dealers not to publish anything else on the same subject. For example he paid George Cruikshank £100 'in consideration of a pledge not to caricature His Majesty in any immoral situation' (RA, 19 June 1820). When it became known that Carlton House was prepared to pay for the suppression of offensive caricatures, however, the number of them naturally increased. Moreover, the pledges were observed more in the letter than in the spirit (BM *Sat*, x, xii, xl–xlvii). Cruikshank's work for William Hone in 1821 displayed the King, if not in an 'immoral situation', as a water scorpion, 'an offensive insect' living 'in stagnant waters, continually watching for prey' and sallying forth 'in search of a companion of the other sex and soon [begetting] an useless generation' (*The Political Showman – at Home!*).

On 17 August the public enquiry began in the House of Lords. The Queen, who had for convenience taken Lady Francis's house in St James's Square, near to Castlereagh's, 'presented herself at the window' in response to the shouts of 'The Queen! The Queen!' from the people in the Square. 'Her appearance called forth from the surrounding multitude the most unbounded marks of applause,' *The Times* reported. 'A short interval only had repassed before the multitude again expressed their wish to see her.' She willingly responded to the calls and appeared once more 'with her wonted dignity'.[68] Soon afterwards she left for the House of Lords in a state carriage drawn by six bays, attended by liveried footmen, cheered by shouts of 'God bless you!' and by protestations of loyalty unto death. 'Alderman Wood preceded her in a carriage and four horses,' the Duke of Wellington noted, 'and his carriage was preceded by a fellow on horseback carrying a *Green Bag*!'[69]

The crowds in the Square that morning and on each subsequent day of the 'trial' – as most people referred to the proceedings in the House – were both noisy and immense. People clambered onto the roofs of carriages and rented standing room in carters' wagons for a shilling a day to catch a glimpse of the Queen as her postilions whipped the horses out of the Square, down King Street, into Pall Mall, and past Carlton House where, to the delight of the mob, the guard presented arms.[70] She was not an appealing sight, though *The Times* loyally reported her as looking 'extremely well': she had grown very fat during her years of exile, and she wore more rouge than ever upon her naturally ruddy cheeks. Her eyebrows were painted black, and long black curls hung down on either side of her face from her wig. Observers noticed that she had taken to adopting a stern and resolute expression which suited her as ill as her favourite hat, a huge, high-crowned black concoction, banded and bowed, and surmounted by an enormous spray of ostrich feathers. In the House she wisely set this hat aside in favour of a big white veil which almost concealed her face and, falling down from her shoulders, disguised the true proportions of the ample bosom in the bodice of her black dress.

As she entered the chamber of the House, where temporary balconies had been erected above the benches to accommodate the great number of Members who were present, all the peers stood up. Attendance was compulsory except for Roman Catholics, minors, invalids and those peers who were either absent from the country or who could satisfy the Lord Chancellor that a family bereavement entitled them to leave of absence. Despite the recent death of his Duchess, the Duke of York was there, insisting that he would be 'ashamed' not to be present to do his duty, 'painful as it might be'. His brother, the Duke of Sussex, however, evaded the likelihood of his giving further offence to his brother by failing to condemn the conduct of his cousin, and excused himself from attendance on the grounds of his consanguinity to them both.

The proceedings were opened by the Duke of Leinster who rose 'and said in a purely Irish tone that, without making any elaborate speech, and for the purpose of bringing his business to a conclusion, he should move' that the order for the second reading of the Bill of Pains and Penalties should be rescinded. Only forty-one peers out of the 247 present agreed with him, and even these, nearly all of them Whigs, mostly voted so not out of any conviction as to the Queen's innocence but as a protest against the government's ineptitude in endeavouring to prove her guilt. A majority of the leading Whig peers, including Lansdowne, Derby, Spencer, Erskine, Grey and Fox's lifelong friend, Fitzwilliam, voted against Leinster's motion; and subsequently Grey, the most influential of these – presumably in the hope that the Queen might be encouraged to negotiate if made to stand trial on such a charge – asked for a legal opinion as to whether the Queen might be held guilty of high treason notwithstanding the circumstances of her alleged adultery. After a brief deliberation the judges declared that 'there was no statute law or law of the land touching the Queen's case', and so the way now lay open for Brougham to contend that the Bill of Pains and Penalties was quite as repugnant as a trial for high treason.

Within the past few weeks, Brougham had had no reason to change his private opinion that his client, whom he found increasingly dislikable, was guilty; and the Queen seemed to suspect this. Certainly she did not trust him. He had been to see her upon the evening of her return to London, and he had not impressed her with any confidence in his ability to prove her innocence. After he had left her, she had commented disapprovingly to Denman, who still doubted that she was guilty, 'He is afraid.'[71] She tried to persuade Sir James Scarlett, reputedly the best advocate in England, to join her list of counsel; but Scarlett tactfully declined her offer.

Whatever Brougham's apprehensions may have been, however, and despite the disparaging way in which he talked about her outside the House – 'she is pure *in-no-sense*,' he said when asked his opinion of her in private[72] – as her Attorney-General before the Lords, he performed his task brilliantly. Even Mme de Lieven – whose sense of propriety was offended by a 'little attorney', a mere lawyer 'sprung from the lowest ranks of society', presuming to ridicule the government – had to admit that he had an 'astonishing facility'.[73] His opening speech was generally considered a masterpiece. There were those, even amongst dedicated Whigs at Brooks's, who thought that it was rather tasteless at such a time to suggest that a Bill of Pains and Penalties ought to have been brought against the Duke of York in consequence of his adultery with Mrs Clarke eleven years before; and there were others who regretted his oblique references to the King's own 'criminal intercourse'; but most of those who heard his speech 'allowed it to have been excellent'.[74] Lord Fitzwilliam deemed it 'a most strong and powerful speech', though he wondered whether, 'its object being to deprecate any proceedings', it did not carry too much 'the appearance of fearing enquiry'.[75]

Fitzwilliam also thought the speech of the Queen's Solicitor-General, Thomas Denman, who supported Brougham the next day, was equally excellent, 'indeed it was even better', and this in spite of the fact that Denman was suffering from jaundice. It was, in fact, as 'argumentative, impressive and convincing' as could be; 'it made a deep impression on the *whole* House'. Such, in Fitzwilliam's opinion, could not be said of the speeches of either the Attorney-General, Sir Robert Gifford, a plain, shrewd, practical West Countryman, or of the Solicitor-General, John Singleton Copley, the convivial son of the American portrait painter. Indeed, Gifford's speech struck Fitzwilliam as no better than 'a sort of scold', while Copley's was 'a display of theatrical eloquence' which 'produced little effect'.[76]

Fitzwilliam was, of course, listening to the speeches as a confirmed Whig, and his comments did justice neither to Gifford's sound common sense, nor to Copley's effective replies to the Queen's Counsel's eloquent jibes against the King and the royal dukes. But there was no doubt that many supporters of the government as well as most of its Whig opponents agreed with Creevey who wrote from Brooks's on the evening of 18 August, 'The truth is the Law Officers of the Crown are damnably overweighted by Brougham and Denman. . . . Nothing can be more triumphant for the Queen than this day altogether.'[77]

The Queen was clearly enjoying to the full her initial triumphs and growing popularity, although the long legal arguments in the House naturally bored her. In the early days of the proceedings she attended quite regularly, sitting on the special chair provided for her within the bar of the House, accompanied by Lady Anne Hamilton who was wearing the thickest and heaviest of veils. But she soon took to spending the greater part of her time in the retiring room which had been provided for her, a room normally reserved for the chairman of committees, where she played backgammon with Alderman Wood. Once she was observed in the House to fall asleep which led to this epigram by Lord Holland:

> Her conduct at present no censure affords
> She sins not with couriers but sleeps with the Lords.[78]*

While she had been staying at Hammersmith, loyal addresses, presented to her by delegations of earnest supporters, had poured into Brandenburg House from all over the country, from Bath and Bristol, from Nottingham and Norwich, from Leeds and Liverpool; and she replied to them all, under the guidance of Alderman Wood, William Cobbett, and her other advisers, in terms calculated to encourage her admirers to further demonstrations in her support. Now that her trial had begun, she was more popular than ever. Creevey was astonished by the numbers of people who came out into the streets to watch her pass by; where the devil they all came from he could not imagine; by 19 August they were 'prodigiously encreased since the first day'.[79] Mme de Lieven estimated that there were twenty or thirty thousand of them, all of them radicals.[80]

They greeted Ministers with cat-calls and abuse. Wellington was hissed and booed with exceptional vehemence as he rode his horse through the gap in the fence that had been erected around the approaches to the House.[81] 'They look upon him particularly as the Queen's enemy,' Emily Cowper observed. 'I suppose they think he is against everybody's wife as well as his own.'[82] One day upon his return to Apsley House a gang of roadmenders stopped his horse in Grosvenor Place and demanded that he repeat, 'God Save the Queen!' 'Well gentlemen,' he – or some reports say the equally abused Lord Anglesey, or Lord Londonderry or Theodore Hook – replied with characteristic aplomb, 'since you will have it

---

* She was, of course, irresistible as a butt for such jokes. Lord Norbury, when asked how she had enjoyed herself in Algiers replied, 'She was as happy as the Dey was long'. When someone wondered what newspaper she read, Norbury said that she 'took in the Courier' (*Greville Diary*, i, 115).

so, God save the Queen – and may all your wives be like her.'⁸³ Castlereagh
felt obliged to board up his house in St James's Square and to have his bed
installed in the Foreign Office.⁸⁴ Mme de Lieven told Metternich that
curiosity induced her to drive towards the House where the crowds stopped
her, told her to shout the by now obligatory formula, 'Long live the Queen!'
and ordered her servants to take off their hats. 'I was in an open carriage,'
she wrote. 'My heart beat quickly for a moment; but I put a bold face on it
and I did not shout. I had forbidden my servants to take off their hats. The
Russian cockade, which has three colours, gave me a certain constitutional
look, which was a good thing in the circumstances. A smart touch of the
whip set the horses bounding, and I got out of it. . . . Five men were killed
by the soldiers the day before yesterday in front of the Houses of Parliament.
The newspapers say nothing of this; for the Jacobin papers do not want
the occurrence, should it become known, to discourage the mob from
going to the House, and the Ministerial papers themselves are not
anxious to boast about it. The Duke of York told me about it yesterday;
he had got it from the military reports. The Duke is the idol of the mob;
they are all for the Queen and for him. He frowns and does not bow,
because they cheer him by the title of King.'⁸⁵* Fitzwilliam confirmed
that the Duke's popularity had never been higher. He was 'huzzaed
every step he took'.⁸⁶ So, too, with quite as much enthusiasm, was the
Duke of Sussex.⁸⁷ While squads of soldiers on parade had been heard to
shout to the Duke of Gloucester, 'You ought to be our King!'⁸⁸

Vigorous support for the Queen was now far from being limited to the
'radicals', 'mechanicks', 'artisans' and 'hooligans' whom most observers
described as constituting the greater part of the mob that surged around

* According to Emily Cowper, however, the Duke of York was delighted by his
reception. She told her brother, Frederick Lamb, 'He is so pleased at [the calls of]
"Long live Frederick the 1st" – he bows and bows and rides along with his hat in his
hand. I was told the scene was droll yesterday at leaving the House. The Duke of
Richmond came out with Anglesey but managed to shrink back before they reached
the barrier in Palace Yard. The Duke of York was setting off from the House; the
Duke of Wellington hurried after him to go through the mob in his company. The
Duke of York, unwilling to lose his cheers, spurred his horse to avoid his joining him –
so much for the little vanities of mankind! . . . The Duke of Wellington and Anglesey
are violently hissed which makes them very angry. The latter made a speech yesterday
to the mob, saying if all their mouths were bayonets planted at his heart he should do
his duty. This got him a few cheers which I hope will not last, it would make him so
elated' (Palmerston Papers, CIV/4/3, 24 August 1820).

the Houses of Parliament. Thomas Babington Macaulay, then a Cambridge undergraduate, was a passionate Queenite; so, too, to almost wild excess, was General Sir Robert Wilson; so was Coleridge. Byron too, though much less vehemently, continued to hope that the Queen would win, for she had always been 'very civil' to him. Lady Jersey, of course, was 'absolutely in a raging fever', 'quite frenzied', so 'violent' that she was 'at daggers drawn even with the Holland family' and inveighed 'bitterly against the moderate tone adopted by Lord Grey'.[89]

*

Nobody could have been more displeased than Lady Jersey by the proceedings in the House of Lords on the day that the first witness, Teodoro Majocchi, gave his evidence. Majocchi was a respectable-looking, well-dressed man – 'very shrewd and cautious', Lord Fitzwilliam thought – and his damning account of the Queen's behaviour caused the deepest dismay to her friends. The Queen herself, indeed, as though only too well aware of the effect that his evidence would have, rose to her feet 'with the rapidity of lightening' at the sight of him, raised her veil, and looking fiercely at him as she took a few steps towards him, cried out in a furious tone of voice something that sounded like 'Theodore! Theodore! Oh, no! no!' Others thought that she screamed 'Traditore! Traditore! Oh, no! no!' But George Keppel, who was close to her, could not distinguish any words at all. The exclamation seemed to him 'a paroxysm of madness'.[90] Having made her frenzied objection, whatever it was, she then rushed out of the chamber; she was taken so ill that night that she had to be 'copiously bled'.*

'She was thunderstruck at seeing him,' Mme de Lieven commented. 'It made a very bad impression. She explains it as a start of indignation, at the sight of a witness on whose gratitude she thought she could count. But nobody is deceived about the cause of the start. . . . Lord Liverpool immediately sent a messenger to inform the King, treating "Oh Theodore" as a fact of the greatest importance. . . . I have not had the heart to read

---

* Enquiries conducted by the Milan Commission had satisfied its members that Majocchi was 'honest' and 'trustworthy' (RA Geo IV, Box 8, Envelope 8). A letter addressed to the Queen after her death and purporting to be a confession that he had accepted a bribe of '£1,000 English money' to swear falsely against her, a crime for which he was now 'artely sorry', is an obvious forgery (RA Geo IV, Box 11, 8 November 1821).

the evidence; it is too disgusting. Is the Queen really a woman? And how can the House of Lords, uniting as it does all that is most dignified and most exalted in the greatest nation in the world, lower itself by listening to such vile trash? Was there no other way of treating her as she deserves? Worst of all, how could statesmen have allowed things to come to such a pass? One of the Queen's lawyers put the trial in a nutshell when he called it a solemn farce.... At Lady Jersey's ... I heard [Brougham] say of some fantastic action ascribed to the Queen: "I can believe in any folly on the part of that woman. We know quite well she is capable of it." ... I am certain [the Bill] will not be passed. Anyway, the Queen is quite mad, and what surprises me is that they don't question the witnesses about that, or at least ask her doctor. If they pronounced her mad they would avoid all this scandal and be nearer the truth besides.'[91]

Two of Brougham's fellow-counsel, Nicholas Tindal and Thomas Wilde, were so disturbed by Majocchi's evidence about the Queen's visits to Pergami's bedroom, her kissing him, his helping her with her bath and the sleeping arrangements aboard the polacca that they both woke him up in the middle of the night to offer him their advice as to his conduct of the man's cross-examination the next day. They need not have troubled. Brougham was a brilliant cross-examiner, and his treatment of Majocchi was masterly. By the time he had finished with him, the poor man was so muddled, nervous and unconvincing – 'frightened out of his wits', according to one report – that he seemed capable of giving no other answer than 'I do not remember' to every question that Brougham asked him. *'Questo non mi ricordo.' 'Non mi ricordo.' 'Questo non mi ricordo.' 'Non mi ricordo', 'Non mi ricordo.'* The answer became a kind of refrain. In the printed record of Majocchi's cross-examination it occurs eighty-seven times. For months afterwards the phrase, *Non mi ricordo*, was just as popular with satirists and caption-writers as ever the green bag had been with caricaturists; and even in mid-Victorian London it was a catchphrase that had not lost its peculiar meaning.

The principal witnesses who immediately followed Majocchi – Gaetano Paturzo, the mate of the vessel on which the Queen had sailed to the Holy Land; Vincenzo Gargiullo the vessel's master; Meidge Barbara Kress, a chambermaid at one of the inns where the Queen had stayed on her travels; Paolo Raggazoni, a master mason at Villa d'Este; and Paolo Oggioni, a kitchen help – all provided the Lords with much of the evidence that they had given the Milan Commission, and were, as Lord

Fitzwilliam noted, not unduly damaged in cross-examination. Fitzwilliam was convinced that unless the evidence so far given could be contradicted, 'the inference must be adultery'.[92] Lady Cowper thought so too. On 24 August, after the Lords had heard the evidence of Gaetano Paturzo – 'a very good witness' whom '*every* body' thought 'fair and honest and above board' – she decided that the Queen's friends had 'no leg left to stand on'.[93]

After the Italian sailors had been cross-examined, an English naval officer, Thomas Briggs, whose evidence carried more weight with most Members than all the Italians put together, testified that he had taken the Queen from Genoa to Sicily aboard the *Leviathan*, and that she had altered the sleeping arrangements which he had made so that Pergami was provided with a cabin near her own. Briggs's evidence also remained largely undisturbed by the various questions that were put to him.*

When it came to the turn of Louisa Demont, however, the case was quite different. Her examination by the Solicitor-General was convincing enough: she repeated most of her stories about the Queen and Pergami and their presumed love-making, the Queen's abandoned behaviour, and her prurient enjoyment of Pergami's obscene anecdotes. She raised the 'strongest suspicions', so Lord Fitzwilliam told his son, and 'proved the undeniable opportunities for adultery'. But when she was cross-examined by one of Brougham's colleagues, John Williams, her replies were almost as evasive as Majocchi's; one of them, often repeated, was, 'I will not swear it, but I do not recollect it.' It was suggested to her, for instance, that while she was living in London she had passed herself off as Countess Colombiera or Colombrère, which certainly seems to have been the case.[94] But she could not swear to that; she did not recollect it. She did admit, however, that she had been dismissed from the Queen's service for 'saying something about her' – that she was in love with Giuseppi Sacchi – which she afterwards 'confessed to be false'. It also appeared that, after her dismissal, she had written to the Queen asking for 'that

* In a conversation with Admiral Lord Keith in 1818, Captain Briggs had said that the Princess had objected to his arrangement of the cabins with the words, 'You are a very good captain of a ship but do not understand ladies.' Having rearranged the accommodation so that Pergami's cabin was next to her own, she spent much of the day with him, and, for all Briggs knew, the night as well. He begged Lord Keith not to let his conversation with him go any further; but Keith felt he could not withhold it from Bloomfield to whom he communicated these 'facts so extraordinary' (RA Geo IV, Box 8, 13 April 1818).

forgiveness which alone [could] restore [her] to life', and that she had also written to her half-sister, who was still in the Queen's service, in praise of her Majesty's virtues. When asked if she had used such phrases as 'august Princess' and 'generous benefactress' which were contained in these letters, she replied, again, 'I will not swear because I am not sure of it . . . I do not recollect whether I have made use of them; I wrote frequently to my sister; and I do not recollect the expressions.' She was also unable to say with any certainty that the handwriting was hers.

Thomas Creevey was delighted by this evidence from the *chienne* Demont who was 'fifty times nearer the devil' on the second day of her cross-examination than she had been on the first; she had turned out to be everything that one could have wished for; it was all 'most infernally damaging for the prosecution'.

The witnesses who followed Mlle Demont, however, were far more damaging to the Queen than to the prosecution. There was a mason to tell of his seeing Pergami sitting with his arm round the Queen when she was bare to the waist; there was a gardener to tell of their kissing; there was Sacchi to swear what he had seen the Queen and Pergami doing behind the curtains of their carriage. There was, in fact, as Creevey was forced to conclude with regret on the evening of 4 September, after eleven witnesses had been examined in a single day, 'much *dirt* and some *damage* certainly'.

A good deal of further damage was promised by the Attorney-General when the next batch of his witnesses arrived; but on 7 September he felt obliged to close his evidence as there was strong doubt that they ever would arrive. Terrified by reports of what had happened to previous witnesses on their landing at Dover, they had refused to continue their journey beyond Beauvais and had scurried back to Italy where reports of the 'Dover massacre' were spread far and wide by the Pergami family and their friends. It was said that Italians had been set upon and severely wounded by the wild Englishmen of Dover, that Sacchi had been assassinated, Demont imprisoned for life, and that Queen Caroline, now placed upon the throne, had given orders for the arrest of all those who had given evidence against her.[95]

It was true that witnesses against the Queen had been abused by the people of Dover and that some of them had been stoned on the road; yet this had been interpreted in Italy, so Colonel Browne complained, 'as the decided execration of a whole nation'.[96] The King's advisers had therefore considered it necessary to ask Giuseppe Rastelli, the Milan Commission's courier, to return to Italy to assure the worried families of the witnesses that no harm would come to them in England. His efforts had not so far been successful.

Among the witnesses who refused to go to England was one who might well have proved to be the most damaging of all. This was Jacinto Greco, a Calabrian who had worked as cook in the Princess's household during her stay in Sicily. According to a former employer, interviewed by the Milan Commission, he had an 'excellent character'; and one Innocenza Biancha, 'a most respectable merchant of Syracuse', also spoke very highly of him.

In the statement he gave to the Commission, Greco claimed to have seen the Princess and Pergami *in flagrante delicto* on a sofa in the saloon of their Sicilian palazzo.[97] But when asked to go to England to repeat this story Greco firmly refused. His wife had been told that if he did so his head would be cut off by the English mob, and he appeared to believe it. In no circumstances was he prepared to leave Italy.[98]

12

'The Queen For Ever!'

1820

*

'The town is literally drunk with joy'

While Rastelli was endeavouring to persuade the reluctant witnesses to return with him to England, the Queen's agents in Italy were busily trying to collect evidence with which to refute their testimony. These agents had found several people willing to testify to the effect that they had seen nothing in the Queen's behaviour to suggest impropriety; but one of the agents, Samuel Fyson, was 'very worried', so he confessed to the Queen's solicitor, Henry Vizard, about the witnesses' 'quality'. Most of them were no more credible than the worst of the witnesses that the King's agents had managed to produce. The prosecution had got up their evidence 'badly', but he feared that the defence's would be '*worse*'. Nor did Fyson think that his colleague, Jabez Henry, had examined the witnesses carefully enough. Admittedly everything had had to be done in a great hurry, as so little time had been allowed for the preparation of the defence, but Henry had made only the briefest enquiries into the characters of the people whom he had examined and passed as suitable candidates to stand as witnesses. Worse than this, he had paid out huge sums of money which the prosecution, if they discovered them, could easily represent as bribes. There had been much talk of bribes being offered to prosecution witnesses; but the defence were much more open to criticism on that head. 'It is undoubtedly necessary sometimes to bribe a man (if I may use that term) to leave his country,' Tyson concluded in his frank letter to Vizard. 'But I hear of very large sums having been given and I dread the exposure.'[1]

In fact, the King's agents were well aware of the large sums being offered to potential defence witnesses. £10,000 had been made available to Vizard by the Treasury;[2] and a further £20,000 was paid to him in December 1820.[3] But it was believed that the Queen's friends had many other sources of supply. Colonel Browne reported to Powell that 1,600 louis d'or had been offered to Cardinal Albani by Torlonia, the Roman banker, to persuade him to go to England to speak for the Queen. 'There is some *strong secret fund* at work somewhere or another,' Powell believed. Money was being 'thrown about in abundance'.[4] Jabez Henry was living in an apartment costing fifty louis d'or a month, and his courtyard was constantly full of servants, agents and couriers. Despite this he had not 'so far got any persons except bad characters to agree to give evidence in England', Browne reported to Joseph Planta, an official at the Foreign Office, 'a bad lot, of the same class as ours. . . . I fear however that they will make much use of certain difficulties still thrown in their way as to passports, vexations to us in fact and not to them.'[5]*

James Brougham (who was himself paid £2,500 for his expenses while in Italy)[6] agreed that Jabez Henry was paying too much to too many witnesses. 'I did all in my power to prevent this new shoal of witnesses from being sent,' he reported to Vizard on 28 October, 'but the fear of displeasing the Queen who asked them to go operated on Mr Henry's mind as to let them. . . . They are totally useless. . . . Allow me to hint to you privately that Pergami has been spending money among people of no earthly use at Pesaro.'[7] One of these people, in particular, was a woman of notorious character, and what on earth was the good of having a 'woman from Italy speaking to character when she herself is the very worst in every way?' Moreover, his brother had 'very strongly impressed upon him' the danger of there being any imputation of bribery. 'He says nothing could be more fatal to the defence than its coming out that the slightest bribery had been employed,' Brougham warned Jabez Henry, 'and both

---

* As soon as the government heard of these complaints by the Queen's agents and of 'the obstacles interposed in Italy to the departure of witnesses', Castlereagh wrote to Lord Stewart, British Ambassador in Vienna: 'I lose no time in representing to Prince Metternich the propriety and indeed the necessity of regarding every application which Mr Henry, Her Majesty's acknowledged law agent, may have made or may make to the Austrian Government in the same light and in the same force as if it were made by Mr Brougham or by the Queen herself: His Majesty's Government being extremely anxious that every possible facility should be afforded to Her Majesty for procuring all the evidence she may think necessary during the progress of these proceedings' (RA Geo IV, Boxes 11, 11 September 1820 and 13, 15 September 1820).

Pergami and his brother may from unwise zeal have done this – caution them for the future. . . . I need not say that bribing people to keep away from the other side is equally bad. This cannot be too strongly impressed on all concerned.'[8]

Undeterred by criticism, Jabez Henry continued to assemble his 'shoals of witnesses' in accordance with the Queen's instructions. He got former servants of hers to depose that they had never seen the Queen and Pergami in each other's arms, that they had never observed any familiarity in the Queen's bedroom nor any indecent behaviour at the Queen's balls, that the mulatto servant was thrown out of the room when he began his obscene dance, that the Queen and Pergami never sat next to each other in her carriage but always face to face. Jabez Henry found fishermen and gardeners, carpenters and masons who were all prepared to swear that, so far as they had been able to observe, the Queen was – as Thomas Denman, in his opening address, had said she was – 'as pure as unsunned snow'. Giovanni Battista dell' Orto, a young man of twenty-two, living with his father, a baker, provided this characteristic testimony: 'Without hope of gain he is ready to prove: That going two or three times a day (being the baker's son) to her Majesty's Palace [at Como] he never saw anything that would injure her reputation, but she was always dignified in her manner and decently dressed, whether walking, riding on a donkey or in her carriage.'[9]

But James Brougham had to confess that he was not in the least convinced by all these witnesses. 'The more I have examined the case,' he reported to Vizard, 'the less I think our answer to it will depend on any evidence we can hope to have even if one had a year – but it is very strong indeed on theirs.'[10]

It was all very well for Lady Charlotte Lindsay's brother, Lord Guildford, who had seen a good deal of the Queen when she first arrived in Italy, to say that there was 'nothing unusual' in the behaviour of the Queen towards Pergami, 'except the advancement of the individual'.[11] For there were quite as many English witnesses who said exactly the opposite, Lord de Clifford and Lady Clavering amongst them.[12] And it was all very well for the Queen's agents to produce men who claimed that attempts had been made to bribe them to give evidence against her.[13] For there was just as much evidence on the other side – most of it equally unreliable – purporting to show that attempts had been made to bribe witnesses in the Queen's defence.[14]

Admittedly the Queen's representatives were constantly receiving letters disparaging the prosecution witnesses. One William Hughes, a bank clerk in Gloucester, who had known Teodoro Majocchi when he had been in service there, wrote to say that Majocchi had always maintained that the Queen was 'most respectable'. A certain Harvey Warburton informed Vizard that both the Captain and mate of the polacca were 'well known for their roguery to the House of Claude Scott', importers of grain; and Captain Gargiullo's roguery was confirmed in a letter to Alderman Wood by Benedetto Salomone, a former captain in the Italian legion.[15] But then, the King's representatives received quite as many letters in disparagement of the defence witnesses, and many more from people who claimed to be able to prove the Queen's 'indecent familiarity' or 'disgraceful intimacy' with Pergami, yet did not wish to come forward in person 'in the present state of public feeling'.[16]

James Brougham was particularly disillusioned with Pergami. Far from being the *'remarkably good sort of man'* he had at first supposed him to be, he was, in fact, 'a very great liar', almost as bad as his brother, Louis, who was 'the greatest rascal unhung'.[17] Both Samuel Fyson and Jabez Henry were inclined to agree with this estimate. Fyson advised Vizard that Pergami was certainly 'not a *gentleman*' who ought to be produced as a witness: 'He is naturally of a hasty and thoughtless disposition, at the same time that he is extremely impatient. In several instances he has made statements inconsistent with what have proved to be the facts . . . I should not be inclined to make him a witness unless it became indispensably necessary. . . . He is loose-headed and impetuous and would certainly lose his temper.' As for his brother 'his *very looks* would damn the whole family'.[18]

❋

Assured by the blithely confident Jabez Henry that the witnesses he was so cursorily examining were going to 'expose the machinations' of her enemies, the Queen remained the heroine of the London mob, who raced after her every morning as she drove to the House, shouting for joy when 'she directed the barouche to be thrown open' so that they could see her better.[19] The evidence presented in the Lords had not in the least diminished her popularity,[20] although, as Lord Liverpool confided to Canning, the case as now proved against her was in 'certainty a very strong one'.[21]

On the day that the Attorney-General had closed his evidence for the prosecution, she sailed triumphantly down the Thames in her state barge. Lord Erskine, who watched the procession from Blackfriars Bridge, estimated that as many as 200,000 people had collected to see her. There was not a single vessel in the river that did not hoist its colours and man its yards in her honour; and the watermen, who were 'all her partisans', were with the greatest difficulty prevented from destroying the hulk which had been anchored near Parliament Stairs as an added protection for the Italian witnesses who had been herded together for their safety in a guarded house in Cotton Garden.[22]

A few days later, while writing a letter to Miss Ord at Brooks's, Thomas Creevey heard 'a noise of hurraing and shouting in the street'. He 'ran out to see the *Navy of England* marching to Brandenburgh House with an address to the Queen'. 'I have seen nothing like this before – nothing approaching to it,' he continued. 'There were thousands of seamen, all well dressed, all sober – the best looking, the finest men you could imagine. Every man had a new white silk or satin cockade in his hat. They had a hundred colours, at least, or pieces of silk, with sentiments upon them such as "Protection to the Innocent".'[23]

Soon after this the Queen 'received eleven more addresses, accompanied in each case by a deputation of several thousand people carrying banners with the most subversive inscription', Mme de Lieven recorded. 'With all one hears and reads, it is difficult to believe that there are still a King and a Government in this country. Just now, as I was passing by our stables, I read, written in large letters on the wall: "The Queen for ever, the King in the river!" All the walls in town are scrawled over with nice things of this kind. I can't tell you what horrible faces one sees nowadays in the streets and the main roads and how insolently they come up and bawl in one's ears, "The Queen for ever!"'[24] But, as Creevey said, it was not only the poorer classes who demonstrated their support of the Queen and their antagonism towards the Bill: 'The entire middle order of people are against it.'[25] Indeed her cause was warmly adopted by everyone who was in opposition to the King and the government. 'Well, Robinson, you are a Queenite, I hope?' Coleridge asked his friend, Henry Crabb Robinson. 'Indeed, I am not,' Robinson replied. 'How is that possible?' 'I am only an anti-Kingite.' 'That's just what I mean.'[26] 'There is no denying it, the feeling of the people is almost everywhere in favour of the Queen,' Lady Cowper confirmed, 'not merely the rabble, but the respectable middle ranks. All their prejudices are in her favour. They hate the King, disapprove of his moral conduct and think all foreigners are liars and villains.'[27]

As though intoxicated by the partisan adulation accorded her and by the prospects before her, the Queen became more and more provocative in her declarations and in her answers to the addresses that came pouring into Brandenburg House. She was 'as full of revenge as careless of crime', Plumer Ward was assured; she was going the way of Catherine the Great, a favourite heroine of hers, who 'by means of the Guards, murdered her husband and usurped the throne'.[28] She herself announced that that was her exact intention. By God, she said, she 'would blow him off his throne'.[29] It was a possibility that Henry Brougham, for one, did not consider at all unlikely.

*

Brougham opened his defence on 3 October with a speech which Creevey concluded was 'a most magnificent address, nothing but perfection', and which Charles Greville thought 'the most magnificent display of argument and oratory that had been heard for years'.[30] It does not read so well now: its rhetoric seems strained, its sincerity suspect, but there was no doubt of its success with his contemporaries. Lord Fitzwilliam, for one, was convinced that Brougham had 'shewn incontestibly' that 'one and all of the Italian witnesses' were perjured.[31] 'The *monde* at Brooks's talked of nothing but Brougham and his fame, and the comers-in from White's said the same feeling was equally strong there.' His speech had 'not only astonished', but had 'shaken the aristocracy'.[32] Denman considered it 'one of the most powerful orations that ever proceeded from human lips'.[33] Lord Erskine was so overcome by it that he burst into tears.[34]

Brougham's initial triumph was somewhat overcast, however, when his witnesses appeared. Lord Guildford, the first of these, struck Creevey as 'the most ramshackle fellow you ever saw', 'a kind of *non mi ricordo* likewise'; the next was that boring old gossip, Lord Glenbervie; the third was Lady Charlotte Lindsay. The evidence of both Glenbervie and Lady Charlotte was favourable enough, but neither was able to convey any personal affection for the Queen whom – as their diaries made clear when published years later – they did not, in fact, much like. On examination, Lady Charlotte was obliged to disclose that she had spent no more than twenty-four days with the Queen at the beginning of her stay in Italy;

and on cross-examination by the Solicitor-General, who used her, in Lord Fitzwilliam's words, as he would 'a shoplifter at the Old Bailey',[35] she admitted that she might have said that she would have quitted the Queen's service far sooner even than this had she not badly needed the salary. Eventually she burst into tears. The King protested that he never thought he 'should have lived to witness so much prevarication, so much lying, and so much wilful and convenient forgetfulness' as Lady Charlotte had displayed in her examination.[36] And it is certainly true that her evidence gave a very different impression from the private letters she wrote home when on the Continent.[37]

The next witnesses, however, were much more confident and convincing than these early ones. Keppel Craven was 'as distinct and favourable as possible', Sir William Gell 'still more so'. Indeed, by the time Gell stood down, having sworn that upon his honour he never once saw the Queen speak to Pergami except on matters of business in all the three months he spent with them, Lord Fitzwilliam felt bound to conclude that he did not see how Ministers could now proceed with the Bill. 'But if they do, and carry it through the House of Lords,' he told his son, Lord Milton, in one of a long series of letters which were written regularly throughout the proceedings and which accurately reflect the almost daily changes of mood in the House, as witnesses came and went, contradicting each other, swaying opinion now this way, now that, 'I do seriously believe that they will pull down the House of Lords about our ears. In short the tenor of this day's evidence goes far to make me doubt of any crime: it is a foul conspiracy hatched under the wing of an ambitious lawyer, and brooded over by a wicked commission in Milan.'[38]

Fitzwilliam's fellow Whig, Thomas Creevey, agreed with him: 'Gell, cross-examined and examined by the Lords, left everything still more triumphant for the Queen; so much so that Pelham [a friend of the King and Bishop of Exeter] and a few other bishops are gone home to cut their throats. Lord Enniskillen has just said in my hearing that the Ministers ought to be damned for coming out with such a case.... The town is literally drunk with joy at this unparalleled triumph of the Queen. There is no doubt now in any man's mind, except Lauderdale's, that the whole thing has been a conspiracy for money.'[39]

The supporters of the Bill naturally took a different view. 'The opposition affect to consider the Bill as completely defeated,' Mrs Arbuthnot wrote, 'But *we*, on the contrary, feel that no real way has been made as the witnesses as yet have not contradicted any of ours. The Duke of Wellington called on me and told me he thought he had got a clue for exposing the perjuries of Sir William Gell who swore he had never seen any improper conduct in the Queen. The Duke had been sitting for our picture to Lawrence who told him that [Sir Thomas Freeman] Heathcote (the former member for Hampshire) had said that Sir William Gell's evidence was so disgraceful and so in direct opposition to the abusive language he had always held about the Queen that he for one, though a former friend, would never speak to him again.'[40]

By the evening of the next day it certainly appeared that the evidence given by Gell and Keppel Craven was far from reliable. The witness responsible for this change of feeling in the House was an Anglo-Irishman, Lieutenant Flynn RN, known to the Queen – never unduly concerned with the niceties of rank or nomenclature – as Captain Fling and Captain Flint.[41] Great store had been set by this man's evidence: as the Prime Minister told the King, if he should deny the facts to which the prosecution witnesses had deposed 'whether truly or falsely (provided it was done with constancy)' it would be impossible to answer for the consequences.

Lieutenant Flynn had been in command of the polacca of which Vincenzo Gargiullo had been the 'working' captain. He denied most of what Gargiullo and the mate had said, both about the tent on deck and the bath in the cabin; but in cross-examination he floundered so much – maintaining that, although he did not think Pergami slept under the tent with the Princess, he did not know where he did sleep – that it was difficult to credit any part of his evidence. At one point during his cross-examination Copley felt sure he was lying. He stared at him so hard that 'he fainted away and was taken out of court'.[42]

Flynn 'is mad', Creevey decided after this lamentable performance. 'He has perjured himself three or four times over, and his evidence and himself are both gone to the devil. He is evidently a crack-brained sailor.'[43]

'Undoubtedly the whole of his evidence' would have to be thrown overboard, Fitzwilliam told his son. But an even worse witness was yet to come. This was another Lieutenant in the Royal Navy, Joseph Robert Hownam, the son of a royal page, and a young man to whom the Queen had taken a fancy when he was a boy, paying for his education, having him to stay with her at Kensington Palace and supplying him with money 'all along very liberally'.[44] She had arranged for him to join the Navy in which he had served in the *Africaine* under Captain Manby, the officer with whom the Queen was alleged to have had an affair at the time of the 'Delicate Investigation' in 1806. Hownam had been asked to join the Queen at Genoa in 1815 when she was thinking of going to Africa, and had been of her party when she sailed to the Holy Land.

He had hoped to help his patroness by coming over from France, where he was then living, but his answers to questions put to him during his examination and cross-examination damaged her cause severely:

'Where did her Royal Highness sleep on the voyage from Jaffa homewards?'
'Under the tent on deck.'
'By whose direction was the tent put up?'
'By direction of the Princess.'
'What was the occasion of her Royal Highness sleeping under the tent during the return voyage?'
'In consequence of the excessive heat, and the [smell of the] animals on board [in the hold].'
'You have said that you did not know where Pergami slept; upon your oath do you not believe he slept under the tent?'
'I have heard he did sleep under the tent.'
'I do not wish to know what you have heard.'
'And I believe he did sleep under the tent.'
'As you are a married man, would you have any objection, or conceive it improper that Mrs Hownam should so sleep in a tent in the dark with a male person?'
'I trust that every man looks upon his wife without making any comparison or exception; I never made the comparison.'
'Do you say that you see no impropriety . . . in a male and female sleeping so placed in such a tent?'
'I do not conceive there was any impropriety in the thing, because I must have felt it, and I did not feel it; I have seen so many situations that her Royal Highness has been placed in, in the course of her travels, that I do not look upon it as improper.'[45]

By the time that Copley and Gifford had finished with Lieutenant Hownam, 'all unprejudiced men' seemed to think, so Charles Greville said, that the evidence was 'sufficiently proved'.[46] Both the Duke of Portland and Lord Harewood declared themselves satisfied that the case against the Queen had been 'made out'. The fact had been 'proved', and all further proceedings were useless.[47] Lord Lonsdale was 'vehement as to the *proved* guilt of the Queen'.[48]

Within the next few days, however, opinion began to change once again. The defence were able to cast grave, though unfounded, suspicion upon the methods used by the Milan Commission in collecting their evidence and to persuade many Members to believe that Giuseppe Rastelli, the Commission's courier, had been guilty of suborning witnesses for the prosecution. Demands were made for Rastelli to be re-examined on this point; and the defence were able to make much of the fact that he was not available, having been sent back to Italy to allay the fears of the witnesses who had fled home from Beauvais.

In the absence of Rastelli, John Allan Powell, the Lincoln's Inn solicitor who had been a member of the Milan Commission, was summoned to the bar of the House. He explained his reasons for sending Rastelli back to Italy: 'I learned that various reports were propagated in Italy of the dangers which the witnesses for the Bill ran, by coming over to this country. I had heard that reports were propagated in Italy that they had received great personal injuries. I had heard that the families of those persons who were here were exceedingly anxious upon the subject of their relations who were in this country. I had understood Rastelli to be acquainted with the greater part of the families of those persons, and I considered that it would be an act of humanity to those relations and friends, that [he] . . . should report to [them] what their situation really was.'

When the Chancellor asked counsel if they had any questions to ask Mr Powell, Brougham suddenly stood up and said intently, 'My Lords, I wish to ask the witness one question. "Who is your client or employer in this case?"'

To cries of 'Order! Order!' the witness was directed to withdraw. So far the King's name had not been mentioned in this connection. But Brougham was determined to bring it in by implication. He insisted that he had a right to know whose agent Powell was, to be informed against whom he was contending in the case, against the government or against some 'shadowy figure' standing behind them. Not knowing who the party was against whom he appeared, he could not 'fix him with any character', Brougham complained; he could not 'trace his lineaments'. 'I know nothing about this shrouded, this mysterious being – this retiring phantom, this uncertain shape,' he continued to the obvious amusement of many peers in the Chamber, and then, in a quotation from *Paradise Lost* suggested to him by Spencer Perceval's son,[49] he drew a malevolent parallel between the King and the powers of darkness:

> If shape it might be called that shape had none
> Distinguishable in member, joint or limb;
> Or substance might be called that shadow seemed,
> For each seemed either . . .
> . . . What seemed his head
> The likeness of a Kingly crown had on.

The King found the insult impossible to forgive. 'He said that I might at least have spared him the attack on his shape,' Brougham recorded. 'He thought that everybody allowed that whatever faults he might have, his legs were not as I had described them.'[50] It was several years before the King could bring himself to allow Brougham – to whom he afterwards refused to speak – to progress in his profession and to admit him to the ranks of King's Counsel.

The case was now nearing its close. Further attempts were made to show that people had been bribed to appear against the Queen, further witnesses appeared to suggest that, after all, the Queen's behaviour had been 'most regular'. And, although it was difficult to overcome the bad impression left by Flynn and Hownam, some ground was made up. By 19 October Lord Fitzwilliam was firmly of the opinion that a majority of his fellow peers agreed with him in thinking that the Bill ought not to pass. There had been a meeting of the government's supporters, including Lord Harewood, two nights before, 'when they came to a resolution of not supporting the Bill, and several have given Lord Liverpool intimation that he must not expect their support on this occasion. . . . Nevertheless, don't imagine,' Fitzwilliam warned Lord Milton, 'that all, or that a majority of our House are ready to put an end to the Bill: the very contrary, they still adhere to the Ministers, and however ill they think of the measure, their first consideration is the preservation of the Ministers, and by this feeling they regulate their conduct.'[51]

On 24 October Denman began to sum up the evidence on the Queen's behalf in a speech which Lady Harrowby considered was 'in a higher and more *creditable* style than Brougham's'.[52] It was an excellent speech, Fitzwilliam agreed, illustrated 'with beautiful remarks; his conclusion was beyond all description fine'.[53] This opinion of Denman's conclusion

The Coronation Banquet in Westminster Hall, by George Jones.

16 The House of Lords during the Divorce Bill of 1820, by George Hayter.

18 Queen Caroline by Samuel Lane.

17 Henry Brougham by James Lonsdale.

was not, however, widely shared; and Denman himself afterwards profoundly regretted it. For having declared that he knew of no example of a *Christian* King who had thought himself at liberty to divorce his wife for misconduct when his own misconduct in the first instance was the occasion of her fall, but that he found a parallel in the history of Imperial Rome in the case of Nero, Denman went on to quote in Greek the reply of one of Octavia's servants to someone who had tried to suborn her on behalf of the Emperor: 'My mistress's vagina is purer than your mouth.'

This angered the King even more than Brougham's references to Satan; and Denman felt obliged to submit a most humble apology explaining his distress that a quotation which he had intended to apply to Giuseppe Rastelli should have been taken to apply to the King. The King accepted the apology, and eventually agreed to Denman's elevation in his profession but, as in the case of Brougham, he refused ever to speak to him again.

If this misguided quotation of Denman's temporarily harmed his own future, his final quotation harmed the Queen. For having insisted that she was quite innocent of the charges brought against her, he concluded with Christ's words to the adulterous woman: 'If no accuser can come forward to condemn thee, neither do I condemn thee: go, and sin no more.'

This was, of course, too good an opportunity for the Queen's enemies to miss, and it was not long before these lines were quoted everywhere:

> Most gracious Queen, we thee implore
> To go away and sin no more;
> Or if that effort be too great,
> To go away at any rate.

In his reply to the Queen's counsel, the Attorney-General was shrewd and matter-of-fact rather than emotive. He could not enliven his speech 'with the eloquence of his learned friends, nor scatter over it those flowers of imagination in which they had indulged'. But his speech was, perhaps, all the more effective for that; and he was content to leave it to Copley to reply to Denman in Denman's manner.

Copley made much of the defence's failure to call as a witness Pergami's sister, a lady described by one of their witnesses, Lord Guildford, as 'very modest, not particularly vulgar' – 'the precise shades of distinction could not be accurately marked'. For, if anyone could swear to the Queen's innocence, surely she could?*

Copley also took trouble to ridicule the 'very singular' argument that because no one had seen her aboard the polacca with her dress taken off, 'it was to be concluded that there had been no criminality. Was a proposition so monstrous ever urged before any tribunal, more especially before such a tribunal as this?' The Queen had been seen looking out of her tent in a morning-gown, and it appeared that the dress of the other party was a loose Tunisian robe. If such obstructions as these were effectual, 'what,' Copley wanted to know, 'was to become of population? Formerly it had been said that a hooped and whale-boned petticoat was insufficient. . . . Was it credible that the Queen's morning-gown had made a stouter resistance?'

On 2 November the proceedings entered their final phase with a summing up by the Lord Chancellor, Lord Eldon, who was himself satisfied that adultery had taken place aboard the polacca, or at least that 'there were sufficient circumstances to lead a plain man to infer it'. Eldon went on to condemn Brougham, who had throughout the progress of the case treated their Lordships with undisguised disdain, for having suggested in his opening speech for the defence that if their judgement went against the Queen, it would be an act that 'would return to them upon their own heads'. 'Whether an advocate be right in using such language or not,' Eldon said, 'you will allow me to observe, my Lords, that it ought to have no effect upon you. . . . For myself, if I had not a minute longer to live, I would say to your Lordships, "Be just and fear not".'

Eldon was followed by Lord Erskine who, despite his close friendship with the King, was a strong opponent of the Bill, and voiced his disapproval with a vigour too extreme for his age and health. After some minutes 'his voice suddenly ceased . . . and he fell forward senseless on the table'. On his recovery he returned to his attack on the Bill with more vehemence than ever, maintaining that it was supported by 'perjury,

---

* All Brougham's colleagues had wanted to call Countess Oldi, realizing how much the prosecution would make of their failure to do so. But Brougham, knowing her to be as inveterate a liar as her brother, dared not do so. He feared that 'she would lie without scruple'. Brougham also feared that Mariette Brun, Louisa Demont's half-sister, would be an unreliable witness, and he dared not call her either. In his letter to the Queen telling her that he had decided not to call them, he did not mention the real reasons for his decision but said merely that he had thought it better to close the case 'at a very favourable opportunity' (RA Geo IV, Box 11, 23 October 1820).

and perjury alone', and that the 'character of that perjury proved the perfect innocence of her Majesty'.

Lord Grey, in a much less impassioned speech, agreed that the Queen ought to be declared not guilty. 'He fairly avowed that in the outset his prejudices and feelings were unfavourable to the Queen: he did think it possible that a case would be made out that would compel him to vote, however reluctantly, in support of the Bill; but as it now stood, viewing it first as a question of guilt or innocence, and, next, as a matter of political expediency, he was bound to declare that he could never lay down his head in tranquillity in future if he did not do his utmost to resist its progress.' When Grey had finished several peers went down to the bench where he was sitting, 'squeezed his arm and said, "beautiful" '.[54]

It was this matter of 'political expediency' to which Grey referred that seemed uppermost in the mind of most peers who subsequently spoke in opposition to the Bill. Lord Ellenborough, for example, said that he would vote against it because of 'the strong and almost universal feeling which existed against it'; but he could not pass over the Queen's conduct 'without censure'; in her duty of setting the kind of example expected of a Queen of England she had 'utterly failed'. It was a view which was widely shared by Whigs and Tories alike. Grantham spoke for many of them when he declared that he felt bound to vote against the Bill, but he could not put his hand on his heart and say, 'Not Guilty'. In letters to Lord Milton, Lord Althorp expressed a similar view: 'I have no respect for the Queen whatever. . . . She is a woman of the most infamous character. . . . I believe her to be guilty, though I do not think it has been anything like proved. . . . My father and mother [Earl and Countess Spencer] are stout anti-Queenites, and indeed my mother seems almost to forget she is in opposition. . . . I myself should have very little satisfaction in voting the Queen innocent . . . I most fervently wish that the Bill will be thrown out.'[55]

While the Lords continued to discuss her conduct in the House, the Queen was greeted with shouts as enthusiastic as ever when she appeared outside it. On the day that Brougham had brought her defence to a close there was an enormous procession through the streets, 'made up of some thousands of men on foot and in carriages, the pedestrians marching gravely two by two, carrying inscribed banners: "Virtue triumphs!", "Down with the conspirators!", "Non mi ricordo" and shouting "Hurrah!" Next came the guild of workers in crystal. Two hundred masters and apprentices were each carrying in procession on the end of a fork some specimen of their handiwork – a crown, a sceptre, vases, urns . . . all of the very finest workmanship. In the distance, the effect produced was that of walking diamonds; the sun glittered on it; it was really beautiful. Next came the bakers displaying samples of their trade; [then came] the Quakers, accompanied by their wives and daughters – the most moral people in England.'[56]

Almost every day there was a procession such as this. On 25 October, Sir Willoughby Gordon was 'quite sure he saw 40,000 people, with banners, pass through Piccadilly on their way to the Queen'.[57] On 30 October there was a magnificent display by the brassfounders, and Thomas Creevey had 'no notion there had been so many beautiful brass ornaments in all the world. Their men in armour, both horse and foot, were capital; nor was their humour amiss. The procession closed with a very handsome crown borne in state as a present to the Queen, preceded by a flag with the words – "The Queen's Guard are Men of Metal".' Creevey was 'quite sure there must have been 100,000 people in Piccadilly, all in the most perfect order'. He was thankful that they *were* in perfect order. He would not like anyone to tell him, he admitted, what would happen next if these 'organised armies' that marched through the streets four or five abreast should ever lose their temper.[58]

The Queen was still just as eagerly supported by the 'solid middle classes' as by the mob, Mme de Lieven assured Prince Metternich. 'You have to see for yourself what the Queen's escort is like to get an accurate notion of the cheering and the people who cheer. The streets are full of well-dressed men and respectable women, all waving their hats and their handkerchiefs. You see the real mob, too . . . but they are certainly not in the majority. All this shows only too clearly how unpopular the King is and what the people think of his behaviour, and how convinced they are that any woman who was protected and proclaimed guiltless by the venerable George III is bound to be the victim of calumny and vile persecution under George IV. You have to take this into account in trying to understand the inexplicable things that are taking place. . . . Yesterday, the Queen received thirty addresses; meanwhile, she is on trial, and the King is in hiding.'[59]

Towards the end of the month, Whig ladies began to call on the Queen, to the appalled dismay of Mrs Arbuthnot who could not believe that any woman of good conduct would 'condescend to notice a person who [had] been proved to have slept for five weeks with her menial servant'.[60] For the past month Lord Fitzwilliam had been attempting 'to prepare people for the step, even *before* the overthrow of the Bill'. 'We ought all, ladies as well as men,' he told his son, 'to write our names at the Queen's door.'[61] His wife, 'a great lady of the most impeccable reputation',[62] was the first to go, and cleared the way for others to follow her. Lady Jersey, not content with a mere courtesy call, went about 'wearing the Queen's portrait round her neck',[63] and was, as Lady Harrowby said, 'longing to fly into her arms and to pay her every possible honour and attention'.[64] Prince Leopold also called on her, though, in his case, it was felt that he had been driven to it by 'mere cowardice'. 'He ought to have made this gesture on the day of her arrival in England, or not at all,' Mme de Lieven thought. 'No doubt he is afraid of the mob. If he had gone at once, he would perhaps have been wrong as regards his relation with the King; but it would have been to show courage and act on principle; for, after all, the Queen is the mother of his wife. . . . She sent him away without seeing him, and quite right too.'[65]

The redoubtable Mme de Lieven herself certainly did not lack courage in facing the mob. 'I was driving to Bond Street,' she recorded, 'when I met the Queen in a state coach with six horses, being led at a walking pace, and escorted as usual by some hundreds of scallywags. As soon as they saw my carriage, they stopped it and ordered my servants to take off their hats, and me to let the window down. Neither I nor my servants obeyed. I was surrounded by people shouting abuse, whistling and booing. Meanwhile, the Queen passed by throwing me a withering glance. I saw two enormous black eyebrows, as big as two of my fingers put together: the contents of two pots of rouge on her cheeks: and a veil over everything. She looks completely brazen.'[66]

*

The speeches in the House were at last concluded on the afternoon of 6 November, and the voting on the Bill of Pains and Penalties took place. Each peer was asked to say 'Content' or 'Not content'. Ninety-five peers voted 'Not content'; 123 were 'Content'. The usually large government majority was cut to twenty-eight, and such a majority on a matter of state, as Grey commented, was 'tantamount to a defeat'.[67] Grenville thought that the Bill would now have to be abandoned; Liverpool was inclined to agree; other members of the Cabinet, including Lord

Sidmouth, objected; and it was eventually decided that if the majority fell below ten, then the Bill would be withdrawn.[68] The rejoicing that night in the streets was wilder than ever; the mob bore Brougham in triumph to Brooks's.[69]

The next day the House considered the question whether or not the divorce clause should be deleted from the Bill. On this the division was a curious one. Ministers hoped that by dropping the divorce clause they might push the Bill through more comfortably; and most of the bishops also wanted to drop the clause as it sidetracked the jurisdiction of the ecclesiastical courts. All the Whig peers, on the other hand, were prepared to vote for its retention, believing that the Bill was far more vulnerable with the clause remaining; and many Tories were prepared to vote with them, since they wanted the Bill to pass as it was originally drafted. So the motion was defeated by a large majority; and the divorce clause was retained.

On 10 November the voting on the third reading of the Bill took place. When his name was called the Duke of Clarence 'leaned over the rail of the gallery as far into the House as he could, and then halloed – "Content!" with a yell that would quite have become a savage. The Duke of York followed with his "Content" delivered with singular propriety'.[70] The majority that agreed with them was an extremely narrow one: 108 members voted for the Bill, 99 against it. As Lady Harrowby had forecast, the majority was 'so trifling' that it created 'more *embarras* than if the Bill had been thrown out altogether'.[71]

The government were forced to recognize now that there was virtually no chance whatsoever of getting the Bill through the Commons. Indeed, they dreaded the thought of its even being debated in the Commons; Sir Thomas Tyrwhitt had already decided at the beginning of September that there would be a mutiny in the House if the thing went on much longer.[72] Brougham had got hold of a copy of the will which the King had made and in which he had referred to Mrs Fitzherbert as his 'dear wife', and he was threatening to produce it as an argument that the King had forfeited his legal right to the throne.[73] The government also knew that Brougham intended to bring direct recrimination against the King.[74] He had found numerous witnesses to swear to the King's sexual escapades with the daughters of a turnpike man named Hyfield, and to his liaisons with a French courtesan, Mme de Meyer, with a Mrs Crowe whom he kept in a house in Charles II Street, St James's Square, and by whom he had had a child, with a Weymouth boarding-house keeper, Mrs Mary Lewis, and even with a common prostitute.[75]

The Duke of Wellington expressed himself as being quite unimpressed by this recriminatory evidence; he told the Duke of Portland that 'the King was degraded as low as he could be already'.[76] But Ministers, for the most part, feared the dangers of further opprobrium. Rather than expose the King to this damning evidence in the Commons, and accepting the fact that even if no such evidence were to be offered the Bill would not pass there, the government decided to take the matter no further. So Lord Liverpool announced his 'intention to move that the Bill do pass this day six months' – a parliamentary phrase meaning that he would abandon it. At least he could prevent an acquittal by the Commons, having just scraped together a majority to affirm her guilt in the Lords.[77]

The King was profoundly upset when told that the Bill would have to be abandoned, and claimed to have 'serious thoughts of retiring to Hanover, and leaving this Kingdom to the Duke of York'.[78] For weeks past he had been complaining about the progress of the Bill, and the government's handling of it, and in his anxiety he had been venting his ill humour in abuse of his Ministers, his 'language and manner', according to Charles Arbuthnot, being 'those of a Bedlamite'.[79] Lord Castlereagh 'lamented very much the King's indiscretion in talking of those he still retained as his Ministers in so indecorous a manner, and said that such conduct and feelings entirely destroyed any pleasure there might be in serving him. He did not, however, seem to believe that the King had any fixed plan for getting rid of [the government].'[80] Nor did Wellington think the King had 'any settled purpose of changing his government'. He had heard from his sister-in-law, Mrs Wellesley-Pole, one of his Majesty's guests at Brighton, that the King's language was 'beyond anything indiscreet and improper, that the language there now [was] not whether the Ministers [would] be changed but only as to the time'.[81] But Wellington considered it was all just talk: the King liked people to imagine that his Prime Minister was a sort of maître d'hôtel whom he might dismiss any moment it happened to suit him.[82] The King discussed the problem with Lord Lauderdale and with his friend Lord Donoughmore; and to the consternation of Lord Liverpool, who thought that he was certainly about to enter into an intrigue with the Whigs, he sent for Lord Grenville to show him the documents about Princess Charlotte and Captain Hesse and to ask him if, in Grenville's opinion, they ought to be published.[83] Grenville declined to commit himself, but he did offer the opinion that, in any case, the Queen ought still to be excluded from the Liturgy.

After Grenville's departure the King went to dine with Princess Augusta at Frogmore. W. H. Fremantle was also there and the King called him aside to tell him 'how much satisfied he had been with Lord Grenville'. Fremantle gained the impression, however, that 'the interview was more for the purpose of consulting and asking his advice' than for any object of changing the government.

The King 'looked dreadfully dejected and thoughtful', Fremantle thought; 'but when he had dined (professing to have no appetite) and ate as much as would serve me for three days ... together with a bottle of strong punch, he was in much better spirits and vastly agreeable. ... He did not sit a quarter of an hour after [the ladies] left us, and ... not a word was said of politics. He remained till twelve o'clock, and he and Princess Augusta and myself sang glees.'[84]

The government, relieved to learn that the interview with Grenville had not set in motion any negotiation with the Whigs, still held to the view that the Queen's name ought to be excluded from the Liturgy, although they did not expect to carry the point in the Commons. For most of the rest of the year they gloomily anticipated defeat, while the King prepared memoranda which he entitled, 'Advantages supposed to be gained by a new government' and 'The Evils attendant upon a change of government'.[85]

The Queen, for her part, appeared overcome by emotion when she was told the news of the Bill's abandonment. She had 'a *dazed* look more tragical than consternation ... evidently all shuddering'.[86] As she entered her carriage to be taken away to Brandenburg House she was observed to be in tears.[87] It was as though she already realized that the celebrations now reaching their climax would soon die away and she would be forgotten.

For three days and nights the celebrations continued, with fireworks and bonfires, dances and parades. Church bells were rung and apprentices ran wild. In Peterborough, as in several other provincial towns, the magistrates called in the troops to quell the disturbance. Lady Milton was not alone in complaining of the 'rebellious, licentious, disgraceful and revolutionary spirit' that had manifested itself.[88] All the large cities in the country were illuminated; and the state of London, so Creevey recorded, was 'beyond everything'.[89] There had never been such rejoicing since Waterloo; there was to be nothing like it again until the passing of the Reform Bill. The people, so Mme de Lieven said, never stopped cheering in the streets on the night that the Bill was thrown out of the Lords. Two days later, after terrific bursts of cannon and musket fire – the 'English way of rejoicing' – the people were 'still mad with enthusiasm for the Queen, and here and there indulged in looting and all kinds of brutality'.[90] At the head of the tallest mast of the decorated ships in the river was an effigy of a bishop, between twenty and thirty feet in height, hanging by his heels. Wellington was booed more loudly than ever; Castlereagh got 'roughly handled at Covent Garden'. And Brougham was the great hero of the entire country. He was presented with the freedom of numerous cities; public houses were named after him; attorneys loaded him with briefs if only for the honour of talking to him.[91]

In the general enthusiasm, all parties congratulated themselves 'on no longer being faced with the prospect of a revolution'.[92] The trial had been a cathartic experience; in the excitement it engendered, everything else had been forgotten, even Peterloo and the Cato Street Conspiracy. It mattered little that, at the end of it, the government obtained strong support for their motion that the Queen's name should remain excluded from the Liturgy, that she was not to be crowned, nor to live in one of the royal palaces. The people congratulated themselves on having won a great victory; and so, in a sense, they had. They had been on the side of the Whigs and the Whigs had won. After the trial the liberal Whigs were firmly in control of the party; and the Tories had to recognize that they could not very well survive another period of such unpopularity unless they as a party became more liberal too. An age was dawning in which the Reform Bill could become a reality.

PART TWO
1821-1830

13

Coronation
1821

*

'Of the splendour of the whole spectacle it
is impossible for me to give you the
slightest idea'

For months past, carpenters and painters, upholsterers and joiners had
been hard at work in both Westminster Abbey and Westminster Hall. In
the Abbey, tiers of crimson cloth-covered benches, boxes and galleries
had been ranged beneath the western windows looking down upon the
nave. Further seats had been provided in the choir and in the north and
south transepts. Boxes for the Royal Family, the Press and foreign Ministers had been built in the sanctuary. The interior of Westminster Hall,
where the coronation banquet was to be held, had been even more
drastically transformed. A new wooden floor, covered in blue cloth, had
been laid above the stone flags; tiers of seats rose above it against the
cloth-draped walls. At one end a Gothic triumphal arch soared towards
the gallery where the King's band was to play. Facing this arch at the far
end of the Hall was the dais for the King and the royal dukes. Between
dais and arch, across the whole length of the Hall, were the dining-tables
for the privileged and distinguished guests; the backs of the chairs were

in the shape of Gothic arches and covered with scarlet cloth. A raised and covered walk, spread with a vivid blue carpet, led from the Abbey to the Hall and was overlooked by decorated stands, seats in which were being offered for sale at prices ranging up to twenty guineas.

At Carlton House the King studied the arrangements, following the precedents for the coronation of King James II but making such altera- tions and improvements as he considered advisable, 'perfectly absorbed in all the petty arrangements'.[1] Visitors were taken to see the coronation robes, on which over £24,000 had been spent, the ermine alone costing £855.[2] One of these visitors was Count Joseph Boruwlaski, the 2ft 4ins tall Polish dwarf, who came to present a copy of his memoirs and who received in exchange a beautiful miniature watch and seals which the King presented to him with the words, 'My dear friend, I shall read and preserve this book as long as I live for *your* sake; and in return, I request you will wear and keep this watch for mine.'[3] The robes which the dwarf was then taken to see were of an astonishing splendour. The King's crimson velvet train, ornamented with golden stars, was 27 feet long; his huge black Spanish hat was surmounted by sprays of ostrich feathers and a heron's plume.

His Majesty appeared to be on edge. He had set his heart on a splendid ceremony, lavish, dignified and memorable for which Parliament had voted no less than £243,000; but he was haunted by the fear that his wife would spoil it, and the apprehension led to sudden outbursts of exaspera- tion. There were reports that when contradicted one day by Sir Benjamin Bloomfield, now his Keeper of the Privy Purse, he 'seized him by the collar and gave him a good hearty shake'.[4]

His apprehension was well-founded. The Queen no longer commanded the general sympathy that she had done before and during her trial; but she still had supporters enough among the mob – so many, indeed, thought Lady Sarah Lyttelton, that the ceremony might have to be postponed. 'The mob are rather too cross, and too fond of the Queen to [permit] a ceremony in which she is not to take part,' Lady Sarah told Captain Spencer. 'They will make some bustle on the occasion. We are all in a fright about it. As it is they make bustle enough; every day there is a gathering on some account or other. And her Gracious Majesty takes care to keep it up, by showing herself all about London in a shabby post-chaise and pair of *post-horses* and living in the scruffiest house she could think of, to *shew* she is kept out of the palace.'[5] Lord Temple reported that fears of riots were making it difficult to sell seats in the stands along the processional route.[6]

On 18 July 1821 the King's robes were carefully packed and transported to the Speaker's House at Westminster, not far from the church of St Margaret's whose bells, sometimes drowned by the boom of cannon firing across the river, were pealed every half hour from midnight until dawn.

Just before half past ten on the morning of the 19th, while rockets exploded in the sky, the King entered Westminster Hall. He was almost half an hour late as Lord Gwydyr, the acting Lord Great Chamberlain, had torn his clothes while dressing; but his Majesty's entrance was none the less impressive for being delayed. 'Something rustles, and a being buried in satin, feathers and diamonds rolls gracefully into his seat,' Benjamin Robert Haydon recorded. 'The room rises with a sort of feathered, silken thunder. Plumes wave, eyes sparkle, glasses are out, mouths smile and one man becomes the prime object of attraction to thousands. The way in which the King bowed was really royal. As he looked towards the peeresses and foreign ambassadors, he showed like some gorgeous bird of the east.'[7] He was 'in full robes of great size and richness', and wore a brown wig, the thick curls of which fell low over his forehead and over the nape of his neck. He had by now – though many caricaturists were unaware of the fact – discarded the russet whiskers which had until recently bristled on his cheeks, giving his face a rather choleric, bucolic look, and he appeared surprisingly young for a man in his fifty-ninth year.[8] There were many who had expected him to present a slightly ridiculous appearance; and there were some, including Mrs Arbuthnot, who thought that he *did* look ridiculous.[9] But most people were impressed by his magnificent dignity. 'The young people in particular' who had gone 'merely with the expectation of a show', were 'taken by surprise and found themselves affected in a manner they never dreamt of'.[10]

Indeed, the whole scene impressed the spectators with its dignity and splendour. Even the white and blue satin Elizabethan costumes which were worn by those Privy Councillors who were not peers and which Emily Cowper had expected 'to convulse the whole of Westminster Abbey with laughter' appeared perfectly in keeping. 'Separately so gay a garb had an odd effect on the persons of elderly or ill-made men,' admitted Walter Scott, who had been induced to travel down for the occasion by the newly invented steamships which could make the journey from Leith within sixty hours. 'But when the whole was thrown into one general body all these discrepancies disappeared.'[11]

The procession to the Abbey was led by the King's Herb-Woman and her six young attendants who, in accordance with a centuries-old tradition, strewed the way with herbs and heavily scented flowers as a precaution against the plague. The King walked in front of a canopy of cloth of gold which the barons of the Cinque Ports had been instructed not to hold over his head so that he could be seen by the people in the garrets and on the rooftops.[12] He was preceded by three bishops, carrying respectively a paten, a chalice and a Bible. In front of the bishops were the officers of state with the crown, the orb, the sceptre, and the sword of state, regalia for which Messrs Rundell, Bridge & Company were still owed £33,000 the following year.[13] The peers marched along in their state robes, in order of seniority; the dignitaries of the City of London followed in their own no less remarkable attire with their chains and emblems of office. The King stopped for a moment to give his pages time to unfold and display his crimson velvet gold-embroidered train. He said to them twice in a clearly audible tone, 'Hold it wider.'[14]

The procession reached the West door of the Abbey at about eleven o'clock. As the King stepped inside the building the choir began to sing the 'Hallelujah Chorus', and the congregation stood and cheered. 'It was fearfully hot in the Abbey and the King appeared distressed, almost to fainting' as he made his way up the aisle with uneven steps and evident difficulty. A lady in one of the galleries actually did faint and had to be carried out of the building.[15]

The ceremony lasted for almost five hours; and the King, very pale, seemed at any moment likely to collapse, weighed down as he was by his heavy, cumbrous robes. 'Several times he was at the last gasp,' Lady Cowper noticed, 'he looked more like the victim than the hero of the fête. I really pitied him from my heart.' But, revived by sal volatile, he behaved on occasions in the most improper fashion, according to the Duke of Wellington, 'even in the most important and solemn' parts of the ceremony – 'soft eyes, kisses given on rings which everyone observed'.[16] Fortunately these 'follies' and '*oëillades*' – which were noticed also by Lady Cowper who, being 'in the line of fire had a full view' – were abandoned during the sternly admonitory sermon of the Archbishop of York who spoke of a Sovereign's duty to 'encourage morality and religion', to preserve the morals of the people from the 'contagion of vice', and from a 'general depravity' which was 'the last calamity' that could befall a state. Nor did the King falter or make any ambiguous gestures during the crowning ceremony; and when this was over the congregation showed their enthusiasm once more by waving their caps and coronets, their purses and handkerchiefs, and by shouting at the tops of their voices, 'God Bless the King!' His Majesty was clearly 'much gratified', and, some thought, rather astonished by the vociferousness and evident sincerity of their acclamations.[17]

As the premier earl present, the Earl of Denbigh performed homage to the King by repeating the oath of allegiance, kissing his hand and left cheek and touching with a finger the crown on his head.[18] Then, the long and exhausting ceremony at last over, the King withdrew; and as soon as he had gone the peers and peeresses, the foreign ministers and their wives, the musicians and singers rushed out of the Abbey as though it had been on fire. So that when his Majesty reappeared he was greeted by the sight of 'empty benches covered with dirt and litter and the backs of his courtiers expediting their exits with a "suave qui peut"-like rapidity'.[19]

Soon after four o'clock the King, having had further recourse to sal volatile, proceeded to Westminster Hall to join his guests for the last coronation banquet ever to be given in England. The three hundred guests and the spectators in the tiered galleries above them were already there awaiting him.

'Of the splendour of the whole spectacle it is impossible for me to give you the *slightest* idea,' Lord Denbigh told his mother. 'It exceeded all imagination and conception. Picture to yourself Westminster Hall lined beneath with the peers in their robes and coronets, the Privy Councillors, Knights of the Bath and a multitude of different attendants and chief officers of state in most magnificent dresses, and with a double row of galleries on each side above, filled with all the beauty of London, the ladies vying with each other in the magnificence of their apparel and the splendour of their head-dresses. Some of them being literally a blaze of diamonds. Prince Esterhazy is said to have had jewels on his person estimated at *eighty thousand* pounds and the rest of the foreign ministers and their ladies were as splendid as jewels and fine clothes could make them.'[20]

Before the King's arrival flower girls entered the Hall, strewing petals over the floor. 'The grace of their action, their slow movement, their white dresses, were indescribably touching,' Haydon recalled. 'Their light, milky colour contrasted with the dark shadow of the archway, which, though dark, was full of rich crimson dresses that gave the shadow a tone as of deep blood. . . . The distant trumpets and shouts of the people, the slow march, and at last the appearance of the King himself crowned and under a golden canopy, and the universal burst of the assembly at seeing him, affected everybody. . . . We were all huzzaing, and the King was smiling.'[21]

Once he had settled himself down in his appointed place, the meal was brought in by a procession of Household officials, Gentlemen Pensioners, and – on horseback – the Lord High Constable, the Lord High Steward, and the Deputy Earl Marshal, the last of whom unfortunately found it necessary to swear at his horse in a voice that resounded around the Hall.

The next horse to appear was more easily managed, however, the rider having taken the precaution of borrowing from Astley's circus a white charger thoroughly accustomed to confined spaces and cheering crowds. The rider was the son of the King's Champion whose father, the Rev. John Dymoke, a Lincolnshire parson, had decided that his cloth was not compatible with the hereditary office which had descended to him from his ancestor, Sir John Dymoke, Champion of King Richard II. Young Dymoke, in full armour, a 'helmet on his head, adorned with a plume of feathers', trotted through the Gothic arch, rode up to the King, and flung a gauntlet down in front of the royal dais, challenging all comers to impugn his Majesty's title. No one presumed to pick the gauntlet up; and the King contentedly drank his Champion's health out of a cup of gold.

It was now the turn of the peers and bishops at the long tables in the centre of the Hall to drink his Majesty's health which they did with the customary rounds of cheering. The King stood up to thank them for their good wishes and to do them 'the honour of drinking their health and that of his good people'.

The censorious Mrs Arbuthnot, who – having, no doubt, discussed the King's behaviour with her friend the Duke of Wellington – accused him of kissing a diamond brooch to a lady admirer in the Abbey, recorded in her diary that he was 'continually nodding and winking' at this same lady in the Hall.[22] But the Earl of Denbigh, who was standing near him, recalled no such improprieties. 'The King was very gracious to me at the banquet and called me to him,' Lord Denbigh said. 'He gave me his hand to kiss, and desired me to stand opposite to him at table and help him to some turtle soup to which I also helped the rest of the royal dukes. . . . I also helped a dish of quails, and carved a slice out of a capon for the Duke of York. I had not a very arduous office as the royal dukes had dined previously. Lord Chichester was my assistant carver and cut up a pine-apple weighing eleven pounds.'[23]

At about half past seven the King retired from the Hall – to which the Queen had unsuccessfully attempted to gain admittance – and returned to Carlton House, leaving his guests to enjoy the banquet. There were soups and salmon, turbot and trout, venison and veal, mutton and beef, braised ham and savoury pies, daubed geese and braised capon, lobster and crayfish, cold roast fowl and cold lamb, potatoes, peas and cauliflower. There were dishes of mounted pastry, dishes of jellies and creams, over a thousand side dishes, nearly five hundred sauce boats brimming with lobster sauce, butter sauce and mint. The peers and the bishops, having had nothing to eat since breakfast, turned to their plates with relish, while their wives and children looked on hungrily from the rows of seats above them. One peer at least, taking pity on his famished family, tied a cold capon in his handkerchief and tossed it up to them.[24]

*

While fireworks exploded in Hyde Park, rockets hissed past coloured balloons, church bells rang and guns thundered, the King could content himself with the knowledge that he really had received, as Walter Scott put it, a 'general welcome from his subjects'.[25] 'The people were all in good humour,' Lord Denbigh confirmed to his mother. 'The King was *excitedly* and most enthusiastically cheered, and seemed in the highest spirits.'[26] Lord Colchester was also told that the people were in good humour and that the few disloyal voices were 'overpowered by bursts of loyalty'.[27]

It was hard to believe that, so short a time before, the King had been execrated wherever he went, that the hatred he had inspired at the time of the Queen's trial was now submerged if not in love at least in tolerance, that the enthusiasm with which, to Mme de Lieven's astonishment, he had been greeted at a performance of the opera *Artaxerxes* at Drury Lane on 6 February, was not a misleading indication of the state of public opinion. Public opinion *had* changed unmistakably and steadily in recent months, so much so, indeed, that Grenville thought there was arising in the country enough 'of a royalist spirit and feeling to have enabled such a man as Pitt . . . to avail himself of it'.[28] It was now the Queen and her noisy supporters who were more likely to be greeted with groans than the King. She was denounced in the pages of Theodore Hook's new Sunday paper, *John Bull*; she was ridiculed in caricatures which depicted her in quite as unfavourable a light as that in which the King had been shewn before the proceedings against her.[29] Even *The Times* agreed that the King's visit to Drury Lane, the first of his reign, had been a success. He was received with 'immense acclamations'. There had been a few cat-calls from the galleries; Grenville reported that a few people called out 'The Queen!' and that one man shouted, 'Where's your wife, Georgey?' But most of the audience had 'testified their respect by rising immediately; all the gentlemen took off their hats, while numbers, particularly in the pit, waved them in the air with loud acclamations. The ladies in the boxes waved their handkerchiefs. . . . His Majesty looked much paler than usual, but in good health. He bowed repeatedly to the audience, and continued to do so, remaining standing while the acclamations lasted.'[30] He was obviously delighted. On the way downstairs he told Lady Bessborough that he had never been more gratified;[31] and he later made a similar comment to Lord Castlereagh.[32] During the performance of the farce *Who's Who?* which had followed the opera he had been seen to throw himself back in his chair, 'convulsed with laughter'.[33]

After the Bill of Pains and Penalties had been thrown out of the House of Lords, various public meetings had been held for the purpose of 'congratulating her Majesty on the rejection of the Bill'. But they had not been very enthusiastically attended. Lord Althorp had expressed a widespread opinion when he told Lord Milton, 'I have no doubt in common prudence that the Queen ought to be restored to all the rights and distinctions to which she has a legal claim, but I cannot say that with my opinion of her general conduct I should be inclined to take so strong a step in her favour as to originate a county meeting for the purpose of asking this of the King. I hope most sincerely that there will be no meeting in Northamptonshire.'[34]

A public meeting held at Leeds had been very poorly attended by 'the more respectable part' of the population, 'considering how generally the proceedings against the Queen had been disapproved amongst that class in this town'. The general feeling had been overwhelmingly against the two radicals who had spoken at the meeting. Lord Fitzwilliam was assured that the 'influence of these demagogues' was certainly declining.[35]

In London when the Queen had gone to St Paul's to give thanks for the abandonment of the Bill – although *The Times* reported the crowds in the streets as being enormous – the entire proceedings had been 'a contemptible burlesque', the Earl of Donoughmore had assured Sir Benjamin Bloomfield. Alderman Wood 'had talked of the necessity of having seats set apart for the peers and peeresses, and the Members of Parliament who would attend'. But, in fact, the congregation had been limited to the Lord Mayor, two Aldermen, two Sheriffs, Sir Robert Wilson, Samuel Whitbread's son – Whitbread himself had committed suicide in 1815 – two other Members of Parliament, William Austin, Keppel Craven and three Italians. The only female attendant had been Lady Anne Hamilton.[36]

In March 1821 the farce *Tom Thumb* had been performed at Covent Garden. When a character had come on stage to announce, 'Sire, the Queen is drunk,' the reply, 'Damn the Queen!' had been applauded with 'frenzied enthusiasm' by the 'entire audience'.[37] Some time later during a performance at Drury Lane, a man dashed up to Queen Caroline, and, to the evident satisfaction of the audience, called her a 'damned whore'.[38] At another performance 'a set of radicals' demanded 'God save the Queen' instead of 'God save the King'; but the stage manager's refusal to comply with the request obviously met with the approval of the majority of the audience: 'The shouts [of the radicals] from the pit were by no means general.'[39] Her popularity was now 'much on the wane', Emily Cowper reported. 'And the King is as popular as possible. Not only in the theatres he is received with the greatest applause, but also in the avenues to the theatres where he has been hissed before.'[40]

In June at Astley's circus, the Queen 'took an odd mode of procuring applause. At one moment there happened to be a profound silence in the house, of which she took advantage to stand up and curtsey all round. This was answered by some applause, but the majority was against her.'[41]

The Queen still had her supporters, of course, as the King well knew from the secret reports he received from those who were employed to keep a watch on her movements and on the arrival and departure of her guests.[42] The Duke of Sussex was a frequent visitor at her house; so was his messenger who delivered letters at her house sealed with black wax. Alderman Wood, his wife and his little granddaughter, of whom she had grown as passionately fond as she had been of Pergami's daughter, were often there too.[43] Sir Robert Wilson called occasionally, as did Lord and Lady Milton and the Duke of Bedford. One day Lord and Lady Jersey appeared 'in a sedan accompanied by Mr Whitbread on foot'.[44] But she did not have many callers. 'On Saturday two carriages arrived,' ran one of these reports of 'Secret Intelligence' which were regularly sent to Carlton House, 'one with 2 Ladys and the other with a Lady and Gentleman on a visite to her M— but could not be informed who they was. . . . Her M— went this morning to town accumpend by Lord and Lady Wood [*sic*] with young Austin they Returned to Dinner – and at 6 this Evening the Carriage of young Austin took him and an Italian Count and [her Steward, John] Hieronimus surposed to go the play. There is no foreign courier arrived . . . there has not bin many visitors for these Last few days.'[45] Lady Hood, her Lady of the Bedchamber, Lady Anne Hamilton, her Mistress of the Robes; Lord Hood, her Chamberlain; and the Hon Keppel Craven, her Vice-Chamberlain, all still remained in attendance upon her. But it was reported that several members of her Household and most of her servants were growing restless and disaffected.

'The Queen has become very mistrustful', according to a characteristic message of 'Secret Intelligence'. 'The upper servants are quite in despair. They seem to say it's all over, that it is feared the Queen will remain in the discarded state that she is in as long as she remains in England. All the establishment wishes her Majesty would leave England. . . . The Queen has not it appears the highest opinion of Lady Jersey although it is said her Ladyship, as well as Lady Grey, have pledged themselves to use all their exertions in supporting the honour and dignity of her Majesty. On the whole the Queen is very dull and appears to be dissatisfied.'[46]

This report was dated 6 April. A later report of 10 May had it that the Queen was 'in excellent health and spirits'. But she was submitted to 'fresh insults' every day. 'Yesterday again two country-looking men stopped opposite the gate and made use of the most disrespectful language about her Majesty. They said amongst other things, "How does Mrs Innocence get on? How long does she mean to carry on the farce?" "I suppose," says one, "she is at this time of day tippling with some of the humbug Italians."'[47]

A few weeks later a deputation of people arrived to present the Queen with an address. But they were a very different sort of supporter from the people who had cheered her on her way to the House of Lords the year before. Those triumphant days had passed for ever. As early as 22 January, when sixty-five addresses were presented to her at Brandenburg House to the accompaniment of loud music and waving banners, a 'very small proportion' of the spectators 'betrayed an interest in the Queen as formerly by the exhibition of laurel leaves or white favours'.[48] The delegation that arrived at the Queen's house on 15 July were 'of the most miserable appearance' and seemed not in the least disposed to take their mission seriously. 'Their appearance was so truly ridiculous that servants in livery and many others turned them into ridicule. One of them asked one of the deputation what their white favours was for. The other answered, "For Caroline because she knows how to hold up her petticoats to a man".'[49]

By this time the Queen had moved from Brandenburg House. She had allowed it to fall into such disrepair and neglect that she had received fourteen days' notice to quit. 'Indeed,' so the King's spies were informed by various of the Queen's servants who frequented the Swan at Hammersmith, 'Brandenburgh House is now in that state that it is not habitable.'[50] Her Household had prevailed upon her to take another house; and in January, to the King's horror, she had entered into negotiations with Prince Leopold for the purchase of the lease of Marlborough House, which was only a short distance from Carlton House; but eventually, shortly before the coronation, she moved into Cambridge House in South Audley Street, while retaining Brandenburg House as a country retreat.*

Her servants had not looked forward to the coronation with any pleasure. Alderman Wood had been overheard telling Lady Hood that

* 'The Queen is going to take Cambridge House,' Lady Cowper recorded. 'Leopold having at last refused her Marlborough House. He has kept her in suspense three months, and now writes her word that it would offend a certain Personage, as if he cared about that when he went to see her. That's the shabbiest Ass!!' (Lever, 72). When she quit Lady Francis's house in St James's Square, which she had occupied during the trial, the Queen left it in a filthy state. The carpets were so discoloured 'with wax, ink, oil and other things thrown over them' that they were past cleaning. The tassels had been ripped off the curtains; the curtains themselves were badly torn; so were the covers to the drawing-room furniture. The blinds had never been drawn during the day, so the blue silk furniture was all faded. Ornaments and furniture had been broken, lustres smashed, keys lost. The silver was 'much bruized and damaged from the servants always throwing them down on the stone floors when done with'. The bedding and blankets had all to be 'sent to the scourers from total neglect' (RA Geo IV, Box 11). A rumour that the Queen was interested in buying the house next door to the Lord Chancellor's so alarmed Lord Eldon that he bought it himself for £3,000 more than it was worth (RA Coutts Papers, 56/40, 5 September 1820).

there would be 'violent riots', that the people would 'never suffer the ceremony to take place without the Queen'.[51] Fearful of these riots the servants had been reluctant to go out to watch the coronation procession. They had protested that 'they would not for any sum be spectators on any of the platforms', that during the riots which were to take place, the people, far from welcoming them as friends of the Queen, would 'have no mercy on them'.[52]

The Queen herself, however, had been determined to attend the coronation and had written to Stephen Lushington to ask him 'by what means and measures' she could 'obtain her perogatif and privilege to assist as Queen Consort equally as the reste of the royal family to have a place allotted to her sole use'.[53] She had also instructed her solicitor to ask permission of the Dean and Chapter of Westminster 'to inspect any ancient manuscripts amongst the archives of the Chapter relative to the Coronations of Kings or Queens'.[54] Finally she had written to Lord Liverpool informing him that she would be present:[55] she considered it 'as one of her rights and privileges which her Majesty [was] resolved ever to maintain';[56] she wished to be accompanied by 'those ladies of the first rank' whom his Majesty might 'think the most proper to attend' her. 'The Queen, being particularly anxious to submit to the good taste of his Majesty,' she had concluded, 'most earnestly entreate the King to informe the Queen in what dresse the King wishes the Queen to appear in, on that day, at the coronation.'[57]

Lord Liverpool had considered that her threat to attend the coronation was 'wholly undeserving of notice or attention'; but the King, who knew her so much better, had felt sure that she must be taken seriously, and had issued instructions that she must be told that she could not '*under any circumstances appear*'.[58] He had returned the Queen's letter to her unopened, 'in uniformity with a resolution adopted *more than* twenty years ago, *and since invariably adhered to by the King*'.[59] Despite the King's apprehension, Lord Liverpool had still been inclined to take the Queen's letters more lightly, believing that her threats were made 'solely with a view of extorting money'.[60] All the same, to satisfy his Majesty who had become 'excessively exasperated' on the subject, he had thought it advisable to write to her to inform her categorically that the King 'having determined that the Queen [should] form no part of the ceremonial of his coronation, it was his royal pleasure that the Queen [should] not attend the said ceremony'.[61]

This firm rejection of her demands to be present had made the Queen more determined than ever to go to the Abbey, and not as a mere spectator. She could have obtained a spectator's ticket without difficulty; but she would not submit to sitting tamely in the stands as though she were a foreign visitor. The King's spies had reported that they had been told by Mrs Brown, her Majesty's porter's wife, that 'all the Queen's establishment was in one opinion that the Queen would certainly go to the coronation', that the Queen's dressmaker had been to her house very often during the past ten days.[62]

'It appears by the Steward's account that her Majesty is determined on going to the coronation,' another report had confirmed. 'She is to be at Westminster Hall by half past eight o'clock. Heronimus further said that he was quite certain that the Queen would not change her mind – as he had been with her seven years and never knew of one instance of her Majesty's altering her resolution when once she had made up her mind if even it would have cost her her life. But many persons imagine in reality the Queen will not attempt to appear at the coronation, especially the Queen's coach maker. . . . All the persons about the house are strictly forbid any intercourse with their neighbours. It is therefore most difficult to obtain any information about her future intention.'[63]

14

Death of Queen Caroline
1821

*

'I am going to die, Mr Brougham; but it does not signify'

The Queen had set out for the Abbey as planned in her coach of state, drawn by six bays. Lady Hood and Lady Anne Hamilton sat opposite her; Lord Hood and Keppel Craven followed in another carriage. *The Times* reported that 'the soldiers everywhere presented arms with the utmost promptitude and respect, and a thousand voices kept up a constant cry of "The Queen! The Queen for ever!"'[1] Brougham also reported much applause and the waving of handkerchiefs, accompanied by 'hooting and cursing the King'.[2] But less partial observers recorded that the Queen's reception was far from enthusiastic, that most of the spectators in the stands watched her in silence, and that the scattered shouts of 'The Queen for ever!' were drowned by 'loud whistling'.[3] Lord Colchester was reliable informed that 'one attempt to raise a cry of Queen at the corner of a street . . . totally failed'.[4]

As though unsure of herself and discouraged by the attitude of the crowd, the Queen stopped her carriage and looked about her. In a moment or two the carriage moved forward again, and stopped close to the door of Westminster Hall which was 'closed amidst much confusion'. The Queen stepped down and, leaning on Lord Hood's arm, approached two other doors which were also shut in her face and guarded by hefty prize-fighters. She then went up to a door-keeper who requested to see their tickets. The subsequent conversation was recorded in the *Courier*:

Lord Hood: 'I present to you your Queen. Surely it is not necessary for her to have a ticket.'

Door-Keeper: 'Our orders are to admit no person without a peer's ticket.'

Lord Hood: 'This is your Queen. She is entitled to admission without such a form.'

The Queen: (*smiling, but still in some agitation*): 'Yes, I am your Queen. Will you not admit me?'

Door-Keeper: 'My orders are specific, and I feel myself bound to obey them.' (*The Queen laughed.*)

Lord Hood: 'I have a ticket.'

Door-Keeper: 'Then, my Lord, we will let you pass upon producing it. This will let one person pass but no more.'

Lord Hood: 'Will your Majesty go in alone?' (*Her Majesty at first assented, but did not persevere.*)

Lord Hood: 'Am I to understand that you refuse her Majesty admission?'

Door-Keeper: 'We only act in conformity with our orders.' (*Her Majesty again laughed.*)[5]

At this point there appeared on the scene one of the Gold Staffs, Sir Robert Harry Inglis, who had been warned by the Home Secretary that the Queen would attempt to get into the Hall or the Abbey and had been told to do all he could to prevent her.

'I was obliged to squeeze between Lady Anne Hamilton and the wall to get before the party,' he afterwards reported. 'I then turned and stood in the doorway. I found her Majesty accompanied by Lord Hood, presenting herself for admission. I said to her, respectfully, I hope, "Madam, it is my duty to inform your Majesty that there is no place for your Majesty in the Royal box, or with the royal family." (I forget which.) The Queen replied, "I am sorry for it." Some further conversation took place. Her Majesty then said, "How can I get in my carriage?" I answered that I would give directions.'[6]

As the Queen drove away, the roof of her landau open 'by way of exciting the mob',[7] there were a few shouts and hisses from the crowd, a little cruel laughter; a voice here and there called out, 'Shame!' or 'Go away!' or 'Back to Como!' 'Back to Bergami!'[8] But that was all. The incident passed without any of the violence which Alderman Wood had predicted; and the only person to have suffered by it was the Queen herself, that 'Bedlam Bitch of a Queen', as Walter Scott now called her.[9]

It was obvious that her spirit was broken; and it was impossible not to feel pity for her now, not to regret that she had ever left Italy where she had been 'a merry soul', painted and preposterous but happy in her way. 'Nobody cared for *me* in this business,' she lamented. 'This business has been more cared for as a political business, than as the cause of a poor forlorn woman.'[10] In her distress she fell ill, yet having doctored herself with 'laudanum and nervous medicines' without consulting her physicians, she insisted on going to Drury Lane where Robert Elliston had staged a magnificent pageant of the coronation with himself impersonating the King so well it was 'like a portrait'.[11] He took the King's manner 'so exactly' that you could have supposed yourself at the ceremony.[12]

After the performance was over, she 'got up and curtsied to the manager, to the pit, galleries and boxes in a manner so marked – so wild – with a countenance so haggard' that Lady Anne Barnard, who had never liked her, 'burst into tears to see royalty and pride so broken down and humbled'.[13]

On her return home she began to vomit and her pulse grew fast and erratic. It was announced that she had 'an obstruction of the bowels, attended with inflammation'.[14] The pain in her stomach was intense, and she continued to be excessively sick. She was bled profusely and given large doses of opium and immersed in a warm bath. But, despite the opium, she could not sleep and the pain increased in violence. The doctors prescribed further bleeding, further doses of opium, calomel and so much castor oil that Henry Brougham thought it 'would have turned the stomach of a horse'.[15]

She was quite certain that she was going to die. 'Her will and certain deeds had been got all ready by Friday night according to her own instructions. Brougham asked her if it was her pleasure then to execute them; to which she said, "Yes, Mr Brougham; where is Mr Denman?" in the tone of a person in perfect health.' Denman opened the curtain of the bed; and she saw that he was there with Stephen Lushington. 'The will and papers being read to her, she put her hand out of bed, and signed her name four different times in the steadiest manner possible. In doing so she said with great firmness, "I am going to die, Mr Brougham; but it does not signify." Brougham said, "Your Majesty's physicians were quite of a different opinion." "Ah," she said. "I know better than them. I tell you I shall die, but I don't mind it."'[16] '*Je ne mourrai sans douleur,*' she repeated to Lord Hood, '*mais je mourrai sans regret.*'[17]

Stephen Lushington, who went to see her on 7 August, told Brougham that she 'talked incessantly on every subject for three hours; and it [was] very remarkable that the only persons she mentioned were the 'Petite Victorine, Bergami's child and the child of Parson Wood', Alderman Wood's granddaughter.[18]

On 8 August, after yet another sleepless night, the pain became more excruciating than ever, and she became delirious, then comatose. Finally she went into convulsions, her eyes became fixed and her muscles paralysed. Her breathing 'stopped just before half past ten'.[19]

Stephen Lushington, who had been appointed one of the Queen's executors, immediately wrote to Lord Liverpool informing him of her death; he spent much of the night securing 'all the repositories' at Brandenburg House, a task which occupied him until three o'clock the next morning. Then, after lying down for two hours, he rushed to Hampstead where that very day he was to be married. As soon as the ceremony was over he returned to London to meet Lord Liverpool who 'behaved extremely well – said the Government would defray the expense of the funeral'.[20]

Lord Liverpool had already written to the King to advise him that the funeral would take place 'as soon as decency would permit'. 'With respect to the place of internment,' Liverpool continued, 'it appeared to [those few members of the Cabinet who happened to be in town] that Windsor or Westminster Abbey must be selected for the purpose.' And as regards a period of mourning this would be indispensably necessary, 'as in no private family, whatever might have been the faults or sins of the individual [was] mourning dispensed with'.[21] The next day, however, Liverpool was at least able to relieve the King 'from all difficulties' as to the Queen's funeral. For he had now learned that she had asked for the burial to take place at Brunswick and for her body to be transported there 'within three days if possible after her demise'. She had also asked that the following inscription should be placed upon her coffin: 'Caroline of Brunswick, the injured Queen of England.' Such an inscription could obviously not be approved, Lord Liverpool commented, 'by authority or consent of government, nor whilst [the coffin was] in the charge of any officers of government'.[22]

The King entirely agreed, and added that the Hanoverian government, under whose immediate orders the internment was to be conducted, 'could not be parties to such a measure' either. The coffin must be removed quietly from Brandenburg House and transported down the Thames to the warship which was to convey it to the Elbe. 'Moving the body through any part of the country, or even through the town' was to be avoided.[23] As for mourning, that was to be for as short a time as decorum demanded: the King considered that three weeks would suffice and that the Earl Marshal 'should not give any orders for a general mourning' as his Majesty felt 'an objection to render the mourning otherwise than voluntary'.[24]

Despite the King's anxiety about demonstrations and disturbances if the coffin were to be transported overland, orders were nevertheless issued for it to be taken from Hammersmith through Chelmsford to Harwich. Anticipating trouble from 'a considerable cavalcade of blackguards, male and female of all ranks', the Home Department did however direct 'the Life Guards at both barracks to be on the alert'.[25] Instructions were also given to Sir Robert Baker, the chief Magistrate at Bow Street, to form a plan 'for stationing police along the line of march'; while 'the whole of the 1st Life Guards and the Blues, not otherwise on duty, were to be on the alert at their respective barracks'.[26]

The precautions were well advised, for when it became known that the Queen's coffin was not to pass through the City 'a large concourse of people, on foot and on horseback, assembled at Hammersmith' with the evident intention of forcing the *cortège* to follow the road to Temple Bar. They succeeded in doing so; for Sir Robert Baker, certain that 'lives would be lost if it was persisted in not to go through the City', declined to give orders to remove the obstacles that the mob had put across the prescribed route. So the demonstrators, encouraged by Sir Robert Wilson and accompanied towards the end of their journey by the Lord Mayor, aldermen and members of the City's Common Council, had the satisfaction of celebrating their 'triumph over the government and the military' by escorting the funeral *cortège* through Temple Bar, across Ludgate Hill and down towards the Essex Road.[27]

The *cortège*, so the Mail Coach Department reported, slowly proceeded to Chelmsford where the church bells were tolling 'as at all the other towns through which it passed'.[28] The coffin was taken off its carriage and placed on the communion table in the church at Chelmsford where, to the 'astonishment of the spectators', Lady Anne Hamilton and Lord Hood suddenly burst out laughing. For Alderman Wood, who had been carefully hiding under his coat a silver plate, dropped it on the floor. On the plate was written, in accordance with the Queen's instructions, CAROLINE OF BRUNSWICK: THE INJURED QUEEN OF ENGLAND. It was quickly retrieved and, surrounded by mourners, a cabinet-maker 'very dextrously' screwed it onto the coffin. But, after a great deal of argument, Sir George Taylor, a representative of the King, persuaded the churchwarden to prohibit the coffin's removal with the silver plate still fixed to it. So the plate was removed before the coffin continued its interrupted journey to Harwich.[29]

'On arriving at Harwich,' Henry Brougham recorded, 'we found everything ready prepared for immediate embarkation. The scene was such as I never can forget or reflect upon without emotion. The multitudes assembled from all parts of the country were immense, and the pier crowded with them as the sea was covered with boats of every size and kind, and the colours of the vessels were half-masted high, as on days of mourning. The contrast of a bright sun and the gloom on every face was striking, and the guns firing at intervals made a solemn impression. . . . The crimson coffin slowly descended from the pier.'[30]

*

On the day of the Queen's death, the yacht *Royal George* had arrived off Holyhead. One of the passengers, Major-General Sir Andrew Barnard, a Groom of the Bedchamber, reported that his Majesty had been 'in the best health and spirits during the whole passage' from Portsmouth. The sea air agreed with him, and he was obviously looking forward to his forthcoming visit to Ireland.[31]

The following morning, however, he received the first accounts of the Queen's illness; and it was considered advisable for him not to sail straight across to Dublin Bay as had been planned, but to land at Holyhead, to go to stay with the Marquess of Anglesey at Plas Newydd and 'to postpone his public entry till something more decisive should be known as to the Queen's state'.[32] The next bulletin from Hammersmith suggested that she was expected to recover, and the King returned to the yacht only to receive the news of her sudden death. 'Though it would be absurd to think that he was afflicted, he certainly was affected. . . . He walked about the cabin the greater part of the night.'[33] 'He had all the masts of the squadron lowered as a sign of mourning.'[34]

The following day he received a copy of the Queen's will by which William Austin was to receive the whole of her estate on reaching the age of twenty-one; but there were so many demands on the estate that her combined assets in England and Italy were insufficient to satisfy the claims. She was, in fact, insolvent.* William Austin was not left destitute as she had instructed Messrs Coutts in 1818 to invest £200 a year (the rent she received from her house in Blackheath) on his behalf in government stock.[35]† But the members of her Household to which she had wished to give pensions were obliged to look for their money to the King.[36] The King agreed to pay these pensions;[37] but he asked Lord Liverpool to confer with the Lord Chancellor, the Attorney-General and the Solicitor-General as to the best way of reclaiming the jewels which were his property, not hers.[38]

The King, who, when Napoleon had died, was said to have responded to the intelligence that his 'greatest enemy' was dead with the words, 'Is she, by God!', was not expected to display any prolonged grief at his bereavement or to feel less than a profound sense of relief after the first shock was passed. And on his fifty-ninth birthday, 12 August 1821, as he crossed the Irish Sea in the steam boat he was certainly 'in great spirits'.

'We drank his health in sight of Irish land,' General Barnard told his sister-in-law, 'but although in mid-channel and much elated by the occasion we were not quite half seas over.'[39] The Countess of Glengall, however, reported the King as being far more than half seas over. Indeed

---

* The Queen had evidently wanted to bequeath some diamonds to Pergami's child, Victorine; but Brougham and the other lawyers had thought it better to omit this from the will though they planned to send the jewels to her (*Creevey Papers*, 336). The Queen's furniture and effects, which were sold by auction at Cambridge House on 20 February 1822, realized no more than £8,085. According to a marked catalogue of sale the most expensive items of furniture were her billiard table (£42) and 'superb ebonized frame state bedstead' (£45 3s.). A portrait of her by Lawrence fetched no more than £56, a wooden sculpture of the Last Supper £29. The only valuable things in the house were the curtains, the pier glasses, chimney glasses and lustres (RA Geo IV Box 10).

† William Austin died in a lunatic asylum in Chelsea in 1849. In 1819 the Queen had told James Brougham that Austin was not the child of the unemployed dockyard worker, Samuel Austin, and of his wife Sophia Austin, as the Commissioners who conducted the Delicate Investigation of 1806 had concluded. The Queen had said she had 'humbugged' the Commissioners and that William was really the natural son of Prince Louis Ferdinand of Prussia. She repeated the substance of this story to Dr Stephen Lushington on her deathbed (Brougham MSS, 10, 268). Austin himself, however, seems not to have doubted that Samuel and Sophia Austin were his parents. From 1810 to 1821 he wrote regularly to Sophia as his mother, giving her news of his activities on the Continent and making arrangements to see her when he was in England (Goulding Papers, Lincoln).

according to her he was 'dead DRUNK' when he landed and could hardly stand up.[40] This, too, was what Lord Temple heard from William Fremantle. 'The passage to Dublin,' Temple was assured, 'was occupied in eating goose-pie and drinking whiskey in which his Majesty took most abundantly, singing many joyous songs, and being in a state, on his arrival, to double in number even the numbers of his gracious subjects assembled on the pier to receive him. The fact was that they were in the last stages of intoxication.'[41] If this were so, he managed to disguise the worst effects of the wine and whisky punch from the Irish spectators on his arrival with some credit.

He landed at Howth at about half past four in the afternoon. Because of the Queen's death, his landing had not been announced, and there were less than two hundred people on the pier; but as the ship approached the landing place the crowds grew and excitement mounted.[42] He stepped ashore, 'a little browned from the weather', in a plain blue coat with a black cravat and a foraging cap trimmed with gold lace, shook hands with several men who approached him, and greeted the Earl of Kingston with the words, 'Kingston, Kingston, you black-whiskered, good-natured fellow! I am happy to see you in this friendly country.'[43] He then drove off to the Viceregal Lodge in Phoenix Park, escorted by a ragged procession of enthusiastic Irishmen, 'dozens of farmers and gentlemen on horseback, and nearly two thousand pedestrians'. At the gates of the Park the King invited them all into the grounds, told them not to trouble to keep off the grass, and asked them to accompany him to the house where he made them what General Barnard described as a 'short but hearty speech which completely won not only their hearts but has had the same effect wherever it has been repeated'.[44]

He reminded them that he had made a long and rough sea voyage and that 'particular circumstances' had occurred of which it was 'better at present not to speak'. But, all the same, this was one of the happiest days of his life. He had long wished to visit Ireland. His heart had always been Irish; he had loved the country since the 'day it first beat'.[45]

This was a little extravagant; but there was a good deal of truth behind the highflown phrases. He had always felt at ease in the company of most Irishmen, had always professed to a sympathetic understanding of most of Ireland's problems, and had consequently been more popular with most of the Irish people than he had ever been at home. At the time of the Regency Crisis in 1788–9 Irish commissioners had invited the Prince to exercise 'all legal powers, jurisdictions and prerogatives';[46] and in later years the Carlton House group of Members of Parliament derived much of its strength from its dozen or more Irish members. In 1821, the King's popularity in Ireland remained largely unabated, and his visit during the summer undeniably increased it. He charmed the people with his friendliness and approachability, with the easy, natural way he shook them by the hand, talked to them, smiled at them and gave numerous proofs of his generosity. It was easy enough, of course, to present a few peasants with pigs and chickens, to present orphan children with new clothing, to distribute handfuls of guineas to needy labourers, to urge absentee landlords to live on their estates, to praise and to wear Irish wool and Irish cloth. But the fact was that Ireland was the first place he had chosen to visit now that he was King, and no reigning English sovereign had ever paid a state visit there since the time of Richard II. 'I was a rebel to old King George in '98,' said one old man, voicing a common sentiment, 'but by God I'd die a hundred deaths for his son, because he's a real King, and asks us how we are.'[47] Another former Irish rebel, Lord Cloncurry, who had served a term of imprisonment in the Tower of London, wrote of the 'strange madness' that came over all Irishmen during the King's visit. He himself was affected by it; and gave 'a pledge of the sincerity' of his 'waiver of all bygones' by inviting the King to his house.[48]

For the first few days of his visit, the King remained quietly 'in seclusion at the Park' as a mark of respect to his wife, though he made it clear that this was the only notice of his bereavement that he felt inclined to take. Bloomfield, himself an Irishman, had some difficulty in persuading him to wear mourning and to put a crape band round his arm.[49] He remained in excellent spirits, though, and gave way in the end good-naturedly.

John Wilson Croker, another Irishman, who was in Dublin at the time and was a guest at the 'very hot and very dull' dinner party given in the Castle to celebrate the King's birthday, recorded in his journal an example of his good humour. Lord Castlereagh – who had become Marquess of Londonderry on his father's death in April – was reading aloud in the King's presence a letter that had arrived in Holyhead from England. When he came to the words, 'the Duke of York', Castlereagh 'looked horrorstruck and stopped short. "Come, Come," said the King, "You must now go on with it, or I shall think it worse than I dare say it will turn out to be."

Castlereagh was then obliged to stammer on, "*The Duke of York is in despair at an event* [the Queen's death] *which so much diminishes his chance of the crown.*" The King, however, laughed very good-humouredly at it, and afterwards repeated the story with equal good humour.'[50]

On 17 August his Majesty, wearing the Order of St Patrick on his field marshal's uniform, and a mourning crape on his arm, made his public entry into Dublin, escorted by hundreds of carriages and thousands of 'gentlemen on horseback'. It was a lovely sunny day and as he stood up in his open carriage, waving his hat, pointing significantly to the big bunch of shamrock attached to its brim, and then laying his hand on his heart, the immense crowds roared their welcome. For almost an hour his carriage was halted by the dense throng that pressed around it, swaying it about so violently that the King was prevented from falling over only by one of his attendants who held him up under the arms. 'The people shouted,' Croker recalled. 'The Irish, it seems, do not know how to *hurrah* or *cheer*; they have not had much practice in the expression of public joy. After the King had received the addresses on the throne, he sent for me into his private room. He was walking about greatly agitated between pleasure at his reception in Ireland and dissatisfaction at what has occurred in London when the Queen's coffin was taken from Hammersmith. . . . He kept me full half an hour, and talked the whole time, alternately at the triumph of Dublin and the horrors of London. Bloomfield tells me that the King sat up the greater part of the night fretting about this latter affair; it affects him certainly more deeply than I should have expected.'[51]*

The events of the next few busy days, however, restored the King's

---

* General Barnard confirmed how angry the King was when he heard of the disturbances over the Queen's funeral procession during which, although the military had behaved 'with infinite temperance', two demonstrators had been killed (*Barnard Letters*, 295). The government felt obliged to ask Admiral Sir George Cockburn and John Wilson Croker, as Secretary to the Admiralty, 'to draw up a *mémoire justificatif*' of the reasons for taking the coffin overland to Harwich and not by water as the King had suggested. Cockburn justified the Admiralty's decision in a lengthy memorandum which pleaded the difficulties of getting a suitable frigate round to the Nore from Spithead in 'a gale of wind at *west*', as well as the possibility of 'greater mischiefs' if the coffin had been moved down the Thames and under London Bridge than had, in fact, been experienced in conducting it across country (Asp/K, ii, 458–64). The King accepted the excuses; but Sir Robert Baker, the Bow Street magistrate, was dismissed from his office.

spirits. There was a splendid review in the Park on 18 August, another 'wonderfully fine' day;[52] there was a crowded levee on the 20th before which the King received addresses from the Presbyterian clergy, Catholic bishops and the Quakers, answering them all in a manner 'impressive and kind beyond description'.[53] Then there was a Drawing-Room on the 21st when 'above a thousand ladies were presented, and really they were (with a very few and very inconsiderable exceptions), all ladies who might have very properly attended at St James's, and their dresses were both rich and in good taste. . . . By some interruption, about one-third of the company were cut off and prevented coming up with the stream. The attendants thought there were no more to be presented, so the door of the presence chamber was shut, and the King made his bows and retired. In a few minutes it was found that the ante-rooms were again full. . . . What was to be done? The King had retired and was undressed. On the other hand, the ladies were dressed and had no mind to retire; after a good deal of *pourparlers*, the King was told of the circumstances, and with great good nature he put on his fine coat, came back to the presence chamber, and went through the ceremony of kissing those hundred ladies more.'[54]

After this Drawing-Room there was an 'extremely splendid' banquet given by the Dublin Corporation in a room specially built for the occasion and representing 'the interior circular court of a Moorish palace open to the sky; the battlements were a gallery filled with ladies, music and a company of halberdiers, in Spanish dresses of light blue silk, as a guard of honour to the King. It was lighted by a vast circle of lamps, hung by invisible wires, which had a wonderfully fine and curious effect.' The loud cheers that greeted all references to the merits of the guest of honour were echoed by the crowds of people in the streets outside.[55]

This banquet was followed by another at Trinity College, where at the singing of 'Rule Britannia' 'the royal countenance glowed with pleasure'; he beat the time with his hand and vigorously struck the table in front of him 'at every word'.[56] This, in turn, was followed by a public breakfast at Leinster House given by the Dublin Society, by visits to the theatre and the Curragh, by the installation of new Knights of the Order of St Patrick, and by a grand ball at the Castle. And everywhere the King went he was greeted with the same enthusiasm and was made to feel as welcome as he had been on the day of his arrival. 'Were you here you would imagine Ireland to be the richest country in the world,' General Barnard told his sister-in-law, 'such exertions have these poor people made to testify their attachment to George the Fourth.'[57]

His cheerful response to these exertions was considered rather vulgar in some quarters in England. He 'seems to have behaved not like a sovereign coming in state and pomp to visit a part of his dominions,' Lord Dudley commented disapprovingly. 'But like a popular candidate come down upon an electioneering trip.'[58]

So far as the Irish were concerned, however, the single disappointment he caused during the entire visit was at the Dublin Society's breakfast which was held on the day that the Queen was buried in her family tomb at Brunswick. The King did his duty by going 'minutely through the museum' at Leinster House but then left the breakfast abruptly, spending no more than three or four minutes on the lawn where there were tents and 'bands of music in all directions'. Barnard thought that the walk through the museum had tired him out; but Croker considered it just as likely that he had left in a hurry because he was so anxious to get to Slane Castle, the home of the Marquess and Marchioness of Conyngham.[59]

15

Lady Conyngham and William Knighton

1820-1821

*

'The King desires Lord Liverpool distinctly
to understand that whatever appointments the
King may think proper to make in his own
family, they are to be considered as quite
independent of the control of any Minister
whatever'

Lady Conyngham was a fat, kindly, religious, rich and rapacious woman
of fifty-two, the daughter of Joseph Denison, a city banker from a modest
home in Yorkshire, who had come down to London where he had amassed,
by industry and parsimony, a fortune of astonishing magnitude. She had
been married for twenty-seven years and had four grown-up children.
Her beauty was beginning to fade, and she had never been amusing or
particularly intelligent, though she was much more shrewd than people
supposed. The King adored her. For some time past he had been seeing
less and less of Lady Hertford whose grandson, Lord Beauchamp, seeing
the King riding with Lady Conyngham in the Park one day, burst out,
'By God, grandmother must learn to ride, or it is all over with us.'[1]

Lady Hertford herself took the King's neglect very badly, pouring out her
tearful, angry complaints to Mme de Lieven, protesting that she found
'the new love ridiculous in view of the age of the contracting parties'.[2] In
less emotional moods, Lady Hertford would haughtily protest that she
took no interest in her rival – on being asked about her she would reply
coldly that 'intimately as she had known the king . . . he had never
ventured to speak to her upon the subject of his mistresses'.[3]

Most people who knew them both well, however, doubted that Lady Conyngham was in fact the King's mistress, though she had rather a conspiratorial manner and was reported to have had lovers in the past. She was excessively fond of clothes, money, and, above all, jewellery – one of her proudest possessions being a sapphire surrounded by brilliants, which had belonged to the Stuarts and had been given by the Cardinal of York to the King. The King had given it to Princess Charlotte and, on her death, had asked Prince Leopold to give it back to him as it was a crown jewel.*

Some pamphleteers described the King snoring in bed with his 'prime bit of stuff', his 'Vice-Queen'. But others who portrayed them

> Quaffing their claret, then mingling their lips,
> Or tickling the fat about each other's hips

---

* 'Never were such jewels,' commented Emily Cowper after seeing Lady Conyngham at a 'very brilliant and very dull' ball at Carlton House in May 1821. 'The family pearls which she talked of last year have increased greatly. The string is twice as long as it was and such a diamond belt three inches wide with such a sapphire in the centre. By the way I must tell you the history of it. The Cardinal York left it to the King to be added to the jewels of the crown. The King in a fit of parental fondness gave it to Princess Charlotte. When she died he sent to Leopold for her jewels, saying they belonged to the crown. Leopold, *qui n'aime pas rendre les bijoux*, as Mme de Lieven says, murmured that he could not bear to part with anything which had belonged to her. The King insisted, upon which Leo gave in and said he would present them *au roi comme un homage*. The King saying in particular he must have this stone for his coronation as it was to go in the crown – when lo and behold here it has appeared in Lady Conyngham's waist' (Palmerston Papers, C IV/4/3, 3 May 1821; Lever, 79). Payments made to Messrs Rundell, Bridge & Co. alone between January 1821 and January 1829 amounted to £105,618 (RA 32696). This sum included £3,150 for a pearl necklace with 'thirty-seven remarkably large oriental pearls' (RA 26161). In two previous months, February and March 1820, the King paid £400 for a pair of diamond ear-rings, £437 for a pair of pearl bracelets, £530 for an emerald necklace and £740 for a pearl necklace (RA 25997). Lady Conyngham was certainly responsible for a fairly large proportion of this expenditure. Sir Benjamin Bloomfield, Keeper of the Privy Purse, said that he thought the King would go mad such was his infatuation for Lady Conyngham. He told Charles Arbuthnot that it was 'quite shameful the way in which she [was] covered with jewels and that he really [believed] the King [had] given her a 100,000 £s worth!!' (*Arbuthnot Journal*, i, 138). It should be added, though, that after the King's death, Lady Conyngham returned to the Keeper of the Privy Purse various jewels, including the Stuart sapphire, which she had reason to doubt 'his late Majesty ought to have given away' (Wellington Papers, 21 November 1830, 4 December 1830).

were drawing an equally cruel but no doubt more realistic picture of their relationship which seems to have been warmly domestic rather than hotly passionate, to have fulfilled the King's needs for a motherly, affectionate woman to fuss over and fondle and be fussed over and fondled by. In its early flowering the relationship was also highly flirtatious. Lord Burghersh, indeed, thought it 'the most laughable thing that ever was'. The King 'never drank wine without touching her glass with his, holding her hand under the table all the time he was drinking'.[4] As with the Hertfords, it was a relationship that embraced husband and children as well as wife, and most of the Conynghams seemed content with it. Mrs Arbuthnot heard that the King and Lady Conyngham spent their evenings 'sitting on a sofa together, holding each other's hands, whispering and kissing, Lord Conyngham being present'.[5] Less complaisant than her husband was Lady Conyngham's brother, William Denison, senior partner of Messrs Denison, Heywood and Kennard, bankers of Lombard Street, who had vastly increased his father's immense fortune and who, dying unmarried and childless, left most of his own to his nephew, Lord Albert Conyngham, on condition that he took the unsullied name of Denison.[6*]

While William Denison felt his sister's virtue to have been outraged by her association with the King, many others considered the liaison more absurd than scandalous. 'The King made himself very ridiculous with Lady Conyngham,' Mrs Arbuthnot commented disapprovingly after a great ball at Carlton House in May 1821. He 'was devoted to her the whole night and at last retired to one of the rooms with her and placed a page at the door to prevent anyone going in. [Various guests] were going in when the page stopped them and, laughing, told them nobody could be allowed to go in. As the King can see Lady Conyngham every day and

* William Denison had been offered a seat in the Commons by the Regent in 1812 but declined it on the grounds that 'he had no intention of coming into publick life' (RA 20071, 27 September 1812). He had been a Whig member for Camelford from 1796 to 1802, represented Kingston-upon-Hull in 1806–7, and was Member for Surrey from 1818 to 1849. His nephew, Lord Albert Conyngham, who changed his name to Denison in 1849 in accordance with the terms of his uncle's will, and who was created first Baron Londesborough in 1850, was widely rumoured to be King George IV's son, unlikely as this seemed to judge from his lank form and toothy face, which were much more like those of the Marquess of Conyngham. He was born in 1805. Although it is not known for certain that the King knew Lady Conyngham well at this time, she was already by then a conspicuous figure in Brighton society (Musgrave, *Brighton*, 167).

all day long, I really think he might control his passion and not behave so indecently in public.'[7]

Charles Greville was equally disapproving. He described the King, who was said to have gone on a strict diet to make himself more attractive to his loved one, going up to her at Brighton when she had given orders for the saloon to be illuminated, and saying effusively, 'Thank you, thank you, my dear; you always do what is right; you cannot please me so much as by doing everything you please, everything to show that you are mistress here.'[8] Mme de Lieven, who had 'never seen a man more in love', gave Wellington 'a very ridiculous account of a scene that she had had with the King and Lady Conyngham. The King had made her sit by him in the evening, Lady Conyngham being on the other side of him, and had told her that he had never known what it was to be in love before, that he was himself quite surprised at the degree to which he was in love, that he did nothing from morning to night but think what he could do to please Lady Conyngham and make her happy, that he would do anything upon earth for her for that he owed his life to her . . . and that she was an angel sent from heaven for him. *He cried*, Lady Conyngham cried and Mme de Lieven said that, being nervous and easily agitated, she had cried also; and all this passed in a crowded drawing room.'[9] Mme de Lieven also told Metternich how he had had Lady Conyngham – 'a nice enough woman' – and all her family to stay with him at the Royal Lodge, how he used to visit her every afternoon at Brighton, where she had a house at the end of Marlborough Row, and how, in the evenings, he would sit down to dinner with her on his right, her elder daughter, Lady Elizabeth, on his left, her second son, Lord Francis Conyngham – 'dearest Frank' – at one end of the table, and the Marquess himself at the other.[10]*

He loved the Conyngham children dearly. When nominating Lord Francis a Grand Cross of the Guelphic Order, he did so, he said, because he wished not only to remind Lord Francis himself but also to convey to others how much he 'loved and distinguished' him.[11] His attentions to Lady Elizabeth were so marked that it was sometimes said that it was really she with whom he was in love and not her mother. And he wrote to her younger daughter, Maria, his 'most beloved and darling Maria' in the most

---

* Lady Conyngham's eldest son, the Earl of Mount Charles, disapproved of his mother's liaison with the King and so was rarely of the company. The King did all he could to placate him, sending him presents and using his influence to obtain for him desired appointments.

affectionate way imaginable. 'You are ever present in my thoughts,' he told her. 'Believe me, my sweet child, when I tell you, that not only a day does not pass without my thinking of you, but that you are constantly before me, in my imagination and thoughts and you cannot imagine what a relief it is to me: in the midst of the many painful and anxious moments to which I am doomed, when your dear little self... darts before my mind's eye.... Dearest Mater mentioned to me, the day before yesterday, that you complained of being tormented to the greatest degree with chilblains. I instantly sent off to our little friend Barrett at Brighton for his lotion.... I need not say how much I have missed you and how long I have wished to see you... and it is therefore with a delight I have not words to express that I announce to you that upon the arrival of a Knight Errant, who will suddenly arrive, seize upon you, and as suddenly convey you to the Old Castle at Windsor when you may be sure, my beloved child, you will be received with open arms by its old Possessor.'[12]

He told her about the 'pretty little pranks' of a favourite puppy which caressed him with delight, ran about the room from him to Maria's Pater and back, sat up on her hind legs, and 'did everything but speak': 'After she had drank she came instantly back, lay down by the side of my bed, began crying for a moment or two... walked to the door, whining piteously as if to say, "Let me out for I want to go and look after my kind mistress." We watched her and the moment the door was opened, she bolted, poor little thing, as fast as she could fly to your dearest Mater's rooms.'[13]

Maria wrote to him in similar vein: 'How can I express my delight and thanks for your affectionate letter. I kissed it as I could not kiss the dear person that wrote it. I am overjoyed at the thought of seeing you soon.'[14]

The whole correspondence shows how important to him was the family life which the Conynghams were able to share with him, how deeply he regretted never having had such a family of his own.*

The influence of the Conynghams had already been strongly demon-

---

* 'He always was fond of children,' Lord Melbourne told Queen Victoria, 'and took notice of them, etc.' The Queen replied, 'He took notice of me' (RA, Queen Victoria's Journal, entry for August 1838). He bought an enormous amount of playthings to give away as presents. His accounts are replete with bills for dolls and lead soldiers, boxes of ninepins, miniature farm yards, play houses, mechanical animals, rocking-horses, games and toys of every description (RA 29111–29204).

strated when, without consulting the government, the King promised to promote to a vacant canonry at Windsor, the Rev. Charles Richard Sumner, curate of Highclere in Hampshire, who had been tutor to Lady Conyngham's three sons. The Prime Minister protested to Bloomfield that the stalls at Windsor had in the past, 'with scarcely any exception', been given to 'some clergyman of known character and merit, who had already filled some conspicuous situation in the Church, or to persons of family and connection'.[15] Lord Liverpool thought that 'serious inconveniences' might result from the 'intended arrangement'.[16] Lord Castlereagh also wrote to Bloomfield to emphasize how dangerous and 'prejudicial' was the step which the King had taken.[17] And Lord Sidmouth added his warnings to the others by declaring that nothing had given him so much uneasiness since he had the 'honor of becoming a member of the present government'.[18] The King, having taken a strong liking to the handsome and suave Charles Sumner was, however, insistent. He felt bound 'to recall to Lord Liverpool the communication made through Sir Benjamin Bloomfield which expressed "that the nomination of the Rev. Mr Sumner to the vacant Canonry at Windsor would be very acceptable to the King's wishes". The absence of Church preferment in this gentleman does not in the King's mind form a just ground of objection on this occasion; the more particularly as Mr Sumner's strict piety, exemplary conduct and great learning peculiarly recommend him for this mark of royal favour.'[19]

For a time the problem appeared so intractable that it was thought that the government might be forced to resign. 'I left the Brighton Pavilion in a great state of excitement over a little affair which may become a big one,' Mme de Lieven wrote on 17 April 1821. 'The King wants to bestow the Canonry of Windsor on the tutor of Lady Conyngham's children. The Ministers will not tolerate this infringement of their privileges; for they alone have these places in their gift. Within three days Bloomfield made the trip from Brighton to London five times. The King is obstinate, and so are his Ministers; and finally Liverpool went to Brighton yesterday to tell the King that, as long as he is Minister, he will not give way. I do not know what has been decided. The Duke of Wellington said to me this morning: "Perhaps at this very moment, we have already been turned out." It is certain that there are more difficulties ahead. An extraordinary state of affairs – the constant hostility between master and servants.'[20]

Eventually, after Sumner had written to Bloomfield to say that he did not wish to cause the King 'the uneasiness of a single instant',[21] a compromise was reached. The Windsor canonry was given to the King's librarian and chaplain at Carlton House, Dr James Stanier Clarke, whose appointments, together with the private chaplaincy at Windsor, a salary of £300 a year, and 'a capital house opposite the Park gates' were given to Sumner.[22] Soon afterwards Sumner was found a canonry at Worcester, and then, having refused the bishopric of Jamaica and accepted a Deputy Clerkship of the Closet, was consecrated Bishop of Llandaff before becoming Bishop of Winchester.[23] But the way in which his wishes had at first been thwarted by Lord Liverpool 'mortally wounded' the King who felt that he could never forget it.[24]

Scarcely had the crisis over the Windsor canonry been resolved when the King's friendship with the Conynghams involved him in another quarrel with the government. The new disagreement was over the vacancy occasioned by the resignation of the Marquess of Hertford who, in July 1821, handed in his resignation as Lord Chamberlain of the King's Household.[25] Lord Liverpool assured the King that with regard to a successor he was 'earnestly desirous' to meet his personal wishes so far as he could do so 'consistently with the responsibility which necessarily belonged to his situation as his Majesty's First Minister'.[26]

This suggestion that he was not entirely free to choose whomsoever he pleased provoked the King into making an angry response: 'The King desires Lord Liverpool distinctly to understand that whatever appointments the King may think proper to make in his own family, they are to be considered as quite independent of the control of any Minister whatever; and Lord Liverpool must be aware that the present government was framed on that basis alone under him.'[27]

The King, as Lord Liverpool feared, was determined to appoint Lord Conyngham to the vacant post in his Household; and the government was equally determined to prevent him, for Lady Conyngham was known to be intriguing with the opposition and was suspected of exacerbating his differences with his Ministers. It was intimated to the King that the only Household appointment to which the government would agree to Lord Conyngham's being appointed was Groom of the Stole. At a dinner party at the Duke of Wellington's, the King – still incensed with the government over their mismanagement of the Queen's funeral procession as well as the Conyngham appointment – 'behaved with pointed rudeness to Lord Liverpool in the presence of the foreign ministers';[28] and with

Wellington himself he was seen to be no longer on friendly terms. He had recently much annoyed the Duke not only by declining a previous invitation to dinner and then going to dine with the Duke of Devonshire (to whom Lady Conyngham hoped to marry her elder daughter), but also by failing to consult him when the King had authorized a statement that he was going to do so. Thus provoked, Wellington said to him 'in his brusque manner, "If you do not like us, why do you not turn us out?" The King made no answer, and the Duke, after a short pause, made his bow.'[29]

*

Although irritated at finding himself unable to gratify Lady Conyngham's wishes to the extent that he would have liked, the King was 'in excellent tone and spirits' when he came to visit her at Slane Castle in August. He found life there so enjoyable, he said, that he would like to stay in Ireland and have Lord Talbot, the Lord Lieutenant, sent over to London as his representative in England.[30] The three days he spent at Slane seemed to have been amongst the happiest of his life.[31] Indeed the whole of his visit to Ireland afforded him the greatest pleasure. Lord Sidmouth, who had accompanied him 'with a determination to hold the scales even between all parties', had 'not heard an unpleasant word nor seen a sullen look'.[32] The King returned home more ready than ever to protest that he was 'a most determined Irishman'. The Irish themselves had been delighted with him; they had been 'out of their wits with joy', and had 'already voted to build him a royal palace in *Dublin*'; he was 'very likely to be now christened *Paddy* the 1st'.[33] Orangemen and Catholics, temporarily forgetting their differences, had been united in their welcome, and there seemed good grounds to hope that a more promising period in the troubled history of their country had begun. Henry Hobhouse, Under Secretary of State for the Home Department, concluded that 'nothing could have gone off better than the King's visit to Ireland'.[34] Even Daniel O'Connell, convinced that the spirit of reconciliation should be encouraged by every possible means, went so far as to present the King of England with a laurel crown upon his departure. The King accepted the tribute, shook O'Connell cordially by the hand and declared to the crowds gathered at the edge of the shore, 'My friends! When I arrived in this beautiful country my heart overflowed with joy – it is now depressed with sincere sorrow. I never felt sensations of more delight than since I came to Ireland – I cannot expect to feel any superior nor many equal till I have the happiness of seeing you again. Whenever an opportunity offers wherein I can serve Ireland, I shall seize on it with eagerness. I am a man of few words. Short adieux are best. God bless you, my friends. God bless you all.'[35]

'The scene was grand and affecting,' wrote General Barnard who believed that his Majesty's visit would be 'productive of the best consequences' and that it had 'already tended much to sooth those political animosities which so long [had] been the destruction of the country'. 'The shores were covered with people of all descriptions who expressed their feelings on the occasion strongly, several who were nearest the spot followed his barge up to their necks in water.'[36] One particularly enthusiastic supporter who had followed him everywhere 'would have been drowned – for he could not swim – had not the King sent a boat to his assistance'.[37]

As his band played 'St Patrick's Day', and cannon fired in salute, as the crowds cheered and the flags fluttered from the masts of the royal squadron, the King stood waving his hat in the gathering darkness. Then he sat down on a sofa which had been placed for him on deck; and the *Royal George* sailed out to sea.

The voyage home was a fearful ordeal. Soon after the squadron's departure, a gale forced it back to Dunleary; and when at last the ships did get out into the Irish Sea a howling storm tossed the *Royal George* away from the escorts, and it was forty-eight hours before land was reached again at Milford Haven. 'Most even of our crew and company were deadly sick,' the King wrote; 'but the very worst of all was my poor self; and I am now on 10th September for the first time, since we are again at anchor in smooth water, risen from my bed, and not without considerable exertion. . . . I am . . . completely shattered and torn to pieces.'[38]

There was worse yet to come. The roads through Wales and parts of the West Country to London were so primitive and bumpy that it was considered advisable, now that the wind had dropped, to continue the journey by sea round Land's End to Portsmouth. But after a few hours' sailing with 'a most promising breeze', 'a violent hurricane and tempest suddenly arose'. The King, who appears to have displayed an admirable fortitude at such times of physical danger, dramatically recorded the consequences: 'The most dreadful possible of nights and of scenes ensued, the sea breaking everywhere over the ship. We lost the tiller, and the vessel was for some minutes down on her beam-ends; and nothing, I believe, but the undaunted presence of mind, perseverance, experience and courage of Paget [Captain the Hon. Sir Charles Paget, commander of the *Royal George*] preserved us from a watery grave. The oldest and most experienced of our sailors were petrified and paralysed; you may judge somewhat, then, of what was the state of most of the passengers; every one almost flew up in their shirts upon deck in terrors that are not to be described.'[39]

It was not until 16 September that the King arrived home. On his way through Hampshire to London he met Lord and Lady Harcourt on the road. He stopped his carriage, got out 'and sat with them in theirs, on the public highway, recounting all his perils at sea'. Lady Harcourt, so she told her friends, was 'quite edified at his pious acknowledgments of his escape, and there was quite a change to be noticed in his conduct'.[40]

He would have liked to have gone down to Brighton for a while to recuperate; but there was no time, for within eight days he was due to leave for Hanover. Proud of being a Brunswicker as well as a patriotic Englishman, he had been looking forward to this trip. In the early summer he had discussed it enthusiastically and at length with Mme de Lieven who had found him at Carlton House 'lying at full length in a lilac silk dressing-gown, a velvet nightcap on his head, his huge bare feet (for he had gout) covered with a pink silk net'. She had 'spent an hour and a half *tête à tête* with this get-up', talking of 'love, religion, tittle-tattle, politics, plans for the journey'; and, having described to her his itinerary, he gave her 'two smacking kisses'.[41] He was less excited now, though. It was not only that he was not yet feeling up to another long journey, but it had been decided that the Conynghams should not go with him. It was some comfort, however, that he was to be accompanied instead by Sir William Knighton.

*

Sir William Knighton was a remarkable man, industrious, conscientious, understanding and discreet, yet so affected, irritating, staid and touchy that it was a cause of some astonishment in the King's Household that his Majesty was evidently so attached to him. Born in Devon, the son of an impoverished country gentleman who had been disinherited and died young, Knighton had been sent by his widowed mother to a small school at Newton Bushell and then to study medicine under an uncle at Tavistock. Having qualified at an early age he became an assistant-surgeon at the Royal Naval Hospital at Plymouth, but, after marrying the daughter of a captain in the Royal Navy, he moved to London and by 1806 had established himself in practice as a fashionable *accoucheur* in Hanover Square. An occasional patient of his was Moll Raffles, one of Lord Wellesley's several mistresses; and when Lord Wellesley was asked to lead an embassy to Spain in 1809 and decided to take Poll with him, she persuaded her lover to ask Dr Knighton to accompany them. Knighton agreed to go on the understanding that he would receive £5,000 in consideration for a two-years' absence from London; and, on Wellesley returning to England unexpectedly, having paid Knighton only a part of that sum, he strongly recommended him to the Prince of Wales as compensation for the loss of the remainder.[42] Knighton had gone to see the Prince who had struck him then as 'very intelligent . . . proud and overbearing, but with a most fascinating complacency of manner'. The Prince had been suffering from 'a lameness in his hand', caused either from an accident 'or from the use of laudanum'. But Knighton had not felt able to prescribe anything, since the complaint was already being treated by Sir Everard Howe, Sir Walter Farquhar and Henry Cline, the surgeon. All the same, the Prince had been much impressed by Knighton, had kept him talking for twenty minutes, and had afterwards told Farquhar that he was 'the best-mannered medical man' he had ever met.[43] Some time later Knighton had been appointed one of the Prince's physicians-in-ordinary, and within two years he had been created a baronet. Sir William had become by then far more than a doctor. The Regent had grown accustomed to consulting him upon all manner of private concerns, and clearly saw in him a worthy successor to that faithful servant, the wily *débrouillard*, Colonel McMahon, who had died in 1817.

Shortly before McMahon's death, Knighton, it seems, had been sent down to McMahon's country cottage near Blackheath to retrieve from him any incriminating papers concerning the King's past that he might still have in his possession there. Knighton claimed to have found McMahon extremely feeble in both body and mind. His wife had just died. She was 'an ill-educated woman', in Knighton's opinion, 'with but two objects, that of making money and the adoration of her husband'. She took every possible opportunity of profiting from her husband's position and was able to leave him a surprisingly large amount of money. He was shattered by her death, began to drink to excess, and to lose his reason.[44] On arrival at his cottage Knighton gave him some brandy which revived him sufficiently to hand over 'all the King's private letters, early correspondence and other documents'. In reporting his success to the King, Knighton added, 'Nothing can have been more secret or more satisfactory than the accomplishment of this desirable object for no second person has been or need be, unless it shall be your royal Highness's pleasure, brought acquainted with any part of your early correspondence or early documents of any description.'[45]

The discretion with which this confidential duty had been performed evidently increased the King's respect for Knighton, who soon afterwards became Auditor of the Duchy of Cornwall, and Secretary and Keeper of his Royal Highness's Privy Seal and Council Seal. By the time of the visit to Ireland, Knighton, who was then forty-five, was undoubtedly his most trusted confidant, though Sir Benjamin Bloomfield – on Lady Hertford's recommendation – had actually succeeded to the office of Private Secretary on McMahon's death four years before. So heavily had the King begun to rely upon Knighton, indeed, that he felt uneasy when he was not readily at hand, and was in the habit of summoning him to his presence in the most affectionate, not to say effusive terms.

'My dearest and best of friends,' he wrote in one characteristic letter in March 1821, when thanking him for a poem which Knighton, an inveterate poetaster, had written and sent to him for his approval. 'I have at length secured a moment to acknowledge your last kind letter, with the poem which accompanied it.' It was a 'very, very, very *wonderful* poem', he assured him with a wild, incoherent hyperbole – induced, no doubt, by drunkenness – a 'most *beautiful production* of the human mind, perhaps, if not the most grand one certainly of the very grandest and *most elegant* at the same time, that any pen produced, either in our language or in any other. You know I put but little value upon my taste and judgment in these matters, but as far as my opinion goes, dear friend, I never . . .' He never, in fact, had read such a poem; it demanded comparison with Shakespeare, Milton, and Dante; he had read it aloud and wept over it.

'I suppose you have seen Astley Cooper [the surgeon],' he continued in more sober mood, 'and therefore I shall leave everything upon that head till I see you next, which I trust *will be at latest four o'clock* on Tuesday next; when we will get our usual tete a tete together, before I am *condemned* to go to the Opera in *state*. I have much to say to you *then*.'[46]

The King's correspondence is full of such summonses, nearly all of them highly urgent, addressed to his 'dear, very dear friend, his *very dear* and *best* friend'. 'For God's sake come down to me tomorrow morning, at latest by ten o'clock', he begged Knighton on receipt of the news that the baby daughter of the Duke and Duchess of Clarence had died. 'You will be a *great consolation to me*. Ever your most affectionate friend.' 'Nothing but the most *pressing urgency* would induce me, indisposed as you are at the moment, to entreat you to come to me for a few instants,' he wrote after receiving an invitation from the Emperor of Austria to attend a conference in Vienna. 'I have *much, and that too of great importance, as well publicly as privately, and as it relates to myself, which I must with the shortest lapse of time possible discuss and talk over with you.*' 'Come to me here, *be it only for an hour, early* tomorrow morning, *if possible . . . See you I must . . . a very early* visit *tomorrow morning. . . ,* ' run other injunctions. 'There certainly seems as if there were some sort of fatality that inevitably attends upon your leaving London, be it only for a single day, for your back is no sooner turned than some disagreeable and unforeseen *something* is sure almost instantly to start up. . . . Come *immediately . . .* I *must* see you. . . . Always affectionately yours.'[47]

Be it family matters, or foreign affairs, or bishoprics, or threats of blackmail, or negotiations with the Press, Knighton's presence and reassurance seems to have been deemed indispensable. His advice was readily given, and, when in the form of a written communication, usually couched in the fondest terms. 'There are no means within my reach that can adequately convey how much and how truly I am impressed with everything relative to your Majesty,' Knighton assured him in one typical letter. 'I trust that the Almighty will give you peace, and that your afflicted mind will cease to be tortured by the overwhelming inquietudes which have of late made such painful inroads on your health. I feel assured that all will be well. In the meantime let me implore your Majesty to *guard your health and to use every means to protect it in your power.* . . . If you knew, Sir, what I really and sincerely felt, your Majesty would scarcely believe the *extent of my anxiety and misery respecting you. Burn this if you please.* I have the honour to be, Sir, you Majesty's most dutiful and most *affectionately attached devoted servant. Secret.*'[48]

Knighton was careful to cultivate the Conynghams and one of his principal duties in the early days of his appointment, when Lady

Conyngham did not wish to appear with the King in public, was to conduct her clandestinely in a hired carriage to Carlton House at times when Bloomfield was out of the way and consequently would not hear of her visit.[49]

Many of Knighton's own visits to the King's bedroom were made with the same utmost secrecy. 'I hope to be in your Majesty's bedroom by half past twelve to-night,' he once wrote. 'Your Majesty had better let *no one* (with the exception of *the one*) *know that I am coming* – Pray remember this; and it may be as well that every person should be in bed – Be pleased to destroy this letter.'[50]

The longer Knighton remained in his service, the greater was the King's dependence on him. In November 1820, when quarrelling with his Ministers, he submitted to him for his 'dear consideration' his memoranda upon the 'Advantages to be gained by a new government', and went so far as to say that he would do whatever Knighton desired.[51]

While waiting off the Welsh coast to sail to Ireland, the King assured Knighton that it was 'utterly impossible' for him to tell him how '*all abroad, how uncomfortable, and how miserable*' he always felt when he did not have him 'immediately at his elbow'.[52] And on the day after he arrived home the protestations were again repeated. The King had suffered the exhaustion and inconvenience of rising from the bed where he had been so sick 'soley for the purpose' of writing to his 'dearest friend'. 'For I too gratefully feel the warmth of your affectionate heart towards me at all times not only not to neglect you but to prove to you that you are always present in my mind.'[53]*

---

* Henry Hobhouse had 'very much doubted' that the King would go to Ireland at all, since Knighton, who had 'great weight with Lady Conyngham', was very averse to his leaving the country. The King's journey, so Hobhouse recorded in his diary, 'would reduce Knighton to the alternative of declining to accompany his Majesty and thus endangering his influence on him, or going with him and thereby losing the profits (to which he is far from inattentive) of his intermediate practice in London'. Knighton was extremely 'fond of lucre', Hobhouse later recorded and quoted an observation made to him by Lord Lauderdale: 'Knighton's a damned clever fellow, but it is very odd, I have had four conversations with him, and each one of them has ended with his asking me what I thought of the price of stocks' (*Hobhouse Diary*, 75, 76, 94). After he had retired from medical practice Knighton told Canning that he had sacrificed £10,000 a year by doing so (Stapleton MSS – quoted by Aspinall, 'George IV and Sir William Knighton', *English Historical Review*, LV, January 1940, 64).

16

A Continental Journey
1821

*

'At table we heard of nothing but Hanover'

On his visit to Hanover the King was to have the company not only of Knighton but also of the Foreign Secretary, Lord Castlereagh, who was given an excellent opportunity for a meeting with Metternich for talks about a recently erupted quarrel between Russia and the Turks. Declining to pass through Dover, where the Queen had been cheered on landing the year before and where the witnesses who had been sent to give evidence against her were stoned by the mob, the King chose to embark at Ramsgate, where he was greeted with almost as much enthusiasm as he had been in Ireland. He spent the night in Ramsgate at Cliff House, the commodious residence of a rich, genial sea-biscuit manufacturer, banker, former Lord Mayor of London and diehard Tory Member of Parliament, Sir William Curtis, a great favourite with the King, who was often a guest aboard his lavishly fitted yacht. Fortified by Curtis's sumptuous hospitality and rough warm company, the King sailed for Calais where landing was 'effected with great difficulty' owing to the wind.[1]

He was welcomed by the Duc d'Angoulême at the Hotel d'Angleterre, usually known as Dessin's after the proprietor who had made it one of the most celebrated hotels in France. Here at Dessin's, the chosen resting place of thousands of English travellers, the King was presented with some 'excellent Maraschino', a liqueur to which his Majesty was known to be 'extremely partial', by Beau Brummell's valet whose master had settled in Calais as a means of escape from his creditors. But the King was reluctant to renew his friendship with a man who had been so rude to him – and to whom he in turn had been so rude. So, ignoring the signature which Brummell had inscribed in the book at Dessin's by way of emphasizing his contrition, the King left Calais for Brussels without seeing him.[2]

At Brussels he recovered the spirits he had enjoyed in Ireland, evidently enjoying himself immensely at a dinner party given by the King and Queen of the Netherlands at their palace at Laecken. Unfortunately the Prince of Orange was there with the wife he had married after his rejection by Princess Charlotte, the rather flamboyant former Grand Duchess Anna Paulowna, who was glittering with diamonds. The King exchanged a few polite words with the Prince, but to his Russian wife he said abruptly, 'Madame, vous êtes très brillante' and that began and ended the conversation.[3] However, on turning to her parents-in-law, he entertained them delightfully with imitations of an eccentric member of their family, whose voice and gestures he mimicked so well that 'at every moment' they broke out into 'violent convulsions of laughter'.[4] He was, thought the Duke of Wellington, one of the other guests, 'very blackguard and entertaining'.[5]

From Brussels the King went on to Waterloo where Wellington conducted him over the battlefield in pouring rain, indicating the positions of the armies, the farmhouse at La Haye Sainte, Hougoumont and Mont St Jean, the direction of Ney's attack, the place where the Imperial Guard recoiled as Maitland's guardsmen charged into them, the point where Ziethen's Prussia Corps had appeared through the swirling smoke. The King 'took it all very coolly', Wellington disgruntledly told Lady Shelley; 'indeed, never asked me a single question, nor said one word, till I showed him where Lord Anglesey's leg was buried, and then he burst into tears.'[6] Recovering himself, he pottered about for some time, picking at the ground with his stick, hoping to find the bones. Failing to do so he gave orders that a tree whose branches had been shattered by gunfire should be cut down, made into a chair for Carlton House and inscribed with the glorious legend: GEORGIO AUGUSTO EUROPAE LIBERATORI.

Leaving Brussels for Hanover at the beginning of October, the King passed through Düsseldorf – where the garrison received him by torchlight as the band played 'God save the King' – and then took the rutted, jolting road to Osnaburgh. It was more than sixty years since Osnaburgh had been honoured with a visit from a King of Hanover, and its citizens were determined to give an even more hospitable welcome to King George IV than they had given to his great-grandfather. They had illuminated their buildings, thrown arches of leaves and flowers across the roads, hung flags and streamers from the windows, and when his Majesty drove through the gates they appeared 'almost mad with joy'. So did the people of Hanover which he entered on the evening of 7 October as a hundred and one guns roared their salute and the people cheered him as though he were a hero returning triumphant from the wars. They crowded round the cathedral where he was crowned a second time; they watched him review the army; they listened to him delightedly as he spoke to them in German, happy to disregard the foreign accent of which his father had complained; they noticed, with satisfaction, the insignia of the recently instituted Royal Hanoverian Guelphic Order which he wore prominently on his coat, to the exclusion of all other decorations; they observed, with sympathy, the tears that fell down his cheeks as he listened to the address made in his honour at the University of Göttingen where young girls in white, bearing flowers, presented him with a poem on a scarlet cushion. All in all the King's reception had been 'very cordial', Lord Castlereagh thought, and Knighton had also been deeply impressed by it. The 'dearest King' was truly 'beloved' here, if not in England; and apart from a sharp attack of gout which had seized him after spraining his knee as he clambered onto a ceremonial horse, he had stood up to the journey very well.[7]

He had, however, been much displeased by the numbers of rich English people he had found living on the Continent, rejecting their own country in a manner he deemed highly unpatriotic. Lady Charlotte Goold told Lady Bedingfield that when one of these rich expatriates called on him attended by servants in white liveries, he rebuffed him with the comment that since he was able to go about in such splendid style he had much better do so in England.[8] He subsequently indignantly refused to receive an address from a group of English residents on the grounds that 'he could not do so from English persons *on the Continent*'.[9] Perhaps he was particularly cross with them because the gout was 'pinching him' so painfully that he was only too anxious now to get home.

The journey from Berlin to Carlsbad and Vienna, which the King had discussed with Mme de Lieven, was postponed. He had, however, seen Metternich in Hanover and was evidently well pleased to have done so. He liked and admired Metternich who, in London in 1814, had delighted him by conferring upon him, in the Emperor's name, the Order of the Golden Fleece and by creating him honorary colonel of a Hungarian regiment with a particularly splendid uniform. He had hoped to gratify Metternich in turn by asking Mme de Lieven to come out to Hanover to entertain them, by talking to him in the frankest, not to say indiscreet, manner, and by the most extreme forms of flattery, declaring that his greatest achievements stood comparison with those of Minos, Themistocles and Cato, Caesar, Gustavus Adolphus and Marlborough, not to mention – though he did mention – Pitt and Wellington.[10] Although Metternich seemed rather embarrassed by these attentions, the King's well publicized journey to Hanover and his friendly meeting there with the Austrian Emperor's representative undoubtedly did much to thwart Russia's designs on Turkey, and Castlereagh gave him due credit for its success.[11]

His homeward voyage began at the beginning of November and a month later he was back at Brighton, his gout somewhat improved, 'cheerful and happy and good humoured with all the world', so pleased to be back in Lady Conyngham's company that he adopted the eccentric habit of taking snuff from her shoulder.[12] He talked endlessly about his journey. 'Ah, my dear friend, I was longing to embrace you,' he called out one evening at the Pavilion to Mme de Lieven who thereupon received 'three great smacking kisses'. 'At table we heard of nothing but Hannover,' she reported to Metternich. 'He talked to me without stopping, and I hardly had a chance to exchange two words with my neighbour on my right. As for Castlereagh, he had a member of the Opposition next to him, someone who hardly speaks even to his friends; so that poor Castlereagh was reduced to falling on two enormous helpings of roast mutton. . . . He had informed [Castlereagh] that I should be here; that means he thinks there is something between us. He informed me the day before that you were the lover of the Duchess of Cambridge [Princess Augusta of Hesse-Cassel]. At table he told [Castlereagh] to come and sit by me. He has a passion for encouraging the affairs he suspects.'[13]

The next time Mme de Lieven was a guest at the Pavilion, the King was 'in a more talkative mood than ever', mostly upon 'the subject of high politics'.[14] She wished that she could remember 'his ideas and the order in which he gave them'. 'I know that three times I bit my lip so as not to laugh,' she told Metternich, 'and that I ended up by eating all the orange-peel I could find, so as to give my mouth something to do to hide its twitching if the danger grew too great. Everything you had said to him was in his oration – I recognised the substance, I even recognised a few phrases; but everything was plunged in such confusion that it was impossible to disentangle the real text of his speech. We had Poland, mystery-mongers, M. de la Harpe, the Don Cossacks, a great deal about gold, my wit, the Hanoverian sappers, who wear green aprons with gold fringes, Benjamin Constant, and Madame de Deken, the Hungarian infantry and the prophecies of the King in 1814, Jesus Christ and the Emperor Alexander who now sees things more clearly, for Prince Metternich says so, and finally the importance of remaining openly united. The end was the best part. The whole speech was addressed to me; but in a tone of voice which obliged everyone else to listen in silence. We should be there still if Admiral Nagle ['a bold, weatherbeaten tar' who was Groom of the Bedchamber] had not begun to snore so loudly that the King lost patience and broke up the meeting.'[15]

For Prince Metternich's amusement, Mme de Lieven provided an overcoloured, but no doubt far from fanciful example of the King's conversation when in one of these expansive talkative moods:

His Majesty: My dear I'm no ordinary man; and – as for you – you've more intelligence in your little finger than all my subjects put together. I said 'little finger' because I did not want to say 'thumb'. Now you, my dear, who are so intelligent, you must admit I am not a fool.

Myself: Indeed, Sir, I wish I could tell you what I think without descending to commonplace flattery. Obviously your Majesty is a very remarkable man.

His Majesty: That's true. You have no conception of the ideas which sometimes go through my head. I have seen everything in a flash. I'm no mystery-monger (*in the King's vocabulary this word is equivalent to mystic*); but I am a philosopher. Nesselrode [Russian Secretary for Foreign Affairs] is an honest fellow; but Capo d'Istria [Russian statesman from Corfu and Nesselrode's colleague] is a rascal . . . Lieven, I've just been saying that Capo d'Istria is a rascal; but (*sotto voce to me*) one of these days soon I shall be sending the Emperor a certain document – something really memorable – quite unprecedented – a document that will make a tremendous effect. I composed it myself; but I shall not tell you what it is. No good making those charming eyes at me. You won't discover. My dear, if I had a difficult negotiation on hand, I should entrust it to you in preference to anybody else. (*To the*

Princess Augusta) Sister, I drink to your health. Long live wine. I say, long live women. 'Long live wine, long live men', you will retort. Gentlemen (*addressing the whole company*), the finest supporter of the throne the one man . . . (*Here the King stops short, joins his hands, lifts his eyes to heaven and moves his lips as if he were reciting a prayer.*) (*Then to Princess Esterhazy*) My dear child, do you know the story of the tailor who was perpetually dropping his wife into the Seine? Very well, I'm the tailor. You don't understand me, but Madame de Lieven does – I can see that from the corner of her mouth.

Myself: I understand the moral of the story, Sir. (*What story or what moral, I had no idea. But it didn't matter; he had no more idea than I had.*)

His Majesty: That's right – the moral of the story (*Angrily*) *Damn it she takes the words out of my mouth!* My dear, as I have already told you, you're more intelligent than anybody else at table. . . . What's that you're saying, my dear?

Myself: Sir, I am comparing your Majesty to Pyrrhus.

His Majesty: Yes, indeed, he was a great man; but, personally I prefer Henry IV, whom I admire almost to the point of extravagance. He shouldn't have kept Sully though. Sully was a rascal, wasn't he?

Myself: I am sorry to disagree with you, Sir; but I should never have thought that of Sully.

His Majesty: My dear, I assure that I'm well up in the subject; I have read the memoirs of the period, M. de la Fayette, Mme de Sevigné, Mme de Bavière. (*At this juncture he nods at me and we get up from the table.*)[16]

Charles Greville, Clerk-in-Ordinary to the Privy Council and the Duke of York's horse-trainer, was also a guest at Brighton in December 1821. He, too, found the loquacious King in excellent humour, but he found life at the Pavilion tedious. 'The gaudy splendour of the place amused me for a little and then bored me,' wrote this acute, prejudiced, fastidious and observant diarist. 'The dinner was cold and the evening dull beyond all dullness. They say the King is anxious that form and ceremony should be banished, and if so it only proves how impossible it is that form and ceremony should not always inhabit a palace. . . . The King was in good looks and spirits, and after dinner cut his jokes with all the coarse merriment which is his characteristic. Lord Wellesley did not seem to like it, but of course he bowed and smiled like the rest. I saw nothing very particular in the King's manner to Lady Conyngham. He sat by her on the couch almost the whole evening playing at patience, and he took her into dinner; but Madame de Lieven and Lady Cowper were also there and he seemed equally civil to all of them.'[17]

*

It was not only his gratifying reception by the peoples of Ireland and Hanover which had helped to put the King in so cheerful and talkative a mood this winter. He had temporarily settled his differences with his irritable Prime Minister. As recently as two months before, this had seemed too much to hope for. Indeed, in his dissatisfaction with the government, he followed the example of Lady Conyngham and was actually civil to the Whigs, much to the alarm of Brougham who dreaded a change being 'operated by such means'.[18] At Herrenhausen on 12 October the King had complained to Castlereagh that Liverpool's conduct had 'upon very many occasions been so monstrous' that he could 'not consent to a continuance of a system' which rendered his 'life full of inquietude and vexation'.[19] He had again considered the possibility of ridding himself of his difficult Prime Minister; and had reviewed the relative merits of Sidmouth, Wellington and Castlereagh as replacements. Castlereagh he had particularly favoured. There had been a coolness between the King and Castlereagh in the recent past, since not only were Lady Castlereagh and Lady Conyngham not on speaking terms, but the Foreign Secretary was Lady Hertford's nephew. The trip to Hanover, however, had brought them together in a friendship as warm as could be expected between two characters so totally incompatible. Yet, in the end, the King had reluctantly been forced to conclude that Liverpool, with a wider measure of support than Castlereagh or any other member of the Cabinet could command, was indispensable. His indispensability made him all the more objectionable to the King, who was constantly finding fault with him.

The trouble over Liverpool's refusal to agree to the appointment of Sumner to the Windsor canonry, the ill-managed affair of the Queen's funeral *cortège*, and the opposition to Lord Conyngham's being appointed Lord Chamberlain of the Household, had been followed by complaints about the King's creating Knights of the Thistle without taking the Cabinet's advice, and about the difficulties and delays in obtaining the royal signature to state papers.* There had also been a quarrel over the King's determination to appoint the sons of two friends of his to studentships at Christ Church, despite the protests of the Dean – supported by Liverpool – that the appointments ought to be made solely on the grounds of merit.[20] More recently the King had been exasperated by Liverpool's resolve to re-admit to the government the Queen's former intimate friend, George Canning, whom he had not forgiven for leaving the country and resigning from the government at the time of the proceedings against the Queen in the House of Lords. Grudgingly the King allowed that he might perhaps be prepared to make up his mind to this 'painful arrangement' if, 'upon further reflection', the government desired it. It must be understood, though, that Canning must not be given an office which would expose the King to 'personal communication' with him, and that as soon as the Governor-Generalship of India was vacant he should be sent out there. The King added that the government must never deceive itself into supposing that any expediency would ever induce him 'to give up the sacred privilege of naming the personal servants of the Crown'.[21] Lord Liverpool gloomily concluded that the King was determined to keep Canning out of any important post in the government 'for the purpose of the more easily oversetting it when he [thought] fit'.[22]

Hoping to come to a better understanding with the King at a personal interview, Lord Liverpool had humbly solicited his 'Majesty to do him the honour of dining and sleeping at Walmer Castle, which is only seven miles from Dover', on his return from Hanover.[23] But his invitation had met with this cold reply: 'The King cannot avail himself of Lord Liverpool's polite invitation, as it is the King's present intention to proceed either to Ramsgate, or, what is more probable, to pass up the river at once in the steam-boat. It is the King's fixed determination to shew as often as the occasion may offer, the thorough disgust he feels at the unpardonable conduct of such part of his subjects as reside in the town of Dover.'[24]

Since then, however, there had been a *rapprochement*. A compromise, which well satisfied the Conynghams, had been reached over the disputed appointment to the vacant office in the Royal Household. Lord

---

* Lord Lauderdale told Creevey that when Ministers had papers to sign they had 'to write a letter to Bloomfield begging him to get the King's signature'; and Bloomfield, in turn, had 'to solicit Du Paquier, the King's valet, to seize a favourable opportunity. . . . The operation [was] the most difficult possible to get accomplished' (*Creevey Papers*, 368).

Conyngham was not appointed Lord Chamberlain, but he did not have to content himself with being a mere Groom of the Stole. He was made Lord Steward of the Household, and was also sworn in as a Privy Councillor and Constable of Windsor Castle. Lord Cholmondeley, the former Lord Steward, was compensated for vacating the office by the promise of a Blue Ribbon for himself and a peerage for his son. 'The two awkward offices of Chamberlain and Master of the Horse are thus avoided,' Castlereagh told his brother. 'The office of Groom of the Stole would have been a more prudent measure, but the King's objections were insuperable. The present arrangement has been productive of *unmixed satisfaction*, and I am sure the difference between the two offices, assuming confidence in all other matters re-established, could not in the mind of a statesman be a motive for giving the King a sentiment of either power or humiliation. The Duke of Montrose will be Chamberlain. The Duke of Dorset, Master of the Horse.'[25]

Castlereagh had never seen 'his Majesty *apparently* in better humour', after these arrangements in his Household had been made. 'Complete harmony' had been restored between the King and the government and he received Liverpool at Brighton '*with cordiality*'. He said he had '*never* felt *so* happy'. 'Canning will probably go to India,' Castlereagh went on, 'but such is the harmony of the day that nothing deemed necessary upon political arrangements will now be refused. Such a changed man as the King you never saw. He is in the highest spirits and says he, Liverpool, is again! entitled to all his confidence.'[26] The day of his reconciliation with his Prime Minister was he said, the 'happiest of his life'.[27] When Canning was offered and accepted the Governor-Generalship of India, all the King's troubles seemed over.

*

The King's cheerful mood continued well into the New Year, the first few weeks of which he spent very quietly at Brighton, rarely leaving his room except to walk across to Lady Conyngham's house about half past three or four o'clock in the afternoon, and to stroll back at six when he dressed for dinner at half past. On 11 January 1822, Croker, a guest at the Pavilion, found him 'looking remarkably well and stout on his legs; he went round the circle as usual' before dinner.

'The King made us all eat some roast wild boar from Hanover,' Croker recalled. 'It was very good, like pork with a game flavour; he asked me what I thought of it. I said it was to pork what pheasant was to fowl. "There I differ from you," said the King. "Nothing is as good as fowl; if they were as scarce as pheasants, and pheasants as plenty as fowls, no one would eat a pheasant."

'When his Majesty took a glass of wine with Lady Conyngham, he *touched glasses* with her in the old-fashioned way.'[28]

He talked of his journey to Hanover and of a play he had seen at Calais where Admiral Nagle was mightily taken with one of the dancers who 'held her leg *square with her shoulder* in a wonderful manner'. 'But the best of all,' Croker thought, 'was the King's mimicry of the old Duc de la Chartre, explaining to him that these actors and dancers at Calais were second-rate performers. I never heard anything so perfect in the way of imitation of voice, matter, and manner, as his representation of the old mumbling Duke.'[29]

The next evening at dinner, the King was as contented as ever. The conversation turned on Lady Hervey's letters which Croker had edited, using in his notes some anecdotes which the King had told him. 'He was very gracious on this point,' Croker recorded, 'and said that if I had consulted him and let him into my secret, he would have afforded me still more. He was, he said, a great *reservoir* of anecdote, for he had lived not only with all the eminent persons of the last fifty years, but he had had an early acquaintance with several eminent persons of the preceding half-century.'

After dinner they had 'a musical night. He never left the pianoforte; he sang in "Glorious Apollo", "Mighty Conqueror", "Lord Mornington's Waterfall" (encored), "Non nobis, Domini", and several other glees and catches.' Croker did not think his voice was a very good one; and he did not 'sing so much from the notes as from recollection'. Even so he gave 'the force, gaiety and spirit of the glees in a superior style to the professional men' who were of the party. One of these professional men was old Michael Kelly, the former lover of the King's one-time mistress, Mrs Crouch. Kelly was 'wheeled in, in a gouty chair, and sang the solo of "Sleep you or Wake you", with all the force of a broken voice. . . . Lady Conyngham and [her daughter] Lady Elizabeth did not conceal their dissatisfaction at all this music. . . . The King, indeed, left his music but one moment the whole evening.'[30]

Later on in the month Mme de Lieven came down to stay at the Pavilion and she, too, found the King still 'in high good humour'.[31] Although far from being in that 'perfect' state of health which he had been seen to be enjoying three months before, his gout showed no signs of lowering his spirits. The undoubted success of his visits to Ireland and the Continent had not, of course, silenced his critics. In one of several caricatures ridiculing his visit to Germany, William Heath depicted him in a red coat of foreign cut and a round Teutonic cap, smoking a meerschaum pipe and carelessly tossing coins to excited Hanoverian subjects one of whom says, 'He is indeed a Hanoverian at heart', to which another replies, 'No, he is an Irishman, he says', whereupon a third comments, 'Why some years ago he said he and his brother William were the only ones in the family who were *not Germans.*' Behind the cart in which he sits staggers John Bull, a weeping, lame and bony animal, weighed down by huge bundles of taxes.[32]

But most of his critics were much quieter than of late; and, though not many of his champions were prepared to go so far as Thomas Moore who – a monarchist since the visit to Ireland – declared that if he occupied himself about the King at all it would be to praise him with all his heart, most of them seemed prepared to admit that he might, after all, prove to be a better monarch than they had expected.[33]

Before the end of January, however, his gout had grown very much worse and he was becoming increasingly cantankerous. He could scarcely manage to walk to the dining-room table; and when he did get there he ate very little, and could eat nothing at all without previously imbibing cherry brandy in quantities 'not to be believed'.[34] He still sang in the evenings, but with only a shadow of his former verve and force. The Duke of Wellington was a guest at the Pavilion for the first time this winter, and he did not like it there. The rooms were so infernally hot; the air reeked of scent; the lights were dazzling; the guests spent their evening half-lying on cushions listening to music, or playing patience and sipping liqueurs.[35] 'Devil take me,' he exclaimed to Mme de Lieven, 'I think I must have got into bad company.' He behaved, she thought, 'in a lordly way with his master' who nevertheless pressed him to stay when he wanted to leave. Wellington made the excuse that he had to go back for a meeting of the Privy Council. '*Damn the Council,*' was all the King said. The Duke grumbled to Mme de Lieven that he would now have to write a long letter of excuse to his colleagues; so she undertook to do this for him and wrote, '*By his Majesty's command, Damn the Council.*' He signed the note and sent it off.[36]

On the last day of the month Wellington, Mme de Lieven and the other guests returned to London. 'We left the King very ill,' Mme de Lieven recorded. 'He is tortured by gout and employs the most violent remedies to be rid of it. He looks ghastly; he is plunged in gloom; he talks about nothing but dying. I have never seen him so wretched; he did everything he could to pull himself together, but in vain. The favourite is in despair, especially over his temper, which is as sour as can be. . . . The least thing gets on his nerves – and a crooked candle produces a storm of abuse. He treated the Duke of York very badly; I do not think he addressed two words to him. He is always very nice to me.'[37]

Mme de Lieven was trying hard to persuade him not to give up his postponed plans for going to Vienna. But he kept making excuses – 'if I am well, if I live, if European politics permit'. Then he refused to budge unless Lady Conyngham went with him; and she absolutely refused to go. She complained to Mme de Lieven of his growing arrogance and despotism; her son, Lord Francis, was threatening to leave the Household because he could not 'stand it any longer'. 'But she drags the King into every sentence, as if she were a parvenue,' Mme de Lieven told Metternich. 'You cannot imagine what idiocies go on in that household; it is like being in a mad-house.'[38]

One of the King's main causes of irritation was Sir Benjamin Bloomfield, whose sulky moods, bossy behaviour and repeated complaints had become intolerable. His management of the King's financial affairs was far from satisfactory, and his presumption in bowing to the audience in his box at a theatre in Ireland when 'God save the King' was being played had caused the greatest offence.[39] The King had also heard, so Henry Hobhouse recorded, that Bloomfield had been spending up to £100,000 on land in Ireland and he wondered where on earth he had managed to get hold of so much money.[40] So, under pressure from Lady Conyngham, whose dislike of Bloomfield was much increased by his persistent claim that the Privy Purse was exhausted by paying for her diamonds, and under equal though more wily pressure from Knighton, who wanted Bloomfield's appointment for himself, the King wrote to Lord Liverpool to suggest that as the government was now hopefully 'fixed on a settled and firm basis', he was desirous that there should be 'no impediment or interruption' to their 'permanent tranquility'. It had, therefore, occurred to the King that 'it might be desirable to get rid of the office of Private Secretary. This office had always been looked upon 'with a jealous eye, both by the government and the country, and it would, in his opinion, be highly popular if they were 'to break up the *thing altogether*'. 'This, however, cannot be done without making an extended provision for Sir Benjamin Bloomfield,' the King continued, 'because I think it is desirable that he should quit the Privy Purse also, for by thus retiring entirely from my family, it would be the means of saving both himself and the government much inconvenience, arising from the natural consequence of mistaken power and patronage.'[41]

Lord Liverpool agreed with the King that Bloomfield should relinquish the offices of Private Secretary and Privy Purse, and that, as compensation, he should be offered the Governorship of Ceylon.[42] So the King wrote Bloomfield a kind letter, thanking him for the 'attachment, zeal and integrity' he had always displayed in the 'very laborious and confidential duties' which had been imposed upon him, and explaining that it was not from preference to any other individual, nor from want of any personal confidence' that made his resignation advisable: 'But many circumstances have occurred which induce the King to think it highly desirable to place the office of his Private Secretary upon a different footing from that on which it has hitherto existed in the hands of Sir John McMahon and Sir Benjamin Bloomfield. The King, in short, wishes to restore it, as nearly as possible, to what it was when held by Sir Herbert Taylor under the King, his father, and to limit the functions of the situation to the arrangement of his papers, the copying of his letters and the occasional writing what he may think proper to dictate, and afterwards sign, but that in future no communication should be made to the King upon publick affairs except through his Ministers, unless in those cases when the individuals making them are entitled to apply directly to the King.'[43]

Having thus written to Bloomfield, the King wrote to Liverpool again to say that his 'own feelings of affection towards the individual in question' were 'not sufficiently relieved', and that whilst he was fully aware of the prudence of the step which he was about to take for the sake of his government there were 'many painful regrets mixed with it'. He, therefore, wanted Bloomfield to be offered a Red Ribbon as well as an Irish peerage.[44] Liverpool had no objection to Bloomfield having a Red Ribbon, and he was accordingly awarded the Grand Cross of the Order of the Bath on 1 April; but the Prime Minister did object to the grant of an Irish peerage, an honour usually conferred for 'services and *personal consequence* in Ireland'.[45]

In any case, Bloomfield refused to be content with an Irish peerage; and declined 'altogether the proposition respecting Ceylon', preferring to remain 'at home with his present allowances', that was to say 'the salary of both his offices of the Privy Purse and the Secretaryship, his pension, and the Park at Hampton Court'. He also demanded a British peerage, and when Liverpool informed him that that was 'absolutely impracticable', he continued to demand it 'with increased pertinacity',[46] though the King agreed with Liverpool as to its 'impropriety'.[47]

Faced with Bloomfield's rejection of employment in Ceylon, the King repeated the suggestion that the Private Secretaryship ought to be abolished not only because of the 'inordinate power' of the office, but also because of the 'embarrassment and painful distress he suffered in consequence of Sir Benjamin Bloomfield's 'unhappy, uncertain and oppressive temper', and the change that had been 'gradually taking place for the last two years, in his general demeanor'.[48] If, therefore, he did not want to go to Ceylon, it would be very welcome if some other foreign mission could be found for him.[49] He had by now been excluded from the small glass-walled sitting-room in the Pavilion, known as the 'Magic Lantern', where the King's most intimate circle were accustomed to meet;[50] and it was embarrassing to have him in Brighton or London at all. The King indeed had conceived a detestation of Bloomfield since the plan to get rid of him was proving so difficult to accomplish because of the man's exasperating obstinacy. He 'loathed and detested' him so much that he could not bring himself even to write his name,[51] and was 'furious' with anybody who was even 'commonly civil' to him.[52]

Fortunately another foreign mission which Bloomfield deemed acceptable was found for him. Having first of all secured the Governorship of Fort Charles in Port Royal, Jamaica – a sinecure worth £650 a year which Lord Stewart generously relinquished upon Bloomfield's resignation of the Privy Purse[53] – he agreed to go as Minister to Stockholm, provided that when a vacancy occurred in a more southerly capital he would be offered it.[54]

Despite the King's protestations of wishing to abolish the office of Private Secretary once Bloomfield had given up the post, he made it clear that he wanted Knighton to succeed him, if not in name at least to take over most of his duties. Lord Liverpool strongly urged him to do nothing 'in this way at the moment', emphasizing that the appointment 'would very much augment all the difficulties attendant upon the removal' of Bloomfield and 'would create a prejudice very inconvenient to Sir Wm. Knighton himself'.[55] The King was determined to have his way, however, and before the end of the year Knighton was appointed Keeper of the King's Privy Purse, and was given instructions 'to undertake the entire management' of the King's 'private affairs'.[56] Knighton accepted the charge, and entirely gave up his profitable practice as a physician.

His influence now became more pronounced than ever; and it was soon clear that although not Private Secretary in name, that was what in fact he was. The King openly admitted it, asking the Foreign Office to let Knighton have a key to the F.F.F. boxes as he was under the necessity of calling upon him 'to fulfil those duties that would naturally attach to the office of the King's Private Secretary'. The keys were sent.[57] But when the King demanded that Knighton should be appointed to the Privy Council, Lord Liverpool objected. The King was insistent: 'You are already acquainted with my feelings relative to the admission of my invaluable friend Sir William Knighton into the Privy Council. The thing is so proper and just that I wish to have no conversation on the subject; as my first Minister I wish to do nothing but what is in unison with your feelings, as far as I can; nevertheless, there are occasions in which I must use my own judgment.'[58]

Although he thought it might be necessary in the end to give way 'to avoid ill humour and other inconveniences', Lord Liverpool reminded the King that no monarch had ever had a Private Secretary until King George III went blind; and when Sir Herbert Taylor was appointed to the situation, 'the late King, who understood these matters better than anyone', decided he ought to be put on exactly the same footing as an Under-Secretary of State; it was certainly never suggested that Taylor should become a Privy Councillor.[59] Wellington was inclined to allow the King to have his way. But sensing perhaps that his Majesty was not as firm on the point as his letters suggested, Liverpool, supported by Bathurst and Peel, decided to hold firm. Knighton was thoroughly indignant. He disliked Liverpool intensely and was excessively put out by the slight to which he fancied himself subjected. 'The truth is Lord Liverpool and I ought to be like *man and wife,*' he complained to Charles Arbuthnot. 'It may be very improper that there should be any person in my situation; the King perhaps ought not to have a favourite, but he cannot do without me.'[60]

When the King appeared to accept, with perfect equanimity, Liverpool's

20 'Installation of a Knight of the *Bath*,—or delicate recreations on board a *Polacre*': cartoon by 'Selim' of October 1820. Louisa Demont interrupts Pergami bathing Queen Caroline aboard the polacca.

19 'Bat, Cat and Mat. How happy could I be with either': cartoon of 1 June 1821. Caricature by Theodore Lane. Partolommeo Pergami urges Queen Caroline to return with him to St Omer and thence to Italy, while Alderman Matthew Wood presses her to come on with him to Calais and London to claim her rights.

21 'Moments of Pain': caricature by Theodore Lane, 1820. The King, dressed as a mandarin, is overcome by the news that the proceedings against the Queen have been abandoned. Lord Sidmouth is represented as a doctor feeling his pulse. Bloomfield throws up his hands in despair

22 'Moments of Pleasure': caricature by Theodore Lane, 1820. The Queen, sitting beneath a portrait of Pergami, is delighted to hear from a capering Alderman Wood that the Bill of Pains and Penalties has been dropped. At the door Lady Anne Hamilton receives

decision that he should not be a Privy Councillor, Knighton was more annoyed than ever, and went about complaining of his Majesty's ingratitude and selfishness, his changed attitude towards him.[61]

There was certainly a strange ambiguity in the relationship between the two men that intrigued and mystified observers. It was said that what had really attracted the King to Knighton in the first place was the *accoucheur's* willingness to gossip about 'all the complaints of all the ladies that consult him',[62] and that there was some sort of 'secret chain' which bound them unwillingly together.[63] Lord Francis Conyngham told Charles Greville that, despite the reliance the King placed upon Knighton and the affectionate nature of their correspondence, in reality he regarded him with 'a detestation that could hardly be described'. He was afraid of him and that was the reason why he hated him so much. He took a peculiar delight in saying mortifying things about him. Once he cried out, 'I wish to God somebody would assassinate Knighton!'[64] Greville himself had heard the King say at a particularly boisterous party when some Tyrolese singers whom Esterhazy had brought down were kissing him, 'I would give ten guineas to see Knighton walk into the room now.'[65]

Thomas Bachelor, a Page of the Backstairs, agreed that the King hated Knighton, whose influence over him was without any limit. He told Greville, whispering 'as if the walls had ears', that Knighton 'could do anything and without him nothing could be done; that, after him, Lady Conyngham was all powerful, but in entire subservience to him; that she did not dare have anyone dine there without previously ascertaining that Knighton would not disapprove of it.'[66]

Another fascinated observer, Charles Arbuthnot, who, as Joint Secretary to the Treasury and Patronage Secretary, had many opportunities of seeing them together, also thought that the King feared and hated Knighton, 'as a madman hates his keeper'. He was 'perpetually talking at him' and at dinner one afternoon 'jeered at him for not understanding French, which nettled Knighton extremely'.[67] In indignant revolt against such treatment, Knighton evidently declared that the King was 'a great beast who liked nothing so much as indecent conversation and that, in that respect, Lady Conyngham managed him well for he dared not do it in her presence. He said he had no regard for anybody but himself.'[68]

The King afterwards told Arbuthnot that Knighton had actually blackmailed him over the secret papers which McMahon had accumulated, and that he had succeeded in extracting £50,000 from him, not to mention £12,000 which had had to be paid in compensation to the holder of 'a place in the Duchy of Cornwall' which Knighton had wanted for himself.[69]

In retailing this extraordinary story – which, in a rather different form Henry Hobhouse also heard – the King added that, although 'very absurd', very ambitious and 'with no idea of how to behave himself in good company', Knighton was admittedly very clever and organized his affairs 'excessively well'. This at least was true. Knighton was, indeed, a highly capable and conscientious servant, who managed the King's finances with exemplary skill. Bloomfield had estimated that his Majesty's income might 'be averaged at £90,000 as applicable to his private expenditure'.[70] To keep his expenditure within the limit of this income was a severely demanding and not always possible task; but Knighton arranged it as well as anyone could have been expected to do.[71] Knighton, of course, was a man whose peculiar and privileged position naturally made him an object of suspicion and jealousy, particularly to those who had formerly enjoyed a small part of his influence. A typical enemy was Sir Thomas Tyrwhitt, who had himself for several years been Private Secretary to the King when he was Prince of Wales. Tyrwhitt thought Knighton the 'greatest villain as well as the lowest blackguard' that ever lived, and was deeply affronted when this 'most vindictive man, eternally upon the watch', came into the King's room without knocking and 'planted himself at the bottom of the bed', while he, Sir Thomas Tyrwhitt, was enjoying a private tête-à-tête with his Majesty.[72]

Yet for all his faults and affectations, his irritating assumption of privileges, his constant hints at secret knowledge, his 'mysterious way of talking', his undoubted love of intrigue and evident desire for advancement, Knighton was undeniably astute, patient and persevering. Even Mme de Lieven, who spoke of him derisively as 'the man midwife', who thought that everyone was afraid of him, 'from the King downwards', considered him a 'very clever man', one 'who really [had] to be reckoned with.' She never knew what he was thinking: when one day he smiled in his silent mysterious way at several compliments she had paid the King, she could not make out 'if that meant he was laughing at [her] or that he thought [she] was laughing at the King'.[73]

Knighton's supreme usefulness in Greville's opinion was that he was the 'only man who could prevail upon the King to sign papers, etc', and bring his mind to bear on tiresome questions which he would otherwise have chosen to avoid.[74] In this, rather than in blackmail, lay the cause of the King's sudden vituperative attacks. As Knighton himself admitted to George Canning, it was 'a most painful part of his duty to press business upon his Majesty . . . and that his doing so sometimes produced unpleasant scenes'. 'I believe he has as great an esteem and affection for me as anybody living,' Knighton went on; 'but he is uncertain, the creature of impulse. . . . When he has got a particular notion into his head, there is no eradicating it.'[75] Knighton 'could not imagine how business would get on at all' were he not there to press the King to attend to it.[76]

The relationship between the two men resembled more that of an exasperated governess and a wayward charge than that of servant and master. Reliance led to resentment, resentment to outbursts of angry abuse against the person without whose help unwelcome and distasteful duties could not be done. They quarrelled; Knighton complained of the King's ingratitude; the King, peevish and resentful, insulted Knighton and told lies about him; the ill-used servant went away to sulk. But then there would come a cry for help from his 'ever most truly attached and affectionate friend', the King, who insisted that whatever his *very* dear and *best* friend might chuse to think', they still *were* friends.[77] Rather huffily the servant would return; and all would be quiet again until the next eruption.

17

A New Foreign Secretary
1822-1823

*

'The damnedest fellow in the world'

The disagreements and tiresome correspondence first about Bloomfield and then about Knighton had endangered but not entirely broken the King's continuing more friendly association with his Ministers, particularly with Castlereagh, even though Lady Castlereagh and Lady Conyngham were still not speaking to each other. Indeed, it was whispered that he behaved in a particularly affectionate way towards Castlereagh merely to pique Lady Conyngham whom he appeared now to be finding exceptionally irritating and with whom he frequently quarrelled.

Mme de Lieven recorded his behaviour at the opening of Parliament at the beginning of February 1822 when there were 'indescribable oglings'. Mme de Lieven had gone to the House of Lords being, as she confessed, a good courtier and having heard that the King liked 'people to go to look at him with his crown on his head'. 'When he came in, he seemed quite crushed. His heavy robes, his crown slipping down on to his nose, his great train making his fat neck look still fatter – everything conspired to heighten the comic effect. He avoided the steps in mounting; when he was finally seated on the throne, he looked prostrate. A moment later, he caught sight of me – a smile. A row higher, his eyes fell on Lady Cowper – another smile. Higher still, Lady Morley – he beamed. He began letting his glance wander down the rows; but more often he looked up, with his eyelids going hard at it. . . . The signalling never stopped for a second.'[1]

A few weeks later, when the Duke went to stay at the Pavilion, the King was still on poor terms with Lady Conyngham; and Wellington was told that he was 'terribly out of spirits'. For this reason, when the

Cabinet apprehensively approached him with a proposal to reduce the Civil List they expected bitter opposition. They were, therefore, the more delighted to meet with a reception 'exactly the opposite of all they had anticipated. . . . He came to meet them and said that he knew the reason of their visit, that he approved it completely, and that he thought it right and proper that he should accept the sacrifice' since they, too, were taking a cut in their official salaries. The result was 'general good-humour and keen disappointment on the part of the opposition'.[2]

He readily agreed to a cut in the Civil List of £30,000 a year; and he made the gesture 'with more feeling' than the Duke had 'ever known him shew'.[3] But he soon afterwards relapsed into despondency.

By the end of April his quarrel with Lady Conyngham had still not been made up; she did 'not go near him' and did 'nothing but yawn'; and he, for his part, was 'in a frightful state of melancholy', 'bored to death', avoiding people, talking intermittently of his approaching end.[4] There appeared to be a temporary *rapprochement* between the King and Lady Conyngham in May, according to Lady Cowper, who thought that Lady Conyngham was now behaving rather more kindly to him; but there were squabbles still.[5] When the Prince and Princess of Denmark came to London, the King felt obliged to give them a large dinner-party and made out a list of names on which were naturally included those of Lord and Lady Castlereagh. Lady Conyngham declared that if Lady Castlereagh were to be invited, she herself could not possibly attend. The King sulkily replied that if she refused to attend he would cancel the dinner altogether. Eventually he persuaded her to talk the matter over with Mme de Lieven who, with great difficulty, persuaded her to let him have the Castlereaghs.[6]

After this, relations between the King and Lady Conyngham improved. One day in June, on a visit to the Royal Lodge, Lady Cowper saw them driving together in a pony-chaise at Windsor; he seemed in excellent humour, and behaved towards her with unprecedented tenderness.[7] Another day he pointed at Lady Conyngham and sighed, 'Ah, heavens, if she were what I am! . . . If she were a widow, as I am a widower, she would not be one for long.'

'Ah, my dear King how good you are.'

'Yes, I have taken an oath.' Then, turning to Mme de Lieven, he added in a low voice, 'Patience; everything in good time.'[8]

But despite his reconciliation with Lady Conyngham, he soon fell back into gloom once more, seeming to Mme de Lieven not to know what to do with his summer, looking like a man on the point of suicide.[9] One evening he quarrelled bitterly with the Duke of Wellington about the relative merits of the British and French cavalry. Wellington thought the French were best; the King, insisting that the English could beat them any day, eventually rose from the table with the angry comment, 'Well, it is not for me to dispute on such a subject with your Grace.'[10]

He succeeded in appearing with a more cheerful face on 20 June at the annual children's ball at Carlton House to which Croker's adopted daughter, his wife's little sister, had been invited. The King was 'much amused with the children. He walked about, except for about an hour and a half that he sat in the conservatory with Lady Conyngham and Mme de Lieven, while the children – including his niece Princess Victoria – danced before him and the company stood around him.'[11]

At every opportunity the indefatigable Mme de Lieven pursued her endeavours to persuade the King to go to Vienna, where she hoped to contrive another meeting between herself and Metternich; but she found it impossible to tie the King down; he was so like a weathercock; the last person to speak to him carried the day.[12] The government were as anxious that he should not go to Vienna, as Mme de Lieven was that he should. They were afraid, as Wellington told Lady Cowper, that he would again be condemned, as he had been on his return from Hanover, for throwing money about recklessly on the Continent. They also feared the consequences of further meetings with Metternich and of the King's becoming even more deeply identified with Metternich's policies. Lord Liverpool strongly urged him not to go to the Continent again, but to bring forward his visit to Scotland which had been planned for 1823. By the beginning of July, Lord Liverpool had won him over: he would go to Scotland instead of to Vienna.

*

Having made up his mind to go to Scotland, the King called in his tailors and jewellers to fit him out with an appropriate array of fine costumes. This was a task he always enjoyed to the full, and his accounts reveal that he spent quite as much on clothes as he had done in the days when he had been, as Prince of Wales, one of the young arbiters of fashion. Opera pelisses, astrakhan Polish caps, silk bathing gowns, white beaver morning gowns made 'extra wide and very long', 'rich gold marmalouk sword belts', 'rich Muscovy sable muffs', 'super printed blue striped long cloth shirts with full bosoms' by the score, white long gloves by the dozen, prime doe pantaloons, 'superfine scarlet flannel underwaistcoats lined with fine callico', gloves, boots, stockings and black silk drawers were delivered to him in enormous quantities, and at enormous expense.[13] One of his pages told Thomas Raikes that a plain coat would cost £300 before it met with his approbation.[14] And Maria Edgeworth learned that one particular blue silk coat, the repeated alterations to which kept a tailor and two assistants busy at Windsor for three weeks, eventually cost £600.[15] It was scarcely an exaggeration. He was constantly returning clothes to his tailors for alterations, and ordering new clothes while waiting for the work to be done. He bought well over five hundred shirts during the nine years of the Regency, and subsequently ordered at least eight field-marshal's full-dress uniforms.[16]*

For his visit to Scotland, George Hunter of Tokenhouse Yard and Edinburgh supplied the King with a magnificent equipage – a pair of fine gold 'shoe rosettes studded all over with variegated gems', 'a goatskin Highland purse with massive gold spring top'; three black morocco belts; a fine gold head ornament for his bonnet 'consisting of the Royal Scots crown in miniature set with diamonds, pearls, rubies and emeralds'; a 'large gold brooch pin with variegated Scotch gems'; 'a powder horn richly mounted in fine gold'; 'a fine basket hilt Highland sword of polished steel'; 'a pair of fine polished steel Highland pistols'; 'sixty-one yards of royal satin plaid; thirty-one yards of royal plaid velvet; seventeen and a

---

* Uniforms delighted him, as they did the rest of the family, and his knowledge of them was remarkable. His fastidious eye immediately spotted the slightest mistake. 'Good evening, sir,' he once called out to Lord Charles Russell who was negligent enough to appear at a ball in the uniform of the Royal Horse Guards without the regulation aiguillette. 'Good evening, sir, I suppose that you are the regimental doctor.' Breaches of etiquette in civilian dress were equally painful to his eye. One evening at Manchester House, Captain Gronow, who had recently been living in Paris where 'knee-breeches were only worn by a few old fogies', was surprised to be tapped on the shoulder by Horace Seymour. 'The "great man", Seymour told him, 'is very much surprised that you should have ventured to appear in his presence without knee-breeches. He considers it as a want of proper respect for him.' The next morning Gronow 'mentioned what had occurred, with some chagrin', to his Colonel, Lord Frederick Bentinck, who told him not to take it to heart. 'Depend upon it, Gronow,' Lord Frederick said, 'the Prince, who is a lover of novelty, will wear trousers himself before the year is out.' And so he did (*Gronow Reminiscences*, ii, 148).

half yards of royal plaid cashmere'. The total cost, including £32 for 'twelve phial cases of eau de Cologne', was £1,354 18s.[17]

*

His Highland attire and his other clothes packed in a variety of trunks, the King left London for Greenwich on 10 August 1822, making a detour around the City to emphasize his displeasure at the disturbances which had taken place there when the Queen's coffin was on its way to Harwich. At Greenwich he stepped aboard the *Royal George* wearing a blue coat very much plainer than the extremely expensive outfits in the trunks that were loaded in the hold.

To the firing of guns, the cheering of the crowds on the bank, and the strains of a band playing 'God save the King', the *Royal George* was towed down river to Gravesend by the steam packet the *Comet*, attended by the Lord Mayor's barge, drawn by another steamboat. The King stood on deck for a time, acknowledging the cheers of the crowd and then retiring to his cabin with his favourite valediction, 'God bless you all!' Four days later, in pouring rain at about two o'clock in the afternoon, the *Royal George*'s anchor was dropped off Leith.

Despite the efforts of the *Scotsman* and other newspapers to persuade their readers not to emulate the conduct of the Irish, the King's welcome was noisy and ebullient. All afternoon boats sailed around the *Royal George*, and their crews and passengers stood up, ignoring the rain, waving their hats and cheering. The King appeared on deck from time to time, bowing and smiling, the first King to have visited Scotland since the time of Charles II. During the afternoon Sir Walter Scott, who had been asked to supervise the arrangements for the King's reception, came aboard to welcome him to Scotland, to apologize for the appalling weather, of which he was 'perfectly ashamed', and to present him with a silver St Andrew's cross from the ladies of Edinburgh. The King greeting Scott as 'the man in Scotland' he 'most wished to see', accepted the cross gratefully, told Scott he would wear it in his hat, and offered him a glass of cherry brandy. Having drunk the King's health, Scott asked if he could keep the glass in memory of the occasion, and, the request being granted, he put it in his back pocket. He forgot all about it when he got home, sat down in a chair, and suddenly screamed so loudly that his wife thought he had cut his bottom on a pair of her scissors.[18]

Next morning the King, wearing as promised the St Andrew's cross in his hat – together with a big thistle and a small sprig of heather – was brought to the landing stage in the royal barge. He was then driven in state to Holyroodhouse, attended by detachments of the Royal Company of Archers and the Scots Greys. He passed through streets magnificently decorated with crowns and stars, streamers and thistles and placards of welcome, past crowds of cheering people waving plumed and feathered hats and wearing buttons inscribed with some such legend as, 'You Are Welcome, King!' Obviously delighted by his reception and by the garlanded beauty of Edinburgh, he smiled and nodded engagingly as the open carriage rolled along the streets, making an occasional flattering remark, observing more than once, 'They are a nation of gentlemen.'

He stayed at Dalkeith Palace with the sixteen-year-old Duke of Buccleuch whose staff were asked to leave the kitchen and cellars in the more expert care of the royal cooks and butlers. The Duke's table was consequently much improved during the visit, but the King kept a careful and solicitous eye on his host. 'No! No!' he once protested when the Duke was offered a glass of the King's liqueur. 'No! No! It is too strong for his Grace to drink.'

From Dalkeith Castle the King drove out, with remarkable zest for a gouty man of sixty, to drawing-rooms and levees, to a command performance of *Rob Roy*, to the Caledonian Ball where he asked for Scottish reels – 'None of your foreign dances!' – to a civic banquet at which he made one of his adroit and pleasant speeches: 'I am quite unable to express my sense of the gratitude which I owe to the people of this country; but I beg to assure them that I shall ever remember as one of the proudest moments of my life the day I came among them, and the gratifying reception which they gave me. I return you, my Lord Provost, my lords and gentlemen, my warmest thanks for your attention this day; and I can assure you with truth, with earnestness and sincerity that I shall never forget your dutiful attention to me on my visit to Scotland and particularly the pleasure I have derived from dining in your hall this day.'

He proceeded in state, in his field-marshal's uniform, from Holyrood to Edinburgh Castle, as the cannon boomed in the fog. It was raining and windy as well as foggy, but he manfully stood beneath the Royal Standard on the Castle's highest battery smiling and waving his hat.[19]

The only event during the visit which was not entirely successful was the levee at Holyroodhouse on 19 August. The King, though still very proud of his legs, did not really look his best in Highland costume;

and the flesh-coloured pantaloons which – according to Sir David Wilkie who painted him in this attire – he wore under his kilt, did not improve the effect. Far stranger than the King's appearance, though, was that of his jovial, loud and uninhibited friend, the sea-biscuit manufacturer, Sir William Curtis, who appeared, 'a portentous figure', wearing full Highland uniform complete with a kilt of the Stuart tartan.[20]

But although the appearance of these 'gallant Highlandmen' was widely ridiculed, the success of the King's visit was not impaired. When he left Edinburgh at the end of the month, having ensured that a suitably grateful letter was written to Sir Walter Scott and having knighted that other fine Scottish artist, Henry Raeburn, President of the Scottish Academy, he had cause to feel satisfied that the duties of yet another state visit had been well performed.

Lord Melville, the Scottish First Lord of the Admiralty, who was 'firmly persuaded' that his visit would be attended with 'important public benefit', wrote to congratulate him warmly upon 'the determined and deep rooted monarchical feeling which evidently pervaded the great body of the people'.[21] And Sir Walter Scott at Abbotsford told Knighton on 12 September that 'ground for congratulation on the King's visit to Scotland continued to increase daily. It was impossible for anyone to have foreseen its extent among a people who are tenacious to a proverb of the opinion which they adopt.' Scott had no doubt that the good effects of the visit would be long felt after he was 'dead and gone'; he was particularly pleased, he said, that the people had been able to see for themselves that his Majesty was far from being as 'overgrown' as 'lying newspapers and caricatures' had suggested. 'Their delight was extreme at seeing a portly handsome man looking and moving every inch a King.'[22]

*

The pleasures of the visit had been overcast at the outset by distressing news that had reached Edinburgh on 14 August. Two days before, at nine o'clock in the morning, the King's sixtieth birthday, Lord Castlereagh had killed himself. The King was 'horribly upset', 'bitterly lamented his loss', spoke of Castlereagh in the 'warmest terms'; and told Peel that it was the 'greatest loss he had ever sustained'. He had, however, been 'almost prepared' for the news.[23] He had seen Castlereagh the day before he had left London, and had then been so appalled and alarmed by his behaviour that he had been unable to get to sleep that night.

Castlereagh had displayed every sign of being deranged, gripping the King by the arm, accusing himself of all sorts of crimes, kissing his Majesty's hands, weeping, telling him that he was being accused of homosexual practices, that he was going to fly away to Portsmouth 'and from there to the ends of the earth'.[24]

As soon as the King had managed to calm him down and to persuade him to go home, he sent for Lord Liverpool, asking him to come to him 'directly'. 'Either I am mad or Lord [Castlereagh] is mad,' he assured Liverpool. 'I am the more apprehensive on account of the strength of his mind. There is greater danger in these cases from strong minds than from weak ones.'[25]

There had been indications of a possible collapse for some time. Castlereagh had been displaying inordinate suspicion of his colleagues, particularly of Wellington. His brother, Lord Stewart, had declared that he 'had never seen a man in such a state' and had burst into tears at the thought of it.[26] And Mme de Lieven had reported him as looking 'ghastly' in June, as having aged five years in a week, of being a 'broken man'.[27]

As a precaution, all his razors and pistols had been removed from his dressing-room; but, making use of 'a little nail-knife which he carried in his pocket book', he had cut his carotid artery with 'anatomical accuracy'.[28]

The King, who had grown accustomed to Castlereagh and appreciated his skill as a mediator between the Crown and the rest of the Cabinet, now gloomily faced the prospect of having to agree to the appointment of a new Foreign Secretary. On his return to London he asked Croker if Lord Liverpool were in a good humour or not, 'almost as a boy after holidays asks in what temper "Dr Bury may be"'.[29] Well aware that Liverpool would probably suggest Canning, who had not yet sailed for India, as a suitable candidate for the vacant office, the King made it clear that his previous objections still remained, that almost any other candidate would be preferable, and that Canning's 'departure for India should not be interrupted'.[30] Wellington would have been the King's choice, with the Home Secretary, Robert Peel, also a strong candidate, promoted to the Chancellorship of the Exchequer with the leadership of the House of Commons.[31] But Liverpool was convinced that Canning would have to come into the Cabinet as Foreign Secretary if his government were to survive.[32] He would, indeed, have brought him in long before had not grief at Lady Liverpool's death made him feel incapable of coping with the King's intransigence so often and so forcibly expressed to him.[33] Now the King must be overruled. Although opinion in the Cabinet was far from unanimous in Canning's favour, several members had threatened to resign if he were not readmitted; and there was danger of losing much support in Parliament. The Tory government desperately needed bolstering by the kind of liberal support which only Canning could supply. Canning himself had expressed a wish to go to India rather than to accept anything less than Castlereagh's 'whole heritage'; Peel had said that he did not wish to be considered in any sense a rival to Canning.

Having listened to Liverpool's arguments, the King consulted Peel, Wellington, Sidmouth, and other members of the Cabinet. He remained sulky, reluctant and unconvinced, complaining of the difficulty in being reconciled with a man whom 'he had said he never wanted to see again in his life'.[34] Lady Conyngham, who had 'conceived a great antipathy to Canning', urged him to stand firm;[35] but he was beginning to recognize the impossibility of this and burst out irritably, 'Very well, if you like. I will not appoint him; I will change the government and put in the Whigs.'[36]

Wellington's advice was more realistic than Lady Conyngham's: his Majesty would have to forgive Canning, and agree to his appointment. The King protested that his 'honour as a gentleman' prevented him from doing any such thing whereupon Wellington, who disliked the clever, self-confident upstart Canning even more than the King did, replied that his duty as a monarch made it essential for him to take the best man available.[37] On 8 September the King gave way. 'Very well, gentlemen,' he said. 'Since you are determined to have him, take him in God's name, but remember I tell you he will throw you all overboard.'[38] When confirming this decision to Liverpool, he insisted that, in sacrificing his 'private feelings', he was making the greatest sacrifice he had ever made in his life.[39] Without mentioning the Foreign Office, he said in a subsequent letter that he would agree to 'Mr Canning's re-admission into the government'; but he wanted him to be told that the King was aware that the 'brightest ornament of his crown' was the power of extending 'grace and favour to a subject who may have incurred his displeasure'.[40]

This phrase deeply offended Canning who, at first, refused to accept the Foreign Office when it was formally offered to him. It was, he complained, just as though he had been given a ticket to Almack's and found written on the back: '*Admit the rogue*.'[41] Liverpool, however, thought the letter unexceptionable, and assured Peel that he considered it to be 'expressed with as much delicacy as, considering the King's strong personal feelings, could reasonably be expected'.[42] In the end Canning decided to ignore the King's rebuke and to accept office.

As Canning took up his duties the King fell ill again, fretfully apprehensive as to the effect of the new Foreign Secretary's ideas on the kind of conservative monarchical Europe which Castlereagh had favoured, worrying continually about the attacks that were made on him in public and the importunities to which he was subjected in private. In May he had been delighted and astonished, on going to Drury Lane, to be greeted with the greatest enthusiasm, and by the National Anthem being repeated no less than six times. The Duke of Wellington had arrived just before him and had acknowledged the loud cheers of the audience 'with two little nods, as if to say, "how do you do", and then left them to clap their hands sore without giving another look'. The King, by contrast, had spent 'a good quarter of an hour bowing to the audience, as politely and respectfully as if it had been composed of Kings and Queens'.[43] But the people so rarely behaved in this gratifying way in England. Far more often he had cause to complain of the assaults made on him in the Press, particularly in the Sunday papers, and of the 'obscene prints in the form of caricatures' that were still displayed in almost every shop window in London, exposing him 'in some indecent ridiculous manner'.[44]

At the beginning of January 1823 Mme de Lieven 'found the King changed', 'aged a great deal in the last three months', and limping 'noticeably'.[45] Emily Cowper was also much disturbed about him. 'The King is in a strange state of health now,' she reported to Frederick Lamb. 'He suffers dreadfully from rheumatic gout so as hardly to be able to turn in bed without screaming . . . I cannot help feeling that his life is very precarious – one thing after another always starting up and keeping him so weak and ill'.[46] He was, indeed, by then in a 'wretched state of health, suffering from 'irregularity of the pulse, occasional pain about the praecordia, sensation in the left arm and sudden breathlessness'.[47] He was 'bled copiously' as usual; but the doctors feared that his heart was affected. If he adhered to the rules of conduct which they had laid down, they considered that 'his constitution, naturally so good', would 'continue to preserve his invaluable life for years'; but they felt it their duty to record in a 'most confidential private' document that it did sometimes happen that life was 'extinguished suddenly' where such symptoms existed as prevailed 'at present in his Majesty'.[48]

Towards the end of March 1823 Croker reported him as being 'much weakened' by his attacks of gout.[49] A few days later he took to his bed, refusing to see anybody but his doctors.[50] He was still in bed at the beginning of May, and the newspapers were 'trying to make out' that he was going the same way as his father. He got up towards the middle of the month but by the fifteenth he had suffered a relapse, had erysipelas on one foot and a high temperature.[51] Wellington confided in Mme de Lieven that he thought he would be dead in eight months, a verdict with which she was inclined to agree. It was 'a fact that since January 6 [he had] not enjoyed an hour's health, and often, for three or four weeks at a time, he had been very ill indeed'. At his age, it was not easy to recover from such attacks, 'especially with a complete lack of air and exercise'. All eyes were, therefore, on the Duke of York who was concerning himself much with public affairs, though the opposition derived little comfort from that as they had 'nothing to hope for from his reign'.[52]

People were also watching Lady Conyngham who seemed to be 'taking precautions'.[53] According to Mme de Lieven, whose comments upon her were always coloured by resentment at her influence over the King, Lady Conyngham had recently observed, 'What a pity now if all this were to end; for you must admit that it is charming.' As she spoke she looked around her drawing-room which was 'like a fairy's boudoir'. That was the sort of thing she wanted from the King, Mme de Lieven commented. If the King died, what she would regret would be 'his diamonds, pearls, handsome furniture and good dinners', and his ability to advance her family. The King was well aware of this himself, so Mme de Lieven claimed. He once observed to her, 'You see how she takes advantage of her position to push her family. Oh she knows very well when she is well off.' If the King saw through her as clearly as that, Mme de Lieven could not understand how his love for her could last so long. 'But it does last,' she wrote, 'simply because he needs a habit.'[54]

Annoyed to have the habit of Castlereagh broken, he could not get used to Canning, although he had received him politely enough when he had first taken up his appointment.[55] 'I do not like him any better than I did,' he complained in the spring of 1823 to Mme de Lieven, who passed on to

Metternich the kind of conversation most pleasing to him. 'I recognize his talent, and I believe we need him in the Commons; but he is no more capable of conducting foreign affairs than your baby. He doesn't know the first thing about his job: no tact, no judgment, no idea of decorum. But what is to be done? Can I change my Minister? No, for I should only get someone worse. That is the fix I am in. The best is bad; but the worst would be hateful, and there is nothing in between'.[56] He was still talking of Canning in similar terms to Wellington in May 1824 saying that he was 'the damnedest fellow in the world and that he could not bear him', while admitting that it 'would not do to turn him out'.[57] 'Think of that damned fellow wanting me to have the King and Queen of the Sandwich Islands to dinner,' he expostulated the next month, 'as if I would sit at table with such a pair of damned cannibals.'[58] It was all made much worse, he complained to Wellington, by the 'absurd, weak and disgusting conduct' of the Prime Minister, to whom he had 'always had an aversion' and whom, if Wellington had been willing to succeed him, he would have endeavoured to replace:[59] 'Depend upon it that Lord Liverpool, if he lives till Doomsday, will never be corrected, or made fit for the high office, to which I raised him.'[60]*

The King talked endlessly about foreign affairs to Mme de Lieven, to the Duke of York, to Wellington, who agreed that Canning 'knew no more of foreign politics than a child',[61] to foreign ambassadors – notably Prince Esterhazy, the Austrian Ambassador, and Count Münster, the Hanoverian Minister – and to anyone else to whom he cared to elaborate his opinions. Lady Charlotte Greville, after sitting next to him at dinner, was forced to conclude that he really was becoming 'the greatest bore she ever saw'.[62]

He took no trouble to disguise his dislike of Canning, or his regret that Castlereagh was dead. Castlereagh had understood the problems of Europe, and had artfully assured the King that the only other person who understood foreign affairs was his Majesty himself.[63] He had known most

---

* Wellington thought that it was just as much Lord Liverpool's fault as the King's that they could not get on together (*Wellington and his Friends*, 40). As Mrs Arbuthnot said, Liverpool had a 'disagreeable, cold manner and a most querulous temper' which rendered it 'a difficult and unpleasant task to act in public life with him'. He must have been 'a very bad manager,' she thought to be 'so perpetually getting into scrapes' with the King who was quite easily 'managed by those who took the trouble to please him when they could' (*Arbuthnot Journal*, i, 126).

of its sovereigns and leading statesmen personally; he had been controlled, patrician, well-mannered, faithful in defence of the monarchical system, whereas Canning, caustically witty and overtly ambitious, seemed to the King to take a view of foreign policy more in line with the Whigs than that of the Tories.

Of course, Castlereagh, while sympathizing with suppression of revolution in Europe, had been prevented by public opinion from interfering in the affairs of other states, even had he approved of the general right of intervention, which he did not. When revolution broke out in the Kingdom of the Two Sicilies, for example, he recognized Austria's right to crush it before it threatened the Emperor's interests in Italy; but Austria must put down the uprising on her own since it did not endanger the general security of Europe. Castlereagh was 'like a great lover of music who is at church', the Austrian Ambassador in London declared. 'He wishes to applaud, but he dare not.'[64]

Canning continued this policy of non-intervention, but he did not fully share Castlereagh's views of the monarchical principle and he wholly disagreed with his methods. He did not approve of conferences: even had he been able to meet foreign rulers and ministers in the way and on the terms that Castlereagh had done, he recognized the danger of conducting foreign policy over the heads of Parliament and people in the way that the King preferred.

The King firmly believed that the monarchs of Europe shared a common interest, that they ought to support each other in their struggle against the revolutionary movements now once more threatening to engulf them. He told the French *chargé d'affaires*, the Vicomte de Marcellus, that he wholeheartedly supported Marcellus's royal master whose troops intervened in Spain on behalf of the tottering Bourbon, King Ferdinand VII. And when *The Times* reported his indiscreet remarks, commenting that they were scarcely sentiments to be expected from a former disciple of Charles James Fox, the King riposted that he was now a royalist by trade and despised the 'shameful uncertainty' of his Cabinet.[65]

He was extremely well-informed – often, indeed, he was better informed than his Ministers, for he did not hesitate to use his position as King of Hanover to obtain information not available to them through the diplomatic channels of that country. Nor did he hesitate to correspond freely with foreign courts until Canning threatened to expose his letters in Parliament. He even sent Knighton to the Continent on confidential missions necessarily out of tune with Canning's policies; and, encouraged by Mme de Lieven and Wellington, he went so far as to invite Metternich to stay at the Royal Lodge where, as King of Hanover, he could talk to him about foreign affairs without the intervention of his Ministers. Metternich, warned by Canning of the consequences of a visit to England for such a purpose, thought it prudent to decline the invitation.[66]

Thereafter the King took an increasingly perverse pleasure in using his acquired knowledge to discomfit Canning, to make him ill at ease in his presence. He delighted in contradicting him, in making outrageous comments he knew would annoy him. One day in June 1823 at the Royal Lodge where – despite his earlier avowal that he would never receive him – he sometimes included Canning amongst his guests, the conversation turned to Spain and her autocratic ruler. The King was in cheerful and confident mood, having been received at Ascot races that morning 'with a good deal of enthusiasm', and when Canning spoke apprehensively about King Ferdinand's policies, he retorted airily that there was 'nothing to be afraid of. Canning insisted that Prince Metternich wanted to rule the whole world, to wipe out every constitution from the surface of the globe. "No harm in that," said the King, "as long as our constitution is among them." '[67]

The next month, at a ball at Carlton House, the King went out of his way to annoy Canning in front of the French *chargé d'affaires*. On this occasion, too, Canning refused to rise to the provocation; but after the King had moved away he said to Marcellus, 'Representative government has still one advantage that his Majesty has forgotten. Ministers have to endure without answering back the epigrams by which a King seeks to avenge himself for his impotence.'[68]

Later on that summer the King led the after-dinner conversation round to Fouché. 'Instead of taking him for my Minister, as the King of France has done,' he said to Prince Polignac, 'I should have hanged him, and eighty other rascals with him; that is what I should have done with those Jacobins.' Prince Polignac 'pretended to look embarrassed, but was really delighted. He was much more so when the King said, "What an admirable speech M. de Chateaubriand made in reply to all the nonsense that was talked here! What good taste! We admired it greatly . . . " Canning made no movement.'[69]

The differences between the King and Canning were strongly emphasized the following year when the Cabinet proposed negotiating a commercial treaty with Buenos Aires which had ceased to acknowledge the sovereignty of the King of Spain. Encouraged by Wellington, the King informed the Cabinet that he very much regretted this move which would 'carry with it the appearance and promise of an early recognition to the different insurrectionary States of South America'.[70] In a long and forceful letter to Lord Liverpool he roundly condemned the 'new political liberalism' which he considered so dangerous a policy that for a time he refused to talk about it personally to Canning who was required to communicate with him in writing.[71] He reminded the Prime Minister that 'the line of policy pursued by the government . . . at the close of the late war . . . was *unanimity* of cooperation with the great Continental Powers not only for the purpose of putting an end to the existing hostilities, but for preserving the future tranquility and peace of Europe'. Lord Castlereagh, in conjunction with the Duke of Wellington, had 'so effectually accomplished this desirable and great object that the country had taken a position, in relation to her continental policy, that she had never before held'.

'The King supposes it will not be denied,' he continued, 'that the anarchy produced throughout the world by the French Revolution has left a record so instructive that the Councils of the British government should never fail to be regulated by the wholesome remembrance of that terrible event! That we should therefore regard with the utmost suspicion every attempt to revive the example of British America which unhappily for Great Britain ended in a separation from the mother country. France treacherously assisted that successful enterprise and by her fatal policy gave the first impulse to that revolution which entailed, for a quarter of a century, such complicated misery on the whole of Europe.

'The revolutionary spirit of those days, although lulled and suspended, is by no means extinguished; and it would be wisdom to look to the ultimate consequences which the result of our recognition of the independence of the South American provinces may probably produce on the evil and discontented who are even at this moment controlled with difficulty by the established power of regular governments.'

The King concluded by saying that he had long been aware that the principles of his early friends, the Whigs, were 'the bane that threatened the destruction of our happy Constitution and the peace of the world', and that since he had abandoned them – for the good of the country – on his coming to power as Regent, could the present government suppose that he would permit 'any individuals now to force upon him measures of which he entirely disapproved', particularly when 'many members' of the present Cabinet (Wellington, Bathurst, Eldon and Westmorland among them) held the same opinion 'respecting the new political liberalism' as he did himself? 'No such thing! If the present line of policy [was] to be *further* pursued, the King [would] feel himself justified in taking such measures as the government [would] be the least prepared to accept.'[72]

But the threat was an empty one. Commercial and other pressures were too strong to prevent recognition of the independence of Spain's South American colonies. Trade with them had increased fourteen times since the end of the Spanish monopoly. Even Castlereagh had declared that recognition of the new republics was more 'a matter of time than of principle'; and the President of the United States, James Monroe, knowing that Britain would oppose any move by the European powers to help King Ferdinand to recover his Empire, had announced in a statement which Canning described as 'a new doctrine', that an attempt by Europe to impose an unwelcome 'political system' on any part of the Western Hemisphere would be considered as dangerous to America's 'peace and safety'. So, on 31 December 1824, Buenos Aires, Mexico and Colombia – and shortly afterwards Brazil – were all recognized as independent countries.

The King was so annoyed by the government's action that he resolutely refused to read the speech announcing it at the opening of Parliament. He let it be known that his gout was so bad that he could not walk. He could not speak either, so he said, because he had lost his false teeth.[73]

18

Palace and Castle
1823-1826

*

'England ought to pride herself on her plainness and simplicity'

As often as he could the King escaped from London to the privacy of the Royal Lodge, where he surrounded himself with 'the Cottage clique' – Esterhazy and Esterhazy's *chargé d'affaires*, Baron Neumann, Count Münster, Prince Polignac, the French Ambassador, and the Lievens – lamenting with them the new liberalism, the sympathetic attitudes towards self-determination, that were spreading so fast across the world and were destroying the hopes of the men who had redrawn Napoleon's map of Europe at the Congress of Vienna. Mme de Lieven, a guest during August 1823, told Metternich how drearily the days passed in contrast with the 'exceedingly agreeable' time that the Duke of Dorset had spent there three years before. The suite which Mme de Lieven and her husband occupied was below the level of the garden from which the field mice came in to run about the rooms. The King was miserable and limped through the house, sometimes in tears. 'Yesterday evening the King began to sing,' she reported on the 12th, his sixty-first birthday. 'In order to produce the sole musical sound of which his throat is capable, he closed his eyes, shed tears. . . . I stifled my laughter . . . I really thought I should die, especially when I saw how affected the courtiers looked at the sight of the royal tears.'[1]

Sometimes Mme de Lieven was so bored that she felt close to tears herself. She got up at nine, went straight out into the garden and returned to her room at eleven to dress for luncheon with the King. After luncheon she and the other guests went out for a drive or on the river, returning half an hour before dinner. Dinner was followed by music, then by a game of écarté. The conversation was occasionally interesting, but usually 'so

262

stupid' that she began to doubt her own intelligence. Once her mind wandered to a far more exciting evening spent with Metternich. She woke from her reverie to find the King 'gazing' at Lady Conyngham with an expression in which somnolence battled against love; Lady Conyngham was staring at a beautiful emerald on her arm; her daughter was toying with a ruby hanging round her neck.[2]

On another occasion Mme de Lieven's unbearable boredom during the customary silence after grace led to her being seized with 'an uncontrollable fit of laughter'. First Lady Elizabeth Conyngham was infected by it, then Admiral Nagle, who upset a bottle which gave them all an excuse 'to go on laughing' and even get worse. The King was angry, Mme de Lieven said. 'He thought we were laughing at him. I did not mind; for the moment I was beyond caring. He could not scold me, so he scolded the daughter. Afterwards we played fourteen games of écarté and thirty-three games of patience.'[3]

*

Frustrated in his efforts to control Canning's policies, the King could at least comfort himself with the knowledge that he was able to use his influence to more effect in the world of art and letters, that his opinions there did carry some weight, and that artists and writers were deeply grateful for his munificent patronage.

By this time the most important items in his collection had already been assembled. Since his purchase in 1814 of eighty-six splendid pictures from the collection of Sir Thomas Baring, he had been less and less inclined to buy paintings *en bloc*. In 1819 Sir Charles Long – who, with Lord Yarmouth and William Seguier, was one of his principal advisers – had heard that the famous Aynard collection would probably come on to the market in Paris. But the King had decided that it was 'too general'; he was now limiting himself to what he 'actually wanted'; and he purchased only the *Farm at Laeken* by Rubens.[4]

Yet though the quantity of the King's purchases had declined, their quality had not. He had paid a thousand guineas for Dou's *Interior of a Grocer's Shop*; he had bought Mieris's *Fruiterer's Shop*, Schalcken's *Candle-light*, Steen's *Morning Toilet*, De Hooch's *The Card-Players* and *A Courtyard in Delft*. In 1819 Lord Yarmouth had purchased for him Rembrandt's *Lady with a Fan*, a superb companion for Rembrandt's *Shipbuilder and his Wife* which he had acquired, together with fine paintings by Adriaen van de Velde, Wouwermans and Ostades at the Lafontaine sale at Christie's some years before.[5]

The King's collection of pictures by contemporary artists, mostly English, had also continued to grow apace. He had year by year placed more and more commissions for portraits of his family and friends, his distinguished contemporaries and his beloved animals. Portraits by Beechey and Stroehling were added to those by Hoppner, Copley, Gainsborough and Reynolds. Pictures by Schwanfelder, Cooper, Doyle and Ward came to join the Sawreys, Gilpins, Garrards, Marshalls and Stubbses. Military subjects were as welcome as ever; so were genre scenes by artists like William Mulready and William Collins.[6]

No artist was kept so busy as Thomas Lawrence who painted Lady Conyngham's daughters, Sir William Curtis, the Duke of Devonshire, Wellington, Lord Eldon, Canning, Bathurst, Liverpool and Walter Scott, as well as numerous other British and foreign notables, almost all the members of the King's immediate family, and on more than one occasion the King himself.[7] Lawrence was eventually to receive well over £25,000 from the Privy Purse.[8]

Nor were painters alone grateful for his patronage and generosity. The sculptors, John Flaxman and Richard Westmacott, as well as Chantrey, received satisfying commissions. Scott was always pleased to know that his latest work appeared on the King's table; Southey was gratified to learn that his Majesty esteemed his 'distinguished talents and the usefulness and importance' of his 'literary labours'.[9] The Trustees of the British Museum were delighted when his father's library of some 65,000 volumes came into their possession and they received from Parliament a generous grant of £120,000 to build a suitable extension to the Museum in which they could be housed.[10] On making this gift to the nation, the King told Lord Liverpool that as well as 'paying a just tribute' to the memory of his father, he had 'the satisfaction by this means of advancing the literature of the country'.[11]* The advancement of literature was, indeed,

---

* The details of this transference of King George III's library to Bloomsbury are a mystery on which the Royal Archives throw no light. In 1850 an article appeared in the *Quarterly Review* which suggested that the King had originally intended to sell the library to the highest bidder. Richard Heber, the book collector, hearing that the Tsar was interested in buying it, approached Lord Sidmouth who arranged for the money which the King had hoped to receive from the Tsar to be paid to him out of the Droits of Admiralty (*Quarterly Review*, clxxv, 143). The Duke of York, who

a pursuit that the King continued to follow with credit. His interest in the Stuarts which had led to the publication in 1816 of *The Life of James II ... Collected out of Materials by his own Hand*, was followed by the formation of a commission, headed by Sir Walter Scott, to edit the Stuart papers. The biography of Nelson, which the King had encouraged his librarian, James Stanier Clarke, to help to write, formed the basis for Robert Southey's classic *Life* and several later works. In 1820 the King readily and enthusiastically took up a proposal of Thomas Burgess, Bishop of St David's, for the establishment, under royal patronage, of a Society of Literature. He agreed to contribute the sum of a thousand guineas towards its establishment, and to make an annual grant of a hundred guineas. The Bishop mistook the King's meaning, and announced that the entire sum would be given annually.[12] The King did not correct the mistake, and it was therefore settled that he would give a thousand guineas a year from the Privy Purse as pensions to ten Associates of the Society – the first of the ten names on the list being that of Samuel Taylor Coleridge – and to donate an annual prize of 'two medals of fifty guineas each'.[13] A few years later the Society obtained from the Commissioners of Woods and Forests the lease of a site in St Martin's Place, Trafalgar Square, on which to build a house for their headquarters.[14]*

---

was very annoyed with his brother for having parted with their father's property, told Charles Greville that the King 'even had a design of selling the Library collected by the late King, but this he was obliged to abandon' (*Greville Diary*, 8 January 1823). The Duke of Clarence was also 'much vexed' by his brother's action and would never visit the King's Library at the British Museum (Macaulay's Journal, Trinity College, Cambridge, entry for 29 November 1849).

Antonio Panizzi, who was Keeper of Printed Books (1837–56) and Principal Librarian (1856–66) said in his evidence before the Select Committee of the House of Commons in 1836, when he was Assistant Librarian, that it was due to the personal influence of the Trustees that the King's Library came to the Museum. The Trustees 'worked very hard, to get that Library,' Panizzi declared, 'and exerted all their influence, both public and private' (Para. 4901).

Peel, however, who was one of the Trustees and had much to do with the disposal of the King's Library, confirmed in his correspondence with W. R. Hamilton that it was King George IV's personal wish that it should go to Bloomsbury as his father had always been so interested in the Museum (BM Peel MSS).

* The house, designed by Decimus Burton, was demolished when the National Gallery was enlarged in the 1890s. The Society then moved to Hanover Square, then to Bloomsbury Square before settling in Hyde Park Gardens (Records of the Royal Society of Literature).

Many other organizations also profited from the King's spontaneous generosity. The Royal Academy received ten more 'casts of statues from the antique';[15] Trinity College, Cambridge, received a grant of £1,000 towards the building of a new quadrangle to be known as The King's Court;[16] £200 was contributed from the Privy Purse 'for the professional use of the English students at Rome';[17] £500 went towards a statue of James Watt;[18] a suggestion from Peel that his Majesty should command 'two gold medals to be in future annually given as honorary rewards for the best papers sent in to the Council of the Royal Society on Scientific Subjects' was immediately accepted with the proviso that the medals should be of the value of fifty guineas each and not twenty as Peel had proposed.[19] Numerous presents were given to artists, writers and musicians whom the King asked to be presented to him. One of these was Gioachino Rossini who visited England in December 1823, 'a fat, sallow squab of a man', in Lady Granville's opinion. 'The courtiers and the rest of the society were indignant at his familiarity. Being fat and lazy, and consequently averse to standing, he took a chair and sat by the King, who, however, gave him the kindest reception, and, less *petit* than his suite, understood the man, and treated him as his enthusiasm for music disposed him to do.'[20] He insisted on accompanying him, and, though still a pretty good performer, he constantly put the *maestro* out owing to his idiosyncratic notions of keeping time. 'He at last offered an apology which Rossini accepted with civility, and good-naturedly said, "There are few in your Royal Highness's position who could play so well." '[21] Rossini afterwards professed himself much taken with his royal accompanist. He had, he said, met no other monarch, apart from the Tsar Alexander I, nearly so amiable: it was 'scarcely possible to form an idea . . . of the charm of George IV's personal appearance and demeanour'.[22]

A project as dear to the King as any other was the formation of a national collection of pictures to rival those of Italy and France. He had contrived to restore the Royal Collection to the eminent position it had held among the great collections of the world before the Commonwealth government had sold off so many of the valuable paintings collected by Charles I; and he was always happy for the public to see it. 'I have not formed it for my own pleasure alone,' he commented when lending his Carlton House pictures for an exhibition in 1826, 'but to gratify the public taste.'[23] Yet there was nothing in London to compare with the fine galleries in Paris, Florence, or indeed, in several other lesser Continental towns. So, with the idea of forming the nucleus of a national collection, the King urged the government to buy the thirty-eight splendid pictures of his friend John Julius Angerstein, who died in 1823. The government accepted his advice, bought Angerstein's collection for £57,000, added to it sixteen pictures donated by Sir George Beaumont, and housed them all in Angerstein's house in Pall Mall until a more suitable gallery could be built. The site eventually chosen for the national collection was on the north side of Trafalgar Square where William Wilkins's domed and turreted building was to be finished in 1828.[24]

Trafalgar Square had already been planned by Nash as part of that ambitious scheme for the redevelopment of London which was being executed under the King's keenly interested eye. For more years than anyone could then remember the old Royal Mews had stood here, row upon row of stables, harness rooms and grooms' quarters surrounding Hubert Le Sueur's statue of Charles I. Nash envisaged the new square as forming the centrepiece of a fine road extending from the southern end of Regent Street across the bottom of Haymarket and linking up with another road to be built from Whitehall as far as the growing developments in Bloomsbury. Originally Nash had seen Carlton House as an integral part of this design. Carriages would come down Regent Street towards Henry Holland's imposing colonnade, would there turn left and rattle away across Haymarket through Trafalgar Square to Whitehall. But Nash was never able to realize this vision, for his patron decided that Carlton House, splendid as it was, was no longer a suitable residence for a King of England. He complained that its rooms were too small for large receptions, as indeed they were, and that, despite the immense sums which had been spent on it, it was antiquated and decrepit. It certainly appeared so now from the outside. Canova described it as 'blackened with dust and soot', and looking like 'an ugly barn'.[25]

The King would have to have something new. Carlton House would have to be pulled down, terraces of houses built on its site and in its garden, and a fine palace built to replace Buckingham House, the far more modest London home of his parents, known since his mother's death as the King's House, Pimlico. He had had this plan in mind since 1819 when he had estimated that the new palace could be built for £500,000, which was £350,000 more than the 'utmost sum' that the government had in mind.[26] At that time Lord Liverpool had told him that 'in the present circumstances of the country . . . it would be quite impracticable to look to any grant of public money' for the ambitious scheme which his Majesty had in view. 'The only measure which could be resorted to would be to sell or lease' part of the site of St James's Palace; but this would 'not produce any considerable sum' and Parliament would have to be consulted.[27] So the project had had to be dropped, but it was now revived again. The King protested that he was now 'too old to build a palace'; but a palace was what he wanted all the same.

Sir John Soane, Professor of Architecture at the Royal Academy – who had rebuilt the Bank of England, enlarged and enriched the Houses of Parliament, and designed many fine houses in Regency London, including his own in Lincoln's Inn Fields – had hoped to be given the commission as an attached architect to the Board of Works; and, believing that Buckingham House ought to be preserved, he had prepared plans for the new palace in Green Park. But the King did not want to live in Green Park. Pleading that 'early associations' endeared him to the spot, he insisted on the palace being built on the site of Buckingham House, an admirable site for a palace with gardens of forty acres originally laid out by 'Capability' Brown. The King also insisted that the architect must be Nash.

Nash went to work immediately and soon all manner of building materials, including five hundred massive blocks of veined Carrara marble, were unloaded at the site. By the time the original estimate of £252,690 had been increased to £331,973 the work was far from completed. Whole wings had been torn down and rebuilt because they had not struck the right note at their first appearance. Yet even in February 1827 when Creevey 'sallied forth to see the alterations' they still remained in his opinion the 'devil's own'.[28] Other critics complained of the 'square towers at the side and wretched inverted egg-cup at the top', 'a common slop pail turned upside down'. Joseph Hume protested that the Crown of England did not require such splendour: 'Foreign countries might indulge in frippery, but England ought to pride herself on her plainness and simplicity.' How could the Chancellor of the Exchequer justify such extravagance? The Chancellor certainly found it hard to justify; but the work, once begun, could not very well be abandoned. Month after month it went on, the expenditure mounting towards an ultimate total of £700,000, excluding the cost of the Marble Arch, proposed by the King and designed by Nash as the main gateway into the forecourt.[29]* People began to doubt that the King would live long enough to see it finished. His mordant friend, Joseph Jekyll, was reminded of a mausoleum.[30]

*

Sternly criticized for his expenditure on Buckingham Palace, the King was just as severely censured for spending so much on Windsor Castle which was being simultaneously transformed at even greater cost and which, so Wellington complained, absorbed the King's attention to such a degree that he appeared 'not to be the least interested in public affairs'.[31] The King had moved into the Castle in the autumn of 1823 for two months to see what living there was like. He chose to occupy the rooms which his mother and sisters had used rather than the gloomier rooms on the ground floor of the north front where his father had spent his last years. The State Apartments on the first floor of the northern front, rebuilt by Charles II, would henceforward, he decided, be used for the state visits of foreign sovereigns.

Already he had given orders for the demolition of the barracks-like Queen's Lodge which King George III had built for his large family less than half a century before. This would open up a fine view down Charles II's avenue, known as the Long Walk, at the far end of which he planned to place an equestrian statue of his father, commissioned from Richard Westmacott. He had also already given orders for the Terrace to be closed to the public, except on Sundays. Ever since George III's death, the Terrace had been used as a promenade, the people peering through the windows while the children whipped tops and flew kites. His order had caused a good deal of resentment, particularly from the Canons of Windsor who claimed that they had had a '*legal right*' to walk upon the Terrace since the time of Charles II.[32] The King had had to be firm with the Canons, and to insist that he 'would never have chosen Windsor Castle for his

* The Marble Arch – constructed of marble from Seravezza – was ornamented with sculptures by Richard Westmacott and E. H. Baily whose friezes, extolling military and naval glories, were intended for the attic storey. These friezes were placed instead on the face of Buckingham Palace. It was originally intended that a statue of Victory should surmount the Arch; but this idea was abandoned in favour of an equestrian statue of King George IV by Chantrey and Earle. In 1851, to make way for the construction of the east wing of Buckingham Palace, the Arch was removed to its present position at the top of Park Lane; and the statue of the King was taken to Trafalgar Square (Pevsner, *London*, i, 347, 556).

royal residence unless the privacy of the Terrace could have been secured, and his Majesty thereby not exposed to be overlooked and interrupted at all periods of the day'.[33] The local newspaper regarded the closure of the Terrace in a more favourable light than the Canons: the inhabitants of Windsor might 'at first feel this measure as a privation', but at the same time they would 'cheerfully acknowledge' that the Castle was 'entirely wanting in privacy' and would hail the closure as an assurance that the King was 'about to make this glorious palace of his ancestors once more the seat of royalty'.[34]

This, indeed, was what the King decided to do after his brief sojourn in the Castle in the autumn of 1823; but, just as Carlton House was considered unsuitable as a London palace for the King of England, so Windsor Castle was at present far from being an appropriate 'seat of royalty'. So, once again an approach had to be made to Parliament; and Parliament obligingly agreed that the work should be done. Eight commissioners were appointed to supervise it.

The commissioners decided to hold a competition and invited various architects, including Robert Smirke, John Nash and John Soane, to submit plans and estimates. Soane declined to compete, but the others agreed to do so. The winner, however, was a man not as well-known as they – Jeffry Wyatt, the fifty-eight-year-old Derbyshire-born nephew of James Wyatt who had already provided a few romantic Gothic details to the buildings of the Upper Ward. Jeffry Wyatt had done work for the Dukes of Bedford, Beaufort and Devonshire and had built a large country house in Surrey for Samuel Farmer in the style of Henry VIII's palace of Nonesuch. He was an inventive and versatile architect, and the fact that he was rather careless in the matter of costing was not of the slightest interest to George IV who shared his enthusiasm for turning the Castle into a magnificently Gothic structure. Indeed, before Wyatt had been selected for the work, the King asked him to make a few drawings to illustrate his ideas on the subject. Wyatt estimated that the work would cost £122,500; but having arrived at this figure – so he later maintained – he was told by the Chancellor of the Exchequer, one of the Commissioners, that the government were thinking in terms of £150,000; so he adjusted his estimate accordingly.[35]

On 12 August 1824, his sixty-second birthday, the King drove up to the Castle from the Royal Lodge to lay the foundation stone of a new archway on the southern side of the Upper Ward which was to bear his name and was to lead out into Charles II's elm-lined Long Walk. He was met by Wyatt, 'a busy-bustling, vain little man',[36] who had already moved into Winchester Tower which he was to occupy until his death in 1840.[37] Wyatt asked the King there and then, so it is said, if he could change his name to Wyatville, to avoid confusion with other members of his family, some of whom were mere builders. 'Ville or mutton,' the King is supposed to have replied cheerfully, 'call yourself what you like.'[38] Later the King, well pleased with his diminutive architect's work, added a view of King George IV Gate to Wyatville's coat of arms, allowed him to use the word 'Windsor' as a motto, had his portrait painted by Lawrence, and knighted him.

In hopeful anticipation of such honours, Wyatville had set to work with a will. Five hundred workmen had been immediately employed; and two years later the numbers had risen to 709 men regularly occupied on full-time work at Windsor, with thirty-six men doing occasional work, and fifty joiners and twenty plasterers preparing woodwork and ornaments in London, making a total force of 815 men.[39]

On the approach of the King's birthday in 1824, Wyatville had hoped 'a treat might be given to the men' in celebration. His Majesty had suggested sitting them all down to dinner in the Castle grounds, but Wyatville, not trusting the weather, had thought that it would be better to give all the men five shillings each so that they could buy good dinners for themselves 'at the various public houses in Windsor'. 'I proposed to man the towers for a general Huzza! at precisely one o'clock,' he had told Knighton, 'but reflecting on the chance of accident, and that the men would be lost behind the battlements, I decide for assembling them either along the south front or on the new Terrace for that purpose.'[40]

He had chosen the new Terrace, and on the appointed day the men, having been 'provided with dinners at the different inns', had responded to Wyatville's signal by hailing the occasion 'with repeated cheers'. A local journalist thought that 'the effect of this assemblage of happy and industrious artisans was most exhilarating'.[41]

Gradually these industrious artisans transformed the Castle. Walls and towers were demolished; apartments were stripped and rotten timbers torn out; roofs were removed; old towers were rebuilt; new towers were erected; Charles II's windows were replaced by Gothic ones; courts vanished, a state staircase and, eventually, the Waterloo Chamber took their place; a garden was made on the eastern side, an orangery to face the south; the Round Tower was raised by a stone crown 30 feet higher than the former structure; the Grand Corridor, 550 feet in length, provided a magnificent picture gallery as well as a covered way between the north front and the east.

Some observers were appalled by Wyatville's architectural contrivances, the imitation portcullis grooves in his gates, the bogus mortar joints in his freestone blocks, the picturesque machicolations of his new towers. But others – Sir Walter Scott among them – thought that the Gothicization, for all its whimsical extravagance, was successful and impressive. An essentially Gothic structure demanded Gothic treatment; and Wyatville was turning Windsor Castle into one of the most distinctive Gothic monuments in the world. The King himself warmly approved. He was later moodily to grumble about the smallness of the rooms, too cramped for their furniture; and about the lack of privacy, despite the closure of the Terrace.[42] But he never grumbled about the grand design of the Castle's external appearance which he had inspired and which Wyatville had so efficiently executed. It was left to others, of course, to grumble about the cost.

The first £150,000 was soon spent; another £150,000 was as quickly disposed of; the cost soared to £600,000, as more extensive improvements were carried out and more furniture was bought, much of it in Paris. Even then the work was not finished. At times, indeed, it seemed that it never would be finished; for lack of funds more than once brought Wyatville to a standstill.[43] When the total cost reached £800,000, and Parliament was asked to grant a further £100,000, the House of Commons rebelled. Was there to be no 'limit to such extravagance'? Who could say that next year there would not be another demand for £300,000 or £400,000? The Chancellor of the Exchequer protested that leaving the building unfinished would be 'a disgrace to the country'; but he was obliged to withdraw his motion in order to prevent 'a most painful discussion'. And Wellington, for one, was not surprised. 'The question is a bad one,' he told Knighton. 'We are in the wrong for bringing forward for the third or fourth time a vote for a fresh grant without an estimate of the whole expence.'[44]

The proposal was therefore referred to a Select Committee which, while deploring the evident disregard of economy, recommended that the money should be provided since 'the complete repair of this ancient and royal residence' had now become an 'object of national concern'. It was also recommended that Wyatville, a rather harassed witness before the Committee, should remain in charge of the operations, 'for the sake of uniformity of character and design'. The members of the Committee added that they entertained 'a favourable opinion' of his work.[45] So did Mrs Arbuthnot who was 'quite delighted' with the Castle after going over it for the first time. She thought the new apartments would be 'quite beautiful'.[46]

Other visitors to the Castle at the time of its reconstruction were not so complimentary. Lady Holland, who was shown over it in the summer of 1826, while admiring the 'glory of the architecture', thought that the state rooms were 'not spacious enough nor sufficiently numerous'.[47] Charles Greville, after a visit in the summer of 1827, considered that not enough had been 'effected for the enormous sums expended'. It was a 'fine house', to be sure; but it was not a palace to stand comparison with 'Versailles, St Cloud and the other palaces in France'.[48] Croker, who was taken over it by Wyatville early the following year, was inclined to agree with Greville. The 'new works' were 'in many respects handsome, and not inconvenient'; but the rooms were by no means 'what they ought to be'; they were 'neither in number and size what might have been produced for much less expense'.[49]

Creevey was of the same opinion, though he thought the Grand Corridor 'above all price'. 'Mr Wyat-*ville* himself did us the honour of conducting us through all the new apartments,' he told his stepdaughter. 'All the new living-rooms make a very good gentleman's or nobleman's house, nothing more.'

The crotchety and eccentric Lord Dudley thought that it would have been a great deal better if it *had* been more of a house and less of a castle. As one of the earliest guests there after its completion, he angrily scolded Wyatville because he felt so cold. The food was cold, too. Why, he had recently dined with a lady where the soup was *hot*, and there was a decent woodcock on the table! 'Look,' he exclaimed in protest at the Castle fare, 'Look at this wretched snipe.' As for the Castle itself, a large house would have been much better. Why had Wyatville had to make such a damned great fortress of it? The Vikings weren't coming over again, were they?[50]

Wyatville himself was not altogether satisfied with the finished interior which was far more to the King's taste than to his own. He was inclined to agree with Croker who thought it too much in the Louis XIV style to accord with the general character of Windsor; it was altogether too 'French'. But the King, who had driven over regularly to see the works, and to supervise the decorations and the furnishing, had been insistent. He liked his woodwork and plaster sumptuously gilded, his walls richly brocaded; he did not want his beautiful fireplaces and doors from Carlton House to disappear with the rest of the building; those that were not required at Buckingham Palace must be found a place at Windsor. One day the King asked Wyatville to incorporate some armorial stained glass from the conservatory at Carlton House in the windows at Windsor. 'Wyatville hummed and hawed at first a good deal,' the King told Knighton. But eventually he was brought round to say in his still strong Derbyshire accent – which his Majesty could imitate to perfection – that he 'thought he cud pleace soom of't to advantage, though 'e 'ad not joust thin fix'd where'.[51]

Queen Caroline leaving the House of Lords after the trial.

24 George IV in Scots dress by David Wilkie.

25 Wyatville's views of the north front of the Upper Ward, Windsor Castle, after and before alteration.

26 George IV driving a phaeton: engraving by J. Dickenson.

19

The Windsor Recluse
1826–1827

*

'It is unpleasant for him to see a strange face'

'The King,' wrote Lady Shelley in 1826, 'never thinks of anything but building.'[1] As well as in London and at the Castle in Windsor, work was also now in progress at Virginia Water where ornamental temples were being built to decorate the shores of an artificial lake.

This lake had been made by his godfather, William Augustus, Duke of Cumberland, who, as Ranger of Windsor Great Park, had employed gangs of discharged soldiers on such works of improvement on the royal estate. The Duke's Deputy Ranger had been Thomas Sandby, brother of the artist, Paul; and it was to the designs of Thomas Sandby that a Chinese temple had been built at Virginia Water on an island in the middle of the lake.

This temple had suggested to the King the idea of building other decorative Moorish and Chinese pavilions on the shores of the lake; and on the bank in front of one of these, the King was often to be found with Lady Conyngham fishing on summer afternoons – though after the appearance in June 1826 of a popular caricature, 'A King-Fisher', which ridiculed this practice, he all but abandoned it.[2] Still, an afternoon's drive down to Virginia Water became a regular feature of life at the Royal Lodge. 'They meet at three o'clock,' Lady Shelley recorded, 'at which hour five or six phaetons come to the door, each to receive a lady and gentleman who drive about the country until five. At that hour the whole party dine in a hut on the shore of Virginia Water. . . . The party sit at table until between nine and ten o'clock, then they return to the Cottage, dress *presto*, and go into the saloon where they play at écarté and other games until midnight. It is every day the same: Oh! monotony!'[3]

Sometimes, if the weather were fine, the guests would stay down by the lake for supper which was served either in one of the temples or in the shade of a folly, built by Wyatville from a selection of classical remains found in a courtyard in the British Museum and from Greek statues captured in a French frigate during the Napoleonic wars.

On special occasions the appearance of his Majesty would be greeted by 'God save the King' played by his band seated in a boat by the shore; and after a visit to *The Mandarin*, a junk that had been moored in the lake since the Duke of Cumberland's time, dinner would be served in tents erected on the lawns by the water's edge. Dinner usually lasted a long time, for the King still 'ate very heartily' when he was well and could still get through two or three bottles of claret before rising from the table.[4]

Wellington was desperately bored by these parties, this perpetual '*junke thing*' which lasted 'from morning till night'. 'We embarked yesterday at three, and were upon the lake of Como, either in the boat or dining, till nine,' he complained one summer day in 1824 to Mrs Arbuthnot. 'We then returned, dressed as quickly as possible and passed the night at Ecarte and supper from which we broke up about one, thus passing ten hours in company! In my life I never heard so much nonsense and folly or so many lies in the same space of time. . . . One is obliged to listen to [them] with a certain degree of complacency if one does not intend to offend. . . . We are to have a repetition of the same today, as I see that unfortunately it is a fine day. . . . I am not astonished that Lady C[onyngham] is tired out of her life.'[5]

Wellington continued to be a regular visitor at Windsor, however, as he prided himself upon being able to settle differences as well as any man and loved being consulted, as Charles Greville said, and 'mixed up in messes'. He was particularly needed this summer because Lady Conyngham's eldest son, Mount Charles, was dying on the Continent; she wanted to go out to see him, and the King insisted on accompanying her. If he followed her, Wellington protested, the public would have the impression that 'it was neither more nor less than abdication of his high duties'. But the King remained adamant: if she went, he would go too. It appeared to Wellington that he was more in love with her than ever, a state of mind that the Duke found incomprehensible, for he had never seen so vulgar a woman as Lady Conyngham, though he recognized her shrewdness, and the advisability of consulting her before approaching the King on matters of importance. She gave him the feeling that he thought he would have if he were ever 'to experience a revulsion of blood'; 'every time she spoke [he] trembled lest [he] should hear some fresh vulgarity'. He could not conceive why the King wanted to go abroad with her. By the beginning of September the crisis was over; Lady Conyngham had agreed to remain in England, and Knighton had left for France to take Lord Mount Charles to Italy.[6]

The 'more tranquil state' in which Wellington left the King and Lady Conyngham after this matter had been settled did not last long. By the summer of 1826 Wellington felt sure that the King's love for Lady Conyngham was 'at an end'. The King still assured Knighton, with tears in his eyes, that he was 'more in love with her beauty than ever', but neither Knighton nor Wellington believed 'one word of it'. Mme de Lieven was convinced by now that Lady Conyngham did not love him at all, and that the King was aware of this and would certainly have replaced her had he not felt himself too old to contract fresh habits.[7] He admitted as much himself to Wellington. 'With my age and infirmities,' he said, 'it is not worth while looking out for another.'[8]

In fact, Wellington thought, complain though he constantly did of his infirmities, there was nothing the matter with him excepting 'what was caused by the effects of strong liquors taken too frequently and in too large quantities'. 'He drinks spirits morning, noon and night,' the Duke told Mrs Arbuthnot; 'and he is obliged to take laudanum to calm the irritation which the use of spirits occasions. ... The Accoucheur [Knighton] and Halford don't agree about the use of laudanum by the King. The former says it will drive him mad. Halford says spirits will drive him mad if laudanum is not given; and that he will take it in larger doses if it is not administered in smaller.'[9] After an enormous dose of spirits on 2 August, the King exasperated Wellington by being 'very drunk, very blackguard, very much out of temper at times, and a very great bore'.[10]

This was at the time of the visit to Windsor of his little niece, Victoria, the Duchess of Kent's child. Princess Victoria, then aged seven, and a 'clever, pretty, winning child' in Lady Shelley's opinion, was staying with her aunt Mary, the Duchess of Gloucester, at Cumberland Lodge. She was driven over to the Royal Lodge by her mother to see her uncle. 'Give me your little paw,' he said, affectionately taking her hand in his, and then pulled her on to his stout knee so that she could kiss him. It was 'too disgusting', she recalled more than half a century later, 'because his face was covered with grease-paint'. But at the time she had responded to his 'wonderful dignity and charm of manner': he never lost his way of pleasing young children. 'He wore the wig which was so much worn in those days,' she remembered clearly. 'Then he said he would give me something to wear, and that was his picture set in diamonds, which was worn by the Princesses as an order to a blue ribbon on the left shoulder. I was very proud of this – and Lady Conyngham pinned it on my shoulder.'

Next day, while she was out walking with her mother, the King, who was driving along in his phaeton with the Duchess of Gloucester, overtook her. As his horses were brought to a halt, the King called out cheerfully, 'Pop her in!' So she was lifted up and placed between him and her aunt Mary, who held her round the waist as the horses trotted off. She was 'greatly pleased', though her mother appeared 'much frightened', fearful that her daughter would either fall out on the road or be kidnapped.

The King drove her 'round the nicest part of Virginia Water', and stopped at the Fishing Temple. Here 'there was a large barge and everyone went on board and fished, while a band played in another!' Afterwards he had her conducted around his menagerie at Sandpit Gate where she inspected his wapitis, his chamois and his gazelles.*

---

* The animals in the King's menagerie, superintended by Edward Cross, grew in numbers year by year. By 1826 they included gnus and monkeys, roebucks and kangaroos, musk deer and elks, Mandarin horses and Brahmin bulls, a zebra, a leopard, a llama, an 'enormous tortoise' and all manner of birds, including ostriches, parrots, hawks, cranes, eagles, Chinese partridges and Greenland geese, macaws, German hook-bill ducks, Siberian wild swans and an orange-crested talking cockatoo (RA 25583–624). In August 1827, accompanied by two Nubian attendants, there arrived a giraffe, a present from the Pasha of Egypt. This giraffe so took the public's fancy that 'nothing else seemed to be thought of' that summer (WDNS iv, 94, 14 August 1827). It was depicted frequently in caricatures of the King and Lady Conyngham (BM *Sat*, x and xi, 15425, 15521, 15845, 16143). It was a beautiful creature: 'nothing could give an idea of the beauty of her eyes,' a contemporary observer recorded. 'Imagine something midway between the eye of the finest Arab horse and the loveliest southern girl, with long and coal-black lashes, and the most exquisite beaming expression of tenderness and softness, united to volcanic fire' (L. S. Lambourne, 'A Giraffe for George IV', *Country Life*, vol. cxxxviii, 1965). The King was devoted to the animal and one of his last acts of patronage was to commission (for 200 guineas) a portrait of her and her attendants, supervised by Edward Cross, from Jacques-Laurent Agasse (*Animal Painting*, The Queen's Gallery, Buckingham Palace 1966–67, 10, 21–2).

In the evenings Princess Victoria was invited to watch the Tyrolese dancers creating a 'gay uproar' or listen to 'Uncle King's' band playing in the conservatory at the Royal Lodge by the light of coloured lamps. He asked her what tune she would like the band to play next. With precocious tact she immediately asked – as Rossini had done – for 'God save the King!' 'Tell me,' he asked her later, 'what you enjoyed most of your visit?' 'The drive with you,' she said. He was clearly very much taken with her.[11]

As Lady Shelley said, she paid her court extremely well. When giving him a bunch of flowers, she said, 'As I shall not see my dear uncle on his birthday I wish to give him this nosegay now';[12] and when wishing him goodbye she said with appealing gravity, 'I am coming to bid you adieu, sire, but as I know you do not like fine speeches I shall certainly not trouble you by attempting one.'[13] Upon her return home she was most anxious that her mother should send 'her best love and duty to her "dear Uncle King"'.[14]

Later that year, Sir Walter Scott was a guest at Royal Lodge, and he found the King as gracious and kind as Princess Victoria had done. He had recently assumed the debts of a partner in a printing business, and was rather cast down by worry. The King did all he could to make him feel at ease. He 'made me sit beside him and talk a great deal – *too much* perhaps', Scott recorded in his diary. 'For he has the art of raising one's spirits and making you forget the *retenue* which is prudent everywhere, especially at court. But he converses himself with so much ease and elegance that you lose thought of the prince in admiring the well-bred accomplished gentleman. . . . Educated as a prince he has nevertheless as true and kind a heart as any subject in his dominions. . . . He is in many respects the model of a British monarch . . . sincerely, I believe, desires the good of his subjects – is kind towards the distressed, and moves and speaks "every inch a King". I am sure that such a man is fitter for us than one who would long to lead armies, or be perpetually intermeddling with *la grande politique*. A sort of reserve, which creeps on him daily and prevents his going to places of public resort, is a disadvantage, and prevents his being so generally popular as is earnestly to be desired.'[15]

The King's reluctance to show himself in public was, in fact, becoming almost obsessive. Rather than risk the cruel gibes that were unfailingly directed at his stout body and swollen legs, his now hobbling gait and the face whose ageing appearance grease-paint could only partially disguise, he chose to remain in secluded retirement as much as he possibly could.

He moved from London to the country and back again with a secrecy that was hardly less than furtive, and rarely now visited Brighton at all as he felt so exposed there and as Lady Conyngham knew that Brighton people disapproved of her.

As early as 1824 people attending his Drawing-Rooms were forbidden to assemble in the antechambers to watch him pass; and Captain Gronow, when on guard duty at Carlton House, heard him angrily exclaim, 'I will not allow those maid-servants to look at me when I go in and out.' The next day while riding in Hyde Park, Gronow was told by one of the Carlton House staff that the King 'constantly complained of the servants staring at him, and that strict orders had been given to discharge any one caught repeating the offence'.[16]

At Windsor when visitors were being conducted over the Castle they were forbidden 'to turn their eyes to the window, lest the King should be passing under it'; and throughout his reign it had been his practice when driving out in the Park to have a groom ride out in advance 'ordering everybody to retire'.[17] He was reluctant even to attend the Royal Academy before the opening of the exhibitions, pleading that his gout made it so difficult for him to get up all the stairs.[18] He still went to Ascot, where he was invariably greeted with applause as he bowled along the course in his carriage and four, nodding and winking and kissing his hand, just as he had done twenty years before on the Brighton racecourse; but even at Ascot when he got into his stand he was apt to sit in a darkened corner with a plain brown hat cocked over one eye.[19]

If only he would show himself more, Mrs Arbuthnot believed, he would be far more popular. As it was, on the rare occasions when he did appear in public, he seemed now to be offended rather than pleased by the welcome accorded him, however flattering. In December 1826 he was 'excessively well received' when he made one of his rare appearances at Drury Lane where 'the shouts of applause were quite deafening and "God Save the King" was sung again and again'; yet he looked 'very cross and very much bored'.[20]

When, in 1827, his knees, legs and ankles swelled 'more formidably and terribly than ever', and he had to be carried up and down stairs and 'in general to be wheeled about everywhere', he became more of a recluse than ever.[21] At the end of February 1828 the open-railed gate to the garden of St James's Palace was replaced by a close-boarded gate so that the public could not witness the King being carried to and from his carriage.[22] At Windsor, in the relative privacy of the Park or the fields at Virginia Water, servants were constantly instructed to ensure that his Majesty was neither disturbed nor seen.[23]

Prince Pückler-Muskau recorded how nervous his English host was when driving him through the Park to the royal stables. The Englishman, fearing that they might unexpectedly come upon the King, noticed with dismay that his carriages stood already harnessed in the yard. There were seven of them altogether, 'all with very low wheels, almost as light as children's carriages, and drawn by little poneys', the King's with four ponies, the others with two each. 'It is unpleasant for him to see a strange face, or indeed a human being of any kind whatsoever, within his domain,' Pückler-Muskau wrote, explaining his friend's fear of being caught at the stables when the King arrived. 'The Park is consequently (with the exception of the high road which crosses it) a perfect solitude. The King's favourite spots are, for further security, thickly surrounded by screens of wood, and plantations are daily laid out to add to the privacy and concealment. In many places, where the lay of the ground would enable you to get a glimpse of the sanctuary within, three stages of fences are planted one behind the other. . . . My venerable host climbed up on the seat of the carriage and stood there, supported by his wife and me, to look about whether the King might not be somewhere in sight; nor was he perfectly tranquil till the gate . . . closed upon us.'[24]

Living in such seclusion at Windsor, the King, like his guests, was often bored, and, in his boredom, endeavoured to dramatize his life, making up stories about himself and his entourage, affecting to believe that the most unlikely people were in love with one another. He confessed to Mme de Lieven that, bored with Lady Conyngham, he would like her as his mistress instead; he showed her a portrait of herself by Lawrence hanging over his bed, and 'with gestures and passionate looks' begged to be allowed into her room.[25] To Wellington and Knighton he confided the manifold faults of Lady Conyngham of whom he nevertheless pretended to be jealous,[26] while affecting at the same time to be jealous of Wellington's friendship with Mme de Lieven.[27]

*

'The King of England has been very ill,' Mme de Lieven told Prince Metternich in the spring of 1826. 'But bleeding does him no good; it merely gives him an excuse for staying in bed a little longer, which he likes better than anything*. . . . The public of all classes and all opinions have been greatly alarmed; they are afraid of his successor. He is pig-headed and narrow-minded.'²⁸

It was Mme de Lieven's ill-founded opinion that the King was just as much afraid of the Duke as were the public. He was also 'very jealous' of him, she thought, and the realization that he would have to appoint him Regent if he went abroad with Lady Conyngham was one of the main reasons which had persuaded him not to go. 'Their relations are strange,' she wrote. 'They have no affection for one another, no esteem; and yet they are always making up to one another. The Duke of York attaches importance to the King's favour, the King, to his brother's moral support. They make fun of one another; they confide in me on this, as on many other equally delicate subjects.'²⁹

In fact, though they had quarrelled often enough in the past, and had never been as close to each other as they had been as children at Kew, the King and the Duke of York had been on the best of terms for some time past, even if they did make fun of one another and even if the Duke was fond of telling stories against his brother to his racing friends.³⁰ The Duke was always welcome to stay at Brighton for as long as he pleased and to bring with him any society he chose;³¹ and when the Duchess died the King, in writing a letter of sympathy, assured his brother how much it meant to him that for so long there had been 'the most unvarying, the steadiest affection between them'.³² 'Believe me,' the King wrote, 'that from the very bottom of my soul, I do participate and enter into the whole extent of your distress.'³³ They were not empty phrases; he had not got on so well with the eccentric, dog-loving Duchess during the last years of her life as he had done in the early days of her marriage, but his affection for his brother was deeply felt. In December 1823 the King had helped to pay the Duke's debts, mainly incurred through his continuing extravagance on the turf, by presenting him with £50,000 which Knighton had raised through the Rothschilds on the King's income from Hanover.³⁴ And thereafter, although the King did not feel justified in trying to settle fresh debts of about £200,000 incurred by the Duke – mainly in the building of a huge new house to suit the grandiose ideas of his friend the

---

* Knighton told Canning that 'he verily believed that if it were not for the society of Lady C[onyngham] which made it necessary for HM to get up and dress himself for dinner, HM would lay the whole day in bed . . . such was his indolence' (Canning Papers, 103b, 27 April 1825).

Duchess of Rutland[35] – the two brothers had seen a good deal of each other and their past differences seemed to have been entirely forgotten. There had been a certain coolness between them in 1825 after the death of Lord Mount Charles, when Lady Conyngham had left Windsor for a time. For the Duke, who the King supposed had once been attracted to Lady Conyngham himself, had written a letter to her and she had replied to it, thus renewing the King's jealousy.[36] But the trouble had not lasted long.

When the Duke fell seriously ill with dropsy at the end of 1826, the King's concern was unfeigned. He was 'in great anxiety and uneasiness about him', Mrs Arbuthnot noted in her journal. Notwithstanding his jealousy of the Duke's popularity, he loved him 'more than any of his family'.[37] He was grieved beyond measure by his death on 5 January, so 'much depressed in health and spirits', in fact, that he was not expected to be well enough to attend the funeral.[38] No one could conceive the extent of his sorrow, he professed; he 'felt it every instant'.[39] Even Charles Greville, who rarely recorded a word in the King's favour in the malicious pages of his early diaries, agreed that he 'showed great feeling about his brother and exceeding kindness in providing for his servants. . . . He gave £6,000 to pay immediate expenses and took many of the old servants into his own service.'[40] He asked Knighton to go down into the vault beneath St George's Chapel to select a place for the coffin as close as possible to their father who had liked the Duke better than himself.[41]

On 20 January, ignoring the advice of his doctors, the King went down for the funeral to Windsor where it was reported that he was 'most grievously affected' and that 'every minute gun was like a nail driven into his heart'.[42] It was a bitterly cold day, and the congregation which included most members of the Cabinet and of the Royal Family stood shivering in the gloom. There was no matting or carpeting on the floor, and Canning presumed that whoever had filched it had had bets on the duration of their lives.[43] Lord Eldon sensibly followed Canning's advice and stood on his cocked hat and then 'in a niche of carved work where he was able to stand on wood'.[44] But the Duke of Wellington caught a severe cold; so did the Duke of Sussex; so did the Lord Chamberlain of the Household, the Duke of Montrose. Canning contracted rheumatic fever, the Bishop of Lincoln subsequently died, and it was alleged that the soldiers who had made up the guard of honour expired at the rate of half a dozen a day.[45]

Lord Liverpool, at the age of fifty-seven, was already chronically ill. Worried that the widespread distress and the industrial depression must lead to a relaxation of the Corn Laws, and that concessions would have to be made to Roman Catholics, he felt himself unable to cope with the difficulties that faced his government. On the morning of 17 February he had a stroke, and, though he did not die until the end of the following year, he was thereafter totally incapable of continuing in office.

20

The Tory Revolt
1827

*

'There never was anything like the bitterness of the ultras against Mr Canning'

Although he had never been able to like Lord Liverpool, the King was agitated beyond measure when he heard of his fatal stroke. William Denison heard from his sister, Lady Conyngham, that he would 'not permit any one whatever to speak to him upon the subject of Lord Liverpool's illness', or upon the subject of his successor as Prime Minister. For fifteen days he did not leave his dressing-room at Brighton, where he had gone for the therapy of 'warm bathing', refusing to see 'the face of a single human being – servants, tailors and doctors excepted'.[1] 'What the devil is it to come to?' Creevey wondered. 'Was there ever such a child or Bedlamite? Or were there ever such a set of lickspittles as his Ministers to endure such conduct. . . . He is a poor devil.'[2]

The government, already divided on the issues of the Corn Laws, Catholic emancipation and Canning's foreign policy, were now in total disarray. There seemed no possible candidate for the office of Prime Minister who could hold the two wings of the Tory party together as Liverpool had succeeded in doing. Of the likely contenders for the office Peel, who was only just thirty, was considered to be too inexperienced, though he had been Home Secretary for five years and was, in Canning's opinion, the best one that the country had ever had. He was also considered to be rather too advanced in his views, except on the Catholic question. Moreover, the King, whose dislike of him was fostered by Knighton, found his *gauche* mannerisms extremely irritating, particularly his awkward habit of suddenly thrusting out his hands while he talked. 'Mr Peel,' he said to him one night as he imitated the gesture, 'it is no use going on so, thrusting out your arms. The question is who is to be my Minister?'[3]

Wellington, who had succeeded the Duke of York as Commander-in-Chief while retaining, at the King's request, the Master-Generalship of the Ordnance, was not at first supposed to be in the running for such high political office from which, in any case, he was believed to have disqualified himself by accepting command of the Army.[4] Furthermore Canning could not be expected to serve under a Tory of the Duke's persuasion, particularly one who had consistently opposed his foreign policy and had endeavoured to contrive his dismissal. Yet Canning would have to be included in the government somehow, despite the opposition of many influential Tories and of the Duke of Buckingham who had been disappointed in his hopes of becoming Governor-General of India and who now recommended 'a balanced government without Mr Canning's assistance'.[5]

Creevey thought that it was Canning who '*ultimately*' would win. Certainly the King was not nearly so averse to Canning now as he had been a few years before. There had been a sharp disagreement between them in the spring of 1824 when Canning caused the gravest offence by attending a banquet at the Mansion House given by Robert Waithman, the Lord Mayor, a strong supporter of Queen Caroline.[6]* But that seemed now

* Wellington thought that the King had every reason to feel annoyed about Canning's dining 'with Lord Mayor Waithman, his speech, and his apology for the absence of his noble friend, Lord Liverpool. . . . The Corporation of the City of London, or rather a party in the Corporation at the head of which is this very Lord Mayor, have more than once in my presence and in that of Lord L[iverpool] insulted the King. HM cannot visit the Corporation on account of a gross insult wantonly persevered in: their sticking up Queen Caroline's picture in the place of honour in the Common Council Room. . . . Yet these Ministers go to these dinners and court this very Lord Mayor.' Wellington did not 'think any King was ever so ill-treated by his two principal Ministers' (*Wellington and his Friends*, 40). The King himself steadfastly refused to dine in the City, even though assured that the picture of Queen Caroline would be 'hidden from view by scarlet hangings' if the invitation were to be accepted (Parker, i, 317). Wellington also thought that Liverpool had behaved very badly over the Windsor Canons' claim to walk on the Terrace. How could the King be expected to live there with Dean and Canons, wives and children and maids staring in at the windows at all hours of the day and night? Yet instead of refusing their claim, Liverpool had left it to the King to do so, saying that 'the late King had allowed everybody to walk upon the Terrace at all hours'. 'He won't see that the present King is not the late King,' the Duke had commented. 'This is not the way a King ought to be treated by his Minister' (*Wellington and his Friends*, 43).

to have been overlooked. Canning bought a house near the Pavilion at Brighton, and he and his wife sought and obtained permission to take their morning walk under the trees in the Pavilion grounds.[7]

From the end of April 1825 onwards, so Canning's private secretary said, 'nothing could surpass the good faith and kindness which the King manifested in the whole of his conduct towards him'.[8] The gossips noted how Canning, at the King's request, had tactfully appointed Lord Francis Conyngham his Under-Secretary of State – a gesture which placated Lady Conyngham who had 'conceived a great antipathy to the Foreign Secretary'. It was an appointment, however, which Canning had not found difficult to make since the office had already been declined by four other men to whom he had previously offered it.[9]* It was also noted how skilfully Canning had dealt with the problem of the extremely handsome Lord Ponsonby, formerly one of Harriette Wilson's numerous lovers, and a man with whom Lady Conyngham had once been very much in love. Harriette Wilson had got hold of some letters written by Lady Conyngham to Ponsonby and was threatening to publish them.[10] The King had evidently bought the letters to protect Lady Conyngham's name; but no sooner had he done so than Lord Ponsonby had returned to England from Corfu where he had been living on a strictly limited income. Lady Conyngham had met him unexpectedly in Lady Jersey's drawing-room and had displayed signs of still being unduly fond of him. The King had immediately consulted Canning and asked him if he had any suitable foreign posts to offer Ponsonby who, though 'he never in his life had thought of adopting a diplomatic career', readily agreed to become

---

* Lord Francis was naturally abused for accepting the offer. Lord Alvanley now called him 'Canningham' (*Creevey Papers*, 401). And Mrs Arbuthnot referred to him as 'a regular spy' at Court. He certainly kept closely in touch with Sir William Knighton after his appointment. 'Mr C is at present confined to his bed with gout,' Conyngham reported to Knighton in a typical note on 13 December 1823; 'this has prevented him speaking much on the subject; besides, you are aware how irritable such an attack always makes such a person, more especially Mr C., who is never over cool in his mind' (RA 23084–5). 'They call F[rancis] Conyngham "Canning-game" – wit of White's, such as it is!' commented Emily Cowper. 'I don't think he much likes the appointment. Lady C[onyngham] writes to me that they are all grieved to lose him and that at first they were all against his taking it but then considering that he is a younger brother, that it was originally his profession . . . and so forth they had made up their minds to it. He is to live in the Red House next to Carlton House. I think it has a very bad effect for the C[onyngham]s with the public' (Palmerston Papers, C/IV/4/3, 7 January 1823).

Envoy Extraordinary in Buenos Aires when Canning suggested it.[11] According to Mme de Lieven – who thoroughly disliked Canning, though she later courted him 'for political objects'[12] – the King had 'nearly swooned with gratitude. And from that moment everything had been peace and love between them.'[13]

It was also noticed by the gossips how close the relationship was between Canning and Knighton; for years Knighton had been intriguing against Lord Liverpool, having never forgiven him for refusing him both the title of Private Secretary and the office of Privy Councillor.[14]

But there were other reasons for the King's more friendly attitude towards the Foreign Secretary. Much as he had disapproved of Canning's foreign policy in the early stages of its development, he had come to recognize that it had raised rather than lowered the standing of Britain in Europe, that his own reputation had been enhanced in consequence, and that the Foreign Secretary was succeeding in his professed endeavours of making him 'comfortable and happy by placing him at the head of Europe, instead of being reckoned fifth in a great confederacy'.[15] Canning had also succeeded in making him less unpopular in his own country than he had been in the past, and the King was naturally drawn to Ministers who could do that.

By the end of April 1825 the 'continental gossipings' at the Royal Lodge had come to an end and 'the effects of all that system', so Knighton assured Canning, 'were gradually passing away'.[16] In November that year the King was prepared to receive the Minister of the new South American republic of Colombia with charm and courtesy. His Majesty's behaviour on that occasion, Canning assured Granville, was all that he could have desired. Having made a short speech, 'extraordinarily well worded and pronounced', he listened politely to a long response in the most atrocious French. 'Peace, peace, by all means and above all things,' the King declared with relief and enthusiasm when the Minister had at last finished. 'We have had thirty years of convulsions – let us all now conspire to keep the peace.'

'And so the audience ended,' Canning contentedly concluded his letter to Granville. 'And so, behold! The New World established, and, if we do not throw it away, ours!'[17]

Canning owed his success with the King not only to his successful policies and his cultivation of Knighton and the Conynghams. He had gone out of his way to attract the King, who was always susceptible to the charm of Irishmen and always as ready to admire talent as to abhor mediocrity. Canning alleviated his boredom, entertained him with witty accounts of the proceedings in the Commons, artfully gave him credit for the success of policies he had formerly opposed, respectfully asked him if he had anyone to recommend when there was some such appointment as foreign messenger to fill, and never displayed those flashes of irritation to which he was always liable particularly when his gout was troubling him.[18]*

Yet for weeks the King recoiled from making any irrevocable decision regarding a new Prime Minister, hoping that the various contestants would wear themselves out in their conflicting efforts to achieve office, as they had done in 1812, and that a victor – preferably Canning whose claims were insistently pressed by Knighton – would emerge apparently *faute de mieux*. By the end of March it was obvious that the right-wing Tories were failing in their endeavours to form a government and that the path was becoming clearer for Canning. On 28 March the King invited him to come to stay at the Royal Lodge at the same time as Wellington. First he interviewed Wellington, on whose behalf Charles Arbuthnot had written an urgent letter to Sir William Knighton begging him to use his influence on the Duke's behalf. And as the morning wore on and his rival did not reappear, Canning grew more and more gloomy. At luncheon the King continued to show particular attention to Wellington; and after luncheon Canning feared that his hopes were sure to be disappointed when arrangements were made for the guests to drive out in the Park in the little two-seater pony carriages which were brought up from the stables. All the seats were allocated to the satisfaction of the King who, ignoring Canning's presence, said to Mme de Lieven, 'I am sure you and the Duke would like to go out together.' Just as everyone was ready to drive off, and the King was expected as usual to seat himself beside Lady Conyngham, he went up to Canning, took him by the arm, and said, 'I want to talk with you. I shan't go out.'[19]

The talk mainly concerned the Roman Catholic question, about which

---

* 'Mr Canning, although quite ashamed to trouble your Majesty with a third letter on the same day,' runs a characteristic communication, 'cannot forbear humbly requesting of your Majesty that you would be graciously pleased to let him know if there be any person, in whom your Majesty takes an interest, whom your Majesty would wish to be appointed to a Consulship in Spanish America' (Canning Papers, 100, 25 September 1823).

the King had been gradually changing his mind ever since the death of Fox. So long as his father was alive, he had been able to plead that he could do nothing against the well-known and constantly reiterated wishes of King George III, an attitude in which he was strongly encouraged by his friend the Duke of Northumberland, who deprecated the speeches in favour of Catholic Relief made by Lord Moira. In 1811 the King had assured Lord Wellesley that he still shared his views about the justice of Catholic Relief;[20] but by 1813 the Duke of Richmond was 'delighted to find [his Majesty] as steady a Protestant as the Attorney-General' with the 'decided opinion that the Catholics [were] further than ever from their object'.[21]

After his father's death he began to profess that he entertained precisely the same opinion as King George III had done as to the binding injunctions of the Coronation Oath. And when informed that there was no possibility of the Oath's being modified, he had said to Castlereagh, 'Remember, once I take that oath, I am for ever a Protestant King, a Protestant upholder, a Protestant adherent.'[22] 'The sentiments of the King upon Catholic Emancipation,' he had informed Peel; 'are those of his revered and excellent father.'[23]

To Knighton he had written, the 'emancipation of the Catholics [is] a measure entirely opposite to my own conscientious feelings which [have] been strengthened, if I may use the expression, by the pure and exalted spirit of my ever revered father.'[24] He had been relieved when William Plunket's Roman Catholic Disability Removal Bill had been thrown out by the Lords in April 1821 after having been read for a third time in the Commons. And he had been further comforted in May 1825 when Sir Francis Burdett's Catholic Relief Bill had met a similar fate in the Lords after a firm speech by the Duke of York who had said that he considered, and always would consider, that the King was bound by his Coronation Oath to defend the Established Church. Yet the King was well aware that further attempts to emancipate the Catholics were bound to be made, and that the rapidly deteriorating situation in Ireland was rendering emancipation an issue of the utmost importance. Even Lord Eldon, who had formerly advocated postponing the issue, was coming to the view that the time had come when 'some decisive measures ought to be adopted'.[25]*

* In a 'Private Minute respecting the Coronation Oath', Eldon reminded the King that he had sworn to the utmost of his power to 'maintain the laws of God, the true profession of the Gospel, and the Protestant Reformed religion established by law'.

Nevertheless the King was anxious that Canning, a supporter of Catholic emancipation, should be in no doubt that his own views on the matter were as firm as ever. Canning advised him to form a government of men known to share his Majesty's views; but the King replied, as Canning doubtless expected, 'I cannot part with you.' In that case, Canning countered, if an entirely 'Protestant' government were not to be formed, he himself must either be Prime Minister or be recognized as the leader of the government with a titular Prime Minister in the House of Lords.[26]

After this interview, choosing to suppose that he had induced Canning not to press the Catholic question in the event of his being asked to form a government, the King assured Peel that he need have no qualms about serving under Canning's leadership.

Peel did have qualms, however; so did Wellington; so did the Duke of Newcastle and Lords Mansfield and Falmouth; and so did the Duke of Rutland who went down to Windsor to protest in person 'on behalf of himself and brother Tories at Canning being cock of the walk'.[27] The King, who quickly turned the Duke of Rutland away from Canning and on to race-horses, was now in as agitated a state as he had been at the beginning of the crisis. 'I am jaded and quite worn out, and writing from my bed, where I have laid down for a little rest,' he told Knighton on 6 April. 'Little or no advance has as yet been made amidst perhaps almost unravelable perplexities.'[28] In an attempt to escape responsibility he suggested that the Cabinet should decide the matter for him; but the Cabinet declined to do so.[29]

Peel now suggested to Canning that the appointment of Wellington might 'solve all difficulty'.[30] But Canning felt 'obliged in frankness and honesty to say that it [did] not in *his* mind afford any such solution'.[31] The next day, 10 April, the King again talked to Peel, but no satisfactory arrangement could be made with him; and, now thoroughly annoyed with both Wellington and Peel for what he took to be their unreasonable and dictatorial manner, he at last told Canning 'to prepare with as little delay as possible a plan for the reconstruction of the Administration', a rather vague instruction which Canning supposed to mean that he was to be entrusted with its leadership.

A king could not therefore, in consistency with his Coronation Oath, sign a Bill of concession to the Roman Catholics; but, Eldon added, a question worthy of consideration was whether he could sign a Bill enabling his successor to do so (RA 23347–52, undated).

As they had already indicated, neither Peel nor Wellington would serve in a government under Canning; nor would any of the right-wing Tories join it. As Lord Howard de Walden observed, 'there never was anything like the bitterness of the ultras against Mr Canning'.[32] So Canning, unable to form an exclusively Tory government, was forced to turn to the Whigs. The King did all he could to set the Tories' minds at rest. He sent for the Archbishop of Canterbury and the Bishop of London and assured them that his views on the Catholic question remained precisely those of his father, and he authorized a public declaration to this effect. But the 'Protestants' were unconvinced. In the House of Lords, the Earl of Mansfield suggested that, had King George III still been King, he would never have consented to the formation of a government which was to contain a preponderance of 'Catholics' like Canning.[33] This so provoked the King that he wrote to the Archbishop of Canterbury to ask him to tell Mansfield that he did not choose to 'pass unnoticed' this direct calumny on his Protestant faith and honour and that he did not deserve, 'as King of this country, this wicked attempt to misrepresent and falsify them to his Protestant subjects'.[34] Before despatching the letter, the King showed it to Canning who agreed that it should go. Later, however, Canning had second thoughts, and wrote to the King warning him that it might be 'represented in Parliament as an interference with the freedom of parliamentary debate'. He ventured humbly to submit that, if the Archbishop had not already read or shown the letter to Mansfield, it might be better to convey the admonition it contained '*verbally*'.[35] He humbly trusted that his Majesty would not mistake the motives of the advice which he presumed to offer nor doubt of his readiness to '*stand*' by his Majesty, if any such attack should ever be '*made*'.[36]

Warmed by this and subsequent assurances of his Minister's 'most humble and *affectionate* duty', the King soon lost all his previous reservations about Canning. Indeed, he grew extremely fond of him, while relations between the King and Wellington grew worse and worse.[37] Canning's past offences were overlooked; and the King settled down to work contentedly with a man whose great gifts were universally acknowledged and whose respectful treatment of his Sovereign was all the more welcome because it was imbued with a genuine affection, a warmth of feeling quite outside the King's normal experience of relations with his Ministers. He said that he had never had 'any Minister he liked half so well' as he liked Canning.[38] Knighton, who shared Canning's ambition to break the hold of the aristocratic establishment on public life – and who also hoped that Canning might help him to become Chancellor of the Duchy of Lancaster – encouraged the King in his affection and did all he could to gain royal approval for Canning's policies.[39]

The King's regard for Canning made the behaviour of his Tory colleagues all the harder for the King to accept, particularly as the resignations of Wellington, Peel, Westmorland, Bathurst, Eldon and Melville were followed by those of the Duke of Montrose, the Duke of Dorset, and several other members of his Household, including the Marquess of Graham and the Marquess of Londonderry, Castlereagh's brother, a Lord of the Bedchamber.[40] When Wellington resigned as Commander-in-Chief, which was not a political appointment, the King showed his displeasure in the briefest of replies:

'The King assures the Duke of Wellington that the King receives the Duke's resignation of the offices of Commander-in-Chief and Master-General of the Ordnance with the same sentiments of deep regret with which the Duke states himself to offer it. The King abstains from any further expression of his feelings.'[41]

He privately commented that he would keep the command of the Army in his own hands until Arthur recovered his temper.[42] Intensely annoyed that the intransigent attitude of Wellington and Peel and the other 'Protestant' Tories had forced Canning to appoint a decidedly Whiggish cabinet, the King nevertheless was anxious not to remain permanently estranged from Wellington. He had always admired him if he had not always liked him and he had recently given him the first Duke of Marlborough's insignia of the Order of the Garter 'as the only person worthy to wear it'.[43] He expressed his surprise to Wellington's brother, Lord Maryborough, that the Duke had not been to see him all summer. The Duke, having got his friend, Charles Arbuthnot, to write to Knighton asking for a '*command*' to attend so that it could not be imputed against him 'that he had gone to the King without being sent for', then rode over to the Royal Lodge on the anniversary of the King's coronation.[44] He did not stay long, and the conversation was 'for the most part on general topics'; but the King could 'easily perceive, from little expressions which now and then dropped,' so he told Canning, 'that the most assiduous pains had been taken, and are still actively employed to give the strongest jaundiced complexion to the past, as well as the present state of things, and to keep up if not to widen as much as malice and wickedness can contrive it, the breach which exists between [Wellington] and my government'.[45]

Although the Duke was highly gratified by his reception at the Royal Lodge,[46] the interview did little to improve the strained relationship. A few weeks later Lady Cowper found the King 'as bitter as ever against the Tories', and in no mood yet to forgive Wellington.[47] While the Duke, for his part, was 'convinced that no man ever had such a hold upon the King' as that 'charlatan' Canning, whom he now disliked more than ever and whom he constantly denigrated.[48] He was certain that 'Canning and all the present men' had got their hold upon the King by 'indulging him in all his expenses and whims'. Consequently, for the remainder of his life, he would 'be more difficult than ever to manage'.[49]

Canning's hold, however, was soon broken. He had been ill in bed at the time of Liverpool's stroke, and during the first few months of his premiership he had never recovered his strength.[50] The tasks that confronted him were appalling: not only had half the Cabinet resigned but the majority of the Tory party were against Catholic emancipation. Yet he knew that the Catholic question would have to be faced soon, and he had been obliged to tell the King that he 'must be free as air with respect to the question'. He had undertaken to ensure that it was put to sleep for a time, and could only hope that the King might eventually be induced to change his mind.[51] In the meantime his relationship with the Whigs was a very wary one. Although a majority of them were prepared to accept a coalition against the ultra-Tories, there were many who were not, and these included the followers of Grey who viewed Canning – as the son of an actress – with supercilious disdain. It was widely supposed, in fact, that Canning's government could only be considered as a stopgap. They were known as the 'warming Pans'.[52] As Lady Cowper remarked, 'The *Morning Chronicle* says it is like people going to keep places for the first act of a play.'[53]

For the King, indeed for the monarchy, the crisis provoked by Canning's appointment proved cataclysmic. Throughout his reign the power of the crown had been declining, not so much because of the King's indolent character and aversion to uncongenial work as because of the increasing political consciousness of the people.[54] In the past the crown had been sustained by the support of the Tories; but the King's dislike of Liverpool and some of his colleagues, his indiscreet talk about their principles and measures, his brilliant and heedlessly wounding mimicry of their idiosyncrasies and mannerisms, his discussions with advisers beyond their control and influence, all served to undermine their confidence in him. By turning to Canning and the Whigs who supported him, the King lost for good the confidence of the Tories who now abused him, so Lady Cowper said, 'a thousand times worse than the Whigs ever did'.[55] Yet, by spurning the Tories in 1827 he did not regain the trust of the Whigs whom he had rejected in 1812. On both occasions the choice, hesitatingly and painfully made, was forced upon him largely by circumstances. But they were choices which left him in the end without influence in either camp.[56]

*

In July the Duke of Devonshire invited the new Prime Minister to Chiswick for a change of air. But Canning felt no better there; and on 29 July he told the King that he did not know what was the matter with him; he felt 'ill all over'. The next week he died in the room where Fox had died twenty-one years before.[57] 'This may be hard upon me,' he murmured towards the end, 'but it is harder upon the King.'[58]

21

Protestants and Catholics
1827-1829

*

'The most Protestant man in his dominions'

The King, as Canning had expected, heard the news of his death with the utmost sorrow and dismay. He felt he had lost a friend as well as an able and agreeable Prime Minister, and he immediately set about doing all he could for his family and friends. He arranged for Canning's private secretary, Augustus Granville Stapleton, an illegitimate son of their mutual friend, Lord Morley, to become a Commissioner of Customs;[1] he pressed a bishopric upon Canning's old tutor, the Rev. Phineas. Pett;[2] he proposed that his widow should be created a viscountess with remainder to his heirs male, telling her that he could only show through her what his opinion was of 'Mr Canning's splendid talents';[3] he suggested that her brother-in-law, the Duke of Portland, should succeed Lord Harrowby as Lord President of the Council;[4] he arranged for Canning's friend, the Foreign Secretary, Viscount Dudley and Ward, to be granted an earldom;[5] and he sent for two of Canning's closest colleagues, Lord Goderich, Secretary of State for War and Leader of the House of Lords, and William Sturges-Bourne, until recently Home Secretary and now First Commissioner of Woods and Forests, telling them that he wanted the present government to remain in office with a reshuffled Cabinet under Lord Goderich's leadership.[6] It was the King, however, rather than Goderich whose leadership was more evident in the selection of the Cabinet over which the Prime Minister was so ineffectively to preside.

When informing Lord Goderich of his choice, the King, so excited by the arrival at Windsor of the beautiful giraffe which had been sent to him by the Pasha of Egypt, did not trouble to talk about much else.[7] He afterwards thought it as well, however, to make the offer of the premiership conditional upon the new Cabinet agreeing to those principles of governing the country upon which he claimed to have acted from the time he had undertaken the Regency and 'from that hour to the present':

The King distinctly stated to poor Mr Canning (on his becoming Minister) that the King had no desire of forming what is termed an exclusive Tory government, as in that case it would have deprived the King of the distinguished talents of many members of the present Cabinet. Nevertheless there was a distinct understanding between the King and his late lamented Minister (Mr Canning) on many very important points.

The King will begin, for example, by mentioning the question of Parliamentary Reform. The King joined with Mr Canning in giving his decided negative to that destructive project.

The King could not of course require of Mr Canning to abjure his strong and settled opinions upon the subject of Catholic emancipation: but there was a distinct understanding that the King's conscientious feelings should not be disturbed upon that painful question, upon which the King's opinions are unalterably fixed: and moreover if at any time this question was to be forced upon Mr Canning, from that moment the Cabinet was to be considered as dissolved.[8]

To this communication Goderich replied, in the name of the Cabinet, that, as to parliamentary reform, they did not entertain the thought of bringing it forward or supporting it as a measure of government; and, as to Catholic emancipation, they felt the 'deepest anxiety to avoid disturbing' his Majesty's feelings 'upon a question of so much delicacy and importance'. But although they did not consider themselves 'called upon at any time to propound that question in the Cabinet without a conviction of the most urgent necessity', they humbly observed that they thought the matter ought still to remain, as in Mr Canning's day, 'an open question, upon which each member of the Cabinet should be at liberty to exercise his own judgment, either in supporting that question if brought forward by others, or in propounding it'.[9]

These assurances did not go nearly far enough for the King's satisfaction; but as he was 'very desirous of preserving the present government', he agreed to 'accept the note . . . without entering into further detail'.[10] In a subsequent message he suggested to Lord Goderich 'the best and safest mode of filling up the different offices'; and he made it clear that he considered it 'impossible, with any degree of security to the stability of the present government, to admit any further Whig member in the present Cabinet without its being at once designated a *Whig Administration*'.[11] He had 'quite *made up his mind not* to extend the Cabinet with any more members belonging to the Whig Party', he reiterated two days later. He had 'no personal objections to Lord Holland', for whom Lord Dudley was prepared to resign as Foreign Secretary; but he had 'the very strongest objections to run any risk that the present government should bear either the name or even the semblance of a Whig administration': he could not consent 'to reorganize the government except with persons already filling offices'.[12]

To secure a Tory preponderance in the Cabinet he pressed William Sturges-Bourne to return to the Home Office, 'an appointment peculiarly agreeable to the King's feelings';[13] and, when Sturges-Bourne declined both this office and the Chancellorship of the Exchequer, he insisted that John Charles Herries, Financial Secretary to the Treasury and a friend of Knighton, should become Chancellor.

It was a highly unfortunate choice, for although Herries had proved himself an efficient and talented Treasury official, he was also one of the Commissioners for supervising the reconstruction of Windsor Castle, and it was naturally alleged that the King had selected him in order to use him for extracting more money for building from the government. Herries himself did not want the appointment. He had already submitted his resignation as Financial Secretary to the Treasury on account of ill-health and had been persuaded by Canning to remain in that appointment only until a suitable successor could be found. He felt himself 'placed in a very embarrassing situation by this sudden call to an office which had been at no time an object of [his] thoughts or wishes, and which in the present condition of [his] health and strength [he] could not contemplate without dismay'. He entreated Goderich to appoint instead William Huskisson, Canning's President of the Board of Trade.[14]

The Whig supporters of the government were even more strongly opposed to Herries's appointment than he was himself. So firmly opposed were they, in fact, that Goderich, who had agreed with the King that Herries should be Chancellor, felt obliged to submit that his Majesty's service would be 'best promoted by placing in that situation Lord Palmerston', the Secretary at War, and that Herries should be asked to take Palmerston's place without a seat in the Cabinet.[15]

To this arrangement the King fervently objected. He did not like Palmerston; he did like Herries; and his personal feelings had a powerful influence over his actions on all such occasions. Besides, he would have those that were 'proper for their business'; aristocratic 'ornaments' might follow later, if the Cabinet wanted them. 'The office requires ability and not aristocracy,' he wrote in a letter drafted by Knighton as though the ghost of Canning were sitting by their side. 'Only yesterday Mr Huskisson [concurred] that Mr Herries was the fittest man. . . . Is the King therefore to be debarred from fulfilling a duty to the country because it does not suit the fancy or the temper of particular individuals?'[16]

The King summoned Herries to the Royal Lodge, and unsuccessfully endeavoured to force upon him the seals of office. He then sent for the leading opponents to the appointment, explained that there had been a series of blunders which were neither his fault nor theirs, and insisted that they accept Herries as Chancellor. He informed Lord Goderich that 'one of the many agreeable qualities that Mr Canning possessed as the King's First Minister was – that Mr Canning never kept any thing back from the King'. His Majesty was, therefore, well aware of the high opinion Mr Canning had entertained of Mr Herries's talents, and supposed that Lord Goderich must also be sensible of having 'reaped so largely from his services'.[17]

In face of the King's determination, and provoked by an attack on his personal integrity in the Whig newspapers, Herries reluctantly decided that he had 'no choice but to go to Windsor to accept the seals'. He made the journey on 3 September. He was not to remain Chancellor for long.

It was soon evident to everyone, including Goderich himself, that the Prime Minister was hopelessly ill-equipped for the task that faced him. He was an attractive, good-natured, businesslike man, but easygoing, hesitant and indecisive, incapable of controlling the disparate forces in the Cabinet and so little recovered from the death the year before of a beloved daughter that his problems often reduced him to tears. By the beginning of November the King had decided that the government would have to be strengthened by the admission of Lord Wellesley, who had recently been succeeded by the Marquess of Anglesey as Lord-Lieutenant of Ireland. But Lord Lansdowne, the Home Secretary, threatened to resign if Wellesley were admitted without Lord Holland. Goderich agreed that both Lord Holland and Wellesley would have to come in together, and he was persuaded by Lansdowne and by Huskisson, now at the Colonial Office, to write a letter to the King threatening to resign if his Majesty deemed this arrangement 'altogether inadmissible'.[18]

Goderich showed the draft of this letter to Huskisson and Lansdowne, but afterwards, 'quite unnerved and in a most pitiful state', added that he could not conclude his statement without venturing to add how deeply he felt his own inadequacy to discharge the great duties to which his Majesty's 'far too favourable opinion called him'. 'His own natural infirmities have been aggravated by a protracted state of anxiety during the last two years,' he pitifully went on; 'his health is enfeebled, and above all he fears that the health of one dependent upon him for support and strength, is still in a state of such feebleness and uncertainty as to keep alive that anxiety to a degree not easily compatible with the due discharge of duties which require the exertion of all the energies of the strongest mind.'[19]

The King in his reply could 'only regret that Lord Goderich's domestic calamities' unfitted him for his present situation, but over this 'he unhappily [had] no control'.[20] He suggested that the Duke of Wellington might be appointed to a seat in the Cabinet as a counterweight to Lord Holland.[21]

While Goderich was apprehensively considering the implications of this proposal, the King discussed the whole problem with Huskisson. He 'spoke very kindly' of Goderich; but he was clearly of the opinion that he would have to be replaced.[22] He considered replacing him by Lord Harrowby; but Harrowby refused the office and said that Goderich must be compelled to stay, at any rate at present.[23] On hearing a rumour that Lord Grey was endeavouring to come to terms with the extreme Tories in order to turn the government out, the King decided that he must follow Harrowby's advice and keep Goderich in office for the moment.

But eventually a more capable leader would have to be found. Lord Lowther told Knighton that the King would have to form a government 'either exclusively Tory or exclusively Whig'. Englishmen liked a 'plain downright straightforward course' and were now 'quite nauseated with the twistings and patchings of the middle party'. There was no force or energy in the government all of whose plans were 'weakened and drivelled away by the necessity of compromise and accommodation of conflicting opinions'. The King had tried a mixed government in 1812 and it had failed; Canning's character had enabled him to 'amalgamate parties into a phalanx of some strength', but now that he had gone the government would inevitably fall to pieces 'from the discordant nature of its own material'.[24] Knighton himself was already doing his best to hasten the disintegration of Goderich's government by revealing to *The Times* exactly how discordant its material was and how incompetent was its leader.[25] He did not have long to wait now before his wishes were fulfilled.

Two days after Lowther's letter was written, on 8 January 1828, Goderich went to Windsor to tell the King that his government was collapsing. Herries, deeply offended that Goderich and Huskisson had agreed to the nomination of Lord Althorp as chairman of the Finance Committee of the House of Commons without his being consulted, threatened to resign if the nomination were confirmed. Huskisson said *he* would resign if it were not. Goderich felt unable to carry on without either. He broke down and wept when explaining his dilemma to the King. The King offered him his pocket handkerchief and soon afterwards sent for the Duke of Wellington.

Wellington found him in bed wearing a dirty silk jacket and an equally grubby turban night cap. He had not been well for some time, suffering from gout and rheumatism, 'very acute pain in the back and loins and one arm'.[26] His appetite was not what it was; and he rarely managed to enjoy a good night's sleep.[27] Since Christmas he had been suffering from the after effects of 'a general cold and feverish attack, attended with great tightness and oppression upon the chest' for which Halford had bled him without producing 'such entire relief' as to allow him to leave his room.[28] In the middle of February he had still 'not regained sufficient strength' to stand on his legs, 'much less to walk'. He had been asked to give away Princess Victoria's half-sister Feodore at her marriage to Count Hohenlohe-Langenburg, but he was not even able to attend the wedding.[29] He confessed to Knighton that the anxieties that beset him on every side tore his 'poor feelings almost to shreds and drove him for a time almost distracted'. 'To you and to you alone, dear friend, it is that I can and I do look therefore for my relief,' he had written to Knighton from the Royal Lodge on 30 December in a scarcely coherent letter, '*as it is you and you alone who can and who I am sure will (from your real affection and attachment to me) entirely put an end to [my worries], and by your powerful exertions and means, crush and put the extinguisher upon that host of vipers and hornets which seems in particular at this moment to have congregated itself together and purposely to sting me personally.*'[30]

It was not only the political crisis that worried him. Harriette Wilson, now living in Belgium as Mrs Rochfort, was renewing her efforts to extort money from her former lovers. Her *Memoirs* had appeared in four small volumes in 1825 and although they created such a sensation that they had been reprinted over thirty times within the year, the King had been able to ensure that, as Prince of Wales, he appeared in them but fleetingly. She was now making further allegations; and this entirely knocked him up and 'destroyed almost all the little amount of strength' he had.[31] Knighton had already been over to the Continent in the autumn when he had decided the wisest course was to defy 'the enemy to do her worst'. He was to make another journey in March, and in the meantime the King was in perpetual anxiety that sooner or later Mme Rochfort and her 'hellish gang' would publicize some most unsavoury stories.[32]

In addition to this distress, there was the continuing worry about politics. When Wellington, who was now to become Prime Minister, went to discuss the new government with him, however, he seemed momentarily quite cheerful. 'Arthur,' he said, sitting up against the pillows, 'the Cabinet is defunct.' He then entertained the Duke with some hilarious imitations of his former Ministers not merely catching their voices exactly but even contriving to make himself look like them. The Duke had 'never seen anything like it'.[33] But the King's resurgence of spirits did not last long.

Wellington's refusal of office under Canning and his resignation from the Horse Guards still rankled; so did the behaviour at that time of Peel, for whom the King had now conceived a profound distaste and whom Wellington wished to reappoint Home Secretary. Indeed, the King viewed most of Wellington's proposed Cabinet with misgivings, though he had given him *carte blanche* to choose any Ministers he liked, with one exception – Grey.[34] Herries was to be replaced by Henry Goulburn. Lord Carlisle, whom the King considered to be a 'personal and attached' friend, declined to accept office unless Lord Lansdowne was also invited to join the government; and Lord Lansdowne refused to serve under a Prime Minister who was not in favour of Catholic emancipation. The Duke of Devonshire, another 'attached and personal friend', followed Lansdowne's lead in refusing to continue in office under men who had behaved so badly towards Canning, though the King told him that his resignation would 'break his heart and drive him out of his senses'.[35]

Moreover, the King soon realized that the freedom in the exercise of patronage which he had enjoyed in the days of Canning and Goderich was now to be severely curtailed. For the Duke of Wellington seemed even more determined to restrict the King's power than Liverpool had been. Never again was he to be allowed such enjoyable freedom to influence appointments on behalf of his friends and their relations and dependants.

While the King grew increasingly peevish and fretful, constantly disputing with the government about his rights of patronage, and threatening to dismiss them from office as though they were his footmen,[36] Wellington decided that he wished he had never agreed to form a government in the first place: he might have avoided 'loads of misery'. As it was he spent his time, so he complained, 'in assuaging what gentlemen call their feelings'.[37] At the first meeting of the Cabinet, one of his Ministers thought that they all displayed towards each other 'the courtesy of men who had just fought a duel';[38] at subsequent meetings the Cabinet met to debate, to dispute and to separate without coming to any decision.[39] The Duke was particularly saddened that his colleagues considered the office of Prime Minister to be incompatible with that of Commander-in-Chief which he was induced unwillingly to relinquish. His colleagues in turn found him domineering.[40] For his part, the King, who had once complained that Wellington was 'incapable of flexibility', that he 'set about a question like a battery of cannon', now insisted that either 'King Arthur must go to the Devil, or King George to Hanover'.[41]

So far as the King was concerned, the Duke's worst offence was what he took to be his softening attitude towards Catholic emancipation. In July Daniel O'Connell, though disqualified as a Roman Catholic, was elected Member of Parliament for Clare. Wellington, whom Creevey rightly believed to have long been aware of the need 'to do something for the Catholics of Ireland', realized that the question of emancipation could now no longer be shelved.[42] The King, on the contrary, became 'the most Protestant man in his dominions'.[43]

He had been encouraged to remain so by the Duke of Cumberland, whose prejudice against Catholics verged on fanaticism. Writing from Berlin, the Duke had urged him never to 'lose sight of that great question on which the safety and wellfare of the British Monarch and Empire must stand or fall', to show 'publicly, the purity and *staunchness* of your sentiments on the *great* question'. He had told him that their brother William – for whom the office of Lord High Admiral had lately been revived – must have 'done great good' by asserting at an anniversary dinner that he was 'unalterably attached' to the 'sound and strict principles of the Church of England'.[44] He had reminded him of the opinions of their 'late revered father'; and had emphasized the necessity of filling up any vacancies in the Cabinet with staunch Protestants.[45]

Thus encouraged by Cumberland the King's views became more and more intransigent. Wellington believed he had now convinced himself that he held these views sincerely, though he also believed that the King was influenced by his knowledge that they were popular views and that his father and the Duke of York had been widely praised in the country for holding them so staunchly. Wellington did not attempt to argue for emancipation other than as a matter of urgent expediency; but the King declined to listen to arguments of any kind. 'God bless you!' he had said to Anglesey upon his departure to Ireland as Lord-Lieutenant. 'I know you are a true protestant.'[46] And now that Anglesey was proving far from being a true protestant by favouring concessions, he would have to be withdrawn. Wellington advocated a less drastic approach, a letter of remonstrance. But the King persisted: Anglesey's reply in which he attempted to justify himself was 'a proud and pompous *farrago* of the most *outré* bombast'. So eventually the Lord-Lieutenant was brought home.[47]

The Duke, too, was persistent. If inclined to be dictatorial in the Cabinet, as though he were once again a general laying down a plan of operations for his staff, he was far too astute to adopt such tactics with the King. 'I make it a rule never to interrupt him,' he told Charles Greville, 'and when in this way he tries to get rid of a subject in the way of business which he does not like, I let him talk himself out, and then quietly put before him the matter in question so that he cannot escape from it.'[48] It was, even so, extremely difficult to get him to stick to the point for he was 'extraordinarily ingenious in turning the conversation from any subject he did not like'. Also he was becoming increasingly, exhaustingly garrulous. He would begin a conversation with 'a long history of his own life, of his political sentiments, of what his father had said of him, of his honesty, his uprightness, his good temper, his firmness, etc., etc.,' and would talk in this strain 'for an hour and a half till he was out of breath' before asking, 'Now what have you got to say to me?'[49]

Throughout the late summer and autumn of 1828 Wellington persisted in his endeavours to bring the King round to a less rigid view of the Catholic question; while the King avoided him as often as he could, pleading severe illness. Indeed, he frequently was very ill, although, as

Joseph Jekyll remarked, not so desperately so as the newspapers, which gave him 'a mortal disease once a week', liked to make out.[50] His right hand, as Knighton said, was 'full of gouty inflammation and as large as two hands'; his arm, too, was so swollen that his valet could not get it into the sleeve of his coat; he was also suffering from 'attacks of spasms' – which the Duke of Cumberland warned him were caused by *'worry of mind'* – from piles, from inflammation of the bladder, from symptoms of dropsy and from various other ailments for which he took such huge doses of laudanum that Cumberland – who seems to have considered himself something of a medical authority – warned Knighton that he would 'kill himself but, previous to that, palsy himself'.[51]

All the same he was well enough to attend the Jockey Club dinner at St James's towards the end of June. Charles Greville – to whom the King always found time to whisper a few remarks about racing at Privy Council meetings – was there and reported the King as being in very good form. He 'made one or two little speeches' and 'nothing could [have gone] off better'.[52] He was also able to attend Egham Races at the end of August, and, a month later, to welcome to England Donna Maria de Gloria, the nine-year-old *de jure* Queen of Portugal. He greeted her with what Wellington considered to be far too much warmth and affection, for it was the government's view that she had been brought over to England in order to commit public opinion to support her against those who wished to deprive her of her inheritance.[53] The King, to whom personalities were always more important than politics, to whom little girls were always attractive, and to whom Donna Maria particularly appealed as a fellow-royal in distress, took her to his heart. In December, attended by a sovereign's escort of Life Guards, he made his formal entry into Windsor Castle, accepted the keys in a crimson bag from Wyatville, and later conducted the Queen of Portugal round the apartments as though she were a beloved niece as well as an honoured guest.[54] He assured her as he said goodbye that he would 'do all in his power to re-instate her in her rights. The child burst out into a fit of crying, and threw her little arms round his neck.'[55]

As 1828 drew to a close, Wellington gradually began to make ground with the King on the Catholic question. His Majesty still insisted that he had the right to refuse his consent to any Bill which might be passed through Parliament, but by January 1829 he had at least been persuaded to agree that the Cabinet should consider and discuss the problem.[56]

Having got so far, Wellington was dismayed to learn that the Duke of Cumberland, the 'most mischievous fellow' he knew,[57] intended to come home from Berlin. He urged him not to come; he persuaded the King to allow Knighton to go over to Germany to stop him; and the King himself, while assuring Cumberland that he loved and valued him above all his other brothers,[58] begged him to stay in Germany. 'The Duke of Wellington has given me some sensible reasons. . . . I must say that it is a great disappointment to me. But I look forward to the happiness of seeing you, the dearest Duchess and my beloved George [their son, aged nine] in the spring. In the Duke of Wellington's ability to administer the affairs of this country I have every reason to place the greatest reliance.'[59]

The next day the Duke of Wellington wrote to Cumberland to tell him that a Catholic Relief Bill was to be introduced, that there was no doubt that the Duke would be put forward as a leader in the cause against it, and that he would be held responsible for 'all the consequences of the violence of others'.[60]

But Cumberland was not to be dissuaded. Before he received Wellington's letter he told Knighton that he proposed to sacrifice his comfort by coming over on 14 or 15 January and that there was no need to do anything other than order '*good fires*' in his rooms; he would drive down to Windsor as soon as he arrived. Supporters of the Bill dreaded his coming for he was, so Brougham told Grey, 'fuller of spirits and all mischief than ever'.[61] Lord Ellenborough, who thought him a 'Mephistopheles' sure to do all the harm he could, was appalled by the news of his imminent arrival. 'The King is afraid of him,' he wrote in his diary. 'God knows what mischief he may do.'[62]

Ignoring Wellington's advice, Cumberland arrived in England on 14 January welcomed by crowds of cheering Protestants. He drove down as planned to Windsor and was soon as inseparable a companion of the King as he had been in 1811.

His influence over his brother was immediately apparent. All the work that Wellington had done over a period of months was undone in a few days. Cumberland knew just how to work on the King's emotional feelings and how to provoke him to make stands against his better judgement. Wellington explained this by saying that, although the King was afraid of nothing which was 'hazardous, perilous or uncertain', he dreaded ridicule; and the Duke's powers of ridicule were unsurpassed.[63]

'John Bull & the Arch-itect wot builds the arches—&c &c &c': caricature by William Heath, 5 June 1829. John Nash, the architect of the reconstructed Buckingham Palace represented as an illiterate workman, is questioned by a disgruntled John Bull as to the excessive cost of the building and of pulling down unsatisfactory wings. The Marble Arch was removed to its present position at the top of Park Lane to make way for the construction of the East Wing.

'The New Palace, St James's Park': engraving after Pugin of 1827.

29 (*above left*) Lady Conyngham by Sir Thon
Lawrence.

30 (*above right*) Princess Lieven by Sir Thon
Lawrence.

31 (*below left*) Sir William Knighton: mezzotint
S. Cousins after a painting by Sir Thon
Lawrence.

As well as being cruelly sarcastic, Cumberland was clever, insinuating and plausible. He succeeded in deepening all the King's prejudices about the Catholic Relief Bill, in persuading him that his Coronation Oath made it impossible for him to countenance it, that emancipation was not a policy that evoked any enthusiasm amongst the great majority of people in the country, and that feeling against it in some quarters was very strong. Dr Sumner, now Bishop of Winchester, wrote to the King putting forward a well-reasoned case for Catholic relief; but his brother's arguments carried far more weight.[64]

Before the end of the month the King seemed on the verge of becoming as fanatical an anti-Catholic as Cumberland himself. He talked for hours on end on the subject and once he had got on to it there was 'no stopping him'. Lady Holland heard that he 'worked himself up into a fury whenever the subject was mentioned';[65] and Lord Francis Conyngham, who had now succeeded his brother as Lord Mount Charles, 'verily believed he would go mad'.[66]* The King told Lord Eldon that if he were ever made to give way he 'would go to the Baths abroad, and from there to Hanover', would never return to England, and that his subjects might then get a 'Catholic' King in the shape of the Duke of Clarence who had come round to declaring himself in sympathy with the Bill.[67] The King's agitation became even more extreme when it became clear that the Conynghams and his Household generally did not support him in the stand he was taking.

Wellington, knowing that Cumberland was intriguing to bring down the government, went down to Windsor on 26 February to give Knighton a letter to hand to the King as soon as he was awake. If the Duke of Cumberland were to stay in the country, Wellington wrote, the King would do well to recommend an immediate change of government, for if matters were delayed and allowed to remain in their present state the prospect was nothing 'but chaos'.[68] The Duke had heard a rumour that Cumberland was planning to get together a mob of 20,000 Protestants to march on Windsor to petition the King and to frighten him into refusing any concessions. Wellington rather hoped that the rumours were true, for if they were he would have sent Cumberland 'to the Tower as soon as look at him'.[69] It was suggested that a more reliable method of

---

* Some years before Sir William Knighton had told Canning that he had known the King talk himself into such a state when sober as to appear utterly drunk ('Most Secret Memorandum', 27 April 1825, quoted in Stapleton, 440).

getting rid of Cumberland would have been to appoint him Governor of Hanover and bring home the Duke of Cambridge as Commander-in-Chief. But Wellington could not approve of this idea, as Cambridge was 'as mad as Bedlam'.[70]

On 27 February Wellington again went down to Windsor where he found the King 'in a very agitated state'. The audience lasted for over five hours, during which tears were shed and there were renewed threats of abdication. Wellington, firm and unyielding, made a little headway against the King's intransigence and received a kiss upon leaving.[71]

The battle, though, was not yet won. Cumberland was still at Windsor; and Peel, having changed his views about emancipation, honourably offered himself for re-election as Member for Oxford University and was defeated by a concourse of rampantly Protestant Masters of Arts. The King was encouraged by this not to give way, though he would have dearly liked to escape from the problem altogether by going abroad to take the baths at Wiesbaden, a suggestion that alarmed Wellington who knew that he would spend 'such sums of money'.[72] Wearily the Duke went down to Windsor yet again on 2 March.

By then the King was worried to distraction not only by the crisis over the Relief Bill but also by Harriette Wilson's furtive activities and, so Lord Kensington told Creevey, by the fear that Captain Thomas Garth, who was rumoured to be Princess Sophia's son either by old General Garth or even by the Duke of Cumberland, was intent on making further trouble now that Cumberland was in England again.[73] The King became so ill with worry that Ellenborough was told he was in danger of going mad; 'nothing but the removal of the Duke of Cumberland from his presence' would restore him to peace.[74]

Wellington, who was really upset to see 'the poor old man's distress and agitation',[75] also sometimes thought that the King would go mad, if indeed he was not mad already. Several years before, he had baldly stated in a letter to Mme de Lieven that he considered the King to be insane.[76] Since then the Duke and others had been astonished by a habit that his Majesty had developed of pretending that he had taken part in events or experienced emotions that were quite outside his experience. He once said, for example, that when he was a young man Lord Chesterfield had told him, 'Sir, you are the fourth Prince of Wales I have known, and I must give your Royal Highness a piece of advice: stick to your father; as long as you adhere to your father you will be a great and a happy man, but if you separate yourself from him, you will be nothing and an un-happy one.' 'And by God,' the King commented with what appeared to be quite passionate sincerity, 'I never forgot that advice and acted upon it all my life.'[77]

He even, so it was said, took a perverse pleasure in astounding his Minis-ters by pretending that he had fought at Waterloo and had helped to win the Battle of Salamanca, 'when things were looking very black indeed', by leading a magnificent charge of dragoons disguised as General Bock. He had also, so he claimed, ridden 'Fleur-de-Lis' for the Goodwood Cup.[78] When recalling these stirring events the tears would often start to his eyes, and no one was quite sure whether or not he was making some elaborate joke. Sometimes it seemed that he had succeeded in persuading himself that he had actually participated in the sagas he so vividly described. When Wellington called on him on 2 March he found him in one of these strange moods and was much exhausted by an inconclusive interview which lasted for three hours.

The next audience which Wellington, Peel and Lyndhurst all attended on 4 March was even more exhausting, and after it the Duke was more than ever convinced that the King was mad. He had talked almost con-tinuously for five and three quarter hours, constantly sipping brandy and water, threatening to retire to Hanover, explaining that he must consult the Archbishop of Canterbury and the Bishop of London, breaking down and weeping, rambling on about the Coronation Oath which he now appeared 'to confuse with the oath of Supremacy'.[79] Ultimately, in face of his Ministers' unyielding attitude, he asked for their resignation. They gave it and left the room, where Knighton and Lady Conyngham later found him, in a 'deplorable state', lying on a sofa, utterly worn out.[80] Before he went to bed, however, having discussed the matter at length with Knighton and the Conynghams, and having eaten a good dinner, he had accepted the fact that he could not do without Wellington and must accept Catholic emancipation. The ultra-Tory opponents of the Bill were not strong enough to form an alternative government. He would have to recall him. 'My dear Friend,' he wrote wearily. 'As I find the country would be left without an administration, I have decided to yield my opinion to *that* which is considered by the cabinet to be for the immediate interests of the country. Under these circumstances you have my consent to proceed as you propose with the measure. God knows what pain it causes me to write these words. G.R.'[81]

Arthur had won. He really was 'King Arthur' now, the King commented bitterly; O'Connell was 'King of Ireland'; as for himself, he was merely 'Canon of Windsor'.[82] But even so, Wellington's troubles were not over, for he feared that the King would change the government as soon as the Bill was passed or even before it was passed, and he was tempted to resign immediately. He was 'so overworked and so indignant' that he 'abused the King most furiously', saying that he was 'the worst man he ever fell in with in his whole life, the most selfish, the most false, the most ill-natured, the most entirely without one redeeming quality'. Mrs Arbuthnot tried to calm him down, to persuade him not to do anything from temper, that he owed a public duty to the country to remain at his post. But he was 'so angry he did not say much except that he would *be damned* if he would stay'.[83]

Grenville, however, considered the Duke's fears were groundless. The King 'is fonder of abusing his Ministers than of changing them', he told the Duke of Buckingham. 'For a few hard words cost him nothing; but a great political change could not be made, if at all, without much more trouble, fatigue, and worry to the King than he will like to expose himself to.'[84]

Grenville was right. Wellington remained in office; and on 10 April, after much grumbling and muttering, the King gave his consent to the Roman Catholic Relief Act.[85] A week later he received Wellington at Windsor where he was 'sitting for his picture *in a Highland dress*'. The Duke was kept waiting for twenty minutes before the King appeared, still wearing plaid stockings.[86] He 'was not in bad humour but cold', and the Duke remained with him for less than half an hour.

After he had returned to London, Wellington reported: 'I saw Lady Conyngham who was very much alarmed at the prospect of having the Duke of Cumberland there so long. But she told me nothing excepting that the King was more easy since he had given the royal consent to the Bill. I have seen different persons since who have been there.' One of these persons was Sir Henry Halford who told him on 23 April that his Majesty was 'more composed and in pretty good spirits'. Unfortunately, however, the atmosphere in the Castle was bound to be rather unpleasant so long as the Duke of Cumberland remained. Lady Conyngham was 'dreadfully afraid of him and perhaps not without reason'.[87]

'The Duke of Cumberland keeps the whole house in awe, particularly the Lady,' Wellington confirmed. 'She appears to be in perpetual alarm lest he should say something to alarm her; and the King sees the whole. Under these circumstances they say that the residence at the Castle is not the pleasantest that could be found.'[88] Certainly Maria Conyngham found it tiresome enough; and though the King disliked emerging from the seclusion which the Castle afforded him, rather than disappoint her, he went to London in April for the parties which she wanted to attend.[89]

22

The Final Years
1829-1830
*

'A bold man, afraid of nothing if his Ministers would stand by him, and certainly neither afraid of pain or death'

Catholic emancipation was not the only issue which divided the King and the Cabinet. There were also differences over the royal prerogative of mercy, differences which showed the King's character in a more attractive and liberal light. He had always taken particular pleasure in using this prerogative, in doing what lay in his power to ameliorate the harshness of the criminal code, as Lord Sidmouth, Home Secretary between 1812 and 1821, had known well enough. One of the first acts of his reign had been to abolish the legal use of torture in Hanover; and on arriving there in October 1821 he had immediately pardoned a man serving a prison sentence whose destitute wife, the mother of his 'eight little children', had appealed to him for mercy.[1]

He had afterwards been frequently in touch with Peel, Sidmouth's successor, on behalf of some unfortunate felon whose history had excited his compassion or that of Lady Conyngham. It was her influence over the King, so it is traditionally supposed by her descendants, which led to the abolition of the flogging of female prisoners;[2] and it is certain that he himself warmly encouraged other measures taken in his reign to lessen the severity of legal punishment. He was also interested in the protection of animals from cruelty and was a personal friend of Richard Martin – whom he nicknamed 'Humanity Dick' – the Irish Member of Parliament responsible for the first legislation anywhere in the world for the prevention of cruelty to animals and one of the founders of the Royal Society for the Prevention of Cruelty to Animals which was established in 1824.[3]

The King's correspondence with Peel is replete with such requests as these: 'to make every possible enquiry into the case of the boy Henry Newbury, aged thirteen, and to commute his sentence from transportation, in consideration of his youth, to confinement in the House of Correction. . . . The King quite approves of Mr Peel's humane recommendations respecting Davis; but what is to be done concerning Desmond, who is of the same age? Is there any opening for the other poor young man Ward? The King would be truly glad if such could be found. . . . The King has received Mr Peel's note, and he must say, after the deepest reflection, that the executions of to-morrow, from their unusual numbers, weigh most heavily and painfully on his mind. . . . The King therefore desires that . . . four may only suffer . . . for the same crime . . . in the place of eight.'[4]

Peel did not always feel able to accede to the King's requests;[5] and on one occasion, believing that the plea for mercy originated with Lady Conyngham, resolved to resign if the King persisted in it.[6] Nor could Peel agree to a reprieve in the case of Joseph Hunton, a Quaker with ten children who was sentenced to hanging for forgery. The King strongly pressed for a mitigation of the capital sentence and urged Peel to confer with the Lord Chancellor and the Lord Chief Justice whose joint opinion was that 'it would be very difficult hereafter to enforce the capital sentence of the law in any case of forgery if mercy [were to be] extended in this case'.[7]

When he did persuade Peel to pardon a man his delight was endearing. Once when Peel was staying at the Pavilion he received a sudden summons in the middle of the night to go to the King's room. Having induced Peel to believe that mercy was justified in the case that was troubling him, the King kissed him, and then, noticing what a poor dressing-gown he was wearing, he said to him, 'Peel, where did you get your dressing-gown? I'll show you what a dressing-gown ought to be.' And he handed him one of his own.[8]

No one who knew the King well could doubt that his concern for condemned criminals was prompted by a genuine humanity. His servants acknowledged him to be a most considerate master. One of them, a valet on his deathbed, told Count Boruwlaski 'that his Majesty during the course of his . . . illness had never omitted to visit his bedside *twice every day*, not for a moment merely, but long enough to soothe and comfort him, and to see that he had everything necessary and desirable, telling him all particulars of himself that were interesting to an old and attached servant and humble friend'.[9]

Sir Andrew Barnard, who served the King as equerry, was equally attached to him. 'I feel proud and gratified at being one of his servants,' Sir Andrew once declared. 'I trust . . . that the whole people of England will appreciate his great and good qualities in the same manner that those do who have had the happiness of seeing them more closely.'[10] Lady Anne Lindsay, who had married Barnard in 1793, and who had so deeply sympathized with the King in his relationship with the difficult and short-tempered Mrs Fitzherbert, was quite as devoted to him as her husband. She loved him, she confessed, 'very much . . . God bless him!'[11] Although now estranged from him, Lady Holland, too, thought of him with affection: there was 'more good in him than [fell] to the lot of most princes; and had he not been a prince, he would', she was sure, 'have been a most amiable man'.[12]

A characteristic story of the lengths to which he would go to serve his friends was related by Lord Eldon who was constantly badgered by the King, when Regent, to make Joseph Jekyll a Master in Chancery. Eldon admired Jekyll more as a wit than as a lawyer and was reluctant to make the appointment, though the King assured him that Jekyll would make a first-class Master if given the chance. For months Eldon resisted the King's importunities until one day he received a call from him at his house in Bedford Square. The servants informed the King that Eldon was ill with gout and could see no one; but the King stepped inside, walked up the staircase, and knocked at all the bedroom doors until he found the one where Eldon was hiding from him. The King sat down by the bed and embarked upon a long eulogy of his friend Jekyll, his talents and integrity. Eldon remained obdurate.

At last the King threw himself back in his chair exclaiming, 'How I do pity Lady Eldon!'

'Good God!' said the Chancellor. 'What is the matter?'

'Oh, nothing, except that she will never see you again. For here I remain until you promise to make Jekyll a Master in Chancery.'

'Well I was obliged at last to give in,' Eldon recorded. 'I could not help it.' And in the end Jekyll 'got on capitally'.[13]

Artists and writers had particular reason to be grateful for the interest which the King continued to take in them. At a time when he was poor and unhappy and his reputation was overcast, Benjamin Robert Haydon submitted for the King's inspection his canvas *The Mock Election* based on a scene he had witnessed in a debtor's prison. The King bought it for five hundred guineas, a much higher price than most of Haydon's pictures were then commanding. 'We drank the King's health in the large goblet I had painted in his picture,' Haydon told his friend Mary Russell Mitford in high excitement. 'God save the King!'

'A thousand and a thousand congratulations to you and your loveliest and sweetest wife,' Miss Mitford replied no less happily. 'I have always liked the King, God bless him. He is a gentleman – and now my loyalty will be warmer than ever.'[14]

David Wilkie was similarly indebted to the King for his generous support and affectionate concern at a time of adversity. 'Go to Wilkie,' the King instructed Knighton on hearing that Wilkie was ill and worried about some pictures that he was unable to finish. 'He is proud and shy – he may not want money at all, and it would not do to offer him that. Say to him, however, that . . . I entertain [so] confident [an] expectation of his recovery . . . that he has my permission to consider me as his banker. . . . He may draw for what he wants, and repay me . . . at his leisure, in the shape of pictures. I can never have too many Wilkies in my collection.'[15]*

Wilkie did not accept the money, but when he was better and had returned from the Continent, the King, who, as an admirer of Teniers and Ostade was naturally attracted to Wilkie's work, asked him to come and see him. He afterwards bought several of his pictures, including *The Spanish Posada* and *The Defence of Saragossa*.[16] The King's kindness to Wilkie, so the sculptor, Francis Legatt Chantrey said, was 'beautiful'.[17]

Chantrey, who sculpted numerous statues of the King, was himself full of gratitude and affection. He recalled how pleasantly the King had put him at his ease when he sat for him for the first time. 'Now, Mr Chantrey,' he had said with the utmost friendliness, 'I insist on your laying aside

---

* In 1811 the King had asked Benjamin West to commission on his behalf a picture from Wilkie as a companion piece to Edward Bird's *The Country Choristers* which he had bought the year before for 250 guineas. 'Let Wilkie make choice of the subject,' he had said to West, 'take his time in painting it and fix his own price' (RA 20499: Asp/K, i, 235). This commission resulted in *Blind Man's Buff* with which the King was so pleased that he asked Wilkie for 'a companion picture of the same size'. So Wilkie painted *The Penny Wedding* for which the King paid £545 in 1820 (RA 27039 10 February 1820; Millar [*Later Georgian Pictures*], 12, 138).

everything like restraint, both for your own sake and for mine; do here, if you please, just as you would if you were at home. . . . Now Mr Chantrey,' he had added, holding out his wig as the sculptor prepared the clay. 'Which way shall it be? With the wig or without it?'[18]

He had behaved in the same easy, friendly way when he had first met Scott whose work he so much admired and whose presence was always welcome in his library. 'Let us have just a few friends of his own, and the more Scotch the better,' he had suggested to their mutual friend, William Adam, when arranging to have Scott invited to a small dinner party. It was a highly successful party, Adam remembered. The King, then Regent, had been 'particularly delighted with the poet's anecdotes of the old Scotch judges and lawyers, which his Royal Highness sometimes *capped*'.[19] Croker, who was also of the party, said afterwards that the King had been enchanted with Scott, 'as Scott with him; and on all his subsequent visits to London, he was a frequent guest at the royal table'.[20] The King was 'the first gentleman he had seen – certainly the first *English* gentleman of the day,' Scott decided. 'There was something about him which, independently of the *prestige*, the "divinity", which hedges a King, marked him as standing by himself.'[21]

On later occasions when they met, Scott was always deeply gratified to note with what cordiality, with what 'great distinction', the King treated him, how he shook hands with him 'before the whole company'.[22] 'No subject was ever more graciously received by a Sovereign,' Scott proudly recalled, remembering the day he had been created a baronet, 'for he scarce would permit me to kneel, shook hands with me repeatedly, and said more civil and kind things than I care to repeat.'[23]

From that day onward it was 'impossible to conceive a more friendly manner' than the King always used towards Scott, a frequent and honoured guest at his Majesty's table.[24]

As flattered as Scott by the place of honour accorded to him at the King's table was Thomas Lawrence,[25] who, up till the time of his death in 1830, continued to paint for the King as vigorously as ever at a total cost to the Privy Purse of well over £25,000.[26]

Exceptionally generous towards artists, the King, indeed, gave liberally to countless other people who succeeded in arousing his admiration or pity. His 'private benevolence', as Knighton wrote in a 'secret and confidential' letter to the Duke of Wellington, stood unrivalled.[27] His family were particularly fortunate. In addition to the £50,000 he provided for the Duke of York, he found £10,000 in 1826 for the Duke of Clarence, and several lesser sums for Princess Elizabeth.[28] Upon hearing that the affairs of Charles Arbuthnot, who had had to resign the Secretaryship of the Treasury on account of ill-health, were in a 'most desperate and wretched state', he borrowed £15,000 on his behalf and gave it to him with the words, 'Take this and never let the subject be mentioned again and, above all, do not let it cause any shyness or embarrassment between us.' As Mrs Arbuthnot said it showed 'how really kind and good-natured' the King was when he acted 'upon the first impulse' and when he had 'no ill-natured person to check him'.[29]

In the theatre, Michael Kelly, John O'Keefe and Charles Mathews were three of many performers who had occasion to be grateful to him when they were in straitened circumstances.[30] He had only to hear of an actor or indeed of anyone in distress, so Knighton said, and he wished to help them; he had but to hear of a worthy cause, and he was anxious to support it. As well as such outright gifts as £1,000 towards the building of St David's College, Lampeter, a theological college for poor Welshmen, 'a most laudable effort' which he could not praise in 'terms of sufficient commendation',[31] and larger sums to the distressed weavers of Spitalfields, he regularly supported year by year numerous charities from foundling hospitals to orphanages, old people's homes to lunatic asylums, from the British and Foreign School Society to the Royal Infirmary for Diseases of the Eye.[32] Even his adversary, Henry Brougham, praised him for his staunch and generous support of popular education.[33]

*

Once he had given his reluctant consent to the Catholic Relief Bill, the King's relations with his Ministers began to grow less antipathetic, though the improvement was certainly slow. At a ball on 11 June he ignored several members of the Cabinet; and at Ascot he had a 'whole party of Canningites in his house and not one Minister'. He 'gave a bad reception to all the friends of government who went into his stand, and said to Mr Peel that he should have as soon expected to see *a pig in a church* as him at a race! Mr Peel was invited to dine at the Lodge, but he pretended he had no clothes and refused to go.'[34]

As the year progressed, however, relations became almost cordial. The King could not forgive Lord Ellenborough, the Lord Privy Seal, for having opposed the third reading of the King's Property Bill in a speech which caused great offence to Lady Conyngham by questioning the Sovereign's rights to leave property to others apart from his successor. And when he invited the Ministers to dinner, Ellenborough was pointedly omitted from the list of guests.[35] But with the other Ministers, even with Peel, he was now on quite friendly terms. With Wellington, indeed, he was once more on the same footing as he had been in 1823 when he had expressed the opinion that 'it would be difficult to find a man of such consummate integrity, possessing such straightforward, *true* political wisdom, or such unsullied principles that comprehend everything that is noble, everything that is great'.[36] The King still lamented Canning's death, of course, and regretted the passing of those days when he had enjoyed more sense of power than the stern Wellington allowed him; but Arthur was a friend once more, and a great man after all.

Wellington was conscious of the King's attachment to him, and regarded him in turn now with a kind of affection.[37] He told Ellenborough that he would be 'very sorry to hurt him'; he could not 'bear to see the King in distress'.[38] Also he had a genuine respect for his undoubted gifts. He had a 'wonderful knowledge of character',[39] and was 'a bold man, afraid of nothing if his Ministers would stand by him, and certainly neither afraid of pain or death'.[40] To be sure he could on occasions still be so utterly exasperating that the Duke felt like giving him up 'as a bad job'.[41] He was the 'greatest *vagabond* that ever existed', he was once driven to conclude, 'he was always acting a part to himself'.[42]

'He is not happy unless he is ill,' Mme de Lieven commented sardonically;[43] and it was only too true that he was thankful to have an excuse to retreat to his bedroom when some unpalatable duty faced him or some unpleasant decision had to be made. Even when he was well he allowed documents to remain unsigned until there was serious talk of the 'necessity of appointing an officer to affix some kind of signet which should be equivalent to, and supersede, the royal signature'.[44] Peel mentioned at a Cabinet dinner 'the circumstance of the King having signed no commissions for more than two years'. 'He will not sign parchment,' Lord Ellenborough noted. 'There can be no reason why the commissions should not be on thick paper; but they say the King would sign them for the first few days, and then give it up.'[45]

The time that Ministers wasted at Windsor was incalculable. As Wellington reproachfully put it in a letter to Knighton, 'When one goes to Windsor no person can answer for the hour of return.'[46] The accomplished and fastidious Charles Greville was far more explicit in his condemnation. 'His greatest delight,' Greville complained, 'is to make those who have business to transact with him, or to lay papers before him, wait for hours in the ante-room while he is lounging with Mount Charles or anybody, talking of horses or any trivial matter; and when Mount Charles has said, "Sir, there is Watson [Sir Frederick Beilby Watson, Master of the Household] waiting etc.," he replied, "Damn Watson, let him wait." He does it on purpose and likes it. . . . A more contemptible, cowardly, selfish, unfeeling dog does not exist than the King, on whom much flattery is constantly lavished. He has a sort of capricious good nature, arising, however, out of no good principle or good feeling, but which is of use to him, as it cancels often in a moment and at small cost a long score of misconduct. . . . There never was such a man or behaviour so atrocious.'[47]

Although most Ministers did not share this harsh and aggravated judgement, few of them were not on occasion infuriated by the King's conduct, incensed to discover, when they called at the Castle to discuss business with him, that he was incapacitated from doing so by laudanum or cherry brandy. When he emerged from the effects of these overdoses he was in such 'a state of excessive irritation' that it was considered advisable not to see him.[48] Lord Aberdeen, the Foreign Secretary, had experience of this when he went to Windsor to discuss the offer of the throne of Greece which had been made to Prince Leopold.

Prince Leopold had continued to live at Claremont Park after Princess Charlotte's death on the splendid annuity of £50,000 which the government continued to provide for him. He had been a constant source of irritation to the King who had been deeply offended by his having called on the Queen after her 'trial' and having allowed his house in London, Marlborough House, to be illuminated in celebration of her 'acquittal'.[49] The Hon. George Agar-Ellis, Member of Parliament for Seaford, had noticed how cross the King had looked at a party at the Duke of Wellington's when, sitting 'in full blown dignity on a sopha between Lady Conyngham and Madam Lieven', his eye had alighted upon the young and handsome features of his son-in-law.[50]

The King was appalled by the offer of the Greek throne to the suave, calculating 'Marquis Peu-à-Peu', and his dislike of him grew more intense than ever. How could the government be 'such fools as to think he could be of any use'?[51] His Majesty could not 'but *deeply regret* the selection made by France and Russia of Prince Leopold as the Prince to be placed at the head of the Greek Kingdom', he wrote to the Duke of Wellington. 'Without entering into a detail of reasoning, the King considers Prince Leopold *not qualified* for this peculiar station.'[52]

He prepared himself for the interview with Lord Aberdeen by taking a hundred drops of laudanum, and was afterwards so much agitated that his barber 'thought he should have cut him twenty times'.[53] Once more there were rumours that the government were to be dismissed;[54] but when the King saw that further resistance was useless he gave way to Prince Leopold's nomination 'in deference to the desire of the two great Powers',[55] though he did so very 'grumpily'.[56]

He was all the more grumpy and agitated because he had been constantly badgered not to agree to the appointment by the Duke of Cumberland who urged him in the strongest terms not to give way 'to the over-bearing and dictatorial spirit of the Duke of Wellington'.

Three days after he had given way – evidently without daring to tell his brother that he had done so – he received a characteristic letter from him, a letter that shows how fully justified were the government's suspicions of Cumberland:

You must remember that . . . yesterday sennight . . . you stated to me in the clearest and most positive manner that in an audience which you had given to Lord Aberdeen . . . you had gone through the whole matter of the Grecian case, that you had expressed your *astonishment* and at the same time your *displeasure* that negotiations should have gone on for upwards of four months without either the Duke of Wellington or Lord Aberdeen having ever mentioned one word to you on the subject. Lord Aberdeen replied that Prince Leopold was not the nomination of England but of France; this naturally made you feel outrageous, and your reply to Lord Aberdeen was, 'Whether the King of France would not be amazingly astonished if Prince Polingnac [now Charles X's foreign minister] had without the King of France's knowledge, intrigued through the Duke of Wellington to have a son of the Duke of Orleans named as a candidate by the King of England.' Lord Aberdeen admitted the truth of this, and, on talking over the personal merits of Prince Leopold, Lord Aberdeen took pretty good care to say that it was not his choice but the Duke of Wellington's. I do not think it is worth while to call your attention upon the *contradiction*, *falsehood*, and *absurdity* of this excuse; but I have seen enough of Lord Aberdeen in this whole transaction and know enough of his conduct herein to be fully convinced that he is become a most apt scholar of the Duke of Wellington, who, you as well as myself know, will stick at nothing to make good his point. . . .

Now the question stands thus, whether in the eyes of all Europe, and in great parts of this country, George the IVth is to be considered as King and *Master*, having a right to be *consulted* and *informed* upon all great matters of importance, of which there is no doubt the formation of Greece and her sovereign must be a most weighty question, or whether the Duke of Wellington is to proclaim to all Europe that *he* is the *master* and that you must give way to his arrogance whenever he thinks it proper; and I am perfectly convinced that the Duke of Wellington has contributed through his friends to have this whole thing made as public as possible to show *his power* to the world which he makes no disguise in proclaiming.

Cumberland went on to assure the King that Wellington was 'fully determined to show the world' that he did 'not care a farthing' about him or any of his commands. 'If you give way on this point,' Cumberland warned him, 'you are completely ruined for not only it must shake you in the opinion of all Europe, but your giving way on this occasion is neither more nor less than signing and sealing the Duke of Wellington not only as your Minister for the rest of your reign, but as Dictator in the country.' The King had missed his opportunity to get rid of the Duke over the Catholic question; now Providence had furnished him 'with another opportunity' which it was his duty to take.[57]*

Although the King never went nearly so far in his opposition to the Duke of Wellington as Cumberland urged him to do, there were scenes similar to those provoked by Prince Leopold and the Greek question when Wellington refused to allow the King to create Nash a baronet, on the grounds that it was a step which would 'be attended with the greatest inconvenience' in view of the other numerous 'pressing applications' and the public's attitude towards the enormous and continuing expenses of Buckingham Palace.[58] The King was outraged: Nash was being most 'infamously used'. He should be created a baronet *'forthwith'*, not only as an act of justice to himself but to the King's *'own dignity'*.[59] Once again his Majesty was overruled; he took to his bed again.

*

* The Duke of Cumberland's assertions that Wellington was endeavouring to assume dictatorial powers were reflected in numerous contemporary caricatures. A typical one by Heath portrayed Wellington trying on the royal crown in front of a looking-glass while the King, sucking his thumb in a cradle, is rocked to sleep by Lady Conyngham, believed to be one of the Prime Minister's closest allies (BM *Sat*, xi, 15521).

There were pleasant days though, even in that summer of 1829 when his eyesight was failing and he could scarcely write any more by candlelight.[60] In May he gave his annual children's ball which was attended by his 'little friend', the Queen of Portugal, who fell down, cutting her nose on one of her diamonds; she cried a great deal, and he was 'very kind to' her.[61] The next month there was a concert at St James's Palace where he listened with evident satisfaction to the singing of Maria Malibran. Later there was the Jockey Club dinner at which he did not speak much and seemed to be in pain; but the next week Mme du Cayla, formerly the mistress of Louis XVIII, thought him handsome still with a pair of beautiful legs.[62]

At Windsor, where he spent the summer in the Royal Lodge, he still drove out occasionally in his little pony-chaise to visit the animals in his menagerie at Sandpit Gate and to address a few words of comfort to his ailing giraffe; his affection for it and his grief at its death in August were cruelly ridiculed by Heath and Doyle who caricatured him and Lady Conyngham weeping over it sentimentally.[63] Sometimes, when he had inspected the menagerie, he would sit for a time in his chaise with his favourite cockatoo on his arm, sipping a glass of cherry-gin which 'was always kept in preparation for him'.[64]

He now spent the greater part of his time at Windsor, though in bed, remaining there often until dinner-time, after which, enlivened by punch, he would still occasionally sing songs and 'relate anecdotes of his youth'.[65]

The curtains of his room were opened between six and seven in the morning when the newspapers were brought in to him.* Sometimes he had a book read to him, or called upon the pretty actress, Eliza Chester, whom he had appointed his reader, to entertain him with a play. His favourite novelists were still Scott and Jane Austen, but he also enjoyed the works of Lady Morgan and called Croker a 'damn blackguard' for making some adverse comments on her novel, *Florence Macarthy*. He

---

* When his sight was capable of it he 'read every newspaper quite through', so Mount Charles said; and Lord Howick was 'rather surprised to hear from Huskisson', so he noted in his journal in March 1829, 'that the King is in the habit of reading every newspaper that is published' (MS Journal of 3rd Earl Grey, 10 March 1829). Certainly throughout his life his Household had taken deliveries of enormous quantities of newspapers: at Carlton House no less than 546 copies of eight different newspapers were delivered every day (RA 28398–915).

also read a great deal of history, memoirs and travel books, and had 'an extraordinary memory' for the information he gleaned from them, and 'liked to talk of them', so Sir Astley Cooper said. His accounts reveal his catholicity of taste as a book-collector, and his concern to buy almost every book that was published about Napoleon.[66] When Napoleon died, and the library which was sent out to St Helena was returned to London, he asked his librarian to go through it and show him any books which had been annotated. From an inspection of these he came to the conclusion that Napoleon's favourite author was Ossian.[67]

When the King's reading was finished, and after attending to what business he could bring his mind to dwell upon, he would doze and then order something to eat or drink, a glass of chocolate perhaps or a chicken and a goblet of soda water, or sometimes, after several glasses of cherry brandy or punch, he would eat an astonishingly heavy meal with quantities of pastry and vegetables.[68] During the meal he would talk to his pages and *valets de chambre*, to his stud groom, Jack Redford, or to whichever doctor happened to be available. One morning in November 1829 he was to be seen 'in a white cotton night cap and a rather dirty flannel jacket, propped up with pillows, and sipping his chocolate', as he talked alternately to Chantrey about some statues he was making for Windsor, to James Wardrop, his surgeon in ordinary, about the stuffing of the giraffe, and to the Duke of Cumberland and a tailor about the possibility of providing the Guards, and later all the infantry, with new uniforms. A servant interrupted this divan to announce the Duke of Wellington, whereupon he put on a black velvet cap with a gold tassel and a grand blue silk *douillette* and limped into the next room to receive him in the character of King George IV. After half an hour's official talk he returned to his bedroom, and tumbled into bed again to resume the discussion on the Army's coats and breeches.[69]

He was evidently in fairly good spirits that day, but his health was deteriorating fast. He was quite blind now in one eye, and the fear of blindness in the other, upon which an operation for cataract had been proposed, made him 'nervous, sad and troubled', although when Wellington called he put on a brave face and displayed not the least concern. At Christmas he complained to Knighton of being already 'blind as a beetle'.[70] He bought a great number of magnifying glasses and pairs of spectacles with pebble lenses; but they do not appear to have been of much use.[71]

He was also having trouble with his remaining teeth. Years before he had complained of discomfort from his false teeth, as a cure for which Lord Lauderdale had recommended him to place a piece of lint steeped in tincture of myrrh between the gum and the gold on the inside of the plate.[72] Since then his dentist, Samuel Cartwright, had been repeatedly called in to treat him: in 1829 Cartwright was obliged to attend his patient thirty-seven times, charging twenty guineas for each visit to Windsor and three guineas an hour at St James's; his total bill for the period, including mechanical work, came to over £700.[73]

In November 1829 Lady Conyngham also fell ill with what began as 'a bad bilious fever' and then culminated in fainting fits so persistent that she thought she was dying. The King, whose practice it had long been to visit her room for an hour or so's desultory conversation each evening, appeared to be much more concerned about her health than she had been in the past about his.[74] When he seemed really unwell she devoted herself to prayer, and once, on being told that he was 'very ill', she burst into tears;[75] but usually she appeared to have little patience with his various complaints and to believe that his sufferings, apart from his obvious gout and failing sight, were more imagined than real.[76]

She still talked of leaving him as she had done intermittently for years. In June 1823, when the King had grumbled to Wellington that her temper was really 'beyond bearing', she in turn had impatiently complained of being so bored that she could not possibly stand it any longer;[77] and, in October that same year, the Duke had told Mrs Arbuthnot that her conduct was 'shocking', that the King 'was full of attention and quite *aux petits soins* with her and that she shrugged her shoulders at him and seemed quite to loathe him; so much so that everybody observed it. She told the Duke that the whole thing bored her to death and that she would go away and have done with it.'[78]

In March 1825, when she had been in deep affliction because of the death of her eldest son, she did leave Windsor for a time and was 'disposed to give up the thing altogether'. 'It has always been known that the late Lord [Mount Charles] detested and remonstrated against the connection,' Fremantle commented, 'and it is whispered that he left her a written exhortation. Whether this be true or not, I cannot pretend to say; but I can answer for her having resisted all application' to return.[79] Eventually she did so only on condition that she would be allowed to dine alone in her own apartment whenever she chose. 'Considering [the King's] extreme kindness to her,' Mrs Arbuthnot commented, 'she really does make him a most ungrateful return. She detests him, shows it plainly, yet continues to accept all his presents which are of enormous value.'[80]

In the summer of 1825 she had again become 'very restless and impatient' under what she called her 'terrible restraint and confinement'. She had then announced 'her fixed determination to go abroad', and had been prevented from doing so only by the efforts of Lord Lauderdale who persuaded her that 'however blameable it was in her to get into her present situation', now that she *was* in it, it was her 'bounden duty to submit and go through with it'.[81] The same advice was given to her by the Duke of Wellington.[82] In the winter of 1826, more bored than ever, she had thrown herself back on her sofa, declining to speak: it had been the general opinion at that time, so Lady Grey said – though Lady Grey herself did not believe the reports – that she hated 'Kingy'.[83] Now, at the beginning of 1830, recovered from her illness and looking 'twenty years younger',[84] she was once again 'bored to death' and was really thinking of 'removing'.[85]

When she was in this kind of mood the King relied on Knighton to keep her at bay. He was finding Knighton more tiresome than ever, and displayed 'great irritability' in his manner when there was business to discuss.[86] Yet, as Knighton noted in his diary on 6 February 1830, 'the King seemed embarrassed at the thoughts of my absence, not from any feelings towards myself, I am satisfied, but from the contention His Majesty would have with Lady Conyngham. . . . The King talked to me at dinner because I was opposite – but at night on his going to bed there was no desire to talk to me in preference to his eating his supper.'[87]

23

The Last Illness
1830

*

'We have an Herculean constitution to work upon'

In the spring of 1830 the King began to suffer from severe attacks of breathlessness and found it impossible to get to sleep except 'by a good contrivance of pillows and a bed chair'. Throughout the night he would wake up periodically and then, in need of company and reassurance, he would ring his bell and ask a valet to pour him a glass of water, although there was a jug on the table beside his chair. The pains in his bladder were also growing worse, and to alleviate them he took increasingly enormous doses of laudanum.* Laudanum, however, was having less and less effect. In the past he had been known to spend 'the greater part of the twenty-four hours in a state of stupor';[1] now he could take over 250 drops in a period of thirty-six hours and remain quite capable of con-conducting a rational conversation with the Duke of Wellington.[2]

His doctors found him an appallingly difficult patient, combining a nervous apprehension as to his condition with a refusal to adopt a way of life which might improve it. They themselves, though, were far from being in agreement as to how he should be treated. Sir Henry Halford, Sir Wathen Waller, Sir Matthew Tierney, as well as James Wardrop and Benjamin Brodie, the surgeons, and O'Reilly, the apothecary, were all in attendance at different times and seem rarely to have agreed with each other's diagnoses and treatments. The King was sceptical about the skills

---

* 'Nothing can exceed the pain of such attacks,' Knighton had told Canning four years before, when Wellington had dismissed all the King's ills as imaginary. As a cure for the complaint – diagnosed as 'gout, principally confined to the neck of the bladder and all along the course of the urethra' – leeches were applied around the King's pelvis (Canning Papers, 103b).

of all of them, particularly of those of O'Reilly, 'the damnedest liar in the world', whom he appears to have considered more as an amusing purveyor of gossip than as a medical attendant to be taken seriously. When he was really apprehensive about himself he sent for Knighton who, though he had not practised for many years, had not forgotten his medical knowledge: when Halford and O'Reilly advocated the use of a *bougie* for the King's urethral complaint, Knighton was proved right in objecting to it for it made the condition more painful than ever. Knighton also rightly continued to condemn Sir Henry Halford for allowing the King far too much laudanum.[3] But neither Knighton nor any of the other doctors had the least control over their difficult patient, who alarmed them all exceedingly by his dreadful spasms of breathlessness. At first there would be a gurgling in his throat, then not only his face but even the ends of his fingers would turn black as he tried to get his breath.[4] Yet as soon as he felt better he would drink a large glass of brandy, get up and go for a ride round the park.[5]

His mode of living now was 'really beyond belief', so Mrs Arbuthnot learned. One day in April 'at the hour of the servants' dinner, he called the page in and said, "Now you are going to dinner. Go downstairs and cut me off just such a piece of beef as you would like to have yourself, cut from the part you like the best yourself, and bring it me up." The page accordingly went and fetched an enormous quantity of roast beef, all of which he ate, and then slept for five hours.'[6]

'One night he drank two glasses of hot ale and toast, three glasses of claret, some strawberries!! and a glass of brandy. Last night they gave him some physic and, after it, he drank three glasses of port wine and a glass of brandy. No wonder he is likely to die. But they say he will have all these things and nobody can prevent him.'[7] For breakfast on 9 April, Wellington said that he had 'a pidgeon and beef steak pie of which he eat two pigeons and three beef-steaks, three parts of a bottle of Mozelle, a glass of dry champagne, two glasses of port [and] a glass of brandy! He had taken laudanum the night before, again before this breakfast, again last night and again this morning.'[8]

On 14 April he was taking a ride in his pony-chaise when he decided to stop and have a look at his hounds. As he was inspecting them he was seized with a very severe attack of breathlessness.[9] That evening the Duke of Wellington reported him as being 'very unwell', though in 'very good humour', and heavily dosed with laudanum.[10]

'We regret to state,' Halford and Tierney reported next morning in an official bulletin, 'that the King has had a bilious attack. His Majesty, although free from fever, is languid and weak.'[11] Subsequent bulletins, issued at intervals during the following three weeks, were equally vague and non-committal but rather more reassuring: 'His Majesty has passed two good nights and continues better. . . . The King continued as well as his Majesty has been for several days past, until this morning when his Majesty experienced a return of the embarrassment of his breathing. His Majesty is now again better. . . . The King has suffered less from the attacks of embarrassment in his breathing. . . . His Majesty has passed a good night. His Majesty's symptoms are somewhat alleviated. . . . The King's symptoms have not varied. . . . The King's symptoms remain the same. . . .'[12]

In his private reports to Wellington, however, Halford expressed a far deeper concern. The King was greatly alarmed by his attacks of breathlessness, and did not like to be left alone for a moment, clinging anxiously to Halford's hand until the doctor was 'completely knocked up.'[13]

There were occasions when, after large doses of laudanum, massive quantities of ether, and a few hours' sleep, the King professed himself much refreshed; but 'the instant he called upon himself for an exertion, all his difficulties were renewed'; and then 'it was hardly possible to be more distressed than he was'. On 1 May there was a 'gigantic struggle' for breath, after which the doctors' 'whole thoughts' were 'devoted to procuring rest'[41].

The King began to dread the appearance of documents, since the effort of signing them brought on spasms of extreme agitation and breathlessness. He asked if Parliament could pass an Act for saving him the trouble, particularly as he could scarcely see the papers which he was expected to sign. But when Halford told him that Parliament 'would not agree without ascertaining previously from the physicians the cause and extent of this disability', all his habitual fears of making such information public were reawakened and he 'withdrew his proposal instantly and said he would take the earliest opportunity of affixing his royal signature'.[15] Afraid of displaying his weakness in front of the Duke of Cumberland, he signed papers valiantly and without complaint when the Duke was present; but he begged Halford not to leave him on these occasions for fear lest he should become involved in some exhausting political discussion, or better still, not to allow the Duke into his room at all.[16]

So the month wore on. On some days, after Brodie had made punctures in his swollen legs, and 'his Majesty had been able to take such a posture as permitted him to sleep uninterrupted a few hours', there would be a marked improvement. Although he did not ask to have the newspapers read to him – a sure sign of weakness – he did manage to eat a reasonable meal; and when not beset by fears of suffocation he behaved with a courage that Halford profoundly admired.[17]

Others, besides Halford, were much impressed by the King's fortitude in his sufferings, by the way he would speak cheerfully of a speedy recovery between prognostications of his imminent demise. He assured Lady Conyngham that he was about to die at any moment; but that, the Duke of Wellington thought, was merely to 'try and vex' her;[18] and certainly such dire prophecies were in keeping with his practised methods of eliciting concern and sympathy. To the Duke he expressed not the least apprehension, and the Duke admired him for it.[19] So did Croker, who reported that he was contemplating the situation 'boldly'.[20] Even Lord Ellenborough wrote, 'in constitution and mind he is certainly a wonderful man. I have no doubt that the feeling that he is always in representation makes him behave in the face of death as a man would on the field of battle.'[21] Yet although they admired his courage, most of his Ministers regarded his approaching death with little sympathy and less regret. As for his heir, he could not conceal his excitement at the prospect before him. The Duke of Clarence and his brothers wrote suitably dutiful letters to Knighton expressing their anxious wishes for his amendment; but the King well knew that the devotion they all expressed did not go very deep. His sisters really did love him, and always had. The Duke of Cambridge, with whom he had been on the best of terms for twenty years, was also concerned, perhaps.[22] But Clarence and Cumberland were thinking of their own future now, not of his; and Sussex he presumed to be indifferent, even though he did send 'affectionate messages'.[23] The Duke of York might have sincerely grieved for him, and might, too, have made a worthy successor; but the King could not conceive that Clarence would be one. 'Look at that idiot!' he had once whispered in Mme de Lieven's ear at the dinner table, indicating his brother whose red-thatched face – 'like a frog's head carved on a coconut' – could be seen at the other end of the table. 'They will remember me, if he is ever in my place.'[24]

Nearly all those whom he had once thought of as his real friends were dead. Fox was gone and Canning, Gerard Lake and John McMahon,

Payne and Moira, the Duke of Northumberland and the Duchess of Devonshire, Lady Bessborough and Lady Lade. Sheridan, too, was dead; and he could not but deeply regret that they had quarrelled at the end over money which the King had sent to him.*

Mrs Fitzherbert was still alive but when she heard that he was ill she had not at first been sympathetic. She remembered, as she told her adopted daughter the Hon Mrs Dawson-Damer, 'that the King always liked to make himself out worse to excite compassion, and that he always wished everyone to think him dangerously ill when little was the matter with him'. She had supposed that this was now the case. Later, however, she heard from Sir Henry Halford, an old friend, that the King was, in fact, 'excessively ill'. His constitution was 'a gigantic one', and his 'elasticity under the most severe pressure' exceeded everything Halford had witnessed in thirty-eight years' experience. But the worst circumstances in which he had ever witnessed the Dukes of Clarence and Sussex, 'under their attacks of spasmodic asthma', hardly approached the King's distress at times. What the final result would be, Halford could hardly venture to say.[25]

Having received this letter, Mrs Fitzherbert overcame her former reluctance and wrote to him for the last time: 'After many repeated struggles with myself, from the apprehension of appearing troublesome or intruding upon your Majesty, after so many years of continual silence, my anxiety respecting your Majesty has got the better of my scruples, and I trust your Majesty will believe me most sincere when I assure you how truly I have grieved to hear of your sufferings. . . . No one can feel more rejoiced to learn your Majesty is returned to complete convalescence, which I pray you may long enjoy, accompanied by every degree of happiness you may wish for or desire. I have enclosed this letter to Sir

---

* Thomas Moore, in his *Life of Sheridan*, gave a highly tendentious account of this transaction and of the King's offer to Sheridan of £500 when he lay dying, supposedly in great distress. Lockhart, who reviewed the book unfavourably, thought that Moore's treatment of the King was more 'unpardonable than anybody knows – for Croker took care to put him in possession of all the facts of the case long before the book was printed. First and last old Sherry (besides his sinecure) received from the Privy Purse upwards of £30,000 in cash' (*Scott Letter-Books*, 146). Certainly the King had been very patient with Sheridan's vagaries, and there can be little doubt that Sheridan misappropriated the £3,000 which the King had given him to buy a seat in Parliament from the Duke of Norfolk, using the money instead to settle some pressing debts (*Croker Papers*, i, 86–7; Bingham, 351–3).

H[enry] H[alford],' she concluded, emphasizing her disapproval of Sir William Knighton whom she had always disliked and distrusted, 'as your Majesty must be aware there is no person about him through whom I could make a communication of so private a nature accorded with the perfect conviction of its never being divulged.'[26]

Halford noticed how eagerly the King seized the letter when it was given to him, and with what emotion he read it before placing it under his pillow.[27] But the will which he had made in her favour in 1796 he wished now to alter. In 1823 when his life had been threatened by a man named Griffith, he had asked Lord Eldon to go to see him 'upon the subject of a will'. He had then told Eldon that he thought Mrs Fitzherbert ought to have £10,000 a year for life, rather than the £6,000 a year which was already granted to her on the security of the Brighton Pavilion. He had also mentioned a 'natural son, an officer in the East Indies, to whom he thought himself bound to give a legacy of £30,000. . . . He then spoke of a residuary legatee. He said the Duke of York would succeed to a station which made it unnecessary to make him residuary legatee.' In any case, he went on, the Duke had had £50,000 from him; the Duke of Clarence had had £30,000; it 'could not be expected that he should look to the family of the Duke of Kent', nor to the Duke of Sussex. The Duke of Cambridge 'wanted nothing'; and 'he added, naming his several sisters, that he did not think there was a necessity to attend to them as residuary legatees. . . . He then said he should make *a friend* residuary legatee, *not naming the person*, but he certainly meant Lady C[onyngham].'[28]

He repeated his wishes now to Knighton who was desired to inform Lady Conyngham of them. When Knighton had delivered the message, the King asked him, 'Well, how did she receive it?'

'She was very much affected, Sir, and burst into tears.'

'Oh, she did, did she?'[29]

Later, so Agar–Ellis was informed 'in the greatest secrecy' by Lady Lyndhurst whose husband was consulted in the matter, the King formally declared his wishes again 'before three witnesses who were Sir Henry Halford, Sir [Matthew] Tierney and Sir William Knighton: His wishes were that everything he stood possessed of should become the property of Lady C[onyngham]. When this declaration was made about a fortnight before the King died the D[uke] of W[ellington] was told of it and came down to Windsor and threatened Lady C[onyngham] if she took advantage of it. He told her among other *gentlemanlike* speeches that she was like

Madame du Barri, and that Madame du B's conduct brought about the French Revolution.' Agar-Ellis added that they did not mean to execute the will, if they could possibly avoid it.[30]

*

In spite of his weakness and sleeplessness, the pain in his limbs, his rapidly decreasing appetite and his frightening attacks of breathlessness, the King continued to endure his sufferings without undue complaint. He looked 'wasted and wasting'; yet, as the Duke of Wellington noticed, his hand was 'cool and healthy, his eye was lively, and his mind as clear and active as ever, and even his spirits were good; in fact he showed strong vitality'.[31] He asked for the *Racing Calendar*, enquired how work was getting on with the new dining-room at the Royal Lodge which Wyatville had been instructed to begin the previous September,[32] and insisted that it must be finished in time for Ascot races.[33] On 12 May Wellington saw him again and found him 'good humoured and alive, his eyes as brilliant as ever', though 'several quarts of water' had been taken from his feet the day before and his colour was now 'dark and sodden'.[34] He was still talking of going to Ascot on 26 May and of convalescing at Aix-la-Chapelle; he remained in 'very good humour'.[35]

But by now, as the Duchess of Gloucester reported, he was 'enormous, like a feather bed', while the dropsied swelling in his legs had made them 'hard as stone'. His face was drawn, his features pinched. He had attacks of choking, and in speaking of Leopold – against whom he was 'furious' for deciding not to go to Greece after all now that the King's approaching death brought their niece Victoria closer to the throne – he 'had a seizure which threatened to be fatal'.[36] The remedies he had been given for dropsy had upset 'the functions of the stomach', and on 15 May he had eaten nothing for three days.[37]

Yet on the 17 May when Peel went to visit him, he appeared 'lively, intelligent and strong'.[38] At this and at a subsequent, and final, meeting early in June all their past differences were forgotten and they spoke as friends. The King asked Peel to push his day-bed towards the window, saying that he had little time left now in which to enjoy the view over the garden, which, in fact, he could only vaguely discern. Peel's old father had died that month, and the King said, 'You are just returned from your father's funeral. You will soon have to pay the like ceremony to me.'[39] Peel attempted to take his mind from such thoughts by talking about the

Royal Lodge, but the King said sadly, 'Ah, poor Cottage, I shall never see it again.'[40]

On 21 May, after a very bad night, the King's condition rapidly deteriorated, though Halford continued to write admiringly of his patience and bravery.[41] There was 'still power left' in the King's extraordinary constitution'; on 15 June he was actually reported to be in 'very good spirits'.[42]

The King's Signature Bill had now been passed, allowing documents to be stamped not signed; yet he still liked to suppose that this was only a temporary measure, even that he was well on the way to recovery. And when he did talk of his expected demise he was more likely to do so with a kind of reckless cheerfulness than in the mournful tone he thought it appropriate to adopt in discussing the painful subject with Peel. 'You know,' he announced carelessly one day, 'I shall be dead by Saturday.'[43] He was 'as amusing as ever', so Knighton said;[44] and Croker heard that he was 'as clear, as communicative, as agreeable, nay as *facetious* in his conversation as he had ever been'.[45]

Knighton, to whom he was now 'particularly affectionate', had put a Bible on the table beside his bed, and he was seen often to pick it up and look into it.[46] Although in the past he had dutifully attended church on Sunday mornings, had taken the Sacrament at Easter and Christmas and had had a little chapel built in the grounds of the Royal Lodge, he had never been a particularly religious man and had always disliked sermons, except those that gave him 'pleasure and satisfaction'. But, in recent years he had seemed to take his religious duties more seriously and had attended Holy Communion more often. He now appeared really to derive comfort from the Sacrament which, administered to him by the Bishop of Chichester, Dr Robert Carr, a former Vicar of Brighton, he took in his room with Knighton and Lady Conyngham.[47] He also seemed comforted by the prayers for his recovery which were being said in the churches. These prayers, which the Bishop repeated to him, kneeling by his bed, ended with the words, 'Finally grant, O heavenly Father, that when it shall be Thy good pleasure to call him from this world unto Thee, he may receive a glory in Thy everlasting Kingdom; through the merits and mediation of our Lord and Saviour, Jesus Christ. Amen.' '*Amen, Amen, Amen!*' the King repeated fervently when the Bishop had finished.[48]

He later talked of this prayer to a visitor who assured him that the public took a great interest in his state. 'He seemed much pleased, and expressed his own conviction that it ought to be so, for he "had always endeavoured to do his duty", and had never willingly done harm to anyone.'[49] As for the prayer, he added with a touching appreciation of its literary rather than its spiritual merits, it was 'in very good taste'.[50]

Although the public were asked to pray for the King's recovery, they had been given very little information as to what was the matter with him. 'The King's symptoms remain the same', a typical bulletin had stated on 22 May. 'His Majesty has passed a better night.'[51] The *Lancet* was highly critical of the 'vague, unsatisfactory and mysterious' bulletins that emanated from Windsor. The King was clearly suffering from a disease from which there was 'no instance of recovery upon record'; yet his medical attendants seemed unaware 'of the precarious situation of their royal patient'. His death had been predicted 'eight or nine years ago when Sir Henry Halford, Sir William Knighton and Sir Matthew Tierney stated under their hands that the King laboured under an organic disease of the heart which might terminate in sudden death'.[52]

In subsequent issues both the *Lancet* and the *London Medical Gazette* were even more critical of the doctors at Windsor whose methods they deplored. Powerful diuretics, morphia, ether and laudanum had all 'failed to produce the desired effects'.[53]

On 12 June *The Times* quoted the *Lancet*'s criticism of the bulletins which were 'so scandalously, so ambiguously framed'. 'His Majesty', the *Lancet* regretted to say, 'is in as alarming a state as ever. The integuments have been again punctured, but his body and his extremities from the immense collection of water, are still enormously swollen. In the management of the royal sufferer, the attendants experience considerable difficulty in inducing him to take proper medicines, food, and drink. The King does not consider that his case is hopeless. From private information, however, we can only say that although in our opinion ultimate recovery is impossible, immediate dissolution is not inevitable. The medicines which have been administered for some time past have consisted chiefly of *aether* and the *sedative tincture of opium*.'[54]

The King himself declined to accept the fact that ultimate recovery was impossible. As though anxious to show Wellington and Lord Farnborough that he was not to be easily defeated, he paid particular attention to the official papers that were brought to him on 16 June and 'all the arrears, about four hundred documents' were stamped.[55] But thereafter the King grew increasingly weak, 'more languid and poorly'. He continued to see as little as possible of Cumberland whose recent alleged affair with Lady Graves had 'horribly annoyed' him;[56] and did not appear to relish the visits of Clarence; but he looked forward to his sisters' visits 'with the greatest pleasure'.

Towards the end of the third week in June, his doctors expressed their unanimous opinion that his system was now 'giving way at all points'. Yet, as Halford reported to Wellington, almost taking for granted now the resilience of his astonishing patient, he was 'easily satisfied that he would get the better of this illness'.[57] On the day that he saw Wellington for the last time, 'he said he was getting quite well and should be able to move soon'.[58]

At half past eleven the following Friday night, 25 June, the King dismissed Sir Henry Halford and sent him to bed; the pages too retired to the outer room. Soon he fell asleep in his chair, leaning on the table which was customarily placed in front of him, his forehead resting on one hand, his other hand in that of Sir Wathen Waller, who was sitting up with him. At a quarter to two he woke up, asked for his medicine, and then drank a little clove tea. After drinking the tea he fell asleep again, and remained asleep until just before three when he sent for the pages to bring in his night-chair. 'He had instantly a purgative motion,' Waller reported, 'but observed, "I do not think all is right," and then added, a common expression of his, "What shall we do next?" I answered, "Return as soon as possible to your chair."' The King did so and then, feeling faint, he ordered the windows to be opened. He tried without success to drink some sal volatile, whereupon Sir Henry Halford was summoned. He was still holding Waller's hand, 'more strongly than usual', when suddenly he looked him full in the face and, 'with an eager eye', exclaimed, 'My dear boy! This is death!'[59]

He then closed his eyes and lay back in his chair. At that moment Halford entered the room. 'His Majesty gave him his hand but never spoke afterwards and, with a very few short breathings, expired exactly as the clock struck the quarter after three, June 26, 1830.'[60]

'I am truly brokenhearted,' Sir Wathen Waller told his son, 'and have lost one of the most affectionate friends man ever possessed. At my age I can ill spare a friend whose eye ever beamed with pleasure on me for nearly forty long years, but I must not go on, for at this moment I can ill bear it.'[61]

24

Post Mortem
'Un roi grand seigneur'

The doctors who conducted the post mortem concluded that the King had been suffering for many years from arteriosclerosis. They also found that many of his internal organs were in an unhealthy condition; but that 'the immediate cause of his Majesty's dissolution was the rupture of a blood vessel in the stomach'.[1]

In a private letter to his son, Wathen Waller added that a contributory cause of death was 'over excitement and high living. There was also a small stone found in the bladder which accounts for the pain he felt all last winter. . . . His will was opened and there is nothing in it to annoy the present King. . . . He is to be buried the Wednesday after next.'[2]*

The funeral took place, in fact, on Thursday 15 July at Windsor where, though the town was full of visitors, 'the only sign of mourning which [was] visible [was] in their dress'.[3] For six hours the day before, the King's body lay in state in the Castle, attended by various members of his Household, Gentlemen Pensioners and Yeomen of the Guard. Yeomen of the Guard also lined the Grand Staircase which – like the rooms through which the public passed on their way to the State Apartment where the coffin lay – was draped in black. A sheet covered all but the King's face. He 'looked well, as though asleep, but his cheeks were sunken and the abdomen much raised'.[4]

At nine o'clock on the evening of 15 July, the coffin was carried to St George's Chapel between lines of Grenadier Guardsmen, every

---

* The King's will was never proved. Wellington paid off all outstanding debts from the estate and handed over the residue to King William IV. On condition that she continued to receive her allowance of £10,000 a year, Mrs Fitzherbert signed a release of her claims on all the King's personal estate and effects (Wellington Papers, Miscellaneous 31).

fifth one of whom bore a burning flambeau. Its pall was held by six dukes and four eldest sons of dukes. In front of them, leading the procession, were the trumpeters, drummers and fifers of the Guards. These were followed by peers bearing banners, Blanc Coursier King of Arms with the crown of Hanover, and Clarenceux King of Arms with the crown of England. The Duke of Wellington carried the Sword of State. Behind him walked King William IV, in a 'magnificent velvet purple cloak', with the collars of the Orders of the Garter, the Bath, the Thistle, St Patrick and the Royal Hanoverian Guelphic Order around his ample neck.[5]

It was an impressive spectacle. But the scene inside the chapel, so far as it could be discerned in the smoke from the Guardsmen's guttering flambeaux, was far from dignified.

The Times reporters, who could see 'not a single mark of sympathy' amongst the congregation, thought that nothing could have been worse managed. 'It seemed as if the servants of the household, the friends of the carpenters and upholsterers, the petty tradesmen of the town had been admitted to the exclusion of all those who, for public character or official situation, ought to have been allowed free access to the funeral of the Sovereign. We never saw so motley, so rude, so ill-managed a body of persons. They who first entered not only seized the best places, but prevented others from taking any.'[6]

To add to the confusion in the chapel, during the singing of a hymn, a piece of the carved work which hung over one of the stalls, crashed to the ground, striking Sir Astley Cooper on the forehead. The wound bled profusely; but Sir Astley clasped a handkerchief to his head and manfully remained in his place.[7]

To Agar-Ellis, who thought that there was 'too much tinsel magnificence' about the Earl Marshal's ceremonial for it to be moving, nothing seemed more indecorous than the new King's behaviour. Bustling with excitement, he 'talked to the people on both sides of him while coming up the aisle, and afterwards when sitting at the head of the coffin'.[8] He 'talked incessantly and loudly to all about him,' Joseph Jekyll confirmed, 'so that the most frivolous things were overheard.'[9]

King William IV's behaviour was not all that was incongruous, Agar-Ellis thought. 'Sussex and Cumberland looked awfully fierce in their black cloaks. . . . Some of the figures in the chapel were incomparably absurd. The Duke of Buckingham squatting down in a stall

337

exhausted (for he had held a corner of the pall) looked exactly like a giant tortoise, then the vulgar, insolent air of Lord Ellenborough in a coat covered with gold – the greasy importance of Verulam carrying a banner, and old Cathcart with another which he could hardly support – the horrid nervous grimaces of the Duke of Norfolk and the awkward gestures of Lord Conyngham were all in their different ways most ludicrous. . . . Mount Charles was much affected and I think no-one else.'[10] Lord Ellenborough agreed that no one appeared much affected: 'It was considered a mere pageant, even by his household who had lived so intimately with him for years.'[11]

After two hours King William could wait no longer. While the anthem was being sung, he rose from his seat, thanked the Earl Marshal for making all the arrangements and left the chapel.[12]

In the absence of the King, while minute guns boomed in the Long Walk, the body of King George IV was lowered into the grave. He had earnestly asked Wellington, whom he had appointed one of his executors, to ensure that he was buried in his night clothes and 'with whatever ornaments might be upon his person at the time of his death'. Wellington has assured him that this would be done. Afterwards he realized what lay behind the King's request, for noticing a black ribbon around the neck in the open coffin, he had been driven by curiosity to see what was suspended from it. He had drawn aside the collar of the nightshirt to reveal a diamond locket containing a miniature portrait of Mrs Fitzherbert. The Duke blushed deeply as, with some hesitation, he told Mrs Dawson-Damer what his inquisitiveness had led him to discover. When Mrs Dawson-Damer, in turn, told Mrs Fitzherbert that the King had been buried with her picture round his neck, she listened without a word. But presently it was seen 'that some large tears fell from her eyes'.[13]*

*

If Mrs Fitzherbert and his sisters wept, if Waller and Mount Charles and many of his servants grieved for him, and if Mme de Lieven heard the

---

* John Whiting, the King's Page of the Backstairs, told Queen Victoria that the portrait was of Lady Conyngham; but Sir George Seymour, Mrs Dawson-Damer's brother and one of Mrs Fitzherbert's executors, had 'no doubt it was Mrs Fitzherbert's portrait'. Sir Wathen Waller and Sir Frederick Watson both assured him that they had seen it (Sir George Seymour's annotations of Langdale's *Memoirs of Mrs Fitzherbert*, Seymour of Ragley MSS, CR 114/A/536/7).

George IV by Sir Thomas Lawrence, 1822.

33 'Brobdignag Cottage. Rusticating.': caricature by William Heath, 29 March 1824. The King and Conyngham family gardening at the Royal Lodge. Lord Conyngham pulls a roller; Lord Francis pus a wheelbarrow; while Lady Elizabeth directs the jet of water from the portable pump operated by mother.

34 'A fishing party, What great enjoyments rise from trivial things . . .': caricature by William Heath, 27 Ju 1827. The King is escorted down to Virginia Water to fish in the lake in a circular stand on castors (su as those used for toddling children) by Lady Conyngham and Sir William Knighton.

news of his death with 'real sorrow',[14] there were few others amongst the public at large who sincerely mourned their loss. During his protracted illness, a few prints had been issued suggesting that John Bull had 'always liked G[eor]ge' – though he had once had a bit of a quarrel with him – and heartily hoped that he would recover. But these were not truly reflective of the state of public feeling. Most people had seemed indifferent, and the rich principally concerned that his expected death would interfere with their arrangements for the summer.[15] At Brooks's, of course, bets had been lightheartedly laid upon the duration of his life.[16]

When the Privy Council met for the first time after his death, 'there was no grief in the room. . . . It was like an *ordinary levee*.'[17] And after his funeral, 'all Windsor' was drunk, so Joseph Jekyll said. 'Suppers and champagne for parties who remained there, and everything but grief or regret.'[18] Gangs of pickpockets roamed the streets, and the 'quantity of watches, money, etc., that fell into the hands of the marauders [was] of an immense amount in value, almost to surpass belief'.[19]

The crowded London streets had 'more the appearance of rejoicing than mourning'.[20] On the day of the funeral the shops were shut and 'in a great number of instances the shutters even of the private dwellings were up'; the church bells tolled; minute guns fired from the Tower and in St James's Park; but there was no 'solemn expression of feeling nor much decorum of behaviour'.[21] The young Lord Howick, driving between Brooks's Club and the Travellers' and 'all about that part of the town' a few days after the funeral, found the streets still 'excessively crowded'; the people were not in mourning and there was 'no sign of sorrow to be seen except a single shutter before the windows of the shops. It looked much more as if some good news had arrived than anything else.'[22]

The King had 'never sincerely inspired anyone with attachment,' Mme de Lieven thought, 'and had hardly been susceptible to attachment himself'. 'No one trusted him. . . . He was full of vanity and could be flattered at will.' Yet 'unquestionably he had some wit and great penetration; he quickly summed up persons and things; he was educated and had much tact, easy, animated and varied conversation, not at all pedantic. He adorned the subjects he touched, he knew how to listen; he was very polished. For my part I had never known a person like him, who was also affectionate, sympathetic and galant.'[23]

Sir Astley Cooper, the surgeon, who had also known him well, emphasized this fundamental kindness in a man who was, however, 'violent in his temper'. Cooper had been called in to carry out an operation for the removal of a wen on the King's head in 1821, an operation which was much more dangerous than had been expected and which, as Wellington and Henry Hobhouse confirmed, the King had undergone without the least fuss or trouble.[24] Over the subsequent years Cooper had formed a high opinion of the attainments of his extraordinary and contradictory patient. He was 'indolent', he had to admit, 'and, therefore, disposed to yield, to avoid trouble; nervous, and therefore anxious to throw every onus from his own shoulders. Yet he was the most perfect gentleman in his manners and address – possessing the finest person, with the most dignified and gracious condescension, though excessively proud; familiar himself but shocked at it in others. . . . He would sometimes be coarse in his conversation, but again nobody could be more refined and polished when he chose. Every story of a character about town, every humorous anecdote, he was perfectly acquainted with, and was constantly seeking means of adding to his stock, and then took the greatest pleasure in relating them to others. He was himself witty, but the points of his conversation consisted principally in anecdote, and the relation of jokes. . . . If I had wanted to decide upon what I ought to do, nobody would have given me better advice; but he very likely would have practised just the contrary himself, for with respect to himself he was too often guided by prejudice.'

Cooper was particularly impressed by his wide knowledge, especially of history and literature, his 'ability to recount anecdotes of everybody'. He 'had an extraordinary memory – he recollected all that he had read or seen – and had the faculty of quickly comprehending everything. If he saw a steam-engine, he would describe not only its principles of action, but enter minutely into its construction. . . . If [he] observed any medicine that was new to him, he immediately asked its object and was not satisfied until he knew all its properties. He was also fond of inquiring into the uses of the various instruments employed in surgery.' Upon being introduced to a manufacturer of surgical instruments who had invented a new form of saddlebag for Army surgeons, he amazed the inventor by his detailed knowledge of his craft and not only pointed out something that was lacking – a large sponge – but showed him where it could be accommodated. The King, Cooper concluded, would have made 'the first physician or surgeon of his time, the first speaker in the House of Commons or Lords, though, perhaps, not the best divine'.[25]

Those who had known the King less well spoke of him less generously. A few people who had cause to be grateful for his generosity or patronage confessed to lamenting the King's death – Benjamin Haydon and Joseph Jekyll amongst them.[26] A few others – like Creevey – remembering past kindnesses, mourned 'poor Prinney'.[27] Mrs Arbuthnot wrote of the 'strange creature's' occasionally doing 'remarkably good natured things'.[28] A few dutiful sermons were preached, associating the King with the advances, improvements, reforms and brilliant successes of his age. A few dutiful letters were written: Scott expressed to Knighton his 'deep sorrow for the loss of a sovereign whose gentle and generous disposition, and singular manner and captivating conversation, rendered him as much the darling of private society, as his heartfelt interest in the general welfare of the country, and the constant and steady course of wise measures by which he raised his reign to such a state of triumphal prosperity, made him justly delighted in by his subjects'.[29]

A few public men delivered tedious eulogies, emphasizing – as, indeed, was his due – 'his late Majesty's munificence as patron and collector'. A few newspapers recorded the 'triumphs of his Regency and reign', and endeavoured to draw a parallel between these triumphs and the late King's character and attainments. The *Morning Post* went so far as to mourn the 'loss of a monarch so conspicuously endowed with all the qualities calculated to endear him to the hearts of his subjects', 'one of the best and most popular monarchs that ever swayed the sceptre of Britain', 'so good and excellent a King'.[30]

But such effusively extravagant praise was wholly out of tune with the general mood of the country. This mood was more accurately reflected by *The Times* which roundly attacked the King's 'most reckless, unceasing and unbounded prodigality', and his 'indifference to the feelings of others'.

'In the tawdry childishness of Carlton House and the mountebank Pavilion, or cluster of pagodas at Brighton,' *The Times*'s merciless obituary continued, 'His Royal Highness afforded an infallible earnest of what might one day be expected from His Majesty when the appetite for profusion and the contempt for all that deserves the name of architecture, should have reached their full maturity.... Princess Caroline's reception in her husband's house was a stain to manhood. A fashionable strumpet usurped the apartments of the Princess – her rights – the honours due to her – everything but the name she bore.... The heroine has now at least nothing to fear from her destroyer. . . . The late King had many generations of intimates with whom he led a course of life, the character of which rose little higher than that of animal indulgence.'[31]

Three weeks later, after the harshness of these judgements had been compared with the almost fawning tributes which the paper had paid to King William IV, *The Times* returned to the attack, making full amends for the thick black mourning bands which surrounded its columns: 'There never was an individual less regretted by his fellow-creatures than this deceased King,' an editorial insisted the day after the funeral. 'What eye has wept for him? What heart has heaved one throb of un-mercenary sorrow . . . for that Leviathan of the *haut ton*, George IV. . . . If he ever had a friend – a devoted friend in any rank of life – we protest that the name of him or her never reached us. An inveterate voluptuary, especially if he be an artificial person, is of all known beings the most selfish. Selfishness is the true repellant of human sympathy. Selfishness feels no attachment, and invites none; it is the charnel house of the affections. Nothing more remains to be said about George IV but to pay – as pay we must – for his profusion; and to turn his bad conduct to some account by tying up the hands of those who come after him in what concerns the public money.'[32]

King William IV, on the other hand, had already 'gained more upon the English tastes and prepossessions of his subjects by the blunt and unaffected – even should it be grotesque – cordiality of his demeanour' than King George IV had ever done during the sixty-seven years of his existence.[33] The excessive cordiality of King William IV was not to everyone's taste, of course. At his first Privy Council he shortsightedly did his very best to make out the face of every Councillor who knelt before him to kiss his hand, greeting one he recognized with a genial, 'How d'ye do?', obviously restraining himself with difficulty from shaking hands with them all. 'Poor Prinney,' Creevey wrote, noting the contrast, 'put on a dramatic, royal, distant dignity to all.'[34]

It was certainly true that the new King was popular, all the more so because of the contrast between his familiar, gregarious manner and the seclusion in which his predecessor had chosen to spend the last years of his life. So obviously delighted to be King, William IV strode about the London streets, nodding cheerfully to left and right. One day in St James's Street the mob followed him and 'one of the common women threw her arms round him and kissed him'.[35] 'The mob adores him,'

Mme de Lieven thought. 'He goes about openly and treats everyone familiarly – that is enough for John Bull. England is quite a new world, and Wellington said to me quite truly, "This is not a new reign, it is a new dynasty."' All the glories of the past reign were forgotten and the vices of the King who had presided over them were maliciously 'exaggerated'.[36]

As though he wished to emphasize the difference between himself and his brother, and to show that he was quite the bluff, simple, economical Englishman, King William IV pulled down most of the Royal Lodge; he replaced the German band with a smaller English one; he pruned the Windsor Castle staff and dismissed the French cooks; he had the recently installed gas installation pulled out; he sent the animals in the royal menagerie to the London Zoo; he made over a miscellaneous collection of treasures and objects of art to the nation. His brother had been very fond of such 'knicknackery', he explained when inspecting one of his pictures, but he couldn't see much in it himself. Aye, it might be pretty. 'Damned expensive taste, though.'

His brother had not only collected this particular sort of knicknackery. His wardrobes and chests of drawers were found to be crammed with all manner of articles, new and old, with which he had been unable to bring himself to part. As well as his immense collection of coats and suits, waistcoats and shirts, boots and breeches, gloves and hats and walking sticks, there were, so Charles Greville learned, 'five hundred pocketbooks, of different dates, and in every one of them money'.[37]* There were vast numbers of wigs, dirty handkerchiefs and faded nosegays; there were three hundred whips, 'canes without number, every sort of uniform, the costumes of all the orders in Europe, splendid furs, pelisses, etc.' and, among countless other pieces of clothing, a dozen pairs of new corduroy riding-breeches ordered from his tailor long after he had given up riding. There were quantities of women's gloves, and locks of women's hair 'of all colours and lengths, some having the powder and pomatum yet sticking to them', and huge packets of love letters, including copies of his own, 'descriptive of the most furious passion'.[38]†

---

* In 1829 the King spent £228 on a huge variety of pocket-books (RA 28915).

† The bulk of this correspondence, including letters 'expressive of ardent attachment' that had passed between the King and Mrs Fitzherbert, were burned by Knighton and Wellington as the King's executors. Letters which the King had written 'in great abundance' to Lady Jersey had already been burned by her executor, Lord Clarendon,

Even more might have been discovered had not Knighton already taken it upon himself to destroy the most heated and compromising of the letters, and had not Lady Conyngham removed various trinkets to which she felt herself entitled. According to current gossip, indeed, she took more than a few trinkets. She was alleged to have taken whole wagonloads of treasure into the obscurity which thereafter surrounded her until her death in 1861, a widow of ninety-one, at her country house in Kent. Contemporary cartoons portrayed her standing in the Castle between curtains framing shelves of money bags and jewels, and, assisted by her husband and daughter, vigorously packing up her loot.[39] When, soon after the King's death, she and her family left the Castle, Miss Margaretta Brown, sister-in-law of one of the Windsor canons, celebrated her departure by writing in her diary, underlining each word with heavy strokes, '*GOOD RIDDANCE*. I am glad we are going to have a *QUEEN*.'[40]

The departure of the Conynghams was not regretted. But, despite *The Times*'s vilification of their former patron and protector, despite the general public's indifference to his death, there were still those who, years later, were reduced to tears by their affectionate memories of him. Riding out with Sir John Cope's hounds in 1833, Wellington galloped past 'skeletons of the tents' near the late King's fishing temples at Virginia Water. The sight of the ruins made him 'quite unhappy'. 'Alas!'

---

in the presence of her son (*Creevey Papers*, 368). Mrs Fitzherbert, who did not trust Knighton, at first declined to hand over the King's letters in her possession; and it was not until August 1833 that she gave her formal consent to their destruction (Wellington Papers, Miscellaneous 31, 24 August 1833). Soon afterwards nearly all of these letters were burned by Wellington in the drawing-room of her house in the presence of her friend, Lord Albemarle. There were so many of them that after several hours' work Wellington said to Albemarle, 'I think, my Lord, we had better hold our hand for a while, or we shall set the old woman's chimney on fire' (Albemarle, ii, 71). Mrs Fitzherbert insisted on keeping some papers, including those which established her marriage to the King, and these were preserved in Messrs Coutts's vaults until 1905 when they passed into the Royal Archives. Wellington was always determined that they should never be opened, and threatened to move for an injunction from Chancery if any attempt were made to publish them. He told John Gurwood, his private secretary, that 'the publication would be mischievous, as the Prince by marrying a Catholic had by law forfeited the crown'. (Sir George Seymour's annotations to Langdale's *Memoirs of Mrs Fitzherbert*, Seymour of Ragley MSS, CR 114/A/536/7). The King's marriage to Mrs Fitzherbert was not made public until after Wellington's death.

he said to Charles Davis, Huntsman of the Royal Buckhounds, 'The poor King! Many a day have I passed with him in those tents!'

Davis 'burst out crying, and was obliged to pull up his horse'.[41]

Some years before, Wellington had referred to the King as 'a man of universal accomplishments';[42] and at the time of his death he had spoken in the House of Lords of his being acknowledged by all to be 'the most accomplished man of his age'. 'My Lords,' the Duke had declared, 'his Majesty's manners . . . received a polish, his understanding acquired a degree of cultivation, almost unknown in any individual. . . . No man ever approached him without having evidence of his dignity, his condescension, his ability, and his fitness for the exalted station which he occupied. . . . Upon every occasion [he evinced] a degree of knowledge and of talent much beyond that which could reasonably be expected of an individual holding his high station.'[43]

In lapidary inscriptions a man is not on oath; and on listening to these extravagant tributes Lord Grey was observed to 'smile a little'.[44] But Wellington's eulogy was not wholly insincere. He recognized that the nation would always have cause to be grateful to a man who had been 'a most magnificent patron of the arts in this country, and in the world', that with the King's acknowledged faults went many varied virtues. 'He was, indeed,' he eventually decided, 'the most extraordinary compound of talent, wit, buffoonery, obstinacy and good feeling – in short a medley of the most opposite qualities, with a great preponderance of good – that I ever saw in any character in my life.'[45]

It is a fitting epitaph. Prince Talleyrand provided a shorter one, no less apt: 'Kings nowadays are always seeking popularity, a pointless pursuit. King George IV was *un roi grand seigneur*. There are no others left.'[46]

References

For full bibliographical details, see Sources, pp. 389–403.

Abbreviations:

RA	—Royal Archives
BM	—British Museum
BM *Sat*	—*British Museum Catalogue of Political and Personal Satires*
PRO	—Public Record Office
HMCR	—Historical Manuscripts Commission Reports
WSD	—Wellington Supplementary Despatches
WDCM	—Wellington Despatches Correspondence and Memoranda
Asp/P	—Aspinall, ed., *Correspondence of George, Prince of Wales*
Asp/K	—Aspinall, ed., *Letters of King George IV*
Asp (*Charlotte*)	—Aspinall, ed., *Letters of the Princess Charlotte*

*

1 WHIGS OR TORIES? (pages 1–15)

1 *Moore Journals*, i, 255
2 *Gentleman's Magazine*, lxxxi, 587; *The Times*, 21 June 1811; Buckingham *(Regency)*, i, 99–102; *Abbot Diary*, ii, 336–9; Huish, ii, 44–7; Fitzgerald, ii, 46–9; Fulford *(George IV)*, 111–15
3 RA 36568–9, 5 June 1811
4 *Farington Diary*, vii, 200
5 *Berry Journal*, ii, 499
6 *Wilkins*, ii, 122
7 Seymour of Ragley MSS, Sir George Seymour's annotations to Langdale's *Life*, CR 114/A/536/7
8 Brighton Pavilion MSS; Langdale, 89; Seymour of Ragley MSS; Wellington Papers, Miscellaneous 31

References

9 RA (Geo IV Accounts) 29895–903, 30370, 50229; Coutts Archives; Wellington Papers, Miscellaneous, 31, 14 August 1814

10 Egerton MSS, 3262, f 83, quoted in Asp/P, viii, 405

11 *Shelley Letters*, 99–100

12 RA His Royal Highness's Establishment, 1811

13 *Farington Diary*, vi, 244

14 Richardson *(George IV)*, 109

15 *Mitford Letters*, i, 134, 136–7; Richardson *(George IV)*, 112; Fitzgerald, ii, 51–2

16 *Berry Journal*, ii, 471

17 *Ibid.*

18 *Plumer Ward*, ii, 319–20

19 *Farington Journal*, vi, 225

20 *Ibid.*, 204–5

21 *Ibid.*, vii, 22 August 1811

22 Howick MSS, quoted in Asp/P, viii, 52

23 *Glenbervie Journals*, ii, 127

24 Asp/P, viii, 3–4

25 *Creevey Papers*, 148

26 *Ibid.*

27 Grattan, v, 427; Roberts, 360

28 Dalling, *Palmerston*, i, 121

29 *Creevey Papers*, 145–6

30 Asp/P, viii, 3

31 *Ibid.*

32 *Dropmore Papers*, x, 166

33 *Ibid.*, ix, 329

34 *Francis Memoirs*, ii, 371; Roberts, 80–1, 339

35 *Romilly Memoirs*, iii, 12; Asp/P, viii, 7, 53–4; *Parliamentary Debates*, xxi, 911–33

36 RA Perceval Papers, Add MSS 21/11, 19 May 1811

37 Asp/P, viii, 7

38 *Ibid.*, 8

39 *Ibid.*, 9

40 *Creevey Papers*, 148–9

41 RA 47294, 16 July 1811

42 Macalpine and Hunter, 160–1

43 *Creevey Papers*, 148–9

44 *Ibid.*, 150

45 Buckingham *(Regency)*, 145

46 *Leveson Gower Correspondence*, ii, 422

References

47 Buckingham *(Regency)*, i, 145; *Leveson Gower Correspondence*, ii, 426
48 Asp *(Charlotte)*, 16; Macalpine and Hunter, 230
49 Buckingham *(Regency)*, i, 162
50 Asp *(Charlotte)*, 18
51 Buckingham *(Regency)*, i, 178
52 Egerton MSS 3262, f 81, quoted in Asp/P, viii, 232
53 *Farington Journal*, vii, 62
54 Bowood MSS, quoted in Asp/P, viii, 235
55 Howick MSS, quoted in Asp/P, viii, 240
56 Bowood MSS, quoted in Asp/P, viii, 274
57 *Ibid.*
58 *Farington Journal*, vii, 72
59 Buckingham *(Regency)*, i, 178
60 Bowood MSS, quoted in Asp/P, viii, 300
61 *Leveson Gower Correspondence*, ii, 429
62 Egerton MSS 3262, f 89, quoted in Asp/P, viii, 406
63 Harewood MSS, quoted in Asp/P, viii, 459

2   AN ADONIS OF LOVELINESS (pages 16–35)
1 Asp/P, viii, 303
2 Roberts, 371
3 *Dropmore Papers*, x, 212; *Parliamentary Debates*, xii, 39 f
4 Buckingham *(Regency)*, i, 230–1; *Romilly Memoirs*, iii, 11
5 *Dropmore Papers*, x, 213–20; Roberts, 379–80
6 Asp/P, viii, 313
7 Buckingham *(Regency)*, i, 262
8 Dropmore MSS, quoted by Ziegler *(Addington)*, 304; Buckingham *(Regency)*, i, 219
9 Buckingham *(Regency)*, i, 238–9
10 Roberts, 382; Buckingham *(Regency)*, i, 180, 240; Holland *(Further Memoirs)*, 125
11 RA 19330–7, 28 February 1812
12 Leigh Hunt *(Autobiography)*, i, 255–6; *Dropmore Papers*, x, 227
13 RA 19411–12, 17 March 1812
14 RA 19437–8, 20 March 1812, 19486, 26 March 1812
15 *Creevey Papers*, 160
16 *Ibid.*, 159
17 Holland *(Further Memoirs)*, 121–4
18 *Parliamentary Debates*, xxii, 85 (19 March 1812)
19 *Ibid.*

20 Buckingham *(Regency)*, i, 250
21 *Creevey Papers*, 146
22 Harrowby MSS, 29 May 1812; Rolo, 90
23 *Parliamentary Debates*, xxiii, 281; Roberts, 384
24 Buckingham *(Regency)*, i, 332
25 *Creevey Papers*, 157; Buckingham *(Regency)*, i, 330
26 WSD, vii, 282; Roberts, 401
27 Roberts, 371–405
28 *Creevey Papers*, 158
29 Brougham *(Memoirs)*, ii, 180
30 *Parliamentary Debates*, xxii, 332–64; Asp/K, i, lix 2
31 RA 18983–4; Asp/P, viii, 278
32 Perceval MSS, quoted in Asp/P, viii, 241
33 Perceval MSS, quoted in Asp/P, viii, 256–7
34 RA 39596–601, 30 December 1811
35 Alnwick MSS, quoted in Asp/P, viii, 240
36 RA 36593, 31 December 1811
37 *Abbot Diary*, ii, 354
38 RA Add, 10, 11, 12 and 13 *passim*
39 Buckingham *(Regency)*, i, 288
40 Aspinall *(Politics and Press)*, 92
41 *Morning Post*, 18 March 1812
42 *Examiner*, 22 March 1812
43 Jackson, iii, 18; Richardson *(George IV)*, 116–17
44 *Byron Letters*, ii, 205–6; *Shelley Letters*, 208, 292; Richardson *(George IV)*, 117, 122
45 Fitzgerald, ii, 92
46 Taylor, i, 208
47 *Gronow Reminiscences*, ii, 12
48 *Ibid.*
49 Jesse *(Brummell)*, ii, 18
50 *Edgeworth Letters*, ii, 106
51 *Glenbervie Journals*, ii, 19; Richardson *(George IV)*, 126
52 Richardson *(George IV)*, 124
53 *Don Juan*, lxxxiv
54 Smiles, 89
55 Fitzgerald, ii, 87
56 *Parliamentary Debates*, xxv, 280f; BM *Sat*, ix, 365
57 *Examiner*, 16 January 1814; *Gentleman's Magazine*, lxxxiv, 88; BM *Sat*, ix, 340–1
58 Pretyman Papers (Ipswich), HA 119 [January 1814]

59 *Ibid.*
60 *Ibid.*
61 Asp *(Charlotte)*, 112
62 *Greville Diary*, i, 4–5
63 *Frampton Diary*, i, 203–4; *Jerningham Letters*, ii, 53–4; Raikes, iii, 57
64 *Creevey Papers*, i, 197
65 *Frampton Journal*, ii, 225
66 Nicolson, 110–11
67 *Ibid.*, 111
68 *The Times*, 22 April 1814; Nicolson, 107
69 Nicolson, 112
70 *Abbot Diary*, ii, 502
71 *Creevey Papers*, 196
72 *Spencer-Stanhope Letter-Bag*, i, 318; *European Magazine*, lxv, 551–3; *Examiner*, 1814, 393f.
73 *Edgeworth Letters*, 333
74 Nicolson, 115–16
75 *Jerningham Letters*, ii, 53
76 *Moore Journals*, ii, 19–20
77 *Examiner*, 18 June 1814

3 PRINCESS CAROLINE (pages 36–46)

1 *Farington Diary*, vii, 19
2 *Bury Diary*, iii, 158
3 Rogers *(Table-Talk)*, 217
4 *Bury Diary*, ii, 16
5 *Ibid.*, 170
6 *Ibid.*
7 Stuart *(Foster)*, 191–2
8 Quoted by Fitzgerald, ii, 127
9 *Bury Diary*, ii, 148
10 HMCR Kenyon MSS, 565–6
11 Asp/K, i, 517
12 *Ibid.*, 518
13 *Bury Diary*, i, 226
14 Asp *(Charlotte)*, 6, 16–17, 18, 22
15 Asp/P, viii, 120
16 Bowood MSS, quoted in Asp/P, viii, 161
17 RA Box 8, 29 September 1812
18 Brougham MSS, 12, 19, 28 September 1812

19 Bowood MSS, quoted in Asp/P, viii, 212
20 *Ibid.*
21 RA Geo IV, Box 8, 4 January 1813
22 *Creevey Papers*, 176
23 *Abbot Diary*, ii, 420; Twiss, ii, 230; New, 98
24 *Knight Autobiography*, ii, 219
25 *Annual Register*, 1813, 344-7
26 Airlie, 17-18
27 New, 96; Aspinall *(Politics and the Press)*, 307
28 Asp/K, i, 228
29 Brougham MSS, 22 May 1814
30 Brougham *(Memoirs)*, ii, 193
31 RA 36693, 23 May 1814
32 RA Box 8, 26 May 1814
33 RA 36696, 24 May 1814
34 Creevey MSS, Brougham to Creevey, 6 June, quoted by New, 103
35 Greenwood, ii, 320-1
36 Canning MS Diaries, Canning Papers, 29d (Leeds)
37 New, 107
38 *Ibid.*
39 *Creevey Papers*, 199-200
40 RA Geo IV, Box 8, 4 July 1814
41 *Ibid.*
42 *Creevey Papers*, 199
43 Brougham MSS, 30 June 1814
44 Creevey MSS, quoted by New, 108; Creevey, 201-2
45 *Creevey Papers*, 202-3
46 Brougham *(Memoirs)*, ii, 254
47 Brougham MSS, quoted by New, 115

4 PRINCESS CHARLOTTE (pages 47-65)

1 Brougham *(Memoirs)*, ii, 172
2 *Glenbervie Journals*, ii, 153
3 *Berry Journal*, i, 192
4 Quoted by Nicolson, 110
5 Quoted by Creston, 126
6 Asp/K, i, 191, 202-3
7 RA Geo IV, Box 8, Envelope 6
8 Asp/K, i, 518
9 *Ibid.*, 519

10 *Ibid.*, 522
11 *Ibid.*, 204
12 *Knight Autobiography*, ii, 198
13 *Ibid.*, 185; *Bury Diary*, i, 193
14 *Ibid.*
15 RA 49854–7, 24 July 1814
16 Luttrell, 155; RA 49771–4, 21–5 January 1813, 49792–3, 13 April 1813
17 RA 49713–17, 9–18 January 1813
18 RA 49808, 30 June 1813
19 Creston, 170–1; *Knight Autobiography*, ii, 227
20 Brougham *(Memoirs)*, ii, 178
21 RA 49147–8 (undated)
22 *Creevey Papers*, 181–2
23 *Ibid.*, 184
24 *Ibid.*; Creston, 175; *Knight Autobiography*, ii, 252
25 *Bury Journal*, ii, 203
26 Grey Papers (Durham), Box 43, File 7
27 *Knight Autobiography*, ii, 230, 254–5
28 Grey Papers (Durham), Box 43, 16 October 1813
29 *Ibid.*, 19 October 1813
30 *Ibid.*, 24, 29 October 1813
31 Brougham *(Memoirs)*, ii, 178–9
32 *Knight Autobiography*, ii, 266–7
33 Asp *(Charlotte)*, 221
34 *Bury Diary*, i, 207
35 *Knight Autobiography*, ii, 274–6
36 Grey Papers (Durham), 2 February 1814
37 *Ibid.*, 7 February 1814
38 *Ibid.*, 9 February 1814, 14 February 1814
39 Asp *(Charlotte)*, 228
40 Webster *(Castlereagh)*, i, 54
41 Holland *(Further Memoirs)*, 198; Buckingham *(Regency)*, ii, 85–7
42 *Bury Journal*, i, 211; Asp/K, i, 444; Creston, 192; Nicolson, 110
43 Grey Papers (Durham), 13 April 1814, 15 April 1814
44 RA Add 22/3, 15 April 1814
45 Grey Papers (Durham), 17 April 1814
46 RA Add 22/4, 18 April 1814
47 Grey Papers (Durham), 6 April 1814
48 RA Add 22/5–6, 22 April 1814
49 RA Add 22/7, 25 April 1814
50 RA Add 22/8–9, 25 and 28 April 1814

51 RA Add 22/10, 27 April 1814
52 RA Add 22/11, 27 April 1814
53 RA Add 22/13, 30 April 1814
54 RA Add 22/13–17, 30 April to 5 May 1814
55 RA Add 22/18–31, 8–15 May 1814
56 Grey Papers (Durham) Box 43
57 *Ibid.*
58 *Ibid.*
59 RA Add 22/33–44, 5–10 June 1814
60 Brougham *(Memoirs)*, ii, 184
61 Quoted by Creston, 203
62 Asp/K, i, 457–8
63 Stockmar *(Memoirs)*, i, 10
64 Brougham MSS, 11 June 1814, quoted by New, 104
65 Brougham *(Memoirs)*, ii, 208–9
66 RA Add MSS, 22/46, 16 June 1814
67 RA Add MSS, 22/47, 18 June 1814
68 Quoted by Creston, 215
69 RA Add MSS, 22/50, 19 June 1814

5 THE WARWICK HOUSE AFFAIR (pages 66–74)

1 *Creevey Papers*, 197–8
2 RA 49834–5, 16 May 1814
3 Pretyman Papers (Ipswich), HA 119, 16 July 1814
4 Asp/K, i, 463–7; *Knight Autobiography*, ii, 301
5 Asp *(Charlotte)*, 175
6 *Greville Diary*, ii, 319
7 Asp *(Charlotte)*, 238
8 *Knight Autobiography*, ii, 301
9 Asp *(Charlotte)*, 239
10 Pretyman Papers (Ipswich), HA 119, 28 July 1814
11 *Ibid.*; Brougham *(Memoirs)*, ii, 227–30; *Edinburgh Review*, October 1838; Twiss, i, 523; Grey Papers (Durham); Asp/K, i, 468; RA Box 13, 12 July 1814; Creston, 218–28; *Knight Autobiography*, ii, 303–5; *Examiner*, 17 July 1814
12 Brougham *(Memoirs)*, ii, 186
13 *Ibid.*, 188
14 *Ibid.*, 195
15 Asp *(Charlotte)*, 137–8
16 Brougham *(Memoirs)*, ii, 253–5

17 *Ibid.*, 258
18 *Bury Diary*, i, 179; Greenwood, ii, 328–31; *The Times*, 17 August 1814
19 Quoted by Fulford *(George IV)*, 151
20 Brougham *(Memoirs)*, ii, 242
21 *Morning Post*, 11 July 1814
22 Quoted by Creston, 229
23 Brougham *(Memoirs)*, ii, 240
24 Yonge, iii, 14

6 IMPRESARIO, COLLECTOR AND PATRON (pages 75–87)
1 RA 19273–4: Asp/K, i, 20
2 *The Times*, 23 July 1814; *Sun*, 23 July 1814; *Morning Post*, 23 July 1814
3 *The Times*, 28 July–2 August 1814; *Morning Post*, 28 July–2 August; *Sun*, 28 July–3 August; *European Magazine*, lxvi, 174–6; *Gentleman's Magazine*, lxxxiv, 2, 179ff.; *Examiner*, 1814, 503–5
4 *Courier*, 3 August 1814
5 Raikes, iii, 58
6 Rogers *(Table-Talk)*, 221
7 *Arbuthnot Journal*, i, 154
8 Cooper, ii, 351
9 Quoted by Creston, 134
10 Francis *(Memoirs)*, i, 218
11 RA 21345: Asp/K, i, 419
12 RA Geo IV, Box 8, 20 June 1815
13 Egerton MSS 3262, f 99, quoted in Asp/P, viii, 424
14 'The Waterloo Despatch'
15 *The Times*, 22 July 1814
16 Musgrave *(Brighton)*, 148
17 *Farington Journal*, vii, 205
18 Finch MSS (Bodleian), d 19, quoted in Richardson *(George IV)*, 131
19 Summerson, 214–22
20 Pückler-Muskau, ii, 38
21 *Edgeworth Letters*, i, 287
22 Steegman, 158–9
23 Morshead *(Royal Lodge)*, 10–38
24 *Farington Journal*, vi, 244
25 Royal Academy, Lawrence Correspondence, iii, 5, quoted by Richardson *(George IV)*, 192
26 *Ibid.*, ii, 32, quoted by Richardson *(George IV)*, 153

27 Cunningham, *Lives of the most eminent British painters*, iii, 59, quoted by Richardson *(George IV)*, 153

28 RA 22025–6: Asp/K ii, 181; Lloyd, 372–3; Richardson *(George IV)*, 153–4

29 Royal Academy, Council Minutes, v, 300 sqq, quoted by Richardson *(George IV)*, 160

30 Millar *(Tudor, Stuart and Early Georgian)*, 47

31 Memes, 375–6

32 Austen-Leigh, 146–8; Chapman, 429–30

7 CRANBOURNE LODGE AND CLAREMONT PARK (pages 88–101)

1 Asp *(Charlotte)*, 184

2 RA, Princess Mary's Memorandum, 1 January 1815: Asp/K, i, 522

3 Brougham *(Memoirs)*, ii, 247

4 Grey Papers (Durham), 5 September 1814

5 Asp/K, i, 491

6 *Ibid.*

7 *Ibid.*, Albemarle, i, 295

8 BM Add MSS 38261, f 28, quoted in Asp/K, i, 491–2

9 *Ibid.*

10 Asp/K, ii, 2

11 *Ibid.*, 60

12 *Castlereagh Correspondence*, x, 64

13 Grey Papers (Durham), 1 January 1815

14 Asp/K, ii, 30–1

15 *Ibid.*, 31–4

16 *Ibid.*, 37

17 *Ibid.*, 39

18 Grey Papers (Durham), Mercer Elphinstone to Earl Grey, 23 September 1814

19 Creston, 239

20 *Ibid.*

21 *Bury Journal*, ii, 17

22 Asp *(Charlotte)*, 186

23 *Creevey Papers*, 425

24 Asp/K, ii, 141

25 Quoted by Creston, 239

26 Quoted by Musgrave *(Brighton)*, 104

27 RA Add 11/270, 19 January 1816

28 Aspinall *(Charlotte)*, 189

29 Asp/K, ii, 146

30 RA 36789, 10 June 1816, 36770–1, 2 March 1816, 36784–5, 14 April 1816
31 RA 36784–5, 4 April 1816
32 RA 21889–90, 3 March 1816
33 RA 21901–2, undated [5 March 1816]; *Parliamentary Debates*, xxxiii, 378–9, 1064–78
34 *Abbot Diary*, ii, 570
35 Creston, 243
36 Foster, 415–6
37 *Bury Diary*, ii, 104
38 *Ibid.*, 163
39 Stockmar *(Memoirs)*, i, 47
40 Crawford Muniments (Balcarres), Lady Anne Lindsay's MSS Memoirs, vi, 73
41 RA 49152 (undated)
42 Macalpine and Hunter, 243
43 *Harcourt Papers*, x, 82
44 Asp/K, i, 522; ii, 60
45 *Ibid.*, ii, 204–5
46 *Ibid.*, 210
47 *Barnard Letters*, 262; *The Times*, 6 November 1817; Twiss, i, 555; Macalpine and Hunter, 241
48 *London Medical and Physical Journal*, 1817, quoted by Macalpine and Hunter, 242–3
49 Green, *Memoirs of her Late Royal Highness Charlotte Augusta*, 386–8
50 *Ibid.*; Macalpine and Hunter, 242
51 *Creevey Papers*, 266
52 Asp/K, ii, 210
53 *The Times*, 10 November 1817
54 Rogers *(Table-Talk)*, 219
55 *The Times*, 20 November 1817
56 RA 22121–2, 15 December 1817
57 RA 36805–6, 20 November 1817
58 RA Add 12/303, 28 November 1817
59 *The Times*, 14 November 1817
60 Quoted by Creston, 264
61 *The Times*, 14 November 1817
62 *Croker Papers*, i, 103
63 Asp/K, ii, 212
64 *Frampton Journal*, 299
65 *Croker Papers*, i, 105
66 Asp/K, ii, 223

67 *Ibid.*, 231
68 Buckingham *(Regency)*, ii, 203

8 ROYAL MARRIAGES (pages 102–19)

1 Brougham *(Memoirs)*, ii, 332
2 Oman *(Gascoyne)*, 93
3 Holland *(Further Memoirs)*, 248
4 Parker, i, 237
5 *Bury Journal*, ii, 92
6 Holland *(Further Memoirs)*, 250
7 *Abbot Diary*, ii, 600
8 Buckingham *(Regency)*, ii, 183
9 *Leadbeater Papers*, ii, 290
10 Adeane *(Early Married Life)*, 401
11 Cobbett, 397
12 *Creevey Papers*, 272
13 *Croker Papers*, ii, 39
14 *Creevey Papers*, 277
15 RA Add 13/53 (undated), 12/190–270, 6 December 1812–16, 11/252, 17 April 1814, 280, 6 July 1817
16 Stuart *(Daughters)*, 115
17 RA Add 10/55, 10/56: Stuart *(Daughters)*, 110–11
18 RA Add 10/59 (undated) [December 1812]
19 RA Add 10/57: Stuart *(Daughters)*, 105
20 RA Add 11/211, 2 December 1812
21 RA 36622–3: Stuart *(Daughters)*, 104
22 RA Add 10/61, 16 December 1812
23 RA Add 11/243, 17 February 1814
24 Asp/K, i, 341; Willis, 117
25 Asp/K, ii, 64
26 *Ibid*, 113
27 *Ibid.*, 90
28 Archives of the Grand Duke of Mecklenburg, quoted by Willis, 140, Duchess of Cumberland to her father, 29 August 1815
29 Asp/K, ii, 89
30 *Ibid.*, 94–5
31 RA 47457–8, 4 September 1815
32 Asp/K, ii, 101
33 *Ibid.*, 103
34 *Bathurst Papers*, 384; Asp/K, ii, 105–6

References

35 Asp/K, ii, Major General Bloomfield's Narrative, 110–11
36 RA 47468–9, 4 September 1815
37 Asp/K, ii, 111, 114
38 Asp/K, ii, 121
39 Archives of the Grand Duke of Mecklenburg, 6 February 1816, quoted by Willis, 148
40 *Ibid.*, 9 April 1816
41 *Ibid.*, 3 May 1816
42 *Ibid.*, 14 April 1816
43 RA 36817–18, 10 April 1818
44 Archives of the Grand Duke of Mecklenburg, 26 July 1818, quoted by Willis, 162
45 Asp/K, ii, 251
46 RA 44307, 26 January 1815
47 Stockmar *(Memoirs)*, i, 52
48 Marples, 152–3; *The Times*, 3 July 1816; Stuart *(Daughters)*, 114
49 Chatsworth MSS, 5 August 1791
50 Asp/K, ii, 227
51 *Knight Autobiography*, i, 282; Asp/P, viii, 205–6; Buckingham *(Regency)*, i, 146; Asp/K, ii, 138; Ziegler *(William IV)*, 112–22; RA 22189
52 *Abbot Diary*, ii, 347
53 Asp/K, ii, 243; Buckingham *(Regency)*, ii, 232
54 *Jerningham Letters*, ii, 118
55 Asp/K, ii, 244
56 BM Add MSS 38574 f 42, quoted in Asp/K, ii, 244
57 BM Add MSS 38574 f 15, quoted in Asp/K, ii, 245
58 RA 22140–1, 22142, 22143–4; Asp/K, ii, 236–8; *Creevey Papers*, 269
59 Webster *(Castlereagh)*, ii, 11
60 *Creevey Papers*, 270–1
61 RA Add 11/282, 4 November 1817
62 RA Add 11/285, 18 December 1817
63 RA Add 11/290, 25 January 1818
64 RA Add 11/294: Stuart *(Daughters)*, 178
65 RA Add 11/295, 29 January 1818
66 *Ibid.*
67 RA Add 11/296, 30 January 1818
68 RA Add 11/297: Stuart *(Daughters)*, 180
69 RA Add 11/300, 5 February 1818
70 RA Add 13/60, 5 February 1818
71 RA Add 11/300, 5 February 1818

72 RA Add 11/301, 6 February 1818, 11/302, 9 February 1818; Stuart *(Daughters)*, 181
73 RA Add 11/304, 17 February 1818
74 *The Times*, 24 February 1818
75 Buckingham *(Regency)*, ii, 226
76 RA Add 11/312, 26 June 1818, 11/328, 2 April 1820
77 RA Add 11/308, 24 May 1818
78 *Morning Post*, 8 April 1818
79 Fitzgerald *(Dukes and Princesses)*, i, 289
80 *Morning Post*, 8 April 1818; *Glenbervie Journals*, 8 April 1818
81 RA Add 11/329, 8 August 1821

9 REPASTS AND RIOTS (pages 120–31)

1 RA 36713–4, 30 October 1814, 36762, 28 December 1815, 36765–6, 27 January 1816
2 RA 36701, 27 June 1814
3 RA 36617, 36619, 36655, 36656, 36658, 36689, 36690, 36734, 36735, 36762, 36803, 13 May 1812–27 January 1817
4 RA 13/63, 30 July 1818
5 *Greville Memoirs*, i, 54
6 RA Sir Herbert Taylor's Papers, 50343–4, 50353, 50354, 50360, 50365, 31 October 1818–17 November 1818
7 RA 50363–4, 17 November 1818
8 *Croker Papers*, ii, 28
9 *Jerningham Letters*, ii, 122
10 RA Add 11/299, 3 February 1818
11 RA Add 21/68, 8 December 1818
12 Musgrave *(Brighton)*, 158
13 RA 21906–10, 15 March 1816
14 *Parliamentary Debates*, xxxiii, 201
15 RA 21917–19 (undated) [20 March 1816]
16 *Sussex Weekly Advertiser*, 10 February 1817, quoted by Musgrave *(Brighton)*, 157
17 Musgrave *(Pavilion)*; Brayley; Steegman, 44–5
18 Musgrave *(Brighton)*, 159
19 RA 33954, 30 June 1821, 31052–7, 8 November 1819; Coutts Archives
20 *Croker Papers*, 8 December 1818
21 Lieven *(Metternich Letters)*, 60
22 *Croker Papers*, 14 December 1818
23 Wilkins, ii, 46; Musgrave *(Brighton)*, 154

24 Fulford *(George IV)*, 178–80
25 *Croker Papers*, 15 December 1818
26 *Creevey Papers*, 279
27 *Wilberforce*, iv, 277
28 Quoted by Musgrave *(Brighton)*, 152
29 RA Coutts Papers, Y 56/22, 31 January 1819
30 *Greville Memoirs*, i, 54
31 RA M4/26, Duchess of Kent to Earl Grey, quoted by Longford *(Victoria)*, 23; Woodham-Smith, 35
32 *Ibid.*
33 RA Coutts Papers, Y56/27, 17 August 1819
34 Reith *(Police Idea)*, 162–3
35 Twiss, ii, 70
36 Butler *(Great Reform Bill)*, 34–5
37 Sidmouth MSS, quoted by Ziegler *(Addington)*, 373
38 RA 48778–9, 48780–1, 12 August 1819
39 *Jerningham Letters*, ii, 155
40 Sidmouth MSS, quoted by Ziegler *(Addington)*, 383; Fitzgerald, ii, 230
41 Fitzwilliam Papers (Delapre Abbey), Althorp to Milton, 15 February 1820

10 THE MILAN COMMISSION (pages 132–44)

1 *Letters to Ivy*, 292
2 RA Geo IV, Box 8, 21 November 1817
3 *Ibid.*
4 *Leveson Gower Correspondence*, ii, 534–5
5 RA Geo IV, Box 8, 19 August 1816, 30 September 1819, 20 February 1817, 15 April 1820
6 RA Geo IV, Box 10
7 Brougham MSS
8 RA Geo IV, Box 8, 2 May 1816
9 RA Geo IV, Box 8, 29 March 1817
10 Asp/K, ii, 252
11 RA Geo IV, Box 23, Browne to Ompteda, 20 November 1818
12 RA Geo IV, Box 23, Browne to Ompteda, 30 December 1818, 8 January 1819
13 RA Geo IV, Box 8, 21 November 1818
14 RA Geo IV, Box 23, Browne to Ompteda, 21 November 1818
15 RA Geo IV, Box 8, 2 November 1818
16 RA Geo IV, Box 9, Report of William Cooke and John A. Powell, 13 July 1819
17 *Report of Proceedings*, i, 450–9

18 *Ibid.*, 25–96
19 *Ibid.*
20 *Ibid.*
21 *Ibid.*, 95–109, 115–29
22 *Ibid.*, 305–421
23 RA Geo IV, Box 9. Evidence of Felice Porta, Giuseppe Merati, Giovanni Fontana, Luigi Galdini, Gaspare Riva, Paolo Raggazoni, Giuseppe Rastelli, Eugenio Bottachi, Genevra Buro, Marco Bergante, Daniele Orsenigo, Giuseppe Galli, Luigi Rossi, Antonio Rossi, Giuseppe Andreoni, Francesca Marrazzi, Pietro Sardella, Pietro Cuchi, Barbara Cress, Maurice Crede, Luigi Majocchi, Alessandro Finetti, Giovanni Antonio Guggiare
24 *Report of Proceedings*, i, 268–83, 422–9
25 RA Geo IV, Box 11: Asp/K, ii, 272–85
26 BM Add MSS 38565, ff 20–22, quoted by New, 230; RA Geo IV, Box 8, 14 June 1819
27 RA Geo IV, Box 13 [March 1819]
28 *Creevey Papers*, 370
29 Buckingham *(George IV)*, ii, 197
30 RA Geo IV, Box 8, 17 June 1819
31 RA Geo IV, Box 8, 10 February 1820
32 Yonge, iii, 38–44

11 THE QUEEN ON TRIAL (pages 145–67)

1 Asp/K, ii, 298–9; RA 44330–1, 20 January 1820, 22363–4, 27 November 1819
2 *Knighton Memoirs*, i, 139
3 *The Times*, 31 January 1820, 1 February 1820
4 *Shelley Diary*, ii, 96
5 Lieven *(Metternich Letters)*, 5
6 *Creevey Papers*, 296
7 *Ibid.*, 298
8 *Ibid.*, 192, 389
9 *Greville Memoirs*, i, 87
10 RA 22410, 7 February 1820
11 *Croker Papers*, i, 157
12 *Ibid.*
13 *Greville Memoirs*, i, 25
14 RA Geo IV, Box 8, 10 February 1820
15 *Greville Memoirs*, i, 89; *Hobhouse Diary*, 26
16 Greenwood, ii, 339

References

17 Canning MS Diaries, 29 d, Canning Papers (Leeds); Stapleton, 291-2, 295
18 Twiss, ii, 3
19 *Hobhouse Diary*, 27
20 *Greville Memoirs*, i, 89
21 RA 22441: Asp/K, ii, 326
22 *Creevey Papers*, 297
23 Brougham MSS, quoted by New, 231
24 BM Add MSS 40344, f 17, quoted by New, 231
25 Brougham MSS, quoted by New, 232
26 Hook MSS, 23 February 1820
27 Brougham MSS, quoted by New, 232
28 BM Add MSS 38565, ff 93-4
29 RA Geo IV, Box 13, 4 June 1820
30 *Ibid.*
31 *Ibid.*
32 RA Geo IV, Box 8, 29 May 1820
33 BM Add MSS 38285, f 172
34 RA Geo IV, Box 13, 6 June 1820
35 *The Times*, 6 June 1820
36 Quoted by Hawes, 149
37 *Greville Memoirs*, i, 94
38 Lieven *(Metternich Letters)*, 30
39 *Croker Papers*, ii, 51
40 *Greville Memoirs*, i, 95
41 RA Coutts Papers, Y56/37, 4 July 1820
42 Buckingham *(George IV)*, i, 53
43 *Ibid.*, 51
44 *Jerningham Letters*, ii, 168-9
45 Quoted by Lean, 118
46 *Hobhouse Diary*, 28
47 *Greville Memoirs*, 23 September 1829; *Arbuthnot Journal*, i, 26
48 Oman *(Gascoyne)*, 207
49 Bartlett, 176
50 *Wilberforce*, v, 56
51 New, 252, 253
52 *Arbuthnot Journal*, i, 64
53 Patterson, *Burdett and his Times* (1931), ii, 518; Brougham *(Memoirs)*, ii, 385
54 Cobbett, 425
55 Lever, 36
56 New, 252-3

References

57 *Croker Papers*, ii, 249
58 *Greville Memoirs*, i, 97, 100
59 Grey-Bennett MSS Diary, quoted by Fitzgerald, ii, 243
60 Royal Academy, Lawrence Correspondence, iii, 48, quoted by Richardson
   (George IV), 207
61 *Scott Letters*, vi, 215
62 New, 252-3
63 Greenwood, ii, 341
64 *Croker Papers*, ii, 204
65 *Greville Memoirs*, i, 99
66 George *(English Political Caricature, 1793-1832)*, 191; Rickwood, *passim*
67 Rush, 311
68 *The Times*, 18 August 1820
69 *Wellington and his Friends*, 8-9
70 Fitzgerald, ii, 251; *The Times*, 18 August 1820; *Hobhouse Diary*, 34
71 Arnold, i, 144-7; *Fox Journal*, i, 50; New, 244; Hawes, 150
72 Lieven *(Metternich Letters)*, 68
73 *Ibid.*
74 *Creevey Papers*, 310; Hawes, 155
75 Wentworth Woodhouse Muniments (Sheffield) G 14, 17 August 1820
76 *Ibid.*
77 *Creevey Papers*, 311
78 *Greville Memoirs*, i, 105; *Fox Journal*, i, 39
79 *Creevey Papers*, 311
80 Lieven *(Metternich Letters)*, 50
81 *Ibid.*; *Creevey Papers*, 306-7
82 Palmerston Papers, C IV/4/3, 22 August 1820
83 Russell, *Collections and Recollections*, 22; Longford *(Wellington)*, 68;
   Anglesey, 366
84 *Hobhouse Diary*, 34; Lieven *(Metternich Letters)*, 150
85 Lieven *(Metternich Letters)*, 48
86 Wentworth Woodhouse Muniments (Sheffield) G 14, 18 August 1820
87 Palmerston Papers, C IV/4/3, 22 August 1820; Fitzgerald, ii, 89
88 Lever, 37
89 *Byron Letters*, v, 60-1; Richardson *(George IV)*, 206-7; Lieven *(Metternich
   Letters)*, 50-1; Randolph, ii, 39; Wentworth Woodhouse Muniments G 14,
   22 August 1820
90 Greenwood, ii, 349
91 Lieven *(Metternich Letters)*, 50-1, 55, 56
92 Wentworth Woodhouse Muniments G 14, 24 August 1820
93 Palmerston Papers (Emily Cowper to Frederick Lamb, 24 August 1820)

94 RA Geo IV, Box 10 (Evidence of Charles Broxholm)
95 RA Geo IV, Box 23, 4 July 1820
96 *Ibid.*
97 RA Geo IV, Box 8, 15 October 1820
98 *Ibid.*

12 'THE QUEEN FOR EVER!' (pages 168–88)
 1 RA Geo IV, Box 23, 29 September 1820
 2 RA Geo IV, Box 10
 3 RA Geo IV, Box 12
 4 RA Geo IV, Box 23, 9 September 1820
 5 *Ibid.*
 6 RA Geo IV, Box 10
 7 *Ibid.*, 28 October 1820
 8 *Ibid.*, 5 September 1820
 9 RA Geo IV, Box 23, 17 August 1820
10 RA Geo IV, Box 11, 25 September 1820
11 RA Geo IV, Box 13 (undated)
12 RA Geo IV, Box 23, 20 August 1820
13 RA Geo IV, Box 10, 4 September 1820
14 RA Geo IV, Box 23, 29 September 1820
15 RA Geo IV, Box 11 (undated)
16 RA Geo IV, Box 9
17 RA Geo IV, Box 10, 5 September 1820
18 RA Geo IV, Box 11, 23 September 1820
19 *The Times*, 25 August 1820
20 Wentworth Woodhouse Muniments (Sheffield) G 14, Letters 11 and 16
21 Yonge, iii, 107
22 *Creevey Papers*, 318
23 *Ibid.*, 321
24 Lieven *(Metternich Letters)*, 61
25 *Creevey Papers*, 316
26 Hawes, 156
27 Lever, 41
28 *Plumer Ward*, i, 56
29 *Bury Diary*, ii, 94
30 *Creevey Papers*, 321; *Greville Memoirs*, i, 102
31 Wentworth Woodhouse Muniments G 14, Letter 23
32 *Creevey Papers*, 322
33 Hawes, 155

34 *Ibid.*
35 Wentworth Woodhouse Muniments G 14, 15 October 1820
36 Asp/K, ii, 371
37 Brougham MSS *passim*
38 Wentworth Woodhouse Muniments G 14, 16 October 1820
39 *Creevey Papers*, 323
40 *Arbuthnot Journal*, i, 41
41 RA Geo IV, Box 13, MS Journal of J. A. Powell
42 Martin *(Lyndhurst)*, 187
43 *Creevey Papers*, 323
44 RA Geo IV, Box 23, MS Journal of J. A. Powell
45 *Report of Proceedings*, ii, 325–88
46 *Greville Memoirs*, i, 104
47 Wentworth Woodhouse Muniments F 64–100, 12 October 1820; *Greville Memoirs*, i, 106
48 *Plumer Ward*, ii, 58
49 *Greville Memoirs*, i, 108
50 Hawes, 158
51 Wentworth Woodhouse Muniments F 64–100, 17–19 October 1820
52 Harrowby MSS, 24 October 1820
53 Wentworth Woodhouse Muniments F 64–100, 23 October 1820
54 *Plumer Ward*, ii, 75
55 Fitzwilliam Papers (Delapre Abbey), 8 October–26 October 1820
56 Lieven *(Metternich Letters)*, 66
57 *Creevey Papers*, 332
58 *Ibid.*, 334
59 Lieven *(Metternich Letters)*, 52, 66
60 *Arbuthnot Journal*, i, 149
61 Wentworth Woodhouse Muniments G 14, 9 October 1820
62 Lieven *(Metternich Letters)*, 68
63 *Ibid.*, 69
64 Harrowby MSS, 24 October 1820
65 Lieven *(Metternich Letters)*, 66
66 *Ibid.*, 72
67 *Ibid.*, 70–1
68 *Hobhouse Diary*, 38, 39
69 Creevey MSS, quoted by New, 259
70 *Creevey Papers*, 339
71 Harrowby MSS, 24 October 1820
72 RA Coutts Papers, Y56/40, 5 September 1820
73 Brougham *(Memoirs)*, ii, 407

74 New, 259
75 RA Geo IV, Box 12
76 *Greville Memoirs*, i, 107
77 Yonge, iii, 108–9
78 *Hobhouse Diary*, 40
79 *Arbuthnot Journal*, i, 53
80 *Ibid.*, 43
81 *Ibid.*, 78
82 *Ibid.*, 79
83 *Hobhouse Diary*, 43
84 Buckingham (*George IV*), i, 83
85 RA22510, 22511–2: Asp/K, ii, 390–1
86 Greenwood, ii, 349
87 New, 260
88 Fitzwilliam MSS (Delapre Abbey), 18 November 1820
89 *Creevey Papers*, 338
90 Lieven (*Metternich Letters*), 73–4
91 New, 260
92 Lieven (*Metternich Letters*), 73

13 CORONATION (pages 189–201)

1 Buckingham (*George IV*), ii, 181
2 RA 29592–3, 6–22 January 1821
3 Mathews, 138–45
4 *Lyttelton Letters*, 236
5 *Ibid.*, 235
6 Buckingham (*George IV*), ii, 183
7 *Haydon Diary*, 339
8 *The Times*, 20 July 1821; Leigh Hunt, *Coronation Soliloquy*, quoted by Fulford, 228
9 *Arbuthnot Journal*, i, 108
10 *The Times*, 20 July 1821
11 *Scott Letters*, v, 38
12 *Abbot Journal*, iii, 233
13 RA Accounts: Asp/K, iii, 499
14 *The Times*, 20 July 1821
15 *Ibid.*
16 Wellington MSS, 29 July 1821; Lever, 86
17 *The Times*, 20 July 1821; *Morning Post*, 20 July 1821; Lever, 86–8
18 Denbigh MSS, 20 July 1821

19 *The Times*, 20 July 1821
20 Denbigh MSS, 20 July 1821
21 *Haydon Diary*, 341
22 *Arbuthnot Journal*, i, 108
23 Denbigh MSS, 20 July 1821
24 *The Times*, 20 July 1821; *Morning Post*, 20 July 1821; Fulford, 225–31; Richardson (*George IV*), 219–24
25 *Scott Letters*, v, 45
26 Denbigh MSS, 20 July 1821
27 *Abbot Journal*, iii, 233
28 Buckingham (*George IV*), i, 94
29 BM *Sat*, x, 14175, 14120, 14191, 14196, 14013
30 *The Times*, 7 February 1821
31 *Greville Memoirs*, i, 114
32 *Arbuthnot Journal*, i, 69
33 *The Times*, 7 February 1821
34 Fitzwilliam Papers (Delapre Abbey), Althorp to Milton, 4 December 1820
35 *Ibid.*
36 RA 22515–16: Asp/K, ii, 396–7
37 Lieven (*Metternich Letters*), 99
38 RA Geo IV, Box 13, 4 April 1821
39 *Ibid.*
40 Palmerston Papers, CIV/4/3, 12 May 1821
41 *Croker Papers*, 21 and 23 June 1821
42 RA Geo IV, Box 13, 10 May 1821–16 July 1821
43 RA Geo IV, Box 8, 3 June 1821
44 RA Geo IV, Box 13, 'Secret Intelligence', 10 May 1821
45 *Ibid.*, 6 April 1821
46 *Ibid.*, 10 May 1821
47 *Ibid.*, 7 May 1821
48 *Hobhouse Diary*, 47
49 RA Geo IV, Box 13, 'Secret Intelligence', 16 July 1821
50 *Ibid.*, 3 March 1821
51 *Ibid.*, 29 May 1821
52 *Ibid.*, 12 July 1821
53 RA Geo IV, Box 8, 12 June 1821
54 RA 22629–30, 22631: Asp/K, ii, 439
55 RA 24920, 29 April 1821
56 RA Geo IV, Box 13, 5 May 1821
57 RA 24919, 29 April 1821; Yonge, iii, 126
58 RA 24921–2, 1 May 1821

59 *Ibid.*
60 RA Geo IV, Box 13, 7 May 1821
61 *Ibid.*
62 RA Geo IV, Box 13, 19 June 1821
63 RA Geo IV, Box 13, 'Secret Intelligence', 16 July 1821

14 DEATH OF QUEEN CAROLINE (pages 202-13)

1 *The Times*, 20 July 1821
2 *Creevey Papers*, 359–60
3 RA Geo IV, Box 13, 'Secret Intelligence', 21 July 1821
4 *Abbot Journal*, iii, 233
5 *Courier*, 19 July 1821
6 RA Geo IV, Box 8, 13 March 1827
7 *Jerningham Letters*, 199–200
8 Denbigh MSS, 20 July 1821; Twiss, ii, 48
9 *Scott Letters*, vi, 505
10 *Bury Journal*, i, 191
11 *Jekyll Correspondence*, 116
12 *Jerningham Letters*, ii, 216
13 *Barnard Letters*, 292
14 *Annual Register*, lxiii, 1821, 118–19
15 *Creevey Papers*, 363
16 *Ibid.*
17 *Ibid.*
18 Brougham *(Memoirs)*, ii, 424
19 *Creevey Papers*, 363; Macalpine and Hunter, 248
20 *Creevey Papers*, 364
21 Asp/K, ii, 452
22 *Ibid.*, 454
23 BM Add MSS, 38191, ff 63–4
24 *Ibid.*
25 RA Geo IV, Box 8, 13 August 1821
26 Asp/K, ii, 455
27 *Ibid.*, 457
28 RA Geo IV, Box 8, 15 August 1821
29 RA Geo IV, Box 8, Envelope 14; *Hobhouse Diary*, 73
30 Brougham *(Memoirs)*, ii, 428
31 *Barnard Letters*, 291
32 *Croker Papers*, 8 August 1821
33 *Ibid.*, 12 August 1821

34 *Jerningham Letters*, ii, 203
35 BM Add MSS 38565, f 106: Asp/K, ii, 496
36 Asp/K, ii, 494–7
37 *Ibid.*
38 Asp/K, ii, 454
39 *Barnard Letters*, 294
40 *Creevey Papers*, 272
41 Buckingham *(George IV)*, ii, 194
42 *Barnard Letters*, 294
43 Fitzgerald, ii, 284
44 *Barnard Letters*, 294
45 S. H. Burke, *Ireland Sixty Years Ago*, quoted by Richardson *(George IV)*, 230
46 Derry *(Regency Crisis)*, 198
47 S. H. Burke, quoted by Richardson *(George IV)*, 94
48 Cloncurry, 277
49 *Croker Papers*, 13 August 1821
50 *Ibid.*, 14 August 1821
51 *Ibid.*, 17 August 1821
52 *Ibid.*, 18 August 1821
53 *Barnard Letters*, 297
54 *Croker Papers*, 21 August 1821
55 *Ibid.*, 23 August 1821
56 Fitzgerald, ii, 286
57 *Barnard Letters*, ii, 297
58 Buckingham *(George IV)*, ii, 207
59 *Barnard Letters*, ii, 298; *Croker Papers*, 24 August 1828

15   LADY CONYNGHAM AND WILLIAM KNIGHTON (pages 214–27)
1 *Greville Memoirs*, i, 96
2 Lieven *(Metternich Letters)*, 28; *Arbuthnot Journal*, i, 10
3 *Greville Memoirs*, i, 96
4 *Arbuthnot Journal* i, 117–18
5 *Ibid.*, 16
6 *Gentleman's Magazine*, 1829, 422; *Croker Papers*, 19 April 1820
7 *Arbuthnot Journal*, i, 9
8 *Greville Memoirs*, i, 118
9 *Arbuthnot Journal*, i, 81
10 Lieven *(Metternich Letters)*, 25–8, 34, 36
11 RA Knighton Papers, 23 April 1823

12 RA Add 3/27, 29, 30 [1822]
13 *Ibid.*, 29
14 *Ibid.*, 28
15 RA 22574-5, 5 April 1821
16 RA 22577, 7 April 1821
17 RA 22584, 9 April 1821
18 RA 22585, 9 April 1821
19 RA 22588, 11 April 1821
20 Lieven *(Metternich Letters)*, 104-5
21 RA 22590 (undated) [11 April 1821]
22 *Hobhouse Diary*, 53-7
23 RA 23168: Asp/K, iii, 76; Sumner, *passim*
24 Mount Charles to Sumner, quoted by Fulford, 265
25 RA 22687, 23 July 1821
26 RA 22688, 24 July 1821
27 RA 22689, 25 July 1821
28 *Hobhouse Diary*, 67
29 *Ibid.*, 69
30 *Arbuthnot Journal*, i, 115
31 *Croker Papers*, ii, 81
32 Bathurst MSS, quoted by Ziegler *(Addington)*, 396
33 Finch MSS, d 2, quoted by Richardson *(George IV)*, 236
34 *Hobhouse Diary*, 74
35 Fitzgerald, ii, 288
36 *Barnard Letters*, 299
37 Cooper, ii, 238
38 Knighton, i, 223
39 *Ibid.*
40 Fitzgerald, ii, 300
41 Lieven *(Metternich Letters)*, 110
42 RA 19045-6, 3 January 1812; Aspinall, 'George IV and Sir William Knighton', 57
43 Knighton Diary: Asp/K, iii, 477-8
44 *Ibid.*, 479-81
45 RA Geo IV, Box 8, 18 August 1817
46 RA Knighton Papers, 16 March 1821
47 RA Knighton Papers, 48-56, 16 March 1821-23 March 1823; RA 24300-2, 24620-1: Asp/K, ii, 418; ii, 527; iii, 355; iii, 340; iii, 289; iii, 177
48 RA 22820-3: Asp/K, ii, 502
49 *Hobhouse Diary*, 29 November 1820
50 RA 294935 (undated)

51 RA 22510, 22511-12; Asp/K, ii, 390-1
52 Knighton, i, 241
53 *Ibid.*

16   A CONTINENTAL JOURNEY (pages 228-45)

1 RA 44342, 26 September 1821
2 Jesse *(Brummell)*, 127-9
3 *Jerningham Letters*, ii, 213
4 Raikes, i, 91
5 *Wellington and his Friends*, 16
6 *Shelley Journal*, ii, 110
7 Knighton, i, 177-82; Huish, ii, 338; Fitzgerald, ii, 108-10; BM Add MSS
   38742, f 71
8 *Jerningham Letters*, ii, 214
9 *Ibid.*
10 Palmer, 207; Fulford, 244
11 Bartlett, 111; Webster, 382; Palmer, 207-8
12 *Lady Holland Letters*, 8
13 Lieven *(Metternich Letters)*, 115
14 *Ibid.*, 102
15 *Ibid.*, 116
16 *Ibid.*, 95-8
17 *Greville Memoirs*, i, 122
18 *Creevey Papers*, 362
19 RA 22740-3, 12 October 1821
20 *Abbot Journal*, ii, 320
21 RA 22740-3, 12 October 1821
22 *Hobhouse Diary*, 65
23 RA 22746, 25 October 1821
24 RA 22747, 1 November 1821
25 Londonderry MSS, quoted in Asp/K, ii, 471
26 *Ibid.*, 472
27 *Arbuthnot Journal*, i, 126
28 *Croker Papers*, 11 January 1822
29 *Ibid.*
30 *Ibid.*, 12 January 1822
31 Lieven *(Metternich Letters)*, 119
32 BM *Sat*, x, 14254
33 *Moore Journals*, iii, 302-3
34 *Arbuthnot Journal*, i, 142

References

35 Lieven *(Metternich Letters)*, 121
36 *Ibid.*, 120
37 *Ibid.*, 121–2
38 *Ibid.*, 122
39 *Creevey Papers*, 447
40 *Hobhouse Diary*, 85
41 RA 22800 (undated)
42 RA 22804, 19 January 1822
43 RA 22805–6 (undated)
44 RA 22811, 21 January 1822
45 RA 22813–14, 22 January 1822
46 RA 24943, 8 March 1822
47 RA 24937–8, 3 March 1822
48 RA 24954–5, 21 March 1822
49 RA 24948, 14 March 1822
50 Lieven *(Metternich Letters)*, 131
51 RA 22856–7; Stapleton MSS, quoted by Aspinall, 'George IV and Sir William Knighton', 71
52 RA 22866–8; *Arbuthnot Journal*, ii, 154
53 RA 22858–9: Asp/K, ii, 525
54 RA 22866–8: Asp/K, ii, 529
55 RA 24939–40: Asp/K, ii, 503
56 Knighton, i, 200
57 RA 23081–2, 23083: Asp/K, iii, 50–1; Canning Papers, 11 December 1823
58 Asp/K, iii, 9
59 WSD, ii, 103, 105
60 *Arbuthnot Journal*, i, 269
61 *Ibid.*, 256, 270
62 *Ibid.*, 187
63 *Greville Memoirs*, i, 236
64 *Ibid.*
65 *Ibid.*, 178
66 *Ibid.*, 273–4
67 *Arbuthnot Journal*, i, 270
68 *Ibid.*
69 *Ibid.*
70 RA 33961, 8 March 1821
71 RA 32695, 14 January 1829
72 *Creevey Papers*, 446
73 Lieven *(Metternich Letters)*, 152, 153, 267, 269
74 *Greville Memoirs*, i, 236

75 Stapleton, 440
76 Canning Papers (Leeds), 27 April 1825
77 RA Knighton Papers 52, 18 December 1821

17   A NEW FOREIGN SECRETARY (pages 246-61)
1 Lieven *(Metternich Letters)*, 123
2 *Ibid.*, 130
3 *Wellington and his Friends*, 20; *Arbuthnot Journal*, i, 150
4 Lieven *(Metternich Letters)*, 129, 130, 136
5 *Ibid.*, 96
6 *Ibid.*, 139
7 *Ibid.*, 98-9
8 *Ibid.*, 145
9 *Ibid.*, 148
10 *Greville Memoirs*, i, 125
11 *Croker Papers*, 21 June 1822
12 Lieven *(Metternich Letters)*, 151
13 RA 29551-638, October 1811–December 1829
14 Raikes, iii, 57
15 Colvin *(Edgeworth Letters)*, 462-3
16 RA 29551-638, October 1811–December 1829
17 RA 29599-600, 20 March–23 September 1822
18 Lockhart, iii, 92; Fitzgerald, ii, 302-3
19 BM MS 'King George IV's Visit to Scotland'; Huish, ii, 346-51; Richardson *(George IV)*, 279
20 Lockhart, iii, 101
21 RA 22884-5, 29 August 1822
22 RA 22902-4, 12 September 1822
23 Parker, i, 320; Lever, 108; Lieven *(Metternich Letters)*, 154; *Hobhouse Diary*, 126
24 Lieven *(Metternich Letters)*, 154
25 *Hobhouse Diary*, 89
26 Lieven *(Metternich Letters)*, 142
27 *Ibid.*, 145
28 *Croker Papers*, 12 August 1822
29 *Ibid.*, 2 September 1822
30 RA 22888-9 (undated); *Hobhouse Diary*, 95; Yonge, iii, 194-5
31 *Hobhouse Diary*, 95
32 Yonge, iii, 143
33 RA 22640, 1 July 1821; *Hobhouse Diary*, 63

34 Lieven *(Metternich Letters)*, 167
35 *Hobhouse Diary*, 61
36 Lieven *(Metternich Letters)*, 166
37 Quoted by Longford *(Wellington)*, 99
38 *Ibid.*
39 Yonge, iii, 199
40 Parker, i, 336; Yonge, iii, 200
41 Lieven *(Metternich Letters)*, 168–9
42 Parker, i, 335
43 Lieven *(Metternich Letters)*, 139
44 Parker, i, 377–8
45 Lieven *(Metternich Letters)*, 176
46 Palmerston Papers, c/iv/4/3, 2 June 1823
47 RA 22913–14: Asp/K, ii, 547
48 *Ibid.*
49 *Croker Papers*, 21 March 1823
50 Lieven *(Metternich Letters)*, 205
51 *Ibid.*, 215
52 *Ibid.*, 217
53 *Ibid.*, 216
54 *Ibid.*, 182
55 *Greville Memoirs*, i, 131
56 Lieven *(Metternich Letters)*, 121
57 *Arbuthnot Journal*, i, 309
58 *Ibid.*, 319
59 *Ibid.*, 262; Longford *(Wellington)*, 107
60 Wellington MSS, quoted in Asp/P, viii, 447
61 *Arbuthnot Journal*, i, 258
62 *Creevey Papers*, 390
63 Bartlett, 201
64 Webster, 326; Woodward, 195–206
65 Shane Leslie *(George IV)*, 140
66 Palmer, 228–9; Temperley, 248–9
67 Lieven *(Metternich Letters)*, 219–20
68 Temperley, 246
69 Lieven *(Metternich Letters)*, 226
70 RA 23422–4 (undated) [November 1824]
71 RA 23154–5 (undated) [1824]
72 RA 23427–46 (undated) [January 1825]
73 Woodward, 211

18 PALACE AND CASTLE (pages 262–74)

1 Lieven *(Metternich Letters)*, 226–7
2 *Ibid.*, 229
3 *Ibid.*
4 *Dutch Pictures from the Royal Collection*, 30
5 *Ibid.*, 23–32
6 Millar *(Later Georgian Pictures)*, 261
7 *Ibid.*, 289; Garlick, *passim*
8 RA 23132–5, 30225: Asp/K, iii, 491
9 Archives of the Royal College of Physicians, quoted by Richardson *(George IV)*, 264
10 Miller *(Panizzi)*, 83
11 Quoted by Fulford *(George IV)*, 257; Asp/K, ii, 550–1
12 Records of the Royal Society of Literature; Whalley, 'Coleridge and the Royal Society of Literature', *Essays by Divers Hands*, 147; Richardson, 'George IV: Patron of Literature', *Essays by Divers Hands*, 128–46; Bradbrook, 7–9
13 Records of the Royal Society of Literature
14 *Ibid.*
15 Royal Academy, Council Minutes, vi, 305, 26 October 1822, quoted by Richardson *(George IV)*, 265
16 RA 22971, 6 August 1823
17 Royal Academy, Lawrence Correspondence, iv, 36, 14 April 1823, quoted by Richardson *(George IV)*, 271
18 Fitzgerald, ii, 89
19 Raikes, i, 387
20 Richardson *(George IV)*, 276
21 *Gronow Reminiscences*, ii, 108
22 Edwards, 262; Richardson *(George IV)*, 277
23 Buckingham *(George IV)*, ii, 419
24 *Annual Biography and Obituary*, 1824; Pevsner, 296–7; Colvin, 675–7; Hibbert *(London)*, 13
25 *Gronow Reminiscences*, ii, 92
26 BM Add MSS 38278, f 358; Asp/P, viii, 431
27 Yonge, iii, 402–3
28 *Creevey Papers*, 493
29 *Buckingham Palace*, 30–1; Hibbert *(London)*, 133–4
30 *Jekyll Correspondence*, 231
31 *Arbuthnot Journal*, i, 295
32 RA 23042, 23 October 1823
33 RA 23043, 23 October 1823

34 *Windsor and Eton Express*, 27 August 1820, quoted by Morshead *(Windsor)*, 84

35 Wyatville's evidence before the Select Committee of the House of Commons, 1830

36 *Frampton Journal*, 337

37 Morshead *(Windsor)*, 86

38 *Ibid.*, 86

39 RA 23570-1, 10 August 1826

40 RA 23568-9, 8 August 1826

41 *Windsor and Eton Express*, quoted by Morshead *(Windsor)*, 86

42 Dalling *(Palmerston)*, i, 299; Morshead *(Windsor)*, 97

43 RA 51343: Asp/K, ii, 402-3

44 RA 24812-13: Asp/K, iii, 475

45 Report of the Select Committee of the House of Commons, 1830

46 *Arbuthnot Journal*, ii, 150

47 *Lady Holland Letters*, 46

48 *Greville Memoirs*, i, 181

49 *Croker Papers*, 30 March 1828

50 *Lady Holland Letters*, 93

51 RA 51308, quoted by Morshead *(Windsor)*, 92

19   THE WINDSOR RECLUSE (pages 275-84)

1 *Shelley Diary*, ii, 41

2 *Ibid.*, 146

3 *Ibid.*

4 *Creevey Papers*, 431

5 *Wellington and his Friends*, 48

6 *Ibid.*, 22, 46-8; Lieven *(Metternich Letters)*, 271

7 Lieven *(Metternich Letters)*, 271

8 Oman *(Gascoyne Heiress)*, 191

9 *Wellington and his Friends*, 70

10 *Ibid.*, 67

11 *Queen Victoria's Letters, 1st Series*, i, 16-17; Longford *(Victoria)*, 29; *Shelley Diary*, ii, 146-7; Fulford *(George IV)*, 254-5

12 *Shelley Diary*, ii, 147

13 *Ibid.*; Morshead *(Royal Lodge)*, 28

14 Asp/K, iii, 296

15 Lockhart, vi, 354-61

16 *Gronow Reminiscences*, ii, 192

17 Buckingham *(George IV)*, i, 60

18 Royal Academy, Lawrence Correspondence, v, 9, 29 April 1826, quoted by Richardson *(George IV)*, 300
19 *Creevey Papers*, 419, 430
20 *Arbuthnot Journal*, i, 70
21 Knighton, i, 375–6
22 *Croker Papers*, 2 March 1825
23 Pückler-Muskau, iv, 141
24 *Ibid.*
25 Lieven *(Metternich Letters)*, 304–5, 307–8
26 Oman *(Gascoyne Heiress)*, 176, 191; *Arbuthnot Journal*, ii, 24
27 *Wellington and his Friends*, 67
28 Lieven *(Metternich Letters)*, 299–300
29 *Ibid.*, 273
30 *Greville Memoirs*, i, 150
31 RA 44284–5, 31 August 1814
32 RA 44337, 16 August 1820
33 RA 44359 (undated)
34 RA 24002–9: Asp/K, iii, 48, 242
35 *Abbot Journal*, iii, 438; *Hobhouse Diary*, 121
36 *Arbuthnot Journal*, i, 378
37 *Ibid.*, ii, 28
38 *Jekyll Correspondence*, 169; *Shelley Diary*, ii, 149–51
39 *Greville Memoirs*, i, 167, 170
40 *Ibid.*
41 Knighton, ii, 48
42 *Shelley Diary*, ii, 149
43 Gash, 425
44 Stapleton, 578
45 Gash, 425

20 THE TORY REVOLT (pages 285–95)

1 *The Times*, 24 January 1827
2 *Creevey Papers*, 450–1
3 Fitzgerald, ii, 370
4 Aspinall *(Canning's Ministry)*, xxxi–xxxii; *Croker Papers*, i, 363
5 WSD, iii, 161
6 RA 23160, 4 May 1824, 23161, 5 May 1824, 23162–7: Asp/K, iii, 72–5
7 RA 23564: Asp/K, iii, 153
8 Stapleton, 444–5
9 *Hobhouse Diary*, 98; Asp/K, ii, 547–8

10 *Greville Memoirs*, i, 349
11 Lieven *(Metternich Letters)*, 293
12 *Wellington and his Friends*, 69
13 Lieven *(Metternich Letters)*, 293
14 *Hobhouse Diary*, 76, 83–5; Aspinall *(Canning's Ministry)*, xiii, 105, 127–30
15 Stapleton, 438
16 *Ibid.*, 439
17 *Ibid.*, 447
18 RA 23084–5, 13 December 1823; Rolo, 130
19 Lieven *(London Letters)*, 286–7
20 Holland *(Further Memoirs)*, 396–7
21 Parker, i, 107
22 Fulford *(George IV)*, 272
23 Parker, i, 349
24 RA 22511–12: Asp/K, ii, 391
25 *Parliamentary Debates*, NS, xvii, 451, 2 May 1827, quoted by Aspinall *(Canning's Ministry)*, xxvii
26 Stapleton, 582–6
27 *Creevey Papers*, 452
28 Knighton, ii, 109
29 Asp/K, iii, 212
30 RA 23853, 9 April 1827
31 *Ibid.*
32 *George Canning and his Friends*, ii, 382
33 *Parliamentary Debates*, NS, xvii, 470
34 RA 23912: Asp/K, iii, 228
35 RA 23913–14: Asp/K, iii, 228
36 *Ibid.*
37 Parker, ii, 5; *Arbuthnot Journal*, ii, 31
38 *Lady Palmerston Letters*, 174
39 Aspinall, 'George IV and Sir William Knighton', 71–2
40 RA 23875–6, 14 April 1827, 23877–8, 14 April 1827, 23879–80 (undated) [April 1827]
41 Fulford *(George IV)*, 278
42 *Shelley Diary*, ii, 155
43 *Abbot Journal*, ii, 395
44 RA 24082–5: Asp/K, iii, 269–71; WSD, iv, 63
45 Fulford *(George IV)*, 279
46 *Arbuthnot Journal*, ii, 132
47 Lever, 174
48 Stapleton, 401

49 Parker, ii, 18
50 Stapleton, 577–9
51 Aspinall *(Canning's Ministry)*, xliv, 118; Stapleton, 585
52 *Arbuthnot Journal*, ii, 109
53 Aspinall *(Canning's Ministry)*, 206; Rolo, 154
54 *Ibid.*, xxv
55 Lever, 165
56 Aspinall (*Canning's Ministry*), xxvi–xxxvii
57 Buckingham *(George IV)*, ii 237
58 Petrie *(Canning)*, 228

21   PROTESTANTS AND CATHOLICS (pages 296–311)
 1 RA 24128–9: Asp/K, iii, 281–2
 2 Goderich Papers (Aylesbury), O.90
 3 RA 24158–9: Asp/K, iii, 288
 4 Goderich Papers, F.88
 5 *Ibid.*, F.92
 6 *Ibid.*, F.67–9; RA 24112; Asp/K, iii, 276
 7 WSD, iv, 94; *Arbuthnot Journal*, ii, 142
 8 RA 24110–11: Asp/K, iii, 275–6; Goderich Papers, F.67
 9 RA 24113–16: Asp/K, iii, 276–8
10 Goderich Papers, F.68
11 *Ibid.*, F.69
12 *Ibid.*, F.71, F.73
13 *Ibid.*, F.69
14 Herries, i, 131–56
15 RA 24153–4: Asp/K, iii, 286
16 RA 24134–41: Asp/K, ii, 291–2
17 *Ibid.*
18 Goderich Papers, O.108; RA 24267–71: Asp/K, iii, 344–6
19 Goderich Papers, O.108
20 *Ibid.*, F.93
21 *Ibid.*
22 BM Add MSS 38752, f 223, quoted in Asp/K, iii, 347
23 Asp/K, iii, 351
24 RA 24308–9: Asp/K, iii, 358–9
25 Aspinall *(Politics and Press)*, 195
26 RA 23101: Asp/K, iii, 57; Aspinall, 'George IV and Sir William Knighton',
    76
27 RA 23323–4: Asp/K, iii, 104

28 RA 24300–1: Asp/K, iii, 355–6
29 RA M 4, 8–10, 19 December 1827, 17 January 1828, 14 February 1828
30 RA 24300–1: Asp/K, iii, 355–6
31 Asp/K, iii, 368
32 RA 24755–6, 14 November 1829
33 Raikes, iii, 94; *Croker Papers*, i, 430–1
34 *Wellington and his Friends*, 81
35 RA 24366–8, 19 January 1828; Aspinall, *English Historical Review*, October
  1935, 639 *et seq.*
36 *Arbuthnot Journal*, ii, 151, 167
37 Woodward, 76
38 *Ibid.*
39 Dalling, i, 147
40 *Ibid.*, 154; Peel, ii, 262
41 Lieven *(London Letters)*, 152; Longford *(Wellington)*, 105
42 *Creevey Papers*, 454; WDCM, ii, 592
43 *Ellenborough Diary*, i, 139
44 RA 24066–70: Asp/K, iii, 264
45 Asp/K, iii, 446
46 *Greville Memoirs*, i, 292
47 *Ellenborough Diary*, i, 257, 264, 281
48 *Greville Memoirs*, i, 301
49 *Arbuthnot Journal*, ii, 245
50 *Jekyll Correspondence*, 186
51 Asp/K, iii, 430, 432, 453
52 *Greville Memoirs*, i, 213
53 WSD, NS, 74, 83
54 Asp/K, iii, 451
55 Holland *(Letters)*, 93
56 Parker, ii, 82
57 *Wellington and his Friends*, 39
58 Wellington MSS, quoted in Asp/P, viii, 480
59 RA Add 15/25, 1 February 1829
60 WSD, v, 482–3
61 Brougham MSS
62 *Ellenborough Diary*, i, 173–4
63 *Greville Memoirs*, i, 302
64 RA 24673–6: Asp/K, iii, 455
65 Holland *(Letters)*, 77
66 *Greville Memoirs*, i, 236
67 Parker, ii, 76

68 RA 24668–9: Asp/K, iii, 454–5
69 *Arbuthnot Journal*, ii, 254
70 *Ibid.*, 253
71 *Ellenborough Diary*, i, 366, 368; *Arbuthnot Journal*, ii, 246
72 *Arbuthnot Journal*, ii, 253
73 *Creevey Papers*, 538–42; Brougham MSS, March 1829
74 *Ellenborough Diary*, i, 370
75 *Arbuthnot Journal*, ii, 246
76 Lieven *(Metternich Letters)*, 111
77 *Greville Memoirs*, i, 301
78 *Ibid.*, 327
79 *Ellenborough Diary*, i, 377
80 *Ibid.*, 376–7, 384–5
81 WSD, v, 467
82 Lieven *(London Letters)*, 187
83 *Arbuthnot Journal*, ii, 266
84 Buckingham *(George IV)*, ii, 395
85 *Statutes at Large*, LXXX, iii, 49–59, 10 Geo IV, C.47
86 *Ellenborough Diary*, ii, 15
87 Wellington Papers, Miscellaneous 31, 23 April 1829
88 RA 24684–6: Asp/K, iii, 458–9
89 Holland *(Letters)*, 103

22   THE FINAL YEARS (pages 312–25)
 1 Knighton, i, 170
 2 1 Geo IV, C.57; Musgrave *(Brighton)*, 167; Sitwell, 18
 3 3 Geo IV, C.71; 8 Geo IV, C. 18; Shane Leslie *(George IV)*, 136
 4 Parker, i, 315–17, ii, 42–3; ii, 147–51; *Abbot Diary*, iii, 297; *Hobhouse Diary*, 17, 87
 5 RA 25042, 25648–9; Parker, *passim*
 6 Parker, i, 317
 7 RA 246002: Asp/K, iii, 449; Parker, ii, 42–3
 8 Fulford *(George IV)*, 288
 9 Mathews, 138–45
10 *Barnard Letters*, 284
11 *Ibid.*, 296, 302
12 Holland *(Letters)*, 77
13 Twiss, i, 533
14 *Mitford Letters*, ii, 250–1; Millar *(Later Georgian)*, 48–9; Haydon, *Autobiography*, i, 419–23

15 Knighton, ii, 204

16 Bayne, 120-1, 133-4; Richardson *(George IV)*, 292-3; Millar *(Later Georgian)*, 137-42

17 *Scott Letter-Books*, 157

18 Jones, 113-17; Richardson *(George IV)*, 318

19 Lockhart, iii, 340-1

20 *Ibid.*

21 *Ibid.*, 344

22 *Scott Letters*, vi, 368

23 *Ibid.*, 173

24 *Ibid.*, xii, 35

25 Royal Academy, Lawrence Correspondence, v, quoted by Richardson *(George IV)*, 319

26 Asp/K, iii, 491

27 RA 24002-7: Asp/K, iii, 242-3

28 *Ibid.*

29 *Arbuthnot Journal*, i, 277; Wellington Papers, 26 November 1823

30 RA 29604-30234

31 RA Add 3/14

32 RA 29644-30723

33 New, 85

34 *Arbuthnot Journal*, ii, 284-8

35 *Ellenborough Diary*, i, 10, 143-4, 295, 297

36 RA 23050-2: Asp/K, iii, 38-9

37 *Ellenborough Diary*, i, 374

38 *Ibid.*, 375

39 *Croker Papers*, i, 430-1

40 *Ellenborough Diary*, ii, 225

41 *Ibid.*, 100

42 Oman *(Gascoyne Heiress)*, 175-6

43 Lieven *(Palmerston Correspondence)*, 6

44 *Croker Papers*, i, 430-1

45 *Ellenborough Diary*, i, 102

46 RA 24709-10: Asp/K, iii, 460

47 *Greville Memoirs*, i, 236-7, 262

48 *Ellenborough Diary*, ii, 35

49 Airlie *(Lady Palmerston)*, i, 73

50 Dover Papers (Delapre Abbey), 24 June 1824

51 *Ellenborough Diary*, ii, 172

52 RA 24771: Asp/K, iii, 468

53 *Ellenborough Diary*, ii, 167

54 *Ibid.*, 173
55 RA 24771: Asp/K, iii, 468
56 *Ellenborough Diary*, ii, 174
57 Eldon Papers, copy in Royal Archives under reference RA 21/179/321, 20 January 1830, RA Add 21/179, 20 January 1830
58 RA 24703-4: Asp/K, iii, 460
59 Summerson, 218-22
60 RA 24721-2: Asp/K, iii, 461
61 *Greville Memoirs*, i, 293
62 *Ibid.*, 305
63 BM *Sat*; xi, 15839, 15845
64 Huish, ii, 360
65 *Gronow Reminiscences*, ii, 292
66 RA 28395-959
67 Fulford *(George IV)*, 256
68 *Greville Memoirs*, i, 324
69 *Scott Letter-Books*, 158-9
70 Lieven *(London Letters)*, 198; *Ellenborough Diary*, ii, 100; Asp/K, iii, 467
71 RA 29206-9
72 RA 23098-9: Asp/K, iii, 56
73 Asp/K, iii, 500
74 Lieven *(Palmerston Correspondence)*, 9
75 *Arbuthnot Journal*, ii, 352
76 *Ibid.*
77 *Ibid.*, i, 242-3
78 *Ibid.*, 271
79 Buckingham *(George IV)*, ii, 209
80 *Arbuthnot Journal*, i, 383
81 *Creevey Papers*, 431
82 *Arbuthnot Journal*, i, 243
83 *Creevey Papers*, 438
84 *Jekyll Correspondence*, 226
85 *Ellenborough Diary*, ii, 168
86 Knighton, ii, 103-4
87 Asp/K, iii, 470

23   THE LAST ILLNESS (pages 326-35)

1 *Arbuthnot Journal*, ii, 48, 79
2 *Ellenborough Diary*, ii, 224-5; Parker, ii, 145
3 RA 24623-4, 3 January 1829

4 *Ellenborough Diary*, ii, 252
5 *Arbuthnot Journal*, ii, 352
6 *Ibid.*
7 *Ibid.*
8 *Wellington and his Friends*, 90
9 *Croker Papers*, ii, 56
10 Parker, ii, 149–51
11 RA Add 18/1, 15 April 1830
12 RA Add 18/1, 18/6, 18/14, 18/28, 18/46, 18/52, 15 April–13 May 1830
13 RA Add 18/4, 26 April 1830; *Ellenborough Diary*, ii, 253
14 *Ellenborough Diary*, ii, 235
15 RA Add 18/30, 3 May 1830
16 RA Add 18/54, 14 May 1830, 18/61, 16 May 1830
17 RA 18/29–42, 2–9 May 1830
18 *Ellenborough Diary*, ii, 234
19 *Ibid.*, 225, 234, 244
20 *Croker Papers*, ii, 57–8
21 *Ellenborough Diary*, ii, 266
22 RA 48625–51, 5 November 1812–4 May 1830
23 *Ellenborough Diary*, ii, 239
24 Lieven *(Metternich Letters)*, 309
25 Wilkins, i, 214
26 RA 50227: Asp/P, viii, 482
27 Wilkins, ii, 216; Langdale, 136
28 Eldon MSS, quoted in Asp/P, viii, 482–4
29 Oman *(Gascoyne Heiress)*, 176
30 Dover Papers (Delapre Abbey), Lord Dover's MS Journal, 17 July 1830
31 RA Add 18/44–61, 9–16 May 1830; *Ellenborough Diary*, ii, 238–9; *Croker Papers*, ii, 57–8, 61
32 RA 24745
33 *Ellenborough Diary*, ii, 257–8
34 *Ibid.*, 244
35 *Ibid.*, 258
36 *Ibid.*
37 Lieven *(London Letters)*, 220–1
38 Gash, 629
39 *Ibid.*
40 *Croker Papers*, ii, 233
41 RA Add 18/86–100, 30 May–7 June 1830
42 RA Add 18/101, 7 June 1830, 112, 14 June 1830
43 *Arbuthnot Journal*, ii, 352

44 *Ellenborough Diary*, ii, 266
45 *Croker Papers*, ii, 64–5
46 Knighton, ii, 140
47 RA Add 18/110, 14 June 1830
48 Knighton, ii, 143
49 *Croker Papers*, ii, 64–5
50 *Ibid.*
51 RA 242820, 22 May 1830
52 *Lancet*, 4 June 1830
53 *Lancet*, 12 June 1830; *London Medical Gazette*, 12 June 1830
54 *The Times*, 12 June 1830
55 *Ellenborough Diary*, ii, 270
56 *Greville Memoirs*, i, 362
57 RA Add 18/124–130, 19–22 June 1830
58 Oman *(Gascoyne Heiress)*, 177
59 Waller of Woodcote MSS (Warwick), CR 341/202
60 *Ibid.*, CR 341/206
61 *Ibid.*, CR 341/204

24   POST MORTEM (pages 336–45)
1 Waller of Woodcote MSS, CR 341/207
2 *Ibid.*, CR 341/206/2
3 *The Times*, 16 July 1830
4 *Morning Chronicle*, 28 June 1830
5 Ceremonial for the Interment of his late Most Sacred Majesty King George
   the Fourth, 12 July 1830; *Jekyll Correspondence*, 242; *The Times*, 16 July 1830
6 *The Times*, 16 July 1830
7 *The Times*, 17 July 1830
8 Dover Papers (Delapre Abbey), Lord Dover's MS Journal, 15 July 1830
9 *Jekyll Correspondence*, 242
10 Dover Papers (Delapre Abbey), Lord Dover's MS Journal, 15 July 1830
11 *Ellenborough Diary*, ii, 312
12 *The Times*, 16 July 1830
13 Wilkins, ii, 221–3; *Frampton Journal*, ii, 13–14; Seymour of Ragley MSS,
   Sir George Seymour's annotations to Langdale's *Memoirs of Mrs Fitzherbert*,
   CR 114/A/536/7
14 Lieven (*London Letters*), 221
15 *Frampton Journal*, ii, 344
16 Brooks's Archives; *Spencer-Stanhope Letter-Bag*, ii, 134
17 *Ellenborough Diary*, ii, 276, 279, 280

18 *Jekyll Correspondence*, 242–3
19 *The Times*, 26 July 1830
20 *Spencer-Stanhope Letter-Bag*, ii, 135–6
21 *The Times*, 16 July 1830
22 Earl Grey Papers (Durham), MS Diary of 3rd Earl Grey
23 Lieven *(Palmerston Correspondence)*, 249
24 *Greville Memoirs*, i, 322; *Arbuthnot Journal*, i, 95; *Hobhouse Diary*, 47
25 Cooper, ii, 347–57
26 Taylor, ii, 25; *Jekyll Correspondence*, 236
27 *Creevey Papers*, 553
28 *Arbuthnot Journal*, ii, 365
29 Knighton, ii, 151–2
30 *Morning Post*, 28 June 1830, 27 June 1830
31 *The Times*, 28 June 1830
32 *Ibid*, 15 July 1830
33 *Ibid.*
34 *Creevey Papers*, 553
35 *Arbuthnot Journal*, ii, 373
36 Lieven (*London Letters*), 224–6
37 *Greville Memoirs*, ii, 23
38 *Ibid.*
39 BM *Sat*, xi, 16143, 16157
40 MS Diary of Margaretta Brown (extracts printed in *Report of the Society of the Friends of St George*, 1960, by Olive Hedley)
41 *Wellington and his Friends*, 105
42 Oman *(Gascoyne Heiress)*, 93
43 *The Times*, 29 June 1830
44 *Ellenborough Diary*, ii, 291
45 Raikes, i, 92
46 Oman *(Gascoyne Heiress)*, 80

Sources

(These include sources for *George IV: Prince of Wales, 1762–1811*)

MANUSCRIPT

Royal Archives (Windsor Castle); British Museum – Fox MSS; Holland House MSS; Hickleton Papers; Add. MSS, 13714, 28063, 29179, 29764, 29915, 33132–3, 33629, 34453, 34992, 37062, 37282, 37296, 37297, 37414, 37728, 37847, 38191, 38242, 38264, 38278, 38285, 38564, 38565, 38574, 38716, 38742, 38752, 38760, 40306, 40344, 41857, 43727, 47560, 47570, 47579, 51520, 51457; Brighton Pavilion MSS; Hurd MSS (Hartlebury Castle); Mary Robinson MS Memoirs and Letters (Chequers); Chatsworth MSS; Wentworth Woodhouse Muniments (Sheffield); Finch MSS (Bodleian); Crawford Muniments (Balcarres); Fremantle Collection (Aylesbury); Goderich Papers (Aylesbury); Earl Grey Papers (Durham); Fitzwilliam Papers, Brook Records and Lord Dover's Papers (Delapre Abbey); Palmerston Papers (Winchester); Petworth House Archives (Chichester); Ragley MSS (Warwick); Pretyman Papers (Ipswich); Markham Papers (York); Capell Manuscripts (Hertford); Goulding Papers (Lincoln); Harrowby Papers (Sandon Hall); Wellington Papers (Stratfield Saye); Farquhar Correspondence and Hook MSS (Bucklebury); Denbigh MSS (Pailton House); Canning Papers (Leeds); Brougham MSS (University College, London); Lord Chamberlain's MSS (Public Record Office); Brooks's Club Archives; Coutts & Co. Archives.

NEWSPAPERS AND JOURNALS

Adam's Weekly Courant, Brighton Gazette, Brighton Herald, Courier, Daily Advertiser, The Diary, European Magazine, Evening Mail, Examiner, The Gazeteer and New Daily Advertiser, General Advertiser, General Evening Post, Gentleman's Magazine, John Bull, Lloyd's Evening Post, London Advertiser, London Chronicle, London Evening Post, London Gazette, London Packet, London Recorder or Sunday Gazette, Morning Chronicle and London Advertiser, Morning Post, Morning Herald, Morning Star, Oracle, Parker's General Advertiser, Public Advertiser, St James's Chronicle, Sun, Sussex Advertiser, The Times, True Briton, The World

Sources

HISTORICAL MANUSCRIPT COMMISSION REPORTS

The Manuscripts of the Earl of Lonsdale (13th Report, Appendix, Part VII); The Manuscripts and Correspondence of James, 1st Earl of Charlemont (13th Report, Appendix, Part VIII); The Manuscripts of the Earl of Carlisle (15th Report, Appendix, Part VI); The Manuscripts of the Duke of Rutland (14th Report, Appendix, Part I); The Manuscripts of J. B. Fortescue preserved at Dropmore (13th Report, Appendix, Part III, 14th Report, Appendix, Part V); The Manuscripts of the Marquess of Ailesbury (15th Report, Part VII)

PRINTED

Abbot Diary: Colchester, Charles, Lord, ed., *The Diary and Correspondence of Charles Abbot, Lord Colchester* (3 vols, 1861)

Account of the Visit of HRH the Prince Regent to the Corporation of London in June 1814 (1815)

Account of the Visit of HRH the Prince Regent to the University of Oxford in June [1814] (1815)

ADEANE, J. H., ed., *The Girlhood of Maria Josepha Holroyd, Lady Stanley of Alderley* (1896)

—— *The Early Married Life of Maria Josepha Holroyd, Lady Stanley of Alderley* (1899)

AIRLIE, Mabel, Countess of, *In Whig Society* (1921)

—— *Lady Palmerston and her Times* (2 vols, 1922)

ALBEMARLE: George Thomas, Earl of Albemarle, *Fifty Years of my Life* (2 vols, 1876)

ANGELO, Henry [Domenico Angelo Malevolti Tremanondo], *Reminiscences of Henry Angelo with Memoirs of his Late Father and Friends* (2 vols, 1830)

ANGLESEY, Marquess of, *One-Leg, The Life and Letters of Henry William Paget, 1st Marquess of Anglesey* (Cape, 1961)

Arbuthnot Journal: Wellington, Duke of and Francis Bamford, eds., *The Journal of Mrs Arbuthnot* (2 vols, 1950)

ASPINALL *(George III Correspondence):* Aspinall, A., ed., *The Later Correspondence of George III* (5 vols, Cambridge University Press, 1962–70)

ASPINALL *(George IV Correspondence):* Aspinall, A., ed., *The Letters of King George IV, 1812–30* (3 vols, Cambridge University Press, 1938)

ASPINALL *(Prince's Correspondence):* Aspinall, A., ed., *The Correspondence of George, Prince of Wales 1770–1812* (8 vols, Cassell, 1963–71)

ASPINALL *(Princess Charlotte's Letters):* Aspinall, A., ed., *Letters of the Princess Charlotte* (Home & Van Thal, 1949)

ASPINALL and SMITH: Aspinall, A., and Smith, E. Anthony, eds., *English Historical Documents 1783–1832* (Eyre & Spottiswoode, 1959)

Sources

ASPINALL, A., ed., *The Correspondence of Charles Arbuthnot* (Camden Third Series, vol. lxv, Royal Historical Society, 1941)

ASPINALL, A., *Politics and the Press*, c. *1780–1850* (Home & Van Thal, 1949)

—— *The Formation of Canning's Ministry, February to August 1827* (Camden Third Series, vol. lix, Royal Historical Society, 1937)

——'George IV and Sir William Knighton' *(English Historical Review, 1940)*

—— *Lord Brougham and the Whig Party* (1927)

Auckland Correspondence: Bath and Wells, Bishop of, ed., *Journal and Correspondence of William, Lord Auckland* (4 vols, 1861–2)

AUSTEN-LEIGH, J. E., *A Memoir of Jane Austen* (1870)

Authentic Account of the Visit of HRH the Prince Regent to Oxford (1814)

AYLING, S. E., *George III* (Collins, 1972)

BAGOT, Josceline, ed., *George Canning and his Friends* (1909)

BAKER, Herschel, *John Phillip Kemble* (Harvard University Press, 1942)

Barnard Letters: Powell, Anthony, ed., *Barnard Letters 1778–1824* (Duckworth, 1928)

BARTLETT, C. J., *Castlereagh* (Macmillan, 1966)

BAYNE, William, *Sir David Wilkie* (1903)

BELL, Robert, *The Life of the Right Honourable George Canning* (1846)

Berry Journals: Lewis, Lady Theresa, ed., *Extracts of the Journals and Correspondence of Miss Berry* (3 vols, 1865)

BINGHAM, Madeleine, *Sheridan: The Track of a Comet* (Allen & Unwin, 1972)

BIRKENHEAD, Sheila, *Peace in Piccadilly: The Story of Albany* (Hamish Hamilton, 1958)

BLAKISTON, Georgiana, *Lord William Russell and his Wife, 1815–1846* (Murray, 1972)

Bland Burges Letters: Hutton, James, ed., *Selections from the Letters and Correspondence of Sir James Bland Burges* (1885)

BLOOMFIELD, Georgina, Lady, *Memoir of Benjamin, Lord Bloomfield* (2 vols, 1884)

Book, or the Proceedings and Correspondence upon the Subject of the Inquiry into the Conduct of the Princess of Wales, The (edition printed by Richard Edwards, 1813)

BOULTON, William B., *Thomas Gainsborough: His Life, Work, Friends and Sitters* (1905)

BRAYBROOK, Edward W., *The Royal Society of Literature of the United Kingdom* (1897)

BRAYLEY: Edward Wedlake, *Illustrations of His Majesty's Palace at Brighton: formerly the Pavilion* (1838)

British Museum Catalogue of Satires (see George, M. D.)

Sources

Brock, M. G., 'George Canning' *(History Today,* August 1951)

Brock, W. R., *Lord Liverpool and Liberal Toryism, 1820–27* (Frank Cass, 1967)

Brooke, John, *King George III* (Constable, 1972)

Brougham *(Statesmen):* Brougham, Henry, *Historical Sketches of Statesmen who Flourished in the Time of George III* (3 vols, 1845)

Brougham *(Memoirs):* Brougham, Henry, *The Life and Times of Henry Lord Brougham written by Himself* (3 vols, 1871)

Bryant, Arthur, *The Age of Elegance* (Collins, 1950)

Buckingham Memoirs: Buckingham and Chandos, The Duke of, *Memoirs of the Court and Cabinets of George the Third* (2 vols, 1855)

Buckingham *(George IV):* Buckingham and Chandos, Duke of, *Memoirs of the Court of George IV* (1859)

Buckingham *(Regency):* Buckingham and Chandos, Duke of, *Memoirs of the Court of England during the Regency* (1856)

Buckingham Palace: John Russell, John Harris, Geoffrey de Bellaigue, Oliver Millar, *Buckingham Palace* (Nelson, 1968)

Burke, S. Hubert, *Ireland Sixty Years Ago* (1885)

Burke Correspondence: Copeland, Thomas, W., gen. ed., *The Correspondence of Edmund Burke* (9 vols, Cambridge University Press, 1958–70)

Bury Diary: Steuart, A. Francis, ed., *The Diary of a Lady in Waiting by Lady Charlotte Bury: Being the Diary Illustrative of the times of George IV* (2 vols, 1808)

Byron Letters: Prothero, R. E., ed., *The Works of Lord Byron. Letters and Journals* (1898)

Calvert: *An Irish Beauty of the Regency* (1911)

Campbell: Campbell, Lord, *Lives of the Lord Chancellors and Keepers of the Great Seal of England* (1846)

Candid Enquiry into the Case of the Prince of Wales, A (1786)

Cannon, John, *The Fox-North Coalition* (Cambridge University Press, 1970)

Castlereagh Correspondence: Londonderry, 3rd Marquess of, ed., *Memoirs and Correspondence of Viscount Castlereagh* (1848–53)

Cecil, Lord David, *The Young Melbourne* (Constable, 1939)

Chapman, R. W., ed., *Jane Austen's Letters to her Sister Cassandra and others* (Oxford University Press, 1952)

Chenevix Trench, Charles, *The Royal Malady* (Longmans, 1964)

Chiffney, Samuel, *Genius Genuine* (1804)

Childe-Pemberton, W. S., *The Romance of Princess Amelia . . . Including Extracts from Private and Unpublished Papers* (1910)

Christie, Ian R., *Myth and Reality in Late Eighteenth Century Politics* (Macmillan, 1970)

Sources

CHRISTIE, Ian R., *The End of North's Ministry, 1780–82* (Macmillan, 1958)

CLARK, Mrs Godfrey, ed., *Gleanings from an Old Portfolio* (3 vols, 1896)

CLARKE, Mary Anne, *The Rival Princes* (2 vols, 1810)

CLONCURRY, Lord, *Personal Recollections* (1849)

COBBETT, William, *History of the Regency and Reign of King George the Fourth* (1830)

COLERIDGE, Ernest Hartley, *The Life of Thomas Coutts, Banker* (2 vols, 1920)

COLERIDGE, S. T., *Letters, Conversations and Recollections* (1836)

COLVIN, Christina, ed., *Maria Edgeworth: Letters from England* (Clarendon Press, 1971)

COLVIN, H. M., *A Biographical Dictionary of English Architects, 1660–1840* (John Murray, 1954)

CONNELL, Brian, *Portrait of a Whig Peer* (Deutsch, 1957)

COOPER, Bransby Blake, *The Life of Sir Astley Cooper, Bt.* (2 vols, 1843)

Cornwallis Correspondence: Ross, Charles, ed., *Correspondence of Charles, first Marquess Cornwallis* (3 vols, 1859)

Creevey Papers: Maxwell, Sir Herbert, ed., *The Creevey Papers: A Selection from the Correspondence and Diaries of the Late Thomas Creevey, M.P.* (1905)

CRESTON: Creston, Dormer, *The Regent and his Daughter* (Eyre & Spottiswoode, 1952)

Croker Papers: Jennings, Louis, J., ed., *The Croker Papers* (3 vols, 1884)

CROLY, George, *The Personal History of His Late Majesty King George the Fourth* (2 vols, 1841)

DALLING, Lord, *Life of Lord Palmerston* (2 vols, 1870)

D'Arblay Diary: Barrett, Charlotte, ed., *Diary and Letters of Madame D'Arblay* (4 vols, 1876)

D'ARBLAY, Mme, *Memoirs of Dr Burney* (1832)

DARVALL, F. O., *Popular Disturbances and Public Order in Regency England* (1934)

DERRY, John W., *The Regency Crisis and the Whigs, 1788–9* (Cambridge University Press, 1963)

—— *Charles James Fox* (Batsford, 1972)

Devonshire Diary: The Diary of Georgiana, Duchess of Devonshire [printed in Walter Sichel's *Sheridan*, 399–426 (1909)]

Dutch Pictures from the Royal Collection (The Queen's Gallery, Buckingham Palace, Lund Humphries, 1971)

Edgeworth Letters: Hare, Augustus, ed., *The Life and Letters of Maria Edgeworth* (1894)

EDWARDS, H. S., *The Life of Rossini* (1869)

EHRMAN, John, *The Younger Pitt* (Constable, 1969)

Ellenborough Diary: Colchester, Lord, ed., *A Political Diary, 1828–50 by Edward Law, Lord Ellenborough* (2 vols, 1881)

Elliot Letters: Minto, the Countess of, ed., *Life and Letters of Sir Gilbert Elliot, First Earl of Minto* (3 vols, 1874)

ELWIN, Malcolm, see *Noels and Milbankes*

ERREDGE, John Ackerson, *History of Brightelmston* (1862)

Farington Diary: Grieg, James, ed., *The Farington Diary by Joseph Farington RA* (8 vols, Hutchinson, 1922–28)

FITZGERALD, Percy, *The Life of George the Fourth* (2 vols, 1881)

FOORD, Archibald, S., *His Majesty's Opposition, 1714–1830* (Clarendon Press, 1964)

FORTESCUE *(George III Correspondence)*: Fortescue, Sir John, ed., *The Correspondence of King George the Third, 1760–83* (6 vols, 1927–28)

FOSTER, Vere, ed., *The Two Duchesses* (1898)

FOTHERGILL, Brian, *Sir William Hamilton* (Harcourt, Brace and World, 1969)

Fox Correspondence: Russell, Lord John, ed., *Memorials and Correspondence of Charles James Fox* (4 vols, 1853–57)

Fox Journal: Ilchester, Earl of, ed., *Journal of Henry Edward Fox, afterwards 4th Earl Holland* (2 vols, 1923)

Frampton Journal: Mundy, Harriot Georgiana, ed., *The Journal of Mary Frampton* (1885)

Francis Letters: Francis, Beata and Eliza Keary, eds, *The Francis Letters by Sir Philip Francis and Other Members of the Family* (n.d.)

Francis Memoirs: Merivale, Herman, ed., *Memoirs of Sir Philip Francis* (2 vols, 1867)

FULFORD, Roger, *George the Fourth* (Duckworth, 1935)

—— *Royal Dukes: The Father and Uncles of Queen Victoria* (Duckworth, 1933)

—— *Samuel Whitbread, 1764–1815: A Study in Opposition* (Macmillan, 1967)

Fulke Greville Diaries: Bladon, F. McKno, ed., *The Diaries of Colonel the Hon. Robert Fulke Greville* (Lane, 1930)

GALT, J., *George III, His Court and Family* (1820)

GARLICK, Kenneth, *Sir Thomas Lawrence* (Routledge & Kegan Paul, 1954)

GASH, Norman, *Mr Secretary Peel* (Longmans, 1961)

GEORGE, M. Dorothy, *Catalogue of Personal and Political Satires* (vols v–xi, British Museum, 1935–54)

—— *English Political Caricature to 1792* (Clarendon Press, 1959)

—— *English Political Caricature 1793–1832* (Clarendon Press, 1959)

Sources

Georgiana: Bessborough, Earl of, ed., *Georgiana* (John Murray, 1955)

GILLEN, Mollie, *The Prince and His Lady* (Sidgwick & Jackson, 1970)

Glenbervie Journals: Bickley, Francis, ed., *The Diaries of Sylvester Douglas (Lord Glenbervie)* (Constable, 1928)

GORE, John, *Creevey's Life and Times* (1934)

Granville Leveson Gower Correspondence: Granville, Castalia Countess, ed., *Lord Granville Leveson Gower (First Earl of Granville) Private Correspondence 1781–1821* (2 vols, 1916)

GRATTAN, Henry, *Memoirs of the Life and Times of Henry Grattan* (1839–46)

GRAY, Denis, *Spencer Perceval* (Manchester University Press, 1963)

GREENWOOD, Alice Drayton, *Lives of the Hanoverian Queens of England* (vol. ii, 1911)

Greville Memoirs: Strachey, Lytton, and Fulford, Roger, eds., *The Greville Memoirs, 1814–1860* (Macmillan, 1938)

Gronow Reminiscences: The Reminiscences and Recollections of Captain Gronow (2 vols, 1892)

HAMILTON, Edwin, *A Record of the Life and Death of HRH the Princess Charlotte* (1817)

Hamilton Letters: Anson, Elizabeth and Florence, eds., *Mary Hamilton ... At Court and at Home ... 1756–1816* (1925)

Harcourt Papers: Harcourt, Edward William, ed., *The Harcourt Papers* (14 vols, 1880–1905)

HAWES, Frances, *Henry Brougham* (Jonathan Cape, 1957)

Hawkins Memoirs: Hawkins, Laetitia, *Anecdotes, Biographical Sketches and Memoirs* (2 vols, 1822)

HAYDON, B. R., *Correspondence and Table-Talk* (1876)

Haydon Diary: Pope, Willard Bissel, ed., *The Diary of Benjamin Robert Haydon* (Harvard University Press, 1960)

HAYTER, John, *The Herculanean and Pompeian Manuscripts* (n.d.)

—— *A Report upon the Herculanean Manuscripts* (1811)

HAYWARD, A., *Diaries of a Lady of Quality from 1797 to 1844* (1864)

HERRIES, Edward, *Memoir of the Public Life of J. C. Herries* (1880)

Historical Account of his Majesty's Visit to Scotland, An (1822)

Historical Account of the Public and Domestic Life and Reign of George IV, An (1830)

History of the Life and Reign of George the Fourth, The (3 vols, 1831)

Hobhouse Diary: Aspinall, A., ed., *The Diary of Henry Hobhouse, 1820–1827* (Home & Van Thal, 1947)

HOBHOUSE, Christopher, *Fox* (John Murray, 1934)

395

Sources

HOLLAND *(Further Memoirs)*: Stavordale, Lord, ed., Holland, Henry, Richard, Lord, *Further Memoirs of the Whig Party, 1807–1821* (1905)

HOLLAND *(Journal)*: Ilchester, the Earl of, ed., *Journal of Elizabeth, Lady Holland 1791–1811* (2 vols, 1908)

HOLLAND *(Letters)*: Ilchester, Earl of, ed., *Elizabeth, Lady Holland to her Son, 1821–1845* (Murray, 1946)

HOLLAND *(Memoirs)*: Holland, Henry Edward, Lord, ed., Holland, Henry Richard, Lord, *Memoirs of the Whig Party During my Time* (2 vols, 1852–4)

HORN, D. B., and RANSOME, Mary, eds., *English Historical Documents, 1714–83* (Eyre & Spottiswoode, 1957)

HUISH, Robert, *Memoirs of George the Fourth* (2 vols, 1831)

HUNT, James Henry Leigh, *Autobiography* (1885)

HUNTER, Richard, see Macalpine

ILCHESTER, Countess of (with Lord Stavordale), *The Life and Letters of Lady Sarah Lennox* (2 vols, 1901)

JACKSON, G. A., ed., *Brougham and his Early Friends* (1908)

JEFFERYS, Nathaniel, *A Review of the Conduct of His Royal Highness, the Prince of Wales* (1806)

—— *A Letter Addressed to Mrs Fitzherbert in Answer to a Complaint that her Feelings have been Hurt by the mention of her Name in the Review of the Conduct of the Prince of Wales* (1787)

Jekyll Correspondence: BOURKE, Algernon, ed., *Correspondence of Mr Joseph Jekyll . . . 1818–38* (1894)

Jerningham Letters: Castle, Egerton, ed., *The Jerningham Letters: Being Excerpts from the Correspondence and Diaries of the Hon. Lady Jerningham and of her Daughter Lady Bedingfield* (2 vols, 1896)

JESSE, Captain, *The Life of Beau Brummell* (1854)

JESSE, J. H., *Memoirs of the Life and Reign of King George III* (5 vols, 1901)

JONES, George, *Sir Francis Chantrey* (1849)

JONES, Wilbur Devereux, *'Prosperity Robinson': The Life of Viscount Goderich* (Macmillan, 1967)

Journal of an English Traveller or Memoirs and Anecdotes of HRH Caroline of Brunswick Princess of Wales (1817)

KILVERT, Rev. Francis, *Memoirs of the life and Writings of the Rt Rev Richard Hurd* (1860)

King's Visit to Scotland, The (British Museum, 1876, e, 24)

Knight Autobiography: Kaye, Sir J. W., and Hulton, J., eds., *The Autobiography of Miss Cornelia Knight* (2 vols, 1861)

KNIGHTON, Lady, *Memoirs of Sir William Knighton* (2 vols, 1838)

Sources

Lamb Letters: Lamb, Charles, *Letters* (1945)

LANDON, H. C. Robbins, ed., *The Collected Correspondence and London Notebooks of Joseph Haydn* (Barrie & Rockcliff, 1959)

LANGDALE, Hon. Charles, *Memoirs of Mrs Fitzherbert* (1856)

Leadbeater Papers, The (1862)

LEAN, E. Tangye, *The Napoleonists: A Study in Political Disaffection, 1760–1960* (Oxford University Press, 1970)

Leeds Memoranda: Browning, Oscar, ed., *The Political Memoranda of Francis Fifth Duke of Leeds* (1884)

LENNOX, Lord William Pitt, *Fifty Years' Biographical Reminiscences* (1863)

—— *My Recollections from 1806–1873* (1874)

—— *The Story of my Life* (1854)

LESLIE, Anita, *Mrs Fitzherbert* (Hutchinson, 1960)

LESLIE, Shane, *George the Fourth* (Ernest Benn, 1926)

—— *The Life and Letters of Mrs Fitzherbert* (2 vols, Burns & Oates, 1939–40)

Letter to the House of Peers on the Present Bill, depending in Parliament, relative to the Prince of Wales' debts by A Hanoverian (1795)

Letter to the Prince of Wales on a Second Application to Parliament to Discharge Debts Wantonly Contracted since May 1787, A (1795)

LEVER, Sir Tresham, *The Letters of Lady Palmerston* (John Murray, 1957)

Lieven (Grey Correspondence): Le Strange, G., ed., *The Correspondence of Princess Lieven and Earl Grey* (3 vols, 1890)

Lieven (London Letters): Robinson, Lionel G., ed., *Letters of Dorothea, Princess Lieven during her Residence in London, 1812–1834* (1902)

Lieven (Metternich Letters): Quennell, Peter, ed., *The Private Letters of Princess Lieven to Prince Metternich 1820–26* (1948)

Lieven (Palmerston Correspondence): Sudley, Lord, ed., *The Lieven-Palmerston Correspondence, 1828–1856* (Murray, 1943)

LINDSTRUM, Derek, *Sir Jeffry Wyatville: Architect to the King* (Clarendon Press, 1973)

LLOYD, H. E., *George IV, Memoirs of his Life and Reign* (1830)

LOCKHART, J. G., *Memoirs of the Life of Sir Walter Scott (1837–38)*

LONGFORD, Elizabeth, *Victoria R.I.* (Weidenfeld & Nicolson, 1964)

—— *Wellington: Pillar of State* (Weidenfeld & Nicolson, 1972)

LUTTRELL, Barbara, *The Prim Romantic: A Biography of Cornelia Knight, 1758–1837* (Chatto & Windus, 1965)

Lyttelton Correspondence: Wyndham, Hon. Mrs Hugh, ed., *Correspondence of Sarah Spencer Lady Lyttelton, 1787–1870* (1912)

MACALPINE, Ida, and HUNTER, Richard, *George III and the Mad-Business* (Allen Lane The Penguin Press, 1969)

MACFARLANE, Charles, *Reminiscences of a Literary Life* (1917)

MACKAY, William, and ROBERTS, W., *John Hoppner R.A.* (1909)

Malmesbury Diaries: Malmesbury, 3rd Earl of, ed., *The Diaries and Correspondence of James Harris First Earl of Malmesbury* (4 vols, 1844)

Markham Memoir: Markham, Sir Clements, *A Memoir of Archbishop Markham, 1719–1807* (1906)

MARPLES, Morris, *Six Royal Sisters: Daughters of George III* (Michael Joseph, 1969)

MARSHALL, Dorothy, *The Rise of George Canning* (Longmans, 1938)

MARTIN, Sir Theodore, *Life of Lord Lyndhurst* (1883)

MATHEWS, Anne, *A Continuation of the Memoirs of Charles Mathews* (1839)

MELVILLE, Lewis, *Beau Brummel, His Life and Letters* (1924)

MEMES, J. S., *Memoirs of Antonio Canova* (1825)

Memoirs of His Royal Highness the Prince of Wales (1808)

MILES, W. A., *A Letter to his Royal Highness the Prince of Wales with a Sketch of the Prospect before him* (1808)

MILLAR, Oliver, *The Tudor, Stuart and Early Georgian Pictures in the Collection of her Majesty the Queen* (Phaidon Press, 1963)

—— *Later Georgian Pictures in the Collection of her Majesty the Queen* (Phaidon Press, 1969)

MITCHELL, L. B. G., *Charles James Fox and the Disintegration of the Whig Party, 1782–1794* (Oxford University Press, 1970)

Mitford Letters: Chorley, Henry, ed., *Letters of Mary Russell Mitford* (1872)

MOLLOY, J. Fitzgerald, ed., *Memoirs of Mrs Robinson* (1894)

Moore Journals: Russell, Lord John, ed., *Memoirs, Journal and Correspondence of Thomas Moore* (1853)

MOORE, Thomas, *Intercepted Letters; or The Twopenny Post-Bag* (1813)

MOORE *(Sheridan)*: Moore, Thomas, *Memoirs of the Life of the Right Honourable Richard Brinsley Sheridan* (2 vols, 1825)

MORSHEAD, Owen, *George IV and Royal Lodge* (Regency Society of Brighton and Hove, 1965)

—— *Windsor Castle* (Phaidon Press, 1957)

MUNK, William, *The Life of Sir Henry Halford, Bt* (1895)

MURRAY, Hon. Amelia, *Recollections of the Early Years of the Present Century* (1868)

MURRAY, Robert H., *Edmund Burke* (Oxford University Press, 1931)

MUSGRAVE, Clifford, *Life in Brighton* (Faber, 1970)

—— *The Royal Pavilion: An Episode in the Romantic* (Leonard Hill, 1964)

NAMIER, Sir Lewis, *Crossroads of Power* (Hamish Hamilton, 1962)

NEW, Chester W., *The Life of Henry Brougham to 1830* (Clarendon Press, 1961)

NICHOLLS, John, *Observations on the Situation of His Royal Highness the Prince of Wales* (1795)

NICOLSON, Sir Harold, *The Congress of Vienna* (Constable, 1940)

NIGHTINGALE, J., *Memoir of the Public and Private Life of . . . Caroline, Queen of Great Britain* (1820)

Noels and Millbankes: Elwin, Malcolm, ed., *The Noels and Milbankes,* (Macdonald, 1967)

Northumberland Diaries: Greig, James, ed., *The Diaries of a Duchess: Extracts from the Diaries of the First Duchess of Northumberland, 1716–1776* (1926)

OLIVER, J. W., *The Life of William Beckford* (Oxford University Press, 1932)

OMAN, Carola, *The Gascoyne Heiress: The Life and Diaries of Frances Mary Gascoyne-Cecil* (Hodder & Stoughton, 1968)

Paget Papers: Paget, Sir Augustus B., ed., *The Paget Papers: Diplomatic and other Correspondence of the Rt Hon. Sir Arthur Paget* (2 vols, 1896)

PALMER, Alan, *Metternich* (Weidenfeld & Nicolson, 1972)

Papendiek Journals: Delves Broughton, Mrs Vernon, ed., *Court and Private Life in the Time of Queen Charlotte: Being the Journals of Mrs Papendiek* (2 vols, 1887)

PARKER, Charles Stuart, *Sir Robert Peel, from his Private Papers* (3 vols, 1891–1899)

Parliamentary History of England, The

PARRY, Edward, *Queen Caroline* (Benn, 1930)

Peel Memoirs: Stanhope, Earl, and E. Cardwell, eds., *The Memoirs of Sir Robert Peel* (2 vols, 1857)

PELLEW, George, *The Life and Correspondence of the Right Honourable Henry Addington, First Viscount Sidmouth* (3 vols, 1847)

PETRIE, Sir Charles, *Canning* (revised edition, 1946)

—— *The Four Georges: A Revaluation* (1935)

—— *Lord Liverpool and his Times* (1954)

PEVSNER, Nikolaus, *The Buildings of England: London* (2 vols, Penguin Books, 1962)

PLUMB, J. H., *The First Four Georges* (Batsford, 1956)

Plumer Ward: Phipps, Hon. Edmund, *Memoirs of the Political and Literary Life of Robert Plumer Ward* (1850)

Porphyria – A Royal Malady: Articles published in or commissioned by the British Medical Journal (British Medical Association, 1968)

PÜCKLER-MUSKAU, Prince, *Tour in England, Ireland and France, 1826–8* (1832)

PYNE, W. H., *The History of the Royal Residences* (1819)

Sources

RAE, William Fraser, *Wilkes, Sheridan, Fox: the Opposition under George the Third* (1927)

RAIKES, Thomas, *A Portion of the Journal Kept by Thomas Raikes Esq. from 1831 to 1847* (4 vols, 1856–7)

RANDOLPH, Herbert, *Life of Sir Robert Wilson* (2 vols, 1862)

REID, Loren, *Charles James Fox: A Man for the People* (Longmans, 1969)

Report of the Proceedings: Nightingale, J., ed., *Report of the Proceedings before the House of Lords on a Bill of Pains and Penalties* (3 vols, 1821)

RICHARDSON, Joanna, *George IV: A Portrait* (Sidgwick & Jackson, 1966)

—— 'George IV, Patron of Literature' in *Essays by Divers Hands*, vol. xxxv (Oxford University Press, 1969)

—— *The Disastrous Marriage: A Study of George IV and Caroline of Brunswick* (Jonathan Cape, 1960)

RICKWORD, Edgell, *Radical Squibs and Loyal Ripostes* (Adams & Dart, 1971)

RIDLEY, Jasper, *Lord Palmerston* (Constable, 1970)

ROBERTS, Henry D., *A History of the Royal Pavilion, Brighton* (Country Life, 1939)

ROBERTS, Michael, *The Whig Party, 1807–1812* (Frank Cass, 1965)

ROBERTS, W., *Sir William Beechey, R.A.* (1901)

Robinson Correspondence: Morley, Edith J., ed., *The Correspondence of Henry Crabb Robinson with the Wordsworth Circle* (1927)

ROGERS *(Table-Talk)*: Bishop, Morchard, ed., *Recollections of the Table-Talk of Samuel Rogers* (Richards Press, 1952)

ROLO, P. J. V., *George Canning: Three Biographical Studies* (Macmillan, 1965)

Romilly Memoirs: Memoirs of Sir Samuel Romilly (3 vols, 1840)

ROSE, John Holland, *Life of William Pitt* (2 vols, 1924)

Rose Diaries: Harcourt, the Rev. Leveson Vernon, ed., *The Diaries and Correspondence of the Rt Hon. George Rose* (2 vols, 1860)

RUSH, Richard, *Memoranda of a Residence at the Court of London* (1933)

RUSSELL, Lord John, *The Life and Times of Charles James Fox* (3 vols, 1859–66)

Scott Journal: J. G. Tait, ed., *The Journal of Sir Walter Scott* (1939–50)

Scott Letter-Books: Partington, Wilfred, ed., *The Private Letter-Books of Sir Walter Scott* (1930)

Scott Letters: Grierson, H. J. C., ed., *The Letters of Sir Walter Scott* (Constable, 1923–37)

Shelley Diary: Edgcumbe, Richard, ed., *The Diary of Frances, Lady Shelley* (2 vols, 1912–13)

Shelley Letters: Ingpen, R., ed., *The Letters of Percy Bysshe Shelley* (1912)

SHERIDAN *(Journal)*: Le Fanu, William, ed., *Betsy Sheridan's Journal: Letters from Sheridan's Sister* (Eyre & Spottiswoode, 1960)

Sources

SHERIDAN *(Letters)*: Price, Cecil, ed., *The Letters of Richard Brinsley Sheridan* (Clarendon Press, 1960)

SICHEL, Walter, *Sheridan* (2 vols, 1909)

SITWELL, Osbert, *Left Hand, Right Hand* (Macmillan, 1945)

Slight Reminiscences of a Septuagenarian from 1802 to 1815 by Emma Sophia, Countess Brownlow (1867)

SMILES, Samuel, *A Publisher and his Friends* (1911)

Southey Correspondence: Southey, Rev. C. C., ed., *The Life and Correspondence of the late Robert Southey* (1849)

Spencer-Stanhope Letter-Bag: Stirling, A. M. W., ed., *The Letter-Bag of Lady Louisa Spencer-Stanhope* (1913)

STANHOPE, Earl, *Life of the Rt Hon. William Pitt* (4 vols, 1867)

Stanhope Memoirs: Memoirs of the Lady Hester Stanhope as related by herself in conversation with her physician (3 vols, 1845)

STAPLETON, A. G., *Political Life of George Canning* (2 vols, 1831)

STEEGMAN, John, *The Rule of Taste from George I to George IV* (Macmillan, 1968)

STOCKDALE, J., *The History and Proceedings of the Lords and Commons . . . with Regard to the Regency* (1789)

STOCKMAR, E. von, ed., *Memoirs of Baron Stockmar* (Trans. Max Müller, 2 vols, 1872–3)

STOKES, Hugh, *The Devonshire House Circle* (1917)

STROUD, Dorothy, *Henry Holland* (Country Life, 1966)

STUART *(Daughters of George III)*: Stuart, Dorothy Margaret, *The Daughters of George III* (Macmillan, 1939)

STUART *(Foster)*: Stuart, Dorothy Margaret, *Dearest Bess: The Life and Times of Lady Elizabeth Foster, afterwards Duchess of Devonshire from her Unpublished Journals and Correspondence* (Methuen, 1955)

Stuart Letters: Johnson, B. B., ed. *The Letters of Lady Louisa Stuart* (1926)

SUMMERSON, John, *John Nash, Architect to King George IV* (Allen & Unwin, 1935)

SUMNER, George Henry, *Life of Charles Richard Sumner* (1876)

TAYLOR, Thomas, *Life of Benjamin Robert Haydon* (2 vols, 1853)

TEMPERLEY, Harold, ed., *The Unpublished Diary and Political Sketches of Princess Lieven* (Cape, 1935)

—— *The Foreign Policy of Canning, 1922–7* (1925)

THOMPSON, E. P., *The Making of the English Working Class* (Gollancz, 1963)

TOOKE, Horne, *A Letter to a Friend on the Reported Marriage of His Royal Highness, the Prince of Wales* (1787)

Sources

Tour to York, A Circumstantial Account of His Royal Highness the Prince of Wales's visit to that City (1789)

TOYE, Francis, *Rossini* (Arthur Barker, 1954)

TROTTER, J. B., *Memoirs of the Later Years of the Rt Hon. Charles James Fox* (1811)

TWISS, Horace, *The Public and Private Life of Lord Chancellor Eldon* (3 vols, 1844)

Two Words of Counsel, and one of Comfort. Addressed to His Royal Highness the Prince of Wales by an old Englishman (1795)

Vindication of the Conduct of Lady Douglas during her Intercourse with the Princess of Wales ... etc. (1814)

VULLIAMY, C. E., *Aspasia: The Life and Letters of Mary Granville, Mrs Delany, 1700–1788* (Bles, 1937)

Walpole Correspondence: Lewis, W. S., ed., *The Yale Edition of Horace Walpole's Correspondence* (34 vols, Oxford University Press, 1937–65)

WALPOLE *(George III):* Barker, G. F. Russel, ed., Walpole, Horace, *Memoirs of the Reign of King George the Third,* (4 vols, 1894)

WALPOLE *(Last Journals):* Steuart, A. Francis, ed., *The Last Journals of Horace Walpole During the Reign of George III* (2 vols, 1910)

WATSON, J. Steven, *The Reign of George III, 1760–1815* (Oxford University Press, 1959)

WEBSTER, Sir Charles, *The Foreign Policy of Castlereagh 1815–22* (2nd edn, 1934)

WEIGALL, Lady Rose, *A Brief Memoir of Princess Charlotte of Wales* (1874)

Wellington and his Friends: Wellington, 7th Duke of, ed., *Wellington and his Friends: Letters of the 1st Duke of Wellington* (Macmillan, 1965)

Wellington Despatches, Correspondence and Memoranda, 1819–32 (8 vols, 1867–80)

Wellington Supplementary Despatches: Wellington, Duke of, ed., *Supplementary Despatches 1794–1818* (15 vols, 1858–72)

WHALLEY, George, 'Coleridge and the Royal Society of Literature' in *Essays by Divers Hands,* vol. xxxv (Oxford University Press, 1969)

WHITE, R. J., *The Age of George III* (History Book Club, 1968)

—— *From Waterloo to Peterloo* (Heinemann, 1957)

WILBERFORCE, Robert Isaac, and Wilberforce, Samuel, *The Life of William Wilberforce* (5 vols, 1838)

WILKINS, W. H., *Mrs Fitzherbert and George IV* (2 vols, 1905)

WILKS, John, *Memoirs of Her Majesty, Queen Caroline* (1822)

WILLIAMS, D. E., *The Life and Correspondence of Sir Thomas Lawrence* (1831)

Sources

Williams Wyn Correspondence: Layard, G. S., ed., *Correspondence of Charlotte Grenville, Lady Williams Wyn and her Three Sons* (1920)

WILLIAMSON, G. C., *Richard Cosway, R.A., and his Wife and Pupils* (1897)

WILLIS, G. M., *Ernest Augustus, Duke of Cumberland and King of Hanover* (Arthur Barker, 1954)

WILSON, Harriette, *Memoirs of Harriette Wilson Written by Herself* (4 vols, 1825)

Windham Papers: Windham, Rt Hon. William, *The Windham Papers* (2 vols, 1913)

WOODHAM-SMITH, Cecil, *Queen Victoria: Her Life and Times* (vol. 1, Hamish Hamilton, 1972)

WOODWARD, Sir Llewellyn, *The Age of Reform 1815–1870* (Oxford University Press, 1961)

WRAXALL: Wheatley, Henry B., ed., *The Historical and Posthumous Memoirs of Sir Nathanial William Wraxall, 1772–1784* (5 vols, 1884)

YONGE, C. D., *Life and Administration of Robert Banks Jenkinson, 2nd Earl of Liverpool* (3 vols, 1868)

ZIEGLER, Philip, *Addington: A Life of Henry Addington, First Viscount Sidmouth* (Collins, 1965)

—— *King William IV* (Collins, 1972)

Index

Aberdeen, George Hamilton Gordon, 4th Earl of (1784–1860), 319, 320

Adelaide of Saxe-Coburg-Meiningen, Princess, Clarence and, 112; Greville on, 114; death of her daughter, 226

Agar-Ellis, the Hon George, *later* 1st Baron Dover of the third creation (1797–1833), on George IV, 319; and George IV's will, 331, 332; on George IV's funeral, 337-8

Agasse, Jacques-Laurent (1780–1849), 278n.

Albani, Cardinal, 169

Albemarle, William Charles Keppel, 4th Earl of (1772–1849), 344n.

Alexander of Soms, Prince, 143

Alexander I, Tsar of Russia (1777–1825), 31; and Louis XVIII, 32; in London, 32-3, 34; and Queen Caroline, 44; Prince Leopold in the suite of, 67; lends Kent money, 114; Princess Victoria's godfather, 128

Althorp, John Charles Spencer, Viscount, *later* 3rd Earl Spencer (1782–1845), on the Cato Street Conspiracy, 131; on Queen Caroline, 181, 196; creates a dilemma, 301

Avanley, William Arden, 2nd Baron (1789–1849), 25, 287n.

Amelia, Princess (1783–1810), 56

Angerstein, John Julius (1735–1823), his collection of pictures, 25, 267

Anglesey, Henry Paget, 1st Marquess of (1768–1854), and the mob, 161-2; his unpopularity, 162n.; his interred leg, 229; Lord Lieutenant of Ireland, 299; and Catholic emancipation, 304

Angoulême, duc d', 2, 228

Angoulême, duchesse d', 2, 3

Anna Paulowna, Grand Duchess, *later* Princess of Orange, her marriage, 92; and George IV, 229

Arbuthnot, Charles (1767–1850), 41n.; on George IV, 185; on George IV and Knighton, 243; and Wellington, 289, 293; George IV's generosity to, 317

Arbuthnot, Mrs Harriett (d. 1834), on Bill of Pains and Penalties, 174-5; on Queen Caroline, 182-3; and George IV at the coronation, 191, 194; on George IV and Lady Conyngham, 216-7; on Liverpool, 257n.; and George IV's popularity 280; on George IV and York, 283; and Lord Francis Conyngham, 287n.; on George IV's kindness, 317, 341; on Lady Conyngham, 324-5; on George IV's mode of living, 327

Artois, Comte d', 2

Ashe, Thomas, 41n.

Auckland, George Eden, Earl of (1784–1849), 113

Augusta of Hesse-Cassel, Princess, *later* Duchess of Cambridge (1797–1889), 113

Augusta Sophia, Princess (1768–1840), 22; Cranbourne Lodge, 94; and Princess Charlotte, 95; writes to George IV, 105-6, 107; and her mother, 106, 122; and Princess Elizabeth, 117; and the Prince of Hesse-Homburg, 118; Frogmore for, 122; George IV and, 186

Index

413

Index

Index